DISENTANGLING

Contributors

ANDREW ARNO
NIKO BESNIER
STEPHEN T. BOGGS
DONALD BRENNEIS
MALCOLM NAEA CHUN
ALESSANDRO DURANTI
DAVID WELCHMAN GEGEO
EDWIN HUTCHINS
LAMONT LINDSTROM
WILLIAM McKELLIN
KAREN ANN WATSON-GEGEO
GEOFFREY M. WHITE

DISENTANGLING

Conflict Discourse in Pacific Societies

Edited by
KAREN ANN WATSON-GEGEO
GEOFFREY M. WHITE

Stanford University Press   1990
Stanford, California

Stanford University Press
Stanford, California
© 1990 by The Board of Trustees of the
Leland Stanford Junior University .
Printed in the United States of America

CIP data appear at the end of the book

Contents

Contributors

ANDREW ARNO is assistant professor of communication at the University of Hawai'i, Manoa. He has degrees in social anthropology from Harvard (Ph.D. 1974) and in law from the University of Texas at Austin (J.D. 1969). He has carried out field research in Fiji, and his interests include law, communication, socio-linguistics, and social theory.

NIKO BESNIER is assistant professor of anthropology at Yale University. He received his Ph.D. in linguistics from the University of Southern California in 1986. He has conducted field research in various areas of Western Polynesia, particularly Nukulaelae atoll (Tuvalu), on language and affect, literacy and orality, the structure and function of gossip, and discourse and syntax. Besnier previously taught at the University of California and the University of Illinois.

STEPHEN T. BOGGS is emeritus professor of anthropology at the University of Hawai'i, Manoa. The author of *Speaking, Relating, and Learning: A Study of Hawaiian Children at Home and At School* (1985), he has carried out research among Polynesian Hawaiians since 1966 and has published on language acquisition/development in relation to culture. He is working on a monograph on Hawaiian life ways, co-authored with Malcolm Naea Chun.

DONALD BRENNEIS is professor of anthropology at Pitzer College, Claremont, California. He has conducted research in Fiji since 1970, focusing on Fijian Indian communities. Brenneis is co-editor with Fred Myers of *Dangerous Words: Language and Politics in the Pacific*, and he has published widely in sociolinguistics, discourse analysis, and language and politics.

MALCOLM NAEA CHUN is currently the executive director of First People's Productions, an organization established for the promotion of native culture and products. He was educated at the University of Hawai'i, St. John's Theological College in New Zealand, and Vancouver School of Theology in British Columbia. He has taught Hawaiian language and folklore at the University of Hawai'i, Manoa, and published several books on traditional Hawaiian culture, particularly translations of primary Hawaiian language sources. Over the past six years, Chun has served in several official positions in the Office of Hawaiian Affairs, a government agency for native affairs.

ALESSANDRO DURANTI is assistant professor of anthropology at the University of California, Los Angeles. He received his Ph.D. in linguistics from the University of Southern California in 1978. His research and publications have concentrated on the relationship between Samoan discourse strategies and local notions of action, intentionality, and self. He has also published on Italian syntax in conversation and on the uses of computer technologies in educational settings. Duranti has taught at the University of Rome, Pitzer College, and the University of California at San Diego.

DAVID WELCHMAN GEGEO is a doctoral student in political science at the University of Hawai'i, Manoa. He earned his B.A. in anthropology at the University of Massachusetts, Boston, and M.S. in communication at Boston University (1986). He is a co-editor of *The Big Death: Solomon Islanders Remember World War II* and has published on language socialization, oral history, and change and development in the Solomon Islands. He is working on a dictionary of his native language, Kwara'ae.

EDWIN HUTCHINS is associate professor of cognitive science at the University of California, San Diego. Trained as a cognitive anthropologist at UC San Diego, where he received his Ph.D. in 1978, Hutchins undertook postdoctoral study in cognitive psychology and worked for several years applying artificial intelligence techniques to problems in education and training. His work earned him a MacArthur Fellowship, awarded in 1985. Hutchins has taken an interdisciplinary approach to research topics ranging from land litigation in Papua New Guinea and traditional navigation in the Western Pacific, to modern navigation aboard U.S. Naval vessels. He is the author of *Culture and Inference: A Trobriand Case Study* (1980) on Trobriand land disputes and debate.

LAMONT LINDSTROM is associate professor of anthropology at the University of Tulsa. He received his Ph.D. from the University of California, Berkeley, in 1981. He has conducted research on Vanuatu since 1978, working primarily on Tanna island. He has published a dictionary of Tanna's Kwamera (Nininife) language and has also published on sociolinguistics, traditional knowledge systems, Pacific drugs, and World War II ethnohistory. Lindstrom has also taught at Rhodes College in Memphis and at the University of Papua New Guinea.

WILLIAM McKELLIN is assistant professor of anthropology in the Department of Anthropology and Sociology, University of British Columbia, Vancouver. He received his Ph.D. from the University of Toronto, where his dissertation was on kinship, social organization, and discourse among the Managalase of Papua New Guinea. His has published on sociolinguistics and discourse analysis.

KAREN ANN WATSON-GEGEO is associate professor of English as a second language and director of the Center for Second Language Classroom Research, at the University of Hawai'i, Manoa, where she earned her doctorate in anthropology. She has co-edited three books, including *Adaptation and Symbolism: Essays on Social Organization.* She has published widely on child language socialization, sociolinguistics and discourse analysis, minority and Third World education, and related topics, and conducted extensive research in the native Hawaiian community and the Solomon Islands. She has been a research associate at the East-West Center and taught for several years at the Graduate School of Education, Harvard University.

GEOFFREY M. WHITE is a research associate at the Institute of Culture and Communication, East-West Center. He received his Ph.D. in anthropology from the University of California, San Diego, in 1978. He has conducted research in Santa Isabel, Solomon Islands, since 1975 and has published widely on language and culture, identity, and ethnohistory. He has also taught at the University of Hawai'i and UC San Diego. His publications include a dictionary of the Cheke Holo language and four co-edited books, including *Person, Self and Experience: Exploring Pacific Ethnopsychologies* (1985).

Preface

THIS BOOK began with our interest in combining approaches from linguistic and psychological anthropology to pursue a series of comparative questions about person concepts, interpersonal conflict, and moral discourse in Pacific societies. Watson-Gegeo first posed antecedents to these questions when attending graduate school at the University of Hawai'i in 1970, when she learned about Hawaiian *ho'oponopono*, discussed by Boggs and Chun in this volume. Her interest in these questions was renewed during field research with David Gegeo on Malaita in 1979, when she witnessed Kwara'ae *fa'amanata'anga* (counseling) for the first time. Just a few years earlier on the neighboring island of Santa Isabel, White was discovering that a type of village meeting called "disentangling" offered insights into a wide range of ethnographic issues.

At the 1979 American Anthropological Association meetings we found ourselves by coincidence on the same panel, with White presenting a paper on A'ara disentangling and Watson-Gegeo and Gegeo on Kwara'ae decision-making meetings (*ala'anga*). The three of us talked briefly about the advantages of combining linguistic and ethnopsychological approaches to conflict resolution processes, and we began to think about a forum that would bring together people with these interests.

In late winter 1981 we met at the meetings of the Association for Social Anthropology in Oceania (ASAO) at Hilton Head, South Carolina, and developed, in consultation with several others, a proposal for a symposium on the topic of "straightening out" contexts. Eventually, through the efforts of Don Brenneis and others, these plans led to an invitation from Pitzer College in Claremont, California, to hold a small conference at that campus. Pitzer, in the person of Dean Ronald Macaulay, generously offered us meeting facilities and travel funds for those coming from outside California. So, on October 15–18, 1983, we convened the

Conference on Talk and Social Inference: "Straightening Out" Contexts in Pacific Cultures at Pitzer College.

Presenters at the conference whose final papers appear in this volume include Besnier, Brenneis, Duranti, Hutchins, McKellin, Watson-Gegeo and Gegeo, and White. In addition, Richard Katz discussed Fijian healing and its relation to resolving interpersonal problems and Karen Ito presented a paper on Hawaiian *ho'oponopono*. A wide range of Pacific cultures were therefore represented in conference presentations: Hawaiian, Samoan, Nukulaelae (Polynesian outlier, Tuvalu), Trobriands, Fijian and Fiji Indian, Managalase (Papua New Guinea), and A'ara and Kwara'ae in the Solomon Islands. Each presenter agreed to address ethnopsychological questions about emotions and the self, and to situate the analysis in the discourse of actual conflict "resolution" events. The two discussants for the conference reflected this union of approaches: Catherine Lutz and Elinor Ochs, as psychological and linguistic anthropologist, respectively. The conference was also attended by Susan Philips, Bambi Schieffelin, and Andrew Pawley, who entered into the discussions in very productive ways.

After the conference the papers underwent substantial revision. During this process we solicited from Lamont Lindstrom a paper he presented at the 1984 American Anthropological Association meetings. His contribution expanded our cultural "sample" to include Tanna in Vanuatu. Andrew Arno, who had been invited to the Pitzer Conference but was unable to attend, contributed a chapter on the Fijian joking debate. And we later solicited a chapter from Stephen T. Boggs and Malcolm Naea Chun on Hawaiian *ho'oponopono*.

We are grateful to Pitzer College, and especially to Dean Ronald Macaulay, for funding and hosting the conference. We would especially like to thank Don Brenneis for skillfully handling all of the conference arrangements, and the Pitzer Anthropology Department's faculty and their families for graciously inviting conference participants to stay in their homes during the conference. We would like to acknowledge generous support for the production of this volume from the University of Hawai'i President's Fund, the University of Hawai'i Program in Conflict

Resolution, the University of Tulsa College of Arts and Sciences and Office of Research, and Pitzer College. Final preparation of the volume was assisted by support from the East-West Center's Institute of Culture and Communication, especially the typing assistance of Carolyn Isono-Grapard, Wesley Oasa, and Edith Yashiki.

K.A.W.-G.
G.M.W.

PART I

INTRODUCTION

Disentangling Discourse

Geoffrey M. White and Karen Ann Watson-Gegeo

TANGLES—interpersonal conflict, disagreements, moral dilemmas—are at the heart of social life. People talk about their troubles, and in seeking solutions through talk, they create valued images of self and community. "Disentangling" refers to cultural activities in which people attempt to "straighten out" their "tangled" relations.[1] In many societies, particularly small-scale communities typical of the Pacific Islands, these activities are enacted in focused, even ritualized, events defined as occasions for discussing and transforming interpersonal conflict. Because conflict can challenge the assumed bases of social life, analysis of the discourse of disentangling may reveal the work of constructing a meaningful and persuasive social order as it occurs.

This volume's focus on discourse signals its concern with interactions among language, culture, and social institutions (cf. Sherzer 1987). Rather than begin with predetermined notions about one-way relations between ideology and practice, we examine their interrelation in the interactively produced meanings of disentangling events. By moving back and forth between close analyses of situated discourse and wider sociocultural horizons, we illuminate processes by which people produce moral accounts within the constraints of a social universe. In the process of disentangling, people not only pose and counterpose interpretations of events, they may also negotiate the premises upon which they act. Disentangling discourse is thus a critical focus for understanding the processes—conceptual, communicative, and institutional—through which people continually create and transform the realities in which they live.

The major theoretical contribution of this volume is its integration of current approaches in linguistic and psychological anthropology. Although the latter are both critically involved in the analysis of social and moral discourse, their methods and approaches rarely inform one another. Whereas sociolinguistic work typically ignores actors' assumptions about the personal meanings of action, psychological approaches often fail to anchor their accounts in the details of everyday interaction. Similarly, much of the work on legal and political process is concerned with talk that is avowedly moral in content. However, without a connection to underlying models of personal significance, these treatments are unable to link their analyses to the phenomenological world of actors' intentions and motivations. Our focus on disentangling combines linguistic and psychological perspectives to examine the instantiation of cultural models in situated communicative practices. We are concerned with interactions between actors' moral assumptions and the socially organized contexts in which those assumptions are enacted and themselves transformed (cf. Bentley 1984; Comaroff and Roberts 1981).

In contrast to event-centered studies, which have tended to exclude structures and events outside situated activity (e.g., Labov and Fanshel 1977), the studies in this volume are all based on a broad range of social, cultural, and linguistic information derived from extended fieldwork. Each one bases its analysis in a record of situated conflict talk and relates that record to other varieties of social and cultural phenomena.[2] The goal is to produce ethnographic accounts that are rich enough to do justice to local forms of understanding and action, while at the same time opening up possibilities for comparison and replication. Disentangling is a universal process with intrinsic sociocultural interest because of the creative and transformative nature of conflict talk. We use "transformation" to refer to change at several levels: evolution of a conflict and the stages through which it evolves; alteration of personal and interpersonal understandings; recasting of social relationships; and, ultimately, the remaking of the social order.

In the literature on the sociology of law, "transformation" has been used to describe the evolution of disputes (Felstiner, Abel, and Sarat 1980–81) and movement through stages in a dispute-handling process (Mather and Yngvesson 1980–81). Unlike our use of transformation, these treatments use formal legal systems as the underlying normative mode. Yngvesson and Mather's (1983) treatment of transformation comes closest to our use of the term. They point to three transformative processes: rephrasing (reformulating a dispute into public discourse), narrowing (reformulating it to fit conventional management procedures), and expansion. Expansion brings together subjects or issues that are typically separated, thus "'stretching' or changing accepted [primarily legal] frameworks for organizing reality" (ibid.: 778–79). Whereas in this approach social change involves expanding legal frameworks, the contributors to the present volume are concerned more broadly with cultural and social frameworks. For us, transformation is not merely a matter of expansion, but of reformulation in the most general sense.

Here we sketch some of the dimensions along which generalization is possible among the ten Pacific communities included in the volume. We explore points of convergence among the following papers by comparing disentangling events, not as exemplars of a single genre (say, "courts" or "gossip"), but as activities aimed at the transformation of problematic circumstances (conflict) into more ideal constructions. We do this by discussing the cultural assumptions that make the disentangling process compelling for participants, as well as the modes of discourse and social organization that make it possible as a collectively orchestrated activity. We first consider the "ethnopsychological" understandings about persons and emotion that frame disentangling activities as meaningful and desirable. We then discuss social structural forces that produce, and are reproduced by, those activities.

Two previous works on Pacific societies establish starting points for our discussion: *Dangerous Words: Language and Politics in the Pacific* (Brenneis and Myers 1984) and *Person, Self and Experience: Exploring Pacific Ethnopsychologies* (White and Kirkpatrick 1985). These volumes contribute, respectively, insights on communicative practices and ethnotheories pertinent to disentangling in Pacific communities. The present volume combines and extends their insights by drawing connections between the conventions of talk about sociopolitical relations and ethnopsychological formulations of person and action. Concepts of "the person," which have been of much interest lately in anthropology but which are often abstractly stated, are here analyzed as elements of culture constituted in interactive contexts where they may be seen to have a determinate role in social process.

Persons, Emotions, and Conflict Discourse

Anthropological writers have frequently observed that small-scale, non-Western societies employ a range of means for handling interpersonal conflict and managing contentious or divisive issues. If formal courts are present at all, they may be narrowly limited in the types of cases they take up, possibly to events involving conflict defined in terms of Western-style laws. In their place, diverse practices varying from gossip to informal village meetings and highly ritualized ceremonial activities function as conflict-regulating and order-maintaining mechanisms. In this spectrum of events, Western observers have noted what seems to them a blurring of genres, of dispute procedures with therapeutic functions (Gibbs 1963), and of religious ceremonies with overtly political messages (Gluckman 1955; Norbeck 1963). Instead of asking just what people themselves think they are up to on these occasions or how one could decide (Frake 1977), the dominant approach has been to explain this multiplicity of forms by imposing theoretical dichotomies such as rational vs. irrational and practical vs. ritual. For example, in works that have been widely influential in social anthropology, Turner (1957) and Gluckman (1955; 1972) suggested that societies deal with "surface" interpersonal conflicts through rational dispute procedures aimed at resolving decidable issues, whereas problems arising from irresolvable structural contradictions (such as between matriliny and virilocal residence) tend to be dealt with through ritual practices that evoke strong emotions in the service of social integration.

Oppositions have their place in exploring cross-cultural reality, but when they are repeated as dichotomies, where one term excludes the other, they mask the complexity of ideas and practices not so easily codified in familiar terms. The complexity of such oppositions, and their usefulness as analytic categories, become clearer as they are examined in relation to Pacific cases. In line with Arno's (1979) observation for Fiji that all dispute processes climax in ritual activity, the studies in this volume find that practical and ritual moves comingle in conflict discourse, as do "rational" and "emotional" appeals to moral judgment. By focusing on concepts of person and the specific strategies of talk used to enact them, we are able to ask ethnographic questions about the significance of practices that are at once social, emotional, and political.

We begin with the premise that cultural concepts of person, emotion, and action are systematically related to a society's ways of formulating conflict and attempting to resolve or manage it. When Gibbs (1963) observed that Kpelle moots dealing with marital disputes exhibit features of Western therapy (citing Parsons 1951), he had uncovered a highly significant property of many "informal" procedures for conflict resolution: they explicitly invoke emotions. Many other examples could be cited, such as the Tolai *varkurai* or moot described by Epstein (1984:29), which comes "to a climax in an emotive appeal to certain highly cathected norms," or the Bunyoro *rukurato* portrayed by Beattie (1957) as a type of "informal judicial activity" held to "finish off people's quarrels and abolish bad feeling" (cited in Gibbs 1963:9). Focused analysis of events such as these, where interpersonal conflict is an avowed topic of discourse, sheds light on concerns of the self as well as on the process of managing sociopolitical relations. The interpersonal situations we examine are all distinguished by their overt concern with other interpersonal events. They are particularly rich in communicative performances aimed at disclosing or disavowing emotions and intentions—data that LeVine (1983) calls for in outlining an ethnographic approach to the study of the self.

Disentangling events also arouse interest because they combine meanings and activities usually kept apart in the more neatly dichotomized Western conceptual world where the political-legal-rational is separated from the psychological-moral-emotional (see Lutz 1988). These parallel oppositions rest upon the edifice of the Western ethnopsychological concept of person as a highly individuated, autonomous actor (cf. Geertz 1984).[3] Here the major lines of definition and discord are drawn along the boundaries of individual persons, such that interpersonal conflicts and moral dilemmas primarily arise from problems in reconciling individual desires and community norms. Dispute resolution and psychotherapy become mirror images of one another: the former a process whereby individuals or factions attempt to impose their own preferred models of reality upon wider collectivities, the latter a matter of replacing a disordered personal experience with a more coherent normative vision. It follows that, in political disputes where the intended outcome is an authoritative version of reality, individual desires and emotions are ideally suppressed and controlled.[4] And, in Western psychotherapy, where the desired outcome is a new personal integration, the individual is sheltered from the inhibiting constraints of social norms and relations so that emotions may be more freely explored, felt, and expressed (see Parsons 1951; Pande 1967; Scheff 1979).

All of this makes good cultural sense in the context of Western assumptions about the nature of persons in the social world. However, as one cultural model among many, it is lacking as a framework for the cross-cultural study of either "disputes" or "therapies." Studies of Pacific ethnopsychologies have found that concepts of person in Pacific cultures tend to be highly relational, with notions of relatedness elaborated in a great variety of ways in social life (White and Kirkpatrick 1985). For example, in all of the societies represented, concepts of shame and practices aimed at creating or alleviating shame were involved in maintaining proper relations and behavior among community members. That many Pacific societies have institutionalized means for straightening out interpersonal tangles and dealing with the problem of shame is further evidence of the salience of the web of interpersonal relations for Pacific persons (cf. Myers 1986:437).

The disentangling practices we examine in this book presume that the person is embedded in a matrix of social relations. Rather than extricate the person from that milieu, as in the legal persona represented in Western courts or the "real self" revealed in psychotherapy, the contexts examined here involve persons as moral actors engaged in interaction with significant others—usually the very same others involved in the precipitating conflicts. Whether the aim of the activity in question is an authoritative statement on contested issues or an emotional rapprochement among family members, the goal inevitably involves the reconstruction of a collective vision of social reality through the mutual involvement of community members. In many instances, emotions are a particularly apt idiom for that involvement. In each case, the *process* by which collective statements are jointly enunciated is itself a product (in some cases, the primary product)—an enactment of identities, relations, and emotions that invoke or produce a desired social reality.

In terms of their overt functions, the cases taken up in this volume may be ordered along a continuum of event types ranging from the political-legalistic to the personal-therapeutic. This continuum, however, is more a matter of event scale than cultural definition. On one end the Samoan *fono* and Tannese and Trobriand "courts" address contested community issues, whereas on the other end Hawaiian *ho'oponopono* and Kwara'ae *fa'amanata'anga* attempt to reconcile intrafamilial conflicts. Despite obvious differences in the types of topics dealt with (the former land rights or leadership status, the latter interpersonal obligations and tensions) and in the status of participants involved (as different as a council of chiefs and a group of family members), all of these events are concerned in some way with the construction and promulgation of moral accounts. The question of what these events are about is not a matter of *either* rational political decision *or* ritual manipulation of emotion. In most instances, they work at multiple levels and purposes, either simultaneously through embedded layers of meaning (overt and covert, recognized and unrecognized) or sequentially, both within and across events.

Many observers have reported on meetings in small-scale societies that do not produce decisions or political directives (e.g., Rosaldo 1973; Brenneis and Myers 1984; Myers 1986; Brison 1989). What is the rationale for recurrent activities that involve discourse on interpersonal conflicts but neither aim for nor achieve specific decisions (as in most cases in this volume)? We argue that the cultural significance of these activities lies in the rhetorics they pose and the realities they create. Seen in this light, particular conflict episodes are part of an ongoing community dialogue in which events and relationships are continually shaped and reshaped in the moral negotiations of everyday life. Of course, these events (with the exception of Nukulaelae gossip and most performances of Managalase allegories) are distinguished from the stream of ordinary interactions as situations overtly concerned with interpersonal problems. They are also marked as speech events that permit discourse genres not possible in other contexts. As recent studies of political language make clear (Brenneis and Myers 1984), much of the genius of such events is in providing a context for communication about topics that are not only problematic in themselves, but frequently cannot even be talked about in ordinary ways (see below on shame). As contexts so marked, these activities provide an opportunity for interactively redefining and transforming problematic circumstances.

Public/Private

All of the contexts we examine facilitate the movement of moral constructions into progressively wider circles of social discourse. In his introduction to a collection of studies of Melanesian dispute processes, Epstein (1974:15) notes that in each society such procedures are concerned with bringing into the open hidden material seen as causing interpersonal tensions. These contexts offer a social analog of the psychodynamic notion of insight—allowing potentially disruptive understandings to enter into collective awareness, just as therapy attempts to bring repressed thoughts into individual consciousness. The achievement of collective insight is easily characterized as the public reworking of private grievances. However, as others have noted (Irvine 1979, 1982; Rosaldo 1984), the public versus private dichotomy bears further scrutiny. Although most cultures probably make some kind of public/private distinction (Moore 1984), the division tends to be sharply dichotomized in cultures viewing the person as the site of inner thoughts and emotions, protected from the gaze of others (or even from the awareness of the thinking subject). In contrast to this private world of the individual stands the public world of shared meanings constructed in interactions with others (Taylor 1979; Todorov 1984). For Westerners, the former is the stuff of psychology, the latter of politics.

Rather than assume that social process adheres to the contours of a dichotomous break between individual and social collectivity, we ask, "What are the major discontinuities in social experience?" and "How are they reproduced and reinforced in interactive settings such as procedures for disentangling?" The events considered here vary in the degree to which they control access to the discourse produced. Some restrict group participation in disentangling (see below); others limit the production and circulation of knowledge. On the one hand, events as disparate as Nuku-laelae gossip, Kwara'ae counseling, Hawaiian *ho'oponopono*, and the Samoan *fono* all foster forms of talk directly addressing moral transgressions that would not be possible in settings where the audience was not restricted according to explicit criteria. On the other hand, Trobriand and Tannese "courts," held as they are in the open air of village or intervillage space, have seemingly un-bounded audiences but definite means for controlling participa-tion. Note, however, that forms that sharply restrict participation do not necessarily limit circulation of their results. Both gossip and chiefly meetings, like formal courts, permit and even en-courage wider circulation of their statements.

A particularly strong implication of the public/private opposi-tion is that emotions reside, ultimately, on the private side of the boundary between individual and society. While recognizing that emotions both affect and are affected by social process, West-erners see them as lodged within the confines of individual ex-perience, fueling the wellsprings of inner motivation. This view tends to obscure the fact that emotions, like knowledge, are the subject of socially organized discourse—a cultural resource that is interactively produced to formulate particular kinds of identity, experience, and moral assertion (see Lutz and White 1986). This is so both in explicit understandings about emotional display (e.g., Bailey 1983; Schieffelin 1983) and in implicit messages encoded in all aspects of language, from voice quality to word order (Irvine 1982; Ochs 1986; Besnier, this volume). It should not be surprising, then, that occasions for disentangling are par-ticularly rich with emotional codes. The role of emotion as moral idiom (Myers 1979; Rosaldo 1984; Lutz 1988) is addressed in several of the studies that follow, ranging from Besnier's analysis of evaluative meanings in the prosodic qualities of gossip to White's discussion of the social meanings created by talk of emo-tion.

In Pacific cultures, where selves tend to be especially perme-able to the experience of others (see Kirkpatrick and White 1985) and where "inner, private" worlds may be elaborated only in rela-tion to interpersonal experience, we might profitably ask, "What are transactions in knowledge and emotion all about for culturally constructed selves?" and, specifically, "How are such transactions managed in the face of perceived risks and rewards?" The answers are indicative of the kinds of cultural rationale that lie behind the "disentangling" activities discussed in this volume.

Catharsis

One of the individual rewards commonly attributed to therapy is catharsis: the release or discharge of pent-up emotions (see Scheff 1979 for a recent statement). As indicated earlier, an overt concern with emotions is seen as one of the hallmarks of therapy, distinguishing it from the more "rational" political process. To produce catharsis is to be therapeutic. The sociological attributes of therapy identified by Parsons (1951), such as permissiveness and support, function especially to facilitate emotional expression. Cross-cultural analyses have frequently drawn upon the concept of catharsis to characterize the psychological functions of ritual events for individuals (e.g., Norbeck 1963; Wallace 1959; Douglas 1970).

Such an omnibus notion of emotional expression or discharge does not discriminate among the emotions operative within the activities considered here. In most cases there is no overt concern for the emotional needs of persons *as individuals* (i.e., as defined separately from relations with others) and little nonverbal evidence that cathartic release is accomplished in some unrecognized way. The events that are most therapeutic in orientation are primarily concerned with reestablishing social and emotional ties among related persons. Except for the weeping exhibited by participants in the Hawaiian-American *ho'oponopono* described by Boggs and Chun, none of the contexts described in this book is regarded as an occasion for bodily displays of felt emotion. While nearly all the cases involve a culturally elaborated discourse *of* emotion, this is distinct from a discourse *for* emotional expression.[5] Even though Santa Isabel "disentangling" is seen as an occasion for talking out problematic feelings, the tone and rhythm of the event are closely modulated to avoid immediate expressions of intense feeling. The Kwara'ae counseling described by Watson-Gegeo and Gegeo is also concerned (in a less direct way) with reviewing the emotions of interpersonal conflict. Yet those embroiled in conflict do not themselves talk about their emotions. Instead, the counselor represents conflicting parties' emotional reactions either directly or indirectly by indexing them with the qualities of his or her own speech (similar to the way the narrator of Nukulaelae gossip described by Besnier infuses his account with moral significance by animating the quoted speech of others).

In these and other contexts taken up here, emotions are not so much an end in themselves as a moral rhetoric put to the task of reconstructing a desired social reality. Even in the case of *ho'oponopono* described by Boggs and Chun, weeping is more a sign of relations restored than of emotions released. The adjustments achieved by *ho'oponopono* and similar contexts involve a moral transformation accomplished through an emotional idiom, and not a generalized purge of the individual psyche. Our analyses of emotion rhetoric in disentangling discourse parallel recent work on affect in socializing contexts (e.g., Miller and Sperry 1987; Ochs 1986) where emotion in language is shown to be an idiom for community moral messages. As in our work, the important theoretical move in the socialization studies has been their search for connections between language practices and sociocultural frameworks of meaning and value.

The studies in this volume examine the meaning and practice of numerous emotions associated with moral conflict and its interpersonal repercussions. The cases of Pacific disentangling examined here indicate that emotions glossed as anger and shame are central to the cultural construction and maintenance of social relationships in the *gemeinschaft* of small communities. These emotions recur again and again in the cases we examine, indicating some degree of cross-cultural convergence in concepts of emotion and their contexts of use. These convergences provide useful "comparative reference points" (Lutz and White 1986:428) for exploring relations among emotion, social structure, interpersonal conflict, and culturally organized attempts at repair. Descriptions of the presence or absence of specific emotions and the degree to which they are elaborated in folk theories, topicalized in discourse, and deployed in social situations all contribute to our understanding of the ways conflict is formulated and managed in the socio-emotional life of a community.

Anger

All the cases taken up here uncover some form of anger as a problematic response to social transgression, to actions perceived as an offense to persons, or as a violation of the moral order. But societies differ in the specific ways they find anger to be problematic and hence a matter to be addressed in procedures for disentangling. Where a transgression goes unredressed or an offense uncompensated, it is commonly seen to produce or intensify anger on the part of the aggrieved person. The manifestations of intensified anger in either an outward expression of moral outrage or an unvoiced resentment pose twin dilemmas for small-scale Pacific Island communities where the continuance of interpersonal relations is a foremost social value. Cultures may selectively emphasize anger suppressed or anger expressed, depending on ideological and social structural factors.[6] It is in this nexus of social and personal processes that ethnopsychological assumptions elaborate the consequences of interpersonal conflict, specifying its significance for persons and collectivities alike.

The dangers of anger and other negative emotions are likely to be articulated in metaphors (Ito 1985), explained by ethnotheories (White 1985), and resolved with culturally constituted procedures. Most of the societies in this volume exhibit clearly delineated ideas about the dangers posed by suppressed anger. Explicit theories about the illness- or misfortune-inducing effects of hidden bad feelings are found in A'ara, Kwara'ae, Hawai'i, and Nukulaelae. Of these, it is those which most elaborate a notion of "inner" self (however linked to the interpersonal world) where disentangling involves personal revelation or discovery, as in the A'ara "opening up" and the Hawaiian "peeling away the layers." These cases are also those which most explicitly topicalize emotion as a focus for conflict discourse. In other cases, such as the New Guinea Managalase or the Malaita Kwara'ae, where persons are conceived as a mosaic of *kulas* extending out into the social world, it is problems of equality and relatedness which are most threatened by perceived anger.

Since all the contexts we examine concern themselves with the transformation of interpersonal conflict, the problem of anger associated with those conflicts impinges upon each of them in some way. Indeed, these activities can be crudely ordered according to the ways they define and deal with perceived anger as a potential source of disruption. For all of them, anger both motivates disentangling and poses a threat to its completion. However, for those activities concerned primarily with moral repair, anger is not so much a force to be restrained as it is a posture to be redefined or transformed. In such events (A'ara disentangling, Fiji Indian *pancayat*, Hawaiian *ho'oponopono*, and Kwara'ae counseling), the work of reconciliation is marked by emotions of pathos. This is in contrast to those activities concerned more overtly with producing statements on contested issues, such as the Samoan *fono* or the Trobriand "court," where anger and violence lurk at the margins as a means of expressing disagreement and challenging the production of authoritative accounts. Mutual acknowledgement of these possibilities allows actors to manipulate, whether playfully or seriously, various emotional postures. The cross-cultural literature is full of examples of anger as an idiom of assertion, a mask of sincerity, a rhetoric for the promotion of moral claims (e.g., Bailey 1983; Schieffelin 1983). But the assertiveness of anger may also contain its own moral risks and ambivalences, as implied by the agitated Managalase big-man who declares, "I am not angry." Various routinized means of dealing with the problem of expressed anger are used, ranging from the Trobriand "bailiff" who drags unruly participants out of the village plaza to the ceremonial decorum of the Samoan *fono*. In contexts where persons are insulated from the moral force of discourse through mechanisms of indirection or ambiguity (as in Managalase allegories, Fijian joking, or Tannese silences), the situational ethos is less marked by passions of conflict.

Shame

Just as concerns with anger are both widespread and variably constructed, so concerns with shame recur in the papers to follow. The emotion of shame, discussed widely in the cross-cultural literature (e.g., Piers and Singer 1971; Levy and Rosaldo 1983; Epstein 1984), is especially interesting because of its moral ambiguity—regarded as positive and necessary for maintaining proper relations (see, e.g., Fajans 1985; Kirkpatrick 1985), yet sometimes intensely problematic, requiring deliberate procedures for its alleviation. In our studies of disentangling, shame emerges as problematic, more as a property of interpersonal relations than individuals. A precipitating transgression may be less the focus in talk of shame than the break in normative relations it implies. As a response to violations of relationship, shame is experienced most acutely in face-to-face situations where the self and the damaged relation are directly exposed. It is the anticipation of moral exposure that commonly leads to mutual avoidance as the parties involved acknowledge the disrupted state of their relations. In this way shame becomes an idiom for interpersonal conflict, signifying continuing disruption in valued relations and motivating their repair. Whereas anger within the moral community is widely seen as a danger that must be alleviated or controlled, shame may be regarded as antithetical to the very relations that make community possible and so must be remedied by somehow reestablishing those relations. It is that "somehow" which concerns the activities we describe in this volume.

In all of the Austronesian societies in our "sample" (i.e., with the exception of Fiji Indian and Managalase), shame enters as a potential by-product of conflict among persons otherwise expected to enjoy enduring and reciprocal relations. As in the case of anger, ethnopsychological notions of shame extend the implications of conflict through cultural time and across social space by specifying its continuing consequence for persons and communities. Levine, for example, notes that shame brackets a form of disentangling or collective "therapy" among the New Guinea Kafe (1982:85). Culturally elaborated shame creates social distance and requires avoidance, affecting daily life by suspending ordinary channels of communication and interaction. Many of the contexts we examine acquire their cultural *raison d'être* as situations facilitating an otherwise impossible communication: face-to-face talk among the principals involved in conflict. This function perhaps best accounts for the visibility of these activities as extraordinary situations marked by distinct forms of discourse. For example, Duranti notes that the "liminality" of the Samoan *fono* as a formal occasion permits direct talk about transgressions of chiefs that would be highly shaming in other settings. Talk of chiefly transgressions is allowed and encouraged by defining the situation as one of decorous discussion among chiefs aimed at reconciliation (see Irvine 1979). Other contexts we consider insulate participants from the potential shame of moral discourse by limiting either its "exposure" (as in the restricted groups engaging in Hawaiian *ho'oponopono*, Kwara'ae counseling, and Nukulaelae gossip) or its moral weight (as in genres of indirect speech such as Fijian joking, A'ara emotion talk, Managalase parables, and the ambiguity of Tannese testimonies, among others). These activities create opportunities for discourse that, by its very enactment, signals an end to burdensome avoidance. The sheer coparticipation of persons entangled in conflict in a process aimed at reconciliation achieves a (rhetorical) realignment of real and ideal social relations in accordance with shared values of mutual involvement and solidarity.

It is here that generalization begins to obscure culturally distinctive ways in which shame acquires social meaning and force. Shame may be variously elaborated as either a *response* of the (collective) self manifest in avoidance or as a *strategy* for challenge, correction, or humiliation of the other. In our studies focused on conflict transformation, cultural concerns with avoidance and means for resolving it are most in evidence.[7] Not only is shaming-as-challenge generally absent from the contexts we examine, but, where it does appear (as in A'ara disentangling and Kwara'ae counseling), the idiom of shame is used for opposite effect: as an appeal for reconciliation, a reminder that the relations disrupted are of the close, valued sort where shame ideally has no place. Within the range of activities considered, two types of concern with shame surface. On the one hand, the small, family-centered activities of Hawaiian *ho'oponopono* and Kwara'ae counseling are concerned with containing conflicts and disagreements that have the potential to produce further, collective shame if they enter wider circles of discourse. On the other hand, activities such as A'ara disentangling and Tannese "courts" seek to redefine events that have already erupted in conflict and thereby to bring an end to shame and avoidance. As Lindstrom notes, the pragmatic outcome of Tannese "courts" is more aptly labeled "avoidance resolution" than "conflict resolution."

It is clear that, however they may be defined, notions of shame are an important idiom for conceptualizing conflict and pursuing its resolution. Numerous writers have suggested that the shape of ethnopsychological concepts of shame may be systematically related to sociopolitical structure and, specifically, to a society's means of handling conflict (e.g., Rosaldo 1984). Thus, Epstein (1984:44) speculates that there is "a close connection between local conceptions of shame, more particularly the means that different societies characteristically employ for promoting and discharging shame, and modes of dispute-management." He goes on to hypothesize that extensive use of shaming techniques occurs in societies lacking clearly developed jural procedures for handling conflict. In other words, shaming provides a functional equivalent for judicial process—a political analog of the social control functions of shame identified by earlier analysts interested in the ways psyches function without clearly developed Western guilt.[8]

Although we do not have a systematic selection of cases, the societies here represented do not support the hypothesis that shame or shaming is most elaborated in places where jural institutions are undeveloped or nonexistent. Indeed, the two cases that give the clearest evidence for the elaboration of shame concepts in political process (Fiji and Samoa) are also those with the most well-developed hierarchical institutions of leadership and decision making. More importantly, our data show shame practices and judicial procedures to fulfill *complementary* rather than equivalent functions in several of these societies. Evoking, intensifying, and resolving shame are, in these cases, pragmatic moves aimed primarily at readjusting social relations rather than asserting decisions or judgments, as is often the function of legal institutions. In one episode described by White, A'ara disentangling is enacted *after* a government court case so that the participants might deal with the interpersonal repercussions of judicial process. This sequence—legal process followed by moral work—is also that of the Fiji Indian *pancayat* discussed by Brenneis, who quotes one man as saying, "The political work is finished; religious work is remaining."

Social Structure, Events,
and the Organization of Discourse

Discourse Analysis

Definitions of "discourse" and approaches to discourse analysis are many (see Harris 1952; Coulthard 1978; Cicourel 1980; van Dijk 1985). A major distinction differentiates those interested in relations between discourse and conceptual schemata (e.g., Hutchins 1980; Quinn and Holland 1987) and those who examine the interactive structuring of discourse in such diverse forms as frames, routines, episodes, and genres (spanning works as different as Goffman 1974; Gumperz 1982; Ochs 1986). Recent interest in the work of the psychologist Vygotsky reflects an increasing concern with bridging cognitive and social functional approaches to discourse (see, e.g., Wertsch 1985; Holland and Valsiner 1988).

Studies in this volume focus on discourse in conflict events as a way of examining both the social ecology of cognition and the cultural framing of interaction. Although each analysis focuses on a text (i.e., a sequence of recorded utterances; see note 2) the power of the analyses lies in their attempt to examine discourse processes as simultaneously interactive and conceptual. Moreover, the analyses point to the mutual relevance of disentangling events and wider societal and historical processes. Although these studies cannot pursue these relations in depth, they do suggest avenues of collaboration between poststructuralist views of discourse as institutional process (e.g., Foucault 1981; Abu-Lughod 1990) and event-centered modes of analysis (see Lindstrom, this volume).

Contemporary analyses of discourse make use of perspectives in linguistics, sociology, anthropology, and literary analysis. Similarly, our studies draw from a range of approaches and show them to be complementary and useful for ethnographic work. We have been primarily influenced by the ethnography of communication in linguistic anthropology and sociolinguistics (e.g., Gumperz and Hymes 1972), by recent work on cultural models (e.g., Holland and Quinn 1987), and by conversational analysis in sociology (e.g., Goffman 1974; Sacks et al. 1974). In particular, all papers examine the interplay of cultural understandings, the characteristics of talk as text, functional relationships between text and interaction, and the structure and role of sociopolitical factors in shaping participation and interpretation.

As Malinowski (1923, 1965) argued from his study of language in Trobriand society and culture, language is a "mode of action." With Malinowski, Bateson (1972), Burke (1966), and others, we view communication (especially speech) as social action and social action as constitutive of social relations (Firth 1975). As Myers and Brenneis (1984:28) note, "Political talk goes beyond persuasion and display. At the heart it compels specific visions of the social world through its own organization." (See also Brenneis 1988.) The role of discourse organization in defining, framing, and shaping disentangling events, adversative talk (Fraser 1985; Grimshaw 1990), emotions, and "visions of the social world" are all concerns of this volume.

In examining the relationships among context, speakers' intent, expectations for interaction, and social meaning, ethnographers of communication focus on speech events (Hymes 1972) and speech activities (Levinson 1979; Gumperz 1982). Following Levinson's definition of "activity type," a culturally recognized speech event or activity is "a goal-defined, socially constituted, bounded event, with *constraints* on participants, setting, and so on, and above all, on kinds of allowable contributions" (1979:368). "Allowable contributions" include speech, gesture, and other forms of meaningful action. By definition, then, such activities are contextually situated and governed by norms of interaction. Speakers come to an activity with a set of background understandings about the nature of the event or activity, what is to be accomplished in it, and how it is to be performed. For example, the speech activities we describe vary in the extent to which they are overtly defined as disentangling activities. Trobriand land litigation, Hawaiian *ho'oponopono*, and A'ara disentangling are all activities clearly demarcated by participants as dealing with conflict. In contrast, Nukulaelae gossip encounters are not locally seen as ways to resolve conflicts (although the act of "talking thoroughly" as reenacted by the gossiper is perceived as such).

Beyond an utterance's propositional content and illocutionary force (Searle 1969), cues about how an utterance is to be socially understood are signaled by and embedded in exchanges among speakers (Gumperz 1970). Both encoding and decoding social meaning depend on shared rules of inference and interpretation (Gumperz 1982). A primary task in discourse analysis is to account for the sociocultural knowledge presumed by speakers and to retrieve the rules of inference and interaction governing their behavior. Although some discourse analysts have argued that social meaning must be located in the interaction itself, our studies show that social meaning is *signaled* but not necessarily manifest in interaction. Interpretation of most socially important discourse is based not only on discourse itself and its immediate context, but also on the larger set of contexts in which both are embedded. These contexts involve a variety of micro- and macroinfluences, including the prior history of interaction among participants, local models of person and action, and institutional constraints such as socioeconomic and political factors.

Hierarchy and Equality in Disentangling Events and in Society

A recurring theme in our volume is the relationship of sociopolitical organization to disentangling processes. The most prominent aspect of this relationship is the role of power and social hierarchy in conflict discourse. The opposition of hierarchy and equality (each necessary to the other) has framed numerous analyses of political systems in Oceania. Marked by Sahlins's (1963) influential use of these terms to contrast Melanesian and Polynesian styles of leadership, many studies have characterized political institutions in terms of big-man and chiefly types. As more and more accounts from the heterogeneous Melanesian area describe chiefly styles of leadership (e.g., Douglas 1979; Friedman 1981; Allen 1984), and as others find big-man attributes in Polynesia (e.g., Marcus 1989), ethnographic debate focuses more closely on the production and reproduction of power in everyday encounters. We examine the process by which status and power are manifest in disentangling events as a way of identifying relations between those events and leadership in the wider society.

Studies of political language in the region have provided the most detailed accounts of the mechanisms of social control and influence commonly used in key performances. Bloch's (1975) landmark essay on political language and oratory attempted to link oratorical or "formalized language" to the function of social control in traditional societies. Myers and Brenneis (1984) have criticized Bloch's position, arguing that "egalitarian" societies in the Pacific seem concerned more with personal autonomy than with social control. They suggest that in societies emphasizing individual autonomy, "the polity is constituted through speech and those events in which it takes place; social order is an achievement and a performance." In societies characterized by relations of dominance and subordination, political order is taken for granted, and there is "considerable concern for public political performance" (p. 28).[9]

In essence, this view poses two related questions: "To what extent does power make context possible?" and obversely, "To what extent does context make power possible?" The first question points to political organization at the societal level and the extent to which hierarchical or more egalitarian political arrangements influence the social organization, modes of discourse, goals, and anticipated outcomes for disentangling activities. The second question points to the role of a socially and symbolically marked context in creating a situated power base for forms of dominance or leadership not necessarily found in other contexts or in the larger society. Specifically, this question suggests a distinction between power relations *in society* that involve institutional arrangements for political leadership and power relations created by and enacted *in specific events*.

We do not find a close fit between sociopolitical organization, forms of political action, and modes of talk in the events examined here, but certain patterns do emerge (see also Watson-Gegeo 1986). For example, in relatively hierarchical Polynesia, as exemplified by Samoa, Tikopia, and Maori (see Duranti, this volume; Firth 1975; Salmond 1975), and in Micronesia (not represented in this volume, but see Black 1983; Silverman 1977; Ward 1980), disentangling or decision-making meetings are more likely to be organized and chaired by leaders, possibly speaking for chiefs in whom real power resides. The Samoan *fono* exemplifies this arrangement, where orators speak on behalf of the chiefs and where tight organization and control are maintained over the proceedings. In Melanesia, where there is great diversity but relatively egalitarian social systems prevail, discussion of conflict and ordinary decision-making meetings frequently do not exhibit hierarchical leadership (colonial-style "courts" are an exception; see essays by Hutchins and Lindstrom). In Santa Isabel, for example, disentangling meetings are virtually without directive leadership.

But there are also cases in which leadership arrangements at the societal level are at variance with the structure of disentangling activities. Fiji Indian society is relatively egalitarian, for instance, yet the *pancayat* is carefully, almost rigidly structured to promote an outcome decided in advance by those who organize and lead it. The control that a Kwara'ae counselor exerts over *fa'amanata'anga* sessions is also in distinct contrast to the egalitarian relations normally obtaining in the wider society. For Fiji Indians (whose egalitarian society belies its hierarchical parentage), the control exerted by *pancayat* leaders over the session is meant to protect disputants from losing face and thus to preserve the egalitarian nature of the larger social structure. In the Kwara'ae case, two explanations are possible. First, the counselor's role may reflect an earlier political structure—Kwara'ae had a chiefdom system which disintegrated perhaps ten generations ago (cf. Douglas 1979). Second, the counselor does not speak as an individual telling others what to do, but as the voice of *falafala* 'culture, tradition'. The cultural meaning of the counselor's role is thus different from its apparent function in the event's organization. These data give additional support to conjectures put forth by Myers and Brenneis (1984) about relations between societal hierarchy and modes of political discourse. If in strongly hierarchical societies such as Samoa and Tikopia (Firth 1975) the power of chiefs makes certain contexts—e.g., *fono* events—possible, then we can say that in egalitarian Kwara'ae, the context created by *fa'amanata'anga* sessions makes power possible in the form of the counselor's complete control.

Yet in both hierarchical and egalitarian political settings, strong constraints limit who may participate. Seen in this light, any simple notion of an egalitarian Melanesia quickly dissolves.

In most of the speech activities we describe, the right to speak is often limited to or greatly controlled by adult males (cf. Lindstrom, this volume). And in similar events reported elsewhere, only important men may speak (see Strathern 1975; Lederman 1984; Goldman 1983; McKellin 1984; Rumsey 1985). Moreover, in many Melanesian societies—exemplified in this volume by Tanna and Kwara'ae—social rank is just as important as in Polynesian societies, albeit with different political and social implications.

The degree of hierarchical structuring of events is also related to their goals and expected outcomes. For example, where recognized hierarchical relations most clearly structure the disentangling event or activity, the expected outcome of the activity is often explicit. Thus, in Hawaiian *ho'oponopono* led by a senior family member such as a parent, and in the Samoan *fono* organized and controlled by chiefs, the goal is frequently to clarify responsibility for actions, and the expected outcome is *apology*.[10] Alternatively, in Trobriand land litigation, where the goal is to clarify the history of a garden's legitimate occupancy, "bailiffs" control the proceedings, and the expected outcome is a *decision* in the form of a chiefly pronouncement about who may legally use the garden. The same set of relations and outcomes obtains for formal and informal public "courts" in the Tolai (Epstein 1974) and Mt. Hagen (M. Strathern 1974) societies of Papua New Guinea, for public meetings in the Micronesian societies of Banaba (Silverman 1977) and Tobi (Black 1983), and for *ala'anga*, public meetings and courts among the Kwara'ae (Watson-Gegeo and Gegeo 1979, 1987). Outcomes in other kinds of events discussed in this volume are much less explicit. In A'ara disentangling, for instance, the overt goal is to talk out hidden feelings and arrive at a collective interpretation, not a public decision, Fiji Indian *pancayat* and Nukulaelae gossip (cf. Lederman 1984).

Establishing an authoritative version of reality subscribed to by all parties is, however, difficult. After all, individuals have a vested interest in what is to be taken as authoritative. Cooperation to the extent of discussing and negotiating the ultimate public account does occur. But adversative talk is not inherently cooperative talk. For all the events we discuss, establishing a desired social reality that exerts moral force beyond the bounds of the meeting itself is problematic. This is so even for those events with explicit outcomes, such as Samoan *fono*, Trobriand litigation, Tanna "witnessing" meetings, and Kwara'ae *ala'anga* village courts. For instance, the Tannese have no explicit mechanisms through which to enforce a decision once taken, and their meetings end in ambiguous silence. In more hierarchical systems, explicit, formal provisions for enforcement may be made. In Kwara'ae *ala'anga* (but not the counseling described by Watson-Gegeo and Gegeo in this volume), decisions are enforced by the weight of public opinion, and in precontact times the elder who convened the court designated provisions for enforcement (Watson-Gegeo and Gegeo 1979).

Nevertheless, situations defined as occasions for talk about interpersonal conflict provide a frame for interactively constructing and collectively understanding the meaning of prior events. When statements are uttered and acknowledged as part of the social life of the group, they may achieve a kind of validity and efficacy not otherwise possible. In some cases, the moral force of collectively constructed accounts is analogous to the power that words achieve in certain ritual contexts where symbol and referent seem to merge in the act of signification (cf. Weiner 1984). The more that the accounts so constructed matter—that is, are seen and heard to be socially, politically, and emotionally powerful—the more they are subject to regulation, management, and rhetorical packaging so as to carefully define and constrain relations among speaker, utterance, and action.

Social Organization and Discourse Mode

Issues of formality, indirection, and modes of discourse organization are related to societal political structure and to the intended purposes and outcomes of disentangling activities. "Formality" refers to certain characteristics of the situation and the structuring of the event itself and the speech accompanying it. The attributes of formality in communicative events outlined by Irvine (1979) are useful to the analyses given here: Formal contexts or events, for instance, are characterized by the invocation of positional and public identities rather than personal identities, an emphasis on social distance over intimacy, a showing of respect for the established social order, the emergence of a central situational focus ("a dominant mutual engagement that encompasses all persons present"; Goffman 1963:164), and a general tone of seriousness. Formal discourse involves increased code structuring (usually through additional rules or conventions governing style, word choice, text sequencing, and participation structure), and greater consistency of choices within or between codes (i.e., stronger co-occurrence constraints).

Formalization of context and speech frequently marks disentangling events, setting them apart from ordinary informal interaction. In Kwara'ae counseling, for example, formalization intensifies the impact of the session's message, a characteristic effectively used by parents in child socialization. Especially in those cases where no overt problem-solving outcome is defined, various rhetorical strategies are employed to facilitate communication on sensitive matters without running contrary to the definition of the situation. Chief among the strategies identified in this volume is *indirection*, which occurs in both formal and informal contexts and discourse. Although widely used to describe speech, "direct" and "indirect" discourse are not yet established analytical constructs, in that analysis of the constituents of direct and indirect speech comparable to that offered by Irvine (1979) for notions of formality has only recently been suggested (see Brenneis 1986). With this caveat in mind, it is nevertheless noticeable that disentangling activities may intend to "straighten out" problems, but the discourse routes to this goal are seldom direct, even where they are said to involve "straight speech." Relatively direct speech is often associated with decision making (whether or not the results are binding), as in the *talanoaga* phase of the Samoan *fono*, Tanna witnessing meetings, Tolai hearings (Epstein 1974), Trobriand courts, and Banaban community meetings (Silverman 1977). In the Tikopia *fono*, held to announce chiefly decisions to commoners, speech is also direct and literal—perhaps reflecting the social relations between chief/orator and commoner and the status of the message (more a proclamation than a topic of debate; see Arno 1986; Firth 1975). Talk in Hawaiian *ho'oponopono* is also relatively direct and sincere, setting this speech activity apart from most other Hawaiian social interactions (with the exception of discipline contexts; see Boggs 1985; Boggs and Chun, this volume). Of the above studies, even where direct speech is the norm, politeness and face-saving remain important.

Reliance almost exclusively on indirect styles of speech is associated with tensions between competing individuals in relatively egalitarian societies and with societies in which the speaker gains or displays prestige through oratory. In Melanesia,where the overt social ideology is often egalitarian and where disentangling activities may be defined as fact-finding, speakers use quoted speech, metaphor, and other devices to avoid direct confrontation and to distance themselves from responsibility for accusations or interpretations (see White, this volume; see also Goldman 1983, Gewertz 1984, Black 1983). In disentangling narratives, causal assumptions, particularly those with strongly moral implications, are usually unstated. On the one hand, this is typical of the cognitive economy of discourse generally. But, leaving moral implications unstated in these contexts creates an ambiguity necessary to the definition of the situation and the successful cooperative negotiation of the event. Our studies provide numerous examples of the cultural patterning of moral inference, ranging from the propositional content of A'ara emotion talk to the Managalase allegories of intention and the nuances of judgment encoded in Nukulaelae gossip or Kwara'ae counseling.

A classic Melanesian example of indirection is the "veiled speech" of the Mt. Hagen (Melpa) area (A. Strathern 1975; Lederman 1984), where oratory is an avenue to political power (see also Rumsey 1985; Merlan and Rumsey n.d.; and compare the Maori of Polynesia, Mahuta 1974; Salmond 1975). Of this volume's ethnographic "sample," the extreme case of indirection is displayed in Managalase ha'a or allegory, one of several forms of indirect speech reflecting the Managalase sensitivity to social tensions and their ambivalence toward personal power. As the "hidden path," ha'a allegories are remarkable for the degree to which they bear alternative interpretations, making them a finely tuned test of the listener's social and cultural knowledge (see also McKellin 1984).

Another kind of indirection is illustrated by Nukulaelae gossip encounters, where speakers avoid direct accusations by reenacting telltale interactions with the intended social message embedded in paralinguistic and gestural cues, as well as in the ordering of the account's events. Similar strategies are undoubtedly found among gossipers in many other Pacific societies.

The role of direct and indirect speech in disentangling must be examined in relation to a society's overall *speech economy* (Hymes 1974), of which the immediate activity or event is apart. Speech economy refers to the formal and functional relationships of modes or ways of speaking, both to each other and to the larger social system. Among the egalitarian Fiji Indians, speech in the *pancayat* is relatively informal and direct, and the goal of the event is to construct a public account and reestablish good relationships.

Such "straight talk" contrasts sharply with the oblique references to issues, events, and personal identities in the "sweet talk" of religious speeches (*parbacan*). Religious speeches—like gossip (Besnier, this volume; Brison 1989; Haviland 1977)—are used to recruit supporters by representing one's opponents as immoral, thereby implying that a private dispute is really a public issue, while at the same time forestalling revenge through oblique talk (Brenneis 1984). Gossip is also indirect and opaque, relying on metaphor, irony, double entendre, innuendo, and reported speech, and rendered without any orienting information (thereby serving as a measure of sociocultural knowledge, much like Managalase allegory). Religious speeches and gossip are ways to manage conflict indirectly where simple avoidance has failed. But when a dispute finally needs arbitration in a *pancayat*, the issues are discussed openly in "straight talk," albeit carefully orchestrated in advance to prevent open conflict and a loss of face for everyone. In this example we see the importance of examining forms and uses of direct/indirect speech in the larger speech economy. Parallel examples are found throughout this volume. Land courts examined by Hutchins emphasize direct speech, described locally as "straight" and "strong" speech. Here the goal is to arrive at a decision on land rights. But indirect speech is extremely important in Trobriand culture, where a personal goal is to protect one's thoughts from penetration by others because exposure is dangerous. Persuasive speech is formalized with a variety of devices to make meaning ambiguous. As discussed by Weiner (1984), the danger of "hard words"—speaking the truth directly—is that immediate and violent repercussions may follow. These understandings give important context to Hutchins's argument that a major unstated goal of land litigation is the control of volatile emotions, especially anger, associated with the direct talk of court situations.

Both direct and indirect speech may occur *within* disentangling contexts as well, as with the distinction between *laauga* and *talanoaga* speeches in the Samoan *fono* referred to above. The Kwara'ae counselor's talk combines indirect statements (usually general statements about culture and behavior, talking about someone else's behavior, making reference to traditional stories, or using metaphors) with direct descriptions of the target subject's behavior or challenges to his or her line of reasoning. Arno similarly reports a distinction between joking debate, where conflict is dealt with indirectly, and gossip, where directness of speech depends on who is talking and who is present (see also Arno 1980).

The Politics of Participation

As with discourse mode, the situational structuring of disentangling events is related to societal organization and reflects the intended purposes and outcomes of the activities. The most important organizational aspect, in this regard, is *participation structure*, which refers to constraints on who can say what to whom, how, and when (Philips 1972). Among the studies in this volume, those contexts defined as the most "problem-solving" (i.e., which appear the most like "disputes") usually allow multiple voices in an interactive dialogue. This is true for Hawaiian *ho'oponopono*, Trobriand land litigation, and the Samoan *fono*, for instance, as well as for the Fiji Indian *pancayat* (even though the interaction is carefully controlled by the interrogating council).

Other contexts focusing more directly on the creation of publicly accepted accounts or socio-emotional reality (e.g., A'ara disentangling, Kwara'ae counseling, and Nukulaelae gossip) feature lengthy interpretive accounts by individual speakers. But most contexts in this volume include both kinds of formats distributed across the various phases of the meeting, sometimes indicating shifts in the definition of discourse. For example, *laauga* speeches meant to establish or reaffirm the Samoan socio-emotional reality occur in the first phase of the *fono* and are formal and indirect (by virtue of tropes, poetic phrases, etc.). Only chiefs and orators deliver them, and the order of speakers is constrained. During the debate portion of the *fono*, *talanoaga* speeches—which are less formal and more direct—may be given by any adult male, and give-and-take interaction is acceptable.

All of the events we examine involve some kind of mediating process, that is, some form of intervention to manage settlement of differences between people. In disputing events where the participation structure is (at least potentially) highly interactive, the mediating process may be institutionalized in a formalized mediator role, as in the Fiji Indian *pancayat*, Tanna witnessing meetings, Trobriand land litigation, Hawaiian *ho'oponopono*, and Kwara'ae counseling. Mediators steer interaction away from confrontation by providing authoritative interpretations of statements and actions and by structuring turn-taking and topic introduction. In other cases, mediation is not invested in an individual but negotiated collaboratively, as in A'ara disentangling where speakers jointly coordinate their efforts to manage topics and turn-taking.

Since the very enactment of disentangling events is, in most cases, a significant socio-moral statement, the question of who participates and how participation is managed is likely to be politically charged. One measure of this concern is the degree to which the event is planned in advance (that is, participants enter the meeting with a mutually agreed upon topic or set of issues to be discussed). Such is the case for A'ara disentangling meetings, Trobriand land litigation sessions, Samoan *fono*, and Fiji Indian *pancayat*. In these cases, setting the topic or issues for discussion is a group task. That process may involve one party bringing a "case" against another, together with a public recognition that a dispute is occurring and must be dealt with, as in Trobriand land litigation. Or the process may involve a collaborative targeting of a socio-moral breach as disruptive to social relationships and the spiritual order so as to threaten the community, as in A'ara disentangling. Shaping the direction of this collectively negotiated naming of topic and issues is of great political consequence, as shown in the median case of Tanna, where the topic of the meeting is negotiated *in situ*, but designation of the witnesses who run the meeting and shape its consensual outcome is a matter for intense maneuvering among disputants.

Even where meeting topics are collectively set, as in land disputes, a challenger's ability to force a meeting may be more important than the plausibility of his or her "case." Despite the seeming mutuality of event planning, the role of socially recognized and politically important opinion leaders may be critical in determining what issues get public attention and how they become resolved.

In the contrasting sort of arrangement, topics of disentangling events are not jointly planned in advance. This is the case with Managalase allegory, Nukulaelae gossip, and Fijian joking debates. Here someone who takes on the self-definition of a wronged person initiates the activity; or else the initiator does so on behalf of a relative, friend, or ally who has been wronged. All three of these activities involve indirect speech, affording the hearer an opportunity to ignore the intended message. Indeed, no genuine resolution can be sought through allegory, gossip, or joking debate. It would seem, then, that the minimum requirement for resolution is a collective agreement on the issue(s) needing to be disentangled.

Kwara'ae counseling is a mixed case, in that it may be held on the counselor's own initiative or mutually negotiated with others. The example given by Watson-Gegeo and Gegeo involves the counselor responding to a request by an intermediary for the wronged person, after which the counselor privately investigated the situation before planning in advance how to do the counseling. Second, once the topic is set, the degree of backstage preparation for disentangling activities also reflects political concern. The most careful management is evident in the Samoan *fono* and the Fiji Indian *pancayat*, which share a similar purpose in constructing a ritualized statement of collective harmony on matters of prior conflict. In the Samoan case, Duranti notes that the statement must not err on the side of *over*–ritualization. In contrast, the *pancayat* is completely ritualized, with the discourse modulated by question-answer pairs in which the answer is already known and even the order of questions is determined in advance by council members who orchestrate the questioning. Such highly controlled events are designed to prevent the dispute from breaking into open conflict in which participants' reputations and relationships could suffer permanent damage. But all events examined in this volume involve varying degrees of planning, whether in terms of the structuring of events or features of planned discourse, in which a disputant lays out in advance a course of argument for himself or herself.

For events in which their occurrence alone goes a long way toward ensuring the desired public outcome (i.e., producing a visible sign that participants mutually acknowledge restored relations), the most critical step may simply be to make the event happen. For example, persuading the parties concerned to convene a ho'oponopono, even though a single such meeting may fail to come to a resolution, signals that participants recognize and value their mutual social relations. Such is also the case with A'ara disentangling and with those cases of Kwara'ae counseling where there has been public arrangement of the session in advance. These kinds of events also underline the fact that when disputes involve interpersonal relationships and ongoing political feuds, "resolution" is temporary at best. It is much more typical that the same issues are returned to again and again, using a variety of activities and strategies to disentangle them.

Variation Within and Across Event Types

Variation in disentangling involves two considerations: variation within specific genres and relationships among genres of conflict-handling across the society. Our studies all describe the prototypic form for a culturally specific disentangling event. Our descriptions are for the most part abstracted from the observation of several cases of the event by attending to its minimal characteristics, stages or phases, and to its socially recognized strategies for participation. Nevertheless, we also show that there is considerable within-genre variation. Boggs and Chun sketch variation in kinds of Hawaiian ho'oponopono as practiced in the past and in the present—among religious groups, in Westernized therapy sessions, and in Hawaiian families. Variants of A'ara disentangling and Kwara'ae counseling depend in part on whether the goal of the session is preventive (held to forestall trouble) or therapeutic (held to resolve problems). Many of the events we discuss continue as emblems and repositories of indigenous moral systems, as ways in which tradition can be maintained and venerated against the pressures of social change. Similarly, colonization and Christianization have altered the original form of some events— including *ho'oponopono*, now undergoing changes influenced by American ethnopsychology, particularly psychotherapy (Ito 1985; Shook 1985).

A second kind of variation involves contrast between genre types used to disentangle conflicts in a given society. Once again the notion of speech economy becomes important. As analytic studies, the papers in this volume represent event-centered ethnography, an approach concerned with micro-analysis of well-defined events used as lenses to scrutinize cultural understandings and principles. Our studies show that, as events concerned with defining, interpreting, evaluating, and negotiating social reality, disentangling events offer special insight into the social order. But we also take the position that the event of focus must be analytically situated in relation to other events, contexts, and interactions that significantly affect its meaning. Moreover, any disentangling event is likely to be only one activity in a conflict process itself embedded in wider social processes. We show that conflict "resolution" should be conceptualized as a spectrum or range of activities, interactions, events, and contexts, involving individuals and collectivities at various points in a temporal process. Strategies and postures adopted in relation to a "conflict" or "problem" vary across this range of interactions/contexts, just as the cultural definition of what is going on also varies. Yet together they form a chain of interactions aimed at progressively transforming conflict. Disentangling activities, therefore, can be seen as episodes located in a temporally sequenced continuum of such episodes and events, with goals, outcomes, and strategies for social action organized accordingly. For instance, Brenneis's study of the Fiji Indian *pancayat* shows the *pancayat* to be a stage in a conflict process where disputants and the larger community formulate a public moral account following a long history of the dispute and earlier attempts at resolution. Similarly, A'ara disentangling occurs in a sequence of attempts to bring about moral repair. Moreover, Nukulaelae gossip sessions can be located at the beginning, middle, and end-points of conflict processes, variously creating, propagating, or dealing with conflict.

The course that a given conflict follows should therefore be carefully described, and the relation of a particular interaction, speech, activity, or event to other social activities and events clarified. Are the described events rare, frequent, or continuous? How are they the same or different from other speaking events in the society? What is the role of ethnotheories of conflict and specific speech forms in the larger society? For example, focusing on the event of Hawaiian ho'oponopono or Kwara'ae counseling requires looking at events that have gone on before or are simultaneously going on with regard to a culturally defined problem. It also requires looking at what *might* go on if the session of focus fails to bring about an expected outcome. These questions are only broached in this volume but challenge future analysts of conflict and discourse processes.

Conclusion

This book takes disentangling discourse as a topic and as a strategy for investigation. We focus on contexts where people talk about their conflicts, and, in attending to what they say and do not say, to what they do and do not do, we begin to understand the social, moral, and emotional universe they invoke and reconstruct in moments of crisis and entanglement.

In the discourse of disentangling people may reformulate cultural ideas, social relations, and personal experience. We assume that every act and every utterance holds possibilities for creating understanding and for moving others to feel and act. These possibilities are most evident in interactional sequences where they are indexed or implied in communicative acts, especially as they are framed and worked out in talk. Disentangling situations offer an intensified version of social reality in the context of marked discourse forms and often heightened feelings. We do not assume that disentangling produces consensus, only that the focused multilogue characteristic of these events reverberates quickly through the collective consciousness of a community. As it does so, multiple voices compete, sometimes in ambiguous and contentious ways, to renew or revise intersubjective understanding. The articulation of structure and event which Sahlins (1985) sees in historical processes of cultural transformation also appears, in microcosm, in the discourse of people attempting to straighten out problematic circumstances through the application of cultural models. Each time a given premise is invoked it raises the possibility of its own revision or restructuring to accommodate disquieting events. When alternative ways of dealing with conflict are discussed in disentangling, and reflexive notions of "tradition" such as the Samoan *fa'a Samoa* or Kwara'ae *falafala* are invoked as emblems of proper conduct, the way is opened for cultural transformation. In the process, assumptions about persons and relatedness coded by those images may find new contexts and meanings as people grapple with the tensions and contradictions of modern life.

But there is more to disentangling practices than moral strategy and structural transformation. For the discourse is an emotional discourse, one of involvement where people discuss issues they find compelling and moving. As such, it affords an important opportunity for the ethnographer to reinject real persons into accounts of sociopolitical process at the same time as situating descriptions of personhood and emotional experience in social events.

Notes

Acknowledgments. In writing this introduction we have profited from discussions with participants at the Pitzer Conference and contributors to the volume. In addition we are especially grateful to John Kirkpatrick and to Niko Besnier, Don Brenneis, David Gegeo, William McKellin, Susan Philips, and Karen Brison for their comments on an earlier draft. The remaining inadequacies are our own.

1. In many Pacific Island societies, the term *disentangling* is a metaphor for deliberate efforts at social problem-solving or moral "straightening." Among the societies taken up in this book, the people of Santa Isabel, Nukulaelae, Malaita, the Trobriand Islands, and Polynesian Hawai'i invoke images of entanglement in their efforts at dealing with interpersonal conflicts. We prefer the label "disentangling" over "conflict resolution" or "dispute management" because disentangling points

to elements of local meaning that organize and guide the activities we examine. To begin with, the notion of disentangling signals a process rather than an end product, indicating that engagement in moral negotiation itself may be more significant than specific decisions or outcomes. Secondly, the image of a tangled net or a knotted line suggests a blockage of purposeful activity, reminding the members of a community that the problem at hand requires attention lest it impede "normal" social life. Disentangling presumes a conception of an unmarked, background state-of-affairs in which the strands of people's lives do not become snarled and ineffective. Whether spoken or implied, these conceptions of "straight" or correct relations may themselves be transfigured in the disentangling process. Despite our wish to examine critically the key terms *conflict* and resolution, we use them throughout this essay to avoid awkward phrasings. Even though we prefer the more metaphoric *disentangling*, we have in places used the phrase conflict resolution as a link to existing literatures.

2. The use of transcripts of recorded discourse is a unifying element in these papers, but there are differences. Authors follow different procedures for rendering speech in transcripts, depending upon the nature and focus of each agenda. In other words, the contributors differ in the ways they *use* transcripts and integrate them into a larger agenda. The limiting case here is the essay by Brenneis, who was not able to use a tape-recorder in the *pancayat* situation but relies on detailed fieldnotes of the interaction. In all other cases, analysis is based on transcripts of tape-recorded material. Boggs and Chun base their analysis on a transcript of the audio portion of a video-taped *ho'oponopono* interaction—a transcript prepared prior to their project (see Shook 1985).

3. We are aware that the category "Western" is a much overused, catch-all category but use it for lack of alternatives as a familiar comparative reference point. The same kinds of cultural critique applied in this volume to differentiate among Pacific practices could be turned on our notion of the West to find a multiplicity of styles and definitions within that unexamined monolith (see, e.g., Kochman 1981).

4. This is not to say, however, that emotions do not play an important and systematic role as a more covert dimension of legal/political discourse. As Bailey (1983) has documented, the "tactical uses" of emotion may be all the more effective as a tacit, unavowed dimension of political rhetoric. In court settings, where the normative view of dispute resolution as rational process is most formalized, emotions are regarded as anathema to truth, seen as best served by a dispassionate recollection of facts and events. As stated by the prosecuting attorney in a recent San Diego murder case, "It's improper to play to emotions" (*Los Angeles Times*, April 14, 1986, II:3).

5. The distinction between felt emotion and cognized emotion can be misleading, deriving as it does from our own dichotomization of "thought" (as abstract reasoning) and "emotion" (as physiologically based feelings) (see Lutz 1987). Talk about emotion in contexts where persons are actively engaged in giving a moral accounting of their own social experience does not simply represent, so much as constitute, its subject matter.

6. Rosaldo's (1984) speculation that broad differences in the social structural requirements of hunter-gatherer societies as opposed to more complex, tribal societies may correspond with different conceptions of anger is suggestive. She hypothesized that the former, with their lack of overlapping mechanisms for binding people together, tend to find the expression of anger intolerable, whereas the latter elaborate the dangers of suppressed anger in theories about the damaging effects of hidden emotions and sorcerous hostility. While the range of cases included here does not span the hunter-gatherer pole of this comparison, these societies do vary significantly in the degree to which political power (authority) is centralized in hierarchical structures. There is, however, little to suggest that differences in this respect correspond with distinct ideologies of anger.

7. Although the gossip session described by Besnier (this volume) would be likely to have shaming effects, as gossip does in many Pacific societies (e.g., Black 1985), there are no examples in this collection of the sorts of overt shaming technique that have been described, especially in Melanesia, as strategies for moral challenge and political maneuver (e.g., Young 1971; B. Schieffelin 1979; E. Schieffelin 1983).

8. The large literature on shame across cultures is dominated by interests in the shame/guilt opposition (e.g., Piers and Singer 1971). Shame has been frequently analyzed as a non-Western analog of guilt, providing a psychosocial mechanism of control where internalized guilt is absent or muted. As a result, the meanings of shame have been systematically skewed toward concerns with responsibility for transgression and away from the relational meanings most evident in this volume. Furthermore, the focus upon the shame/guilt opposition has shifted attention away from differences among varieties of non-Western shame.

9. Arno's proposed typology of persuasive versus impressive speeches is consistent with Myers and Brenneis's (1984) position. Arno (1985) suggests that in egalitarian or individualistic settings where speakers compete for political influence, *persuasive* public speaking will be emphasized, while in more hierarchical situations, *impressive*, non-persuasive speaking will be emphasized. Fijian public speaking is *impressive*, for example, emphasizing common values; but private talk in

the form of joking debate (Arno, this volume) and gossip (Arno 1980) is *persuasive*. It is in the latter contexts that decisions are made and social control manifested, especially among commoners (Arno 1985). Impressive and persuasive speeches may be equally formal, since formality need not involve fixed, formulaic, or highly ritualized formats and speech styles. As Myers and Brenneis argue, the analyst must look at the diversity of political performances within a speech community before characterizing the role of formal and informal language in social control.

The language used in Kwara'ae counseling illustrates the difficulty in arriving at a clear-cut typology, as well as the necessity of examining the relation of speech form to function in conflict events. Counseling is initiated by a code-switch to high rhetoric, the formal level of spoken discourse. As context and event, counseling is formal in Irvine's (1979) terms because of its central situational focus, seriousness, and invoking of positional, public identities (sessions are led by a senior ranking man or woman who speaks as the embodiment of tradition, not as an individual). Although the counselor's talk is constructed around cultural rules and values, named and explained in ritualized ways, counseling is "about" persuading individuals to change their behavior. The counseling event therefore includes impressive and persuasive speaking, both carried out in formal language. In contrast to the Samoan *fono* (Duranti, this volume, and 1983, 1988), which is organized around the distinction between impressive *laauga* speeches and persuasive *talanoaga* speeches (with the two sharply demarcated in form, style, and participants), Kwara'ae counseling talk is constructed precisely on the artful union of the impressive and the persuasive, the counselor's tactics varying according to subtle audience reactions and with the argumentative strategy he or she develops during the session. Although most counselors maintain code consistency (that is, do not mix low and high rhetoric during counseling), examples used to illustrate the effects of behavior are drawn from everyday life and given reality through quoted dialogues rendered in the speech appropriate to the illustration. Emically, in moving from formal, impressive style to informal quoted speech, the counselor shifts from the abstractly cultural to the vividly human (David Gegeo, personal communication).

10. Apology, whether mutual or otherwise, gives at least the appearance of a definitive outcome through specific actions recognized as social repair, as moral resolution. While apology may not necessarily end a conflict, it strikes it from the public record. And, striking conflict from the public record may be perceived locally as more important than actually ending it (Besnier, personal communication; Hickson 1979; Ward 1980).

References

Abu-Lughod, Lila

1990 The Politics of Bedouin Love Poetry. *In* Language and the Politics of Emotion. C. Lutz and L. Abu-Lughod, eds. Cambridge: Cambridge University Press.

Allen, Michael

1984 Elders, Chiefs, and Big Men: Authority Legitimation and Political Evolution in Melanesia. American Ethnologist 11:20–41.

Arno, Andrew

1979 Conflict, Ritual and Social Structure on Yanuyanu Island, Fiji. Bijdragen (Journal of the Royal Anthropological Institute) Deel 135:1–17.

1980 Fijian Gossip as Adjudication: A Communication Model of Informal Social Control. Journal of Anthropological Research 36:343–60.

1985 Impressive Speech and Persuasive Talk: Traditional Patterns of Political Communication in Fiji's Lau Group from the Perspective of Pacific Ideal Types. Oceania 56(2):124–37.

Bailey, F. G.

1983 The Tactical Uses of Passion: An Essay on Power, Reason and Reality. Ithaca, NY: Cornell University Press.

Bateson, Gregory

1972 Steps to an Ecology of Mind. New York: Ballantine.

Beattie, J. H. M.

1957 Informal Judicial Activity in Bunyoro. Journal of African Administration 9:188–95.

Bentley, G. C.

1984 Hermeneutics and World Construction in Maranao Disputing. American Ethnologist 11:642–55.

Black, Peter

1983 Conflict, Morality and Power in a Western Caroline Society. Journal of the Polynesian Society 92:7–30.

1985 Ghosts, Gossip and Suicide: Meaning and Action in Tobian Folk Psychology. *In* Person, Self and Experience: Exploring Pacific Ethnopsychologies. G. White and J. Kirkpatrick, eds. Berkeley: University of California Press.

Bloch, Maurice, ed.
1975   Political Language and Oratory in Traditional Society. New York: Academic Press.

Boggs, Stephen
1985   Speaking, Relating and Learning: A Study of Hawaiian Children at Home and at School. Norwood, NJ: Ablex.

Brenneis, Donald
1986   Shared Territory: Audience, Indirection and Meaning. *In* The Audience as Co-Author. A. Duranti and D. Brenneis, eds. Special issue of Text 6(3):339–47.
1988   Language and Disputing. *In* Annual Review of Anthropology, vol. 17. B. Seigel, ed. Palo Alto: Annual Reviews, Inc.

Brenneis, Donald L., and Fred R. Myers, eds.
1984   Dangerous Words: Language and Politics in the Pacific. New York: New York University Press.

Brison, Karen J.
1989   All Talk and No Action?: How 'Saying is Doing' in Kwanga Meetings. Ethnology 28:97–115.

Burke, Kenneth
1966   Language as Symbolic Action: Essays on Life, Literature and Method. Berkeley: University of California Press.

Cicourel, Aaron V.
1980   Three Models of Discourse Analysis: The Role of Social Structure. Discourse Processes 3(2):101–31.

Comaroff, J. L., and S. Roberts
1981   Rules and Processes: The Cultural Logic of Dispute in an African Context. Chicago: University of Chicago Press

Coulthard, Malcolm
1978   An Introduction to Discourse Analysis. London: Longman.

Douglas, Bronwen
1979   Rank, Power, Authority: A Reassessment of Traditional Leadership in South Pacific Societies. Journal of Pacific History 14:2–27.

Douglas, Mary
1970   Natural Symbols. London: Barrie and Jenkins.

Duranti, Alessandro
1983   Samoan Speechmaking Across Social Events: One Genre In and Out of a Fono. Language in Society 12:1–22.

1988   Intentions, Language, and Social Action in a Samoan Context. Journal of Pragmatics 12:13–33.

Epstein, A. L.

1974   Introduction. *In* Contention and Dispute: Aspects of Law and Social Control in Melanesia. A. Epstein, ed. Canberra: Australian National University Press.

1984   The Experience of Shame in Melanesia: An Essay on the Anthropology of Affect. Royal Anthropological Institute of Great Britain and Ireland. Occasional Paper No. 40. London: Royal Anthropological Institute.

Epstein, A. L., ed.

1974   Contention and Dispute: Aspects of Law and Social Control in Melanesia. Canberra: Australian National University Press.

Fajans, Jane

1985   The Person in Social Context: The Social Character of Baining "Psychology." *In* Person, Self and Experience: Exploring Pacific Ethnopsychologies. G. White and J. Kirkpatrick, eds. Berkeley: University of California Press.

Felstiner, William L. F., Richard L. Abel, and Austin Sarat

1980– The Emergence and Transformation of Disputes: Naming, Blam-
81   ing, Claiming. . . . Law and Society Review 15(3–4):631–54.

Firth, Raymond

1975   Speech-making and Authority in Tikopia. *In* Political Language and Oratory in Traditional Society. Maurice Bloch, ed. New York: Academic Press.

Foucault, Michel

1981   The Order of Discourse. *In* Untying the Text: A Post Structuralist Reader. R. Young, ed. Boston: Routledge and Kegan Paul.

Frake, Charles O.

1977   Plying Frames Can Be Dangerous: Some Reflections on Methodology in Cognitive Anthropology. Quarterly Newsletter of the Institute for Comparative Human Development 1(3):1–7.

Fraser, Bruce

1985   Disputing: The Challenge of Adversative Discourse. Unpublished ms., Boston University.

Friedman, Jonathan

1981   Notes on Structure and History in Oceania. Folk 23:275–95.

Geertz, Clifford
1984 'From the Native's Point of View': On the Nature of Anthropological Understanding. *In* Culture Theory: Essays on Mind, Self and Emotion. R. Shweder and R. LeVine, eds. Cambridge: Cambridge University Press.

Gewertz, Deborah
1984 Of Symbolic Anchors and Sago Soup: The Rhetoric of Exchange Among the Chambri of Papua New Guinea. *In* Dangerous Words: Language and Politics in the Pacific. D. L. Brenneis and F. R. Myers, eds. New York: New York University Press.

Gibbs, James L.
1963 The Kpelle Moot: A Therapeutic Model for the Informal Settlement of Disputes. Africa 33:1–11.

Gluckman, Max
1955 Custom and Conflict in Africa. Glencoe, IL: The Free Press.
1972 Moral Crises: Magical and Secular Solutions. *In* The Allocation of Responsibility. M. Gluckman, ed. Manchester: University of Manchester Press.

Goffman, Erving
1963 Behavior in Public Places: Notes on the Social Organization of Gatherings. Glencoe, IL: The Free Press.
1974 Frame Analysis: An Essay on the Organization of Experience. Cambridge, MA: Harvard University Press.

Goldman, Laurence R.
1983 Talk Never Dies: The Language of Huli Disputes. New York: Tavistock.

Grice, H. P.
1975 Logic and Conversation. *In* Syntax and Semantics, Vol. 3 of Speech Acts, P. Cole and J. L. Morgan, eds. New York: Academic Press.

Grimshaw, Alan D., ed.
1990 Conflict Talk: Sociolinguistic Investigations of Arguments in Conversations. Cambridge: Cambridge University Press (in press).

Gumperz, John J.
1970 Sociolinguistics and Communication in Small Groups. Work-

ing Paper no. 33. Language Behavior Research Laboratory. Berkeley: University of California.

1982 Discourse Strategies. Cambridge: Cambridge University Press.

Gumperz, John J., and Dell Hymes, eds.

1972 Directions in Sociolinguistics: The Ethnography of Communication. New York: Holt, Rinehart and Winston.

Harris, Zellig S.

1952 Discourse Analysis. Language 28:1–30.

Holland, Dorothy, and Jaan Valsiner

1988 Cognition, Symbols and Vygotsky's Developmental Psychology. Ethos 16:247-272.

Holland, Dorothy, and Naomi Quinn, eds.

1987 Cultural Models in Language and Thought. Cambridge: Cambridge University Press.

Hutchins, Edwin

1980 Culture and Inference: A Trobriand Case Study. Cambridge, MA: Harvard University Press.

Hymes, Dell

1972 Models of the Interaction of Language and Social Life. In Directions in Sociolinguistics: The Ethnography of Communication. J. J. Gumperz and D. Hymes, eds. New York: Holt, Rinehart and Winston.

1974 Foundations in Sociolinguistics: An Ethnographic Approach. Philadelphia: University of Pennsylvania Press.

Irvine, Judith T.

1979 Formality and Informality in Communicative Events. American Anthropologist 81(4):773–90.

1982 Language and Affect: Some Cross-Cultural Issues. In Contemporary Perceptions of Language: Interdisciplinary Dimensions. H. Byrnes, ed. Washington, D.C.: Georgetown University Press.

Ito, Karen L.

1985 Ho'oponopono, "To Make Right": Hawaiian Conflict Resolution and Metaphor in the Construction of a Family Therapy. Culture, Medicine and Psychiatry 9:201–17.

Kirkpatrick, John

1985 Some Marquesan Understandings of Action and Identity. In Person, Self and Experience: Exploring Pacific Ethnopsychologies. G. White and J. Kirkpatrick, eds. Berkeley: University of California Press.

Kirkpatrick, John, and Geoffrey M. White

1985   Exploring Ethnopsychologies. *In* Person, Self and Experience: Exploring Pacific Ethnopsychologies. G. White and J. Kirkpatrick, eds. Berkeley: University of California Press.

Kochman, Thomas

1981   Black and White Styles in Conflict. Chicago: University of Chicago Press.

Labov, William, and David Fanshel

1977   Therapeutic Discourse: Psychotherapy as Conversation. New York: Academic Press.

Lederman, Rena

1984   Who Speaks Here? Formality and the Politics of Gender in Mendi, Highland Papua New Guinea. *In* Dangerous Words: Language and Politics in the Pacific. D. L. Brenneis and F. R. Myers, eds. New York: New York University Press.

Levine, Harold G.

1982   Tebe Kre Nentie: Social Learning and Behavior Therapy Among the New Guinea Kafe. Ethos 10:66–93.

LeVine, Robert A.

1983   The Self in Culture. *In* Culture, Behavior, Personality (rev. ed.). R. LeVine. Chicago: Aldine.

Levinson, Stephen C.

1979   Activity Types and Language. Linguistics 17: 365–99.

Levy, Robert I., and Michelle Z. Rosaldo, eds.

1983   Self and Emotion. Ethos (special issue, vol. 11, no. 3).

Lutz, Catherine

1987   Goals, Events and Understanding in Ifaluk Emotion Theory. *In* Cultural Models in Language and Thought. D. Holland and N. Quinn, eds. Cambridge: Cambridge University Press.

1988   Unnatural Emotions. Chicago: University of Chicago Press.

Lutz, Catherine, and Geoffrey M. White

1986   The Anthropology of Emotions. *In* Annual Review of Anthropology, vol. 15. B. Seigel, ed. Palo Alto: Annual Reviews, Inc.

Mahuta, R.

1974   Whaikoorero—A Study of Formal Maori Speech. M.A. thesis,

University of Auckland, New Zealand.

Malinowski, Bronislaw

1923 The Problem of Meaning in Primitive Languages. *In* The Meaning of Meaning, C. K. Ogden and I. A. Richards, eds. New York: Harcourt, Brace and World.

1965 Coral Gardens and Their Magic. Vol. 2, The Language of Magic and Gardening. Bloomington: Indiana University (first published in 1935).

Marcus, George

1989 Chieftainship. *In* Developments in Polynesian Ethnology. A. Howard and R. Borofsky, eds. Honolulu: University of Hawaii Press.

Mather, Lynn, and Barbara Yngvesson

1980– Language, Audience, and the Transformation of Disputes. Law
81 and Society Review 15(3–4):775–821.

McKellin, William H.

1984 Putting Down Roots: Information in the Language of Managalase Negotiations. *In* Dangerous Words: Language and Politics in the Pacific. D. L. Brenneis and F. R. Myers, eds. New York: New York University Press.

Mehan, Hugh

1979 Learning Lessons: Social Organization in the Classroom. Cambridge: Cambridge University Press.

Merlan, Francesca, and Alan Rumsey

n.d. Nebilyer Social Actions: Structure and Events. Cambridge: Cambridge University Press (in press).

Miller, Peggy, and Linda L. Sperry

1987 The Socialization of Anger and Aggression. Merrill-Palmer Quarterly 33:1–31.

Moore, Barrington

1984 Privacy: Studies in Social and Cultural History. Armonk, NY: M. E. Sharpe.

Myers, Fred R.

1979 Emotions and the Self: A Theory of Personhood and Political Order Among Pintupi Aborigines. Ethos 7:343–70.

1986 Reflections on a Meeting: Structure, Language and the Polity in a Small-Scale Society. American Ethnologist 13:430–47.

Myers, Fred R., and Donald L. Brenneis

1984 Introduction: Language and Politics in the Pacific. *In* Dangerous Words: Language and Politics in the Pacific. D. L. Brenneis and F. R. Myers, eds. New York: New York University Press.

Norbeck, Edward

1963 African Rituals of Conflict. American Anthropologist 65:1254–79.

Ochs, Elinor

1986 From Feeling to Grammar: A Samoan Case Study. *In* Language Socialization Across Cultures. E. Ochs and B. Schieffelin, eds. Cambridge: Cambridge University Press.

Pande, S. K.

1967 The Mystique of "Western" Psychotherapy: An Eastern Interpretation. Journal of Nervous and Mental Disease 146:425–32.

Parsons, Talcott

1951 The Social System. Glencoe, IL: The Free Press.

Philips, Susan U.

1972 Participant Structures and Communicative Competence: Warm Springs Children in Community and Classroom. *In* Functions of Language in the Classroom. C. B. Cazden, V. John, and D. Hymes, eds. New York: Teachers College Press, Columbia University.

Piers, Gerhart, and Milton B. Singer

1971 Shame and Guilt: A Psychoanalytic and a Cultural Study. New York: W. W. Norton and Co. (originally published 1953).

Quinn, Naomi, and Dorothy Holland

1987 Culture and Cognition. *In* Cultural Models in Language and Thought. D. Holland and N. Quinn, eds. Cambridge: Cambridge University Press.

Rabinow, Paul, and William M. Sullivan

1979 The Interpretive Turn: Emergence of an Approach. *In* Interpretive Social Science: A Reader. P. Rabinow and W. Sullivan, eds. Berkeley: University of California Press.

Rosaldo, Michelle Z.

1973 "I Have Nothing to Hide": The Language of Ilongot Oratory. Language in Society 2:193–223.

1984 Toward an Anthropology of Self and Feeling. *In* Culture

Theory: Essays on Mind, Self and Emotion. R. Shweder and R. LeVine, eds. Cambridge: Cambridge University Press.

Rumsey, Alan
1985 Oratory and the Politics of Metaphor in the New Guinea Highlands. Sydney Studies in Society and Culture 3. Sydney: University of Sydney.

Sacks, Harvey, Emanuel Schegloff, and Gail Jefferson
1974 A Simplest Systematics for the Organization of Turn-Taking for Conversation. Language 50(4):696–735.

Sahlins, Marshall
1963 Poor Man, Rich Man, Big-man, Chief: Political Types in Melanesia and Polynesia. Comparative Studies in Society and History 5:285–303.

Salmond, Anne
1975 *Hui*: A Study of Maori Ceremonial Gatherings. Wellington: A. H. and A. W. Reed.

Scheff, Thomas J.
1979 Catharsis in Healing, Ritual and Drama. Berkeley: University of California Press.

Schieffelin, Bambi
1979 How Kaluli Children Learn What to Say, What to Do and How to Feel. Unpublished Ph.D. dissertation, Columbia University.

Schieffelin, Edward L.
1983 Anger and Shame in the Tropical Forest: On Affect as a Cultural System in Papua New Guinea. Ethos 11:181–91.

Searle, J. R.
1969 Speech Acts. Cambridge: Cambridge University Press.

Sherzer, Joel
1987 A Discourse-Centered Approach to Language and Culture. American Anthropologist 89:295–309.

Shook, E. Victoria
1985 *Ho'oponopono*: Contemporary Uses of a Hawaiian Problem-Solving Process. Honolulu: University of Hawaii Press.

Silverman, Martin G.
1977 Making Sense: A Study of a Banaban Meeting. *In* Exiles and Immigrants in Oceania. M. Lieber, ed. Honolulu: University of Hawaii Press.

Strathern, Andrew
1975 Veiled Speech in Mount Hagen. *In* Political Language and Oratory in Traditional Society. M. Bloch, ed. New York: Academic Press.

Strathern, Marilyn
1974 Managing Information: The Problems of a Dispute-Settler. *In* Contention and Dispute: Aspects of Law and Social Control in Melanesia. A. Epstein, ed. Canberra: Australian National University Press.

Taylor, Charles
1979 Interpretation and the Sciences of Man. *In* Interpretive Social Science: A Reader. P. Rabinow and W. Sullivan, eds. Berkeley: University of California Press.

Todorov, Tzvetan
1984 Mikhail Bakhtin: The Dialogical Principle. Translated by Wlad Godzich. Minneapolis: University of Minnesota Press.

Turner, Victor
1957 Schism and Continuity in an African Society: A Study of Ndembu Village Life. Manchester: University of Manchester Press.

van Dijk, Teun A., ed.
1985 Handbook of Discourse Analysis (4 volumes). New York: Academic Press.

Vygotsky, Lev Semenovich
1962 Thought and Language. Translated by E. Hanfmann and G. Vakar. Cambridge, MA: MIT Press.

Wallace, Anthony F. C.
1959 The Institutionalization of Cathartic and Control Strategies in Iroquois Religious Psychotherapy. *In* Culture and Mental Health. M. Opler, ed. New York: The Macmillan Co.

Ward, Roger L.
1980 Ponape Apology Rituals: The Persistence of the Apology Pattern in Modern Ponape. Unpublished ms. Pacific Collection, Hamilton Library, University of Hawaii.

Watson-Gegeo, Karen Ann
1986 Language Use in Oceania. *In* Annual Review of Anthropology, vol. 15. B. Seigel, ed. Palo Alto: Annual Reviews, Inc.

1987 The Ethnographic Study of Language Socialization. Occasional Paper, School of Education, Boston University.

Watson-Gegeo, Karen Ann, and David Welchman Gegeo

1979 *Ala'anga*: Settling a Dispute in Kwara'ae. Presented at the Northeastern Anthropological Association Meeting, New England College, Henniker, New Hampshire, March.

1987 Strategic Alternatives and Contextual Variation in Kwara'ae Dispute Settling. Presented at the International Pragmatics Association Meeting, Brussels, August.

Weiner, Annette B.

1984 From Words to Objects to Magic: "Hard Words" and the Boundaries of Social Interaction. *In* Dangerous Words: Language and Politics in the Pacific. D. L. Brenneis and F. R. Myers, eds. New York: New York University Press.

Wertsch, James, ed.

1985 Culture, Communication and Cognition: Vygotskian Perspectives. Cambridge: Cambridge University Press.

White, Geoffrey M.

1985 'Bad Ways' and 'Bad Talk': Interpretations of Interpersonal Conflict in a Melanesian Society. *In* Directions in Cognitive Anthropology. J. Dougherty, ed. Urbana: University of Illinois Press.

White, Geoffrey M., and John Kirkpatrick, eds.

1985 Person, Self and Experience: Exploring Pacific Ethnopsychologies. Berkeley: University of California Press.

Yngvesson, Barbara, and Lynn Mather

1983 Courts, Moots, and the Disputing Process. *In* Empirical Theories about Courts. K. Boyum and L. Mather, eds. New York: Longman.

Young, Michael

1971 Fighting With Food. Cambridge: Cambridge University Press.

PART II

MIND, EMOTION, AND THERAPEUTIC DISCOURSE

Emotion Talk and Social Inference: Disentangling in Santa Isabel, Solomon Islands

Geoffrey M. White

AS BOTH researchers and enculturated members of our own society, we tend to regard emotions as deep, irrational forces that run counter to orderly thought and action. It is widespread, if not universal, to find emotions implicated in people's talk about conflict, about the entanglements of everyday life that challenge ideal conceptions of the social order. As people talk about their entanglements, they frequently invoke cultural understandings of persons, action, and social relations in their attempts to transform events and experience. In this paper I suggest that close attention to the discourse of entanglement, and particularly to talk of action and emotion laden with moral significance, provides an approach to the cultural fabric of social life—the commonsense ways that people construe, negotiate, and experience social reality.

Talk of emotions is advantageously situated at the juncture of personal and social worlds.[1] As cultural signs pointing to experience that is at once individual and collective, emotion words and expressions constitute a unique code for communicating about intentions, motivations, and social relations (Levy 1984; Lutz 1987; Myers 1979). Recognition of the ability of actors to play upon the public meanings of emotion has led to recent work on the role of emotional rhetoric in the management of interpersonal encounters (Bailey 1983; Hochschild 1979). In this study I explore the meanings of a particular emotion discourse, not only as moral rhetoric, but as a window onto social experience. In doing so I find the method of analyzing discourse pioneered by Hutchins (1973, 1980) and extended by Quinn (1987), Lutz (1987), and others to be especially useful in unpacking the cultural understandings that speakers use to develop a line of reasoning and promote a point of view (see Holland and Quinn 1987). The power of such an analysis is enhanced by locating the process of understanding within a culturally defined situation where actors may be seen to actively negotiate their interpretations within the constraints of a socially organized environment.

My discussion focuses on a well-defined, routinized activity that A'ara-speaking peoples of Santa Isabel (Solomon Islands) refer to as "disentangling"—a type of meeting with the avowed purpose of facilitating talk about bad feelings and interpersonal conflict. The situational focus has both advantages and disadvantages. While necessitating a certain myopia with regard to other sorts of activities and contexts, it establishes a vantage point from which to consider what actors think they're up to when they engage in disentangling. This, in turn, gives greater leverage to the task of interpretation by making transparent (or at least less opaque) the overt definition of the situation that frames their discourse.

While disentangling generates explicit talk about persons, feelings and events, the full meaning and effect of what is said depends upon much that is unsaid—relying upon culturally patterned inferences to fill in unstated propositions (Tyler 1978; Hutchins 1980). As the discussion will show, talk of emotion, of felt responses to events, is particularly dense with implied meaning. The analytic task, then, begins with the question, "What are the (unspoken) inferences that give a particular emotion attribution its social and moral significance in this context?" In addition to asking about the meanings that cohere in emotion attributions, this study asks, "What is the folk theory or ideology of disentangling which gives the activity its publicly avowed purpose?" and, second, "How is the event organized as an interactive social occasion aimed at fulfilling this purpose?" Convergences in the answers to these questions lend greater credence to the ensuing interpretations by linking them to both ideology and social practice.

The study proceeds by first examining the cultural rationale for disentangling—the "what is it all about?" question. This is done by exploring the conceptualization of "entanglement" embodied in metaphor and local theories of conflict and misfortune (see also White 1985a). I then briefly describe the social organization of disentangling, suggesting that the collaborative management of topics and turn-taking work to sustain the definition of the situation as one that avoids confrontation and animosity. Finally, two cases of disentangling are examined to analyze the meanings of talk about emotion in this context. The analysis suggests that the rhetoric of emotion not only fulfills the purpose of disentangling, but also allows speakers to create and transform socio-emotional reality as they ply their own interpretations of events.

Setting

Santa Isabel is one of five major islands in the Solomon Islands. The population in 1986 was well over 14,000 people. Half of the population speak variants of the A'ara language (also known as *Cheke Holo* 'bush language'; see White *et al.* 1988). Nearly everyone engages in subsistence gardening, and many are involved in agricultural development projects. While economic changes have been slow in coming, cultural changes on the island associated with contact with European society have been more dramatic. Undoubtedly the most significant agent of change has been the Anglican Melanesian Mission (now the Church of Melanesia), which by 1920 had completed its work of converting the island population. The Mission was received eagerly at the end of the nineteenth century by the Isabel people, who had been severely victimized by marauding headhunters from the Western Solomon Islands (White 1979a). Conversion entailed major changes in residential patterns in which people formerly scattered throughout the bush migrated to coastal villages of unprecedented size (100–200 people), with ceremonial life centered on the village church (White 1988).

Prior to these changes at the turn of the century, social organization was based largely on kinship relations and regional alignments in which local leaders (*funei*) were the focal point for intergroup feasting and raiding. The idiom of descent is distinctively matrilineal, and descent groups were formerly identified with territorial regions marked by shrines where propitiatory offerings were made to the spirits of deceased ancestors. Ceremonial life has been almost entirely recast in the framework of Christian activities. More importantly for this paper, contemporary social and moral ideals are frequently expressed in the rhetoric of Christian ideology.

Disentangling: Model and Metaphor

A'ara speakers recognize disentangling (*gruarutha*, from the verb *rutha* 'disentangle, undo') as a distinct type of activity in which people talk among themselves about interpersonal conflict and bad feelings in their community. The avowed purpose of disentangling is to talk out (*cheke fajifla*) bad thoughts and feelings which, if they remain hidden, pose a danger to personal and community well-being. Such dangers come in the form of illness, injury, or failure of important activities such as hunting and fishing. Disentangling may take two forms: a therapeutic activity aimed at the psychosocial causes of illness or misfortune and a preventive measure used to dispel bad feelings that could interfere with collective projects such as turtle hunting.

At first glance, disentangling bears some resemblance to our Western notions of both psychotherapy (or group therapy) and conflict resolution. Yet it is neither. To label disentangling as either therapy or conflict resolution is to miss the more fundamental question of what it is all about as a culturally constituted activity, an activity that derives meaning from cultural beliefs about persons, emotions, and social experience. Somewhat like Western psychotherapy, disentangling can be used to ferret out social and emotional sources of illness. In both cases, persons are urged to review their feelings associated with past events. But unlike psychotherapy (Pande 1968), disentangling is eminently social, conducted in a community milieu, usually with the very same others who figure in the entanglements under review. While both entail the revelation of personal thoughts, the "therapy" of disentangling lies precisely in the telling, in the act of giving a certain kind of public account, and only secondarily in the reorganization of mind or personality (in this respect, it is less *explicitly* concerned with socializing than the Kwara'ae *fa'amanata'anga* discussed by Watson-Gegeo and Gegeo elsewhere in this volume).

The preventive type of disentangling takes the form of a village (or intervillage) meeting. In this setting, the activity resembles other types of village meetings aimed at discussion (*roghe*), or problem-solving (*fapuipuhi*, from *puhi* 'action' or 'way', literally, 'make a way'). Meetings called to air (if not resolve) community disputes also involve the public recitation of accounts of social conflict. Yet the accounts recited in dispute meetings attempt to influence village leaders who formulate authoritative versions of reality (as in the courts described by Duranti, Hutchins, and Lindstrom in this volume). For disentangling meetings, the outcome is in the performance of narrative discourse. At least in the normative model of disentangling, what you say is what you get. No comments, evaluations, or judgments from third parties are necessary. Perhaps more like the Fiji Indian *pancayat* described by Brenneis than other, more deliberate forms of conflict resolution, disentangling manifests an emotional aesthetic.

The difference between disentangling meetings and the more straightforward sorts of conflict resolution is perhaps best indicated by the fact that A'ara speakers themselves do not see them as comparable. When I asked one informant about disentangling, he compared it to Holy Communion service. Given the discrepancy in the formats of these activities, the comparison seems odd at first. It is, however, in their perceived *functions* that similarities emerge. Both are viewed as a kind of moral cleansing—an instrumental means of expiating personal conflicts that could prove injurious. Being allowed to receive the Sacrament presupposes that one is free of serious moral transgression and hence may participate in church ritual aimed at ensuring well-being and avoiding misfortune. Similarly, disentangling puts a symbolic seal on old wounds and conflicts, certifying that one's social relations and personal thoughts/feelings are in reasonable harmony.

The functional similarity between disentangling and Communion services should not, however, obscure the obvious differences between them as *social* activities. First of all, disentangling is far less "scripted" than the highly ritualized and formulaic quality of Communion services (which require only passive involvement of participants). Secondly, disentangling is primarily an interpersonal activity, with spirit forces in the background, if present at all. The issue of a supernatural component of disentangling (such as the belief that failure to disentangle could invoke ancestral or godly retribution) is an open question (cf. Watson-Gegeo, this volume). Most evidence points to a fundamentally interpersonal definition of the situation which has admitted Christianization in some aspects (such as the now customary presence of a priest to listen as people speak their minds).[2] Because of our own assumptions about causal agents mediating cause and effect (Needham 1976), there is a tendency to (wrongly) insert supernatural beings in the chain of reasoning that links socioemotional conflict with misfortune.

Disentangling as Cultural Model

In the local theory of disentangling, personal thoughts and feelings have explanatory efficacy. Like the Western theory of psychosomatic disorder, which attributes psychosocial causes to maladies that show no obvious somatic cause, or that do not respond to conventional medical cures, the disentangling theory attributes socio-emotional factors in cases of illness that persist despite the application of usual treatments. For example, in the case of a woman suffering from uterine pains and bleeding who had been treated without success by a variety of traditional remedies over a period of six weeks, a village leader finally said that he could see that ordinary treatments were not working because of problems between the woman and her husband. In the leader's words, it was "their thinking which blocked the work of the other treatments," and thus they needed to disentangle their thoughts and feelings.

The most significant difference between the disentangling theory and Western theories of psychosocial disorder is the distinctly interpersonal or social character of the A'ara model. For example, disentangling theory includes the premise that one person's socioemotional entanglements may cause illness or misfortune for third parties—for significant others or for the community as a whole. In the words of one informant, "if two people, husband and wife, are always arguing, then their child will continually be sick." Such reasoning appears to be extremely widespread in traditional models of illness (e.g., Besnier, this volume; Boggs and Chun, this volume; Harris 1978; Ito 1985; Turner 1964; Watson-Gegeo and Gegeo, this volume).

The explanatory efficacy of emotions also extends beyond illness to various kinds of social misfortune. The failure of an important community enterprise such as fishing or hunting may be attributed to some lingering "bad feeling" which obstructed or blocked success, similar to a curse (*tibri*) which could have the same effect. One of the most common examples involves domestic pigs that become lost in the forest. Domestic pigs are usually not kept penned, but are allowed to forage in the forest, where they establish well-known feeding places and can be located and retrieved when needed. On occasion, however, a pig cannot be found, despite the efforts of several men. If after one or two days, the pig is not located, the searchers will conclude that something is "obstructing" their attempt to find it, just as something was "obstructing" the medical treatment of the woman's illness mentioned above. In one case where two brothers and their sister were preparing (together with their respective households) to host a memorial feast for their father, who had died a year earlier, one of their pigs could not be located after a day and a half of searching. So they decided to hold a disentangling meeting in which the three siblings, their spouses, and their mother gathered to "talk out" any bad feelings that might be blocking their efforts. The topics discussed at the meeting included: (1) the mother's regrets about her children's failure to take good care of their father in his old age, (2) a previous argument between the brothers about their responsibilities in preparing for the feast, and (3) a dream by the sister that her father's ghost was playing tricks on the party searching for the pig. Since the pig was located the next day, it was generally inferred that this airing of bad feelings associated with social conflict served to overcome the obstructions.

The preventive uses of disentangling can be seen as an extrapolation of the premises of this theory of illness and failure. Given the premise that bad feelings can cause misfortune or obstruct social activities, disentangling *before* important social ventures is a way to avoid accidents or injuries and help insure success. Before any major feast which demands collective fishing or hunting, a series of intervillage disentangling meetings may be held to air any bad feelings.

Illness and collective failure stand as symbols of dysfunction, both personal and communal. If serious or unexpected, such disorders are likely to be explained in terms of disruptions in the fabric of interpersonal relations (or in terms of malevolent spirit forces). Both harm to the person in the form of illness and harm to the community in the form of, say, a bad catch of turtle may be explained as the result of social conflicts and possibly of the bad feelings they engender. In the interpersonal explanations used by Aʻara speakers to make sense of misfortune, emotions play a mediating role: they are both caused *by* and causes *of* problematic social events (see White 1985a:355). Where emotions figure into interpretations of misfortune it is not just emotions in general, but negative, conflicted feelings harbored within the person that are believed to be most dangerous as possible causes of illness, "accidents," or failure. In this way, the unexpressed disappointments and resentments that accrue from everyday conflicts (the "tangled feelings") take on significance for persons and communities—significance that is important enough to necessitate a culturally constituted remedy in the form of disentangling. How, then, do Aʻara speakers conceptualize this social activity (disentangling) so that it is seen as providing an antidote to problematic emotions? Clues are found in the language, particularly the figurative language, used to talk about such things.

Metaphor

"Entanglement" is a key metaphor in Aʻara ethnopsychology, with a number of entailments indicative of understandings about emotion and social life. Both emotions and interpersonal relations may become entangled (*fifiri*) because of conflicts in everyday life.[3] This ambiguity of reference, both emotional and social, is significant. It reflects the Aʻara outlook on social life, which consistently draws linkages between personal experience and interpersonal relations, rather than boundaries between the psychological worlds of individuals.

The notion of "tangled" feeling subsumes a variety of specific negative emotions such as "angry," "sad," and "shame."[4] However, to talk of "tangled" emotions is to say something more complicated than would be conveyed by any one of the more particular terms. Specifically, to describe feelings as tangled (*fifiri nagnafa*) or knotted (*haru*) is more *evaluatively* ambiguous than describing them as, say, 'angry.'[5] It is particularly in relations with significant others, between persons closely related through kinship or residence where negative emotions are not easily expressed, that problematic feelings are described as entangled.

Yet, the metaphor of entanglement is not just a vague cover term. In the terms of Lakoff and Johnson (1980), it is "productive" insofar as it entails an array of propositions and images used to conceptualize social and moral understandings. Consideration of the range of conventional figurative expressions related to entanglement reveals a set of images linked to underlying understandings of conflict and what to do about it (Quinn and Holland 1987).

Troublesome feelings and social relations in need of moral repair are variously described as tangled (*fifiri*) or blocked (*nagra*). Each term implies its own resolution, forming an opposition between problem state and solution: tangled/untangled (*krutha*) and blocked/clear (*snagla*). These oppositions represent the beginning and ending points of scenarios of everyday problem-solving. Extending the tangling metaphor, persons experiencing such conflicts are said to become entangled (*khale*), in the sense of snared or hung up in, just as a turtle gets caught in a net. By representing socioemotional conflict as a state of affairs that impedes normal purposeful activity, just as becoming entangled restricts movement or a fallen log blocks progress along a path, these images imply that some sort of deliberate attempt at removing the problem or impediment is required. It is against the backdrop of these scenarios that the verbs 'disentangle' and 'clear away obstruction' (*fasnasnagla*) acquire their meaning as active attempts to move from one side of the opposition to the other: from problem state to one that is untangled or clear:

tangled/untangled   ⇒   DISENTANGLE
blocked/clear   ⇒   CLEAR AWAY

In the A'ara view, then, how is disentangling or clearing away obstruction accomplished? Put simply, it is by talking about one's feelings and thoughts in the presence of significant others involved in the entanglement. It is in making the personal public, and doing so in accordance with prescribed formats (described below), that disentangling is culturally constituted. In line with some of their most basic social values (White 1980, 1985a, 1985b), A'ara speakers describe the social aim of disentangling as being of one mind (*kaisei gaoghatho*) or being together (*au fofodu*) in community thought and action. This aim is fulfilled in the very enactment of disentangling, through the *process* of articulating personal thoughts and feelings, which itself creates at least the rhetoric of community-wide solidarity. Not surprisingly, then, clues to the conceptualization of disentangling are to be found in *verbs* that represent this process of articulation, especially as ways of talking.

The notion that certain experiences manifest themselves as thoughts and feelings within the person as an individual is basic to A'ara ethnopsychology (White 1985a). The underlying concept of person is aptly expressed in the metaphor PERSONS ARE CONTAINERS (see Lakoff and Kövecses 1987 for discussion of a comparable English-language proposition and its role in emotion concepts). Thoughts and feelings are said to be *within* the person, sometimes using the locative preposition *ta-* —a form reserved for containers such as a cup or canoe. For example, the emotion term *angry* (*di'a tagna*, literally 'badness within him/her') is built upon this prepositional form, combining *ta-* with an obligatory possessive marker (in this example, third-person singular, *-gna*).[6] Extending this image, bad thoughts or feelings are said to become lodged or stuck (*chakhi*) within the person. The container metaphor, however, is not a static one. Indeed, much of ordinary thinking about social reality is concerned with the means by which personal and public social realities affect one another—especially through talk. Consideration of the specific images used to describe these transactions in knowledge and affect gives a more finely tuned depiction of local understandings of disentangling.

Troubled thoughts and feelings about which one does not readily speak are described as hidden (*phoru*) from others, unless they become revealed (*thakle*) or visible (*kakhana*). As in English, the metaphor of sight is used for knowing: KNOWING IS SEEING. Hence the movement of thoughts and feelings from within the person to the social arena is described as revealing (*fatakle*) or making visible (*fakakhana*). The sight metaphor is also implicated in an UP/DOWN orientational schema used to talk about the movement of thoughts and feelings in the social world. Problematic experiences may be kept down (*pari*), buried (*fruni*), or covered over (*plohmo*) (and hence out of sight), or they may rise up (*hnaghe*) or surface (*thagra*), just as a turtle becomes visible when it comes up for air.

The terms used to talk about disentangling amount to more

than a few ideas expressed in metaphorical expressions. Rather, they signify understandings about knowledge and emotion as dynamic processes traversing personal and social realms of experience. The entailments of the container metaphor produce specific understandings about the means by which thoughts and feelings are made social. By combining the proposition about persons as containers [1] with that about knowledge as a visible object [2], A'ara speakers conceptualize the process by which thoughts/feelings move from personal to social realms as one of *revelation*, as making enclosed objects visible [3]:

[1] PERSONS ARE CONTAINERS
[2] KNOWING IS SEEING
[3] REVELATION IS MAKING ENCLOSED OBJECTS VISIBLE

Given the container metaphor, revelation may be accomplished in a variety of concrete ways. The incidental or unintended way for attitudes to become public knowledge is for them to leak out (*suplu*) through loose talk or gossip, just as a liquid might run out of a permeable container. Disentangling, however, is a more deliberate, purposeful process. Two primary means of revelation are voiced by disentanglers as they variously urge one another to open up (*tora*) or put outside (*fajijifla*) their thoughts and feelings, just as one might open a box to remove its contents or allow others to see inside. In other words, the proposition that revelation is making enclosed objects visible ([3] above) has the more specific entailments:

[3a] REVELATION IS OPENING UP
[3b] REVELATION IS PUTTING OUTSIDE

In the A'ara view, both actions are accomplished through *talk*. In the context of disentangling, talk is made the deliberate definition of the situation. By invoking images of talking out (*cheke fajifla*) or opening up with talk (*cheke tora*), participants in disentangling sessions remind one another that *just by talking* in a certain way one may fulfill the overt agenda of the occasion, of making thoughts and feelings public. This type of talk is not only *seen* as efficacious, it *is* efficacious in transforming that which is 'hidden,' 'inside,' and 'under' to that which is 'visible,' 'outside,' and 'on the surface,' and thus 'clearing away' impediments to desired social ends. To the degree that the representation of emotional experience is linked to social reality, disentangling merges talk with experience.

This discussion of the ways disentangling is conceptualized is intended to illuminate understandings that provide the overt agenda for disentangling as a culturally defined and socially acknowledged activity. However, as a public occasion for talking about problematic events that have given rise to ill feeling, it is inevitable that disentangling sessions will also be used to some extent as a forum for moral *negotiation* in which competing interpretations are posed and counterposed. Indeed, much of the analysis that follows indicates that interlocutors play upon the overt definition of the situation (giving a public accounting of emotions) to manipulate more indirect claims about moral liabilities and the shape of past events. This covert agenda, then, creates certain problems for maintaining the normative definition of the situation (cf. Bailey 1983). There is always the possibility that the assertion of moral claims will evoke counterclaims, and possibly lead to confrontation and animosity—just the type of entanglements that would be anathema to the avowed aim of disentangling. To counter these potentials, participants work cooperatively to frame disentangling discourse by voicing the purpose of disentangling and managing the course of conversational interaction. How, then, is a context constructed which allows for and encourages the kind of disentangling discourse interpreted as straightening out tangled emotions, rather than as disputing contested events? Some of the conversational and interactional devices used to create and sustain the disentangling context are considered briefly below before taking up two example cases.

Creating a Context

This paper's discussion of disentangling is based largely on information about four specific meetings, two of which were tape-recorded.[7] The tape-recorded sessions were of the larger, village-level type. Both were held in anticipation of the same major Christmas feast for the dual purposes of disentangling and planning. The disentangling, then, was preventive, concerned with clearing away emotional obstacles that might block the success of planned hunting and fishing expeditions. Meetings were held in four villages where people were involved in preparations for the feast. Each meeting drew people from more than one village, and some individuals participated in more than one of the sessions. It was the planning and preparing for the feast which occasioned these meetings, rather than any specific conflicts to be disentangled (although most people probably anticipated which events would be raised as topics for disentangling). The meetings began with disentangling but finished as planning sessions discussing feast preparations.

For the preventive purposes of the larger disentangling meetings, the very fact that a meeting occurs goes a long way toward fulfilling its aim. By just staging a session, and getting the protagonists of past conflicts to co-participate, villagers implicitly certify that there are no lingering social rifts that would prohibit people from talking or working together. This implies that participation itself may be problematic. To participate in a disentangling session is to be prepared to offer an account of contested events—an account that must be in line with the harmonizing goals of the occasion. I assume that those unprepared to do so simply don't show up. Indeed, in the second case to be discussed below, the absence of some of the key principals is noted and criticized (appendix, ll. 252–79). Given that knowledge of interpersonal squabbles is widely circulated in gossip, it is likely that most participants have a reasonable idea of what events will be discussed and who will discuss them. From my small sample, it appears that events taken up in disentangling sessions are located far enough in the past (by a matter of weeks or months) that they are unlikely to give rise to unexpected challenges or outbursts.

Both of the recorded meetings took place in the late evening, after people from several villages (who would later be engaged in preparing for the Christmas feast) had gathered in one of the larger village houses. In each instance, floor space inside the house was completely occupied by people sitting on mats, attending to the casual activities of rolling and smoking cigarettes or chewing betel. With only a few small kerosene lamps inside the house, most people (about thirty in number in each case) were only barely visible in the shadows at the periphery. In addition, an indeterminate number remained outside the house, some of these occasionally speaking through the thatched walls. Thus, disentangling meetings place participants in a situation where anyone who speaks can readily be heard by others, but where eye contact is minimized. The physical separation of speakers imposed by darkness and seating arrangements characteristic of these meetings facilitates talk about conflict without evoking confrontation and argumentation.

These features of the physical setting are consistent with the mode of speaking characteristic of disentangling sessions. The greatest proportion of talk at the two recorded meetings consists of long, uninterrupted narrative sequences in which speakers recount past events. Each narration may take five, ten, or even twenty continuous minutes. The narrative mode permits a speaker to develop an account from his or her point of view, as would be expected in light of the purpose of disentangling to provide an occasion for people simply to talk about their thoughts and feelings. Both of the first two disentangling segments analyzed below are begun by speakers who introduce their talk as telling a story (*thoutonu*) (appendix, l. 013 and l. 283).

In addition to the features of physical setting and narrative talk characteristic of these meetings, the rationale for disentangling is underscored by repeated statements about the overt aims of the occasion. Explicit statements about the purpose of disentangling punctuate transitions between narratives, framing their significance as attempts at straightening out, rather than challenging others' interpretations. Although senior men in the village may take the lead in initiating opening remarks (see below), statements aimed at defining the situation and managing the course of interaction are contributed by numerous participants in the encounter. Unlike the social structure of the Hawaiian *ho'oponopono* (Ito 1985; Boggs and Chun, this volume), or Kwara'ae counseling (Watson-Gegeo and Gegeo, this volume), disentangling sessions have no single person who assumes the role of group leader to direct interaction and control speaking rights. Rather, participants collaborate in managing the disentangling event.

The opening of each of the disentangling sessions recorded is marked with direct statements about its purpose. These statements are set off by an increase in volume and topical focus which contrast with the unfocused talk preceding them (cf. Turner 1972). The conversational sequence shown below (ll. 1–9 of the appendix) illustrates the way in which four different participants jointly initiate a disentangling session through four successive turns at speaking:

ARNON

001 Go ahead and disentangle at this time, because it is nearly time for one group to go out (fishing).

002 It's only how many days (away) already?

BASI

003 Maybe Bilo and Pala should disentangle.

004 In order to go to the work, the hunting, (that) would be good.

CHAKU

005 The man who died at Mosu didn't follow the doctrine, collections, didn't stay in the Church (just) followed his own ways.

006 And then he went pig hunting and he died.

007 (They) just accused Fada, (saying that) Fada made sorcery, is what they said about that.

008 That's what is strong (hot) with the Church: collection, prayer, and disentangling before going out fishing, pig hunting, and so on.

DOFU

009 There are always things that bite in the ocean and forest.

This exchange effectively accomplishes a number of pragmatic ends. First of all, the first speaker's utterance marks the beginning of disentangling by referring to the upcoming turtle hunt, which has occasioned the meeting. Secondly, the first case is evoked by the next speaker, who calls upon two people, Bilo and Pala, to "disentangle" so that the collective work may proceed. Most people at the meeting probably expected that Bilo and Pala would discuss their entanglement in the incidents that make up case 1 below. And, indeed, immediately after the quoted sequence, Pala begins his narrative account of the events in question (appendix, l. 010).

The other opening remarks (ll. 005–009) frame the purpose and importance of disentangling by reminding everyone about the harmful consequences of not doing so. The third speaker, Chaku, does this by referring to a recent incident in which a man was gored by a wild pig and died from his wounds. Although the death was commonly attributed to sorcery, Chaku suggests that it may have resulted from moral failure, from failure to adhere to Christian doctrine and practice. He implicitly compares disentangling with Christian practices ("collection, prayer") aimed at maintaining a mantle of spiritual protection against accidents and misfortune. The comparison parallels the functional analogy noted earlier between disentangling and Holy Communion. Chaku thus reminds those present that disentangling is a way of remaining "strong with the Church" before venturing out on risky ventures such as hunting or fishing. Dofu makes the same point somewhat more succinctly by simply noting that "There are always things that bite in the ocean and forest."

This type of talk about the activity of disentangling, its purpose and desirability, is often accompanied by statements that urge people to talk about their "bad feelings." One participant stated at the outset of another meeting that, "If you all have any anger, backbiting, or grumbling, you should talk about it now, because now is the time for disentangling." Recurrent statements urging participants to engage in this type of discourse punctuate the progression of the event, usually at points of transition between speakers, thereby reasserting the appropriate framework for interpretation and encouraging others to speak. For example, during a lull in the meeting that began with the lines quoted above, a priest who had been sitting quietly stated: "Yes, other people must have various wrongs ("dirt"). You should open up and see the source as I do at length in church. Straighten things out well. With all the dirty things, the church can't be powerful . . . I don't always come and sit in your meetings. It is this meeting for disentangling and clearing that I come and sit. . . ."

In addition to these sorts of encouragement voiced by listeners, speakers themselves will frequently characterize their narration as "disentangling" or straightening" and attempt to distance themselves from the actual conflict in a variety of ways, such as talking about their feelings as past, completed responses. So, for example, the first narrative included in the appendix is prefaced:

PALA

010 "Perhaps they (two) should disentangle," you all say.

011 But for myself, that sort of thing that happened is already finished for me myself.

012 But perhaps for my older brother Bilo it is still with him.

013 But I will go through that story again about our (the two of us) going to court.

014 For you all and my older brother Bilo to know, "Ah! That's how it was."

015 I myself have simply finished with that already.

016 I have not a single thought about that which is gone, already finished.

017 All right, that incident that we all know about is the way of all the young (small) men.

The speaker, Pala, thus begins his story by saying that the incident is finished, that he no longer has any thoughts about it, but that he will go ahead and run through the story so that everyone else can hear. Then, after talking for more than fifteen minutes, he concludes by asserting that his story has been aimed at "revealing" his thoughts, as people are about to set out hunting and fishing (ll. 130–33).

The conclusion of this story exemplifies a stereotyped means for closing disentangling narratives. As if to assert that one's talk has had the desired effect, speakers frequently conclude their accounts with an affirmation that thoughts and feelings have been expressed, that the incident in question is finished, and that it has only been brought up in order to "disentangle" and "straighten out." For example, the account given in response to the opening narrative (by the older brother of the first speaker) concludes :

187 That's what that behavior was.

188 These here are the only feelings with me, they are simply finished.

189 No (further) talk, no thoughts about them after these.

190 In order to disentangle these actions, to make them better, these things, those bad things are finished.

191 Those are the thoughts with me.

While utterances such as these are posed as a statement of purpose, they represent an overt "official agenda"—by no means all
that is accomplished in conflict narratives. In addition to the
stated goal of talking about bad feelings, disentangling accounts
promote an interpretation of events—events in which the speaker
has been personally involved. It is not surprising to find that disentangling discourse is also aimed at rationalizing that involvement. The ambiguity in whether a speaker is attempting to
achieve community rapprochement or is asserting a contested interpretation or both is an important feature of disentangling, and
one that is deftly manipulated by participants. Even though the
acknowledged definition of the situation is that of airing bad feelings without engendering further conflict, much of disentangling
is concerned with the negotiation of competing interpretations of
past events.

When the mode of interaction drifts too far into the realm of
challenge and riposte, it is likely to be directed back on course
through the collaboration of other participants. So, for example,
in the first case one of the participants attempts to signal the end
of the exchange between the two brothers, Pala and Bilo, after
each has completed an extended narrative:

192 The two of them are finished.
193 All right, very good.

But when they continue to exchange further remarks, another
participant also attempts a closing:

201 So, it's gone all right, you two.

However, the younger brother, Pala, persists in rationalizing
certain aspects of the case until yet a third participant interrupts
to assert that they are wandering from the relevant subject, and
someone else should quickly initiate a new topic:

217 You two are going to other talk.
218 Someone else go ahead, quickly.

It is not unusual for participants in these sessions to call for others to initiate disentangling, just as did the priest cited previously. However, in this instance, calls for the transition to a new topic are evoked when Pala and Bilo slip out of a narrative mode of speech, into a more confrontational style, marked by a more rapid sequence of turn-taking in which each is responding directly to the other (appendix, ll. 192–218).

The Moral Work of Emotion Talk

Cross-cultural studies are showing that concepts of emotion entail significant social and moral understandings (Lutz and White 1986). It is obvious that talk about emotions does much more than simply label or report feeling states. It also does moral work, with directive force and the ability to transform socioemotional reality. One of the most moral of moral emotions, both in Santa Isabel and cross-culturally, is anger (Harris 1978; Lakoff and Kövecses 1987; Lutz 1988; Poole 1985; Rosaldo 1980; Schieffelin 1985; White 1985b; other essays in this volume). Emotions glossed as anger frequently encode judgments about violations of person and moral order. In light of these understandings, talk about anger becomes an idiom for moral argumentation: it signals the perception of transgression and the possibility of corrective action.

An example of explicit talk about anger as moral judgment occurs in one of the recorded disentangling meetings (not included in the appendix) when an older man, a village catechist, reports an incident in which he chastised one of his neighbors, Edi (also a catechist), for hitting several misbehaving children. The alleged hitting runs counter to a strong proscription on the physical punishment of children and against the generalized ethos of non-aggression (White 1985b). Reporting his own speech on the occasion when he confronted his neighbor, the old man quotes himself,

Catechists shouldn't hit, shouldn't be angry toward children and people, man. (They) should take care of them, just like chiefs, in order to be good. But you were hitting children. . . . I was very angry with you, Edi. Because you are a catechist, you should be teaching people, not hitting. . . .

This passage presents an interesting example of anger attributed to anger. First of all, the speaker's anger is said to be precipitated by a violation of moral strictures—specifically, by his neighbor's angry actions flagrantly ignoring the prohibition against physical punishment. Furthermore, in his prior description of the event, the speaker says that he threatened to "report" his neighbor, implying that his own felt anger was inclined toward some kind of retribution. In this way, the attribution of anger links an antecedent rule violation (hitting) with a possible corrective response (reporting).

It may seem ironic that the speaker says that he got angry at Edi for getting angry. The difference, and it is an important one, is that the two angers are differently contextualized: between adult and child on the one hand, and between mature men on the other. In the A'ara view, sharp anger should not be expressed in relations marked by asymmetries of power. Hence the speaker's analogy between Edi's relation to the children and a chief's relation to his followers. Talk of anger, then, is not only an idiom of moral claims (implying that the events that induce anger constitute rule violations) but also a code for construing social relations (Levy 1984). Another example will illustrate.

In one of the recorded meetings, a man claimed to be angry (di'a tagu) with his sister's son for stealing betel nut from one of his trees. But because he simply expressed anger, without acknowledging either the asymmetry or the close relation of kinship between himself and his nephew, others saw his talk of anger as inappropriate. Two other participants responded, not to the act of stealing, but to the uncle's stated anger toward his maternal nephew. One of the listeners spoke to the uncle, saying, "This kind of talk that you are making is as if you are all separate (soasopa) people. It is better to speak to your nephew to teach him, like I do with my nephew. . . . That kind of (angry) talk can be aimed at other people, but to our own nephews, our own children, it is very bad."

The speaker's reprimand mirrors that of the first example: both are concerned with the social context of expressed anger: one between adult and child, the other between mother's brother and sister's son. This second example is more explicit about the primacy of the social component ("[anger] can be aimed at other people . . .".). Given these assumptions about emotion and morality, it can be seen that the experience of anger poses a dilemma for A'ara speakers: expressed anger is likely to be regarded as contrary to norms of relatedness, while suppressed anger, according to the folk theory of misfortune, poses a danger to self and others.

As an arena for the sanctioned expression of emotion, disentangling would appear to be a culturally constituted solution to the dilemma of suppressed anger. Yet, as the above examples indicate, this is not as straightforward as it might seem. In disentangling as elsewhere, talk of anger in close relations is likely to be disapproved. The disentangling context does not legitimate expressions of hostility untempered by ideals of solidarity and repairing damaged relations. What it does provide is an opportunity for the creation of a social reality in which angry events are rhetorically transformed and damaged relations symbolically repaired. Since talk of anger is an idiom for the assertion of moral claims, it is somewhat out of place in disentangling sessions concerned neither with uncovering transgressions nor with imposing sanctions. Perhaps for this reason talk of anger is relatively infrequent in the recorded sessions. (The examples cited account for most of the instances on those occasions.) Instead, one finds numerous examples of talk about sadness (di'a nagnafa) and shame (mamaja). The analysis below suggests that these attributions are particularly well-suited to the work of transforming angry events to fit the avowed aims of disentangling while at the same time promoting a particular point of view on those events.

Emotion talk is a central component of the rhetorical process by which events and experiences are reconstructed. The attribution of emotion, whether to self or others, obtains social meaning from cultural models of action and experience. Cross-cultural studies show that these models are frequently structured in terms of scenario-like schemata that represent emotions as arising in social situations and compelling certain types of response (see D'Andrade 1987; Lutz 1987). In other words, emotions point backward at antecedent events and forward to expected outcomes. A'ara talk of emotions follows this general pattern, which may be diagrammed in generalized form as a causal or implicational sequence as follows:

SOCIAL EVENT   →   EMOTION   →   ACTION RESPONSE

Conceived as a "prototypical scenario," such sequences are neither invariant nor entirely predictable, but represent only a typical or default course of reasoning about social process (see Lakoff and Kövecses 1987; Quinn and Holland 1987). The generalized schema above captures the general form of more specific knowledge about particular emotions.

For example, consider the emotion term *di'a tagna*, glossed here as '(he is) angry.' The ethnographic vignettes discussed above indicate that talk of anger foregrounds a concern with moral transgression and an unresolved impulse for retribution or redress. It also assumes that, ideally, the social relationship involved is neither close nor sharply asymmetrical. Using the general schema outlined above, these specific understandings about anger form a kind of "retribution schema," represented below as a prototypical event sequence in which a set of preconditions gives rise to anger, which in turn leads to a particular course of action:[8]

TRANSGRESSION
and
DISTANT RELATION   —→   ANGER   —→   RETRIBUTION
and
EQUAL POWER

Although highly simplified and intended only to represent the most basic components of a prototypic anger scenario, the schematic representation is useful in directing attention to the role of emotion attributions in communication. By asserting that some action or event has evoked a specific kind of felt response (such as anger), the speaker gives that action a particular interpretation; he or she implies that it is an instance of that class of happenings that produces anger. At the same time, the emotion attribution implicitly "says" something about the social consequences of those events (in this case, seeking moral correction).

In this way, the cultural model of anger (and of other specific emotions) provides a template for the construction of intersubjective understandings only partially articulated in discourse. By relying on the entailments of an implicit model, interlocutors leave a great deal unspoken. Much of the task of analyzing disentangling discourse involves identifying those unspoken assumptions and inferences which figure importantly in the construction of social reality. As a general strategy, the analysis below proceeds by focusing on specific emotion attributions and asking, "what must be known or inferred in order for a particular attribution to have the meaning it does in this context?" Both the cultural definition of disentangling and the social organization of its enactment place constraints on the kinds of interpretation available to participants. The analysis offered here builds a model of cultural understanding by examining the usage of particular emotion words across numerous occurrences and speakers. This could also be extended to other occasions and situations.

Inference, Indirection, and Multiple Realities

The following discussion examines two cases taken up at one of the recorded meetings. The entire exchange surrounding these cases is given in the appendix. Because they were the first two episodes to be reviewed at the meeting in question, they provide a continuous transcript of disentangling discourse spanning two distinct event-topics.

Case 1

This case was the first one discussed in the disentangling session. It concerns an incident in which a teenage boy was beaten by other boys, causing their parents and other villagers to become embroiled in disagreements about how to deal with the offenders. Most of the disentangling of this case takes the form of narrative accounts by two main principals: the victim's father, Pala, and Bilo, the father of one of the attackers. As in most disentanglements, the principals are closely related, although they live in different villages. Pala and Bilo are matrilateral cousins, or classificatory brothers. Genealogical relations between them, and others in the case are shown in Figure 1.

Nearly one year prior to the disentangling meeting, three teenage boys ganged up on Pala's son, Rubin, and beat him up either as a prank or to settle a score of some kind. In itself, this incident

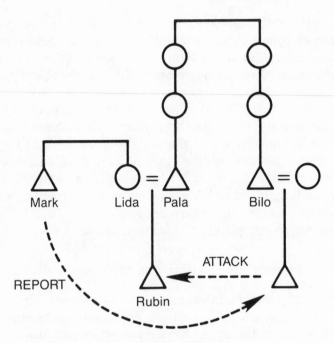

FIGURE 1. Relations among principals in case 1

was not controversial. Everyone agreed that it was a somewhat serious example of adolescent misbehavior. The incident became a problem for the wider community when relatives of the boys attempted to deal with the matter. It appears that Rubin's mother's brother, Mark, reported the attack to the police, who then discussed the matter with various people in the community, including Pala, who agreed to take his son's attackers to court. The three boys were ultimately given fines of up to five dollars (not a trivial amount for many villagers at that time.)

It was this response, reporting the matter to the police and pursuing it in court, which upset the parents of the attackers and others, leading to a more serious rift with repercussions for social relations between people in several villages. As a result of the police intervention, Bilo, father of one of the accused, said that he would withdraw from the upcoming Christmas feast, which was to be staged in his village (although it was sponsored jointly with others). Furthermore, he said he would rather leave the island for wage labor than have to see the people who had taken his son to court. This threat affected a wider network because Bilo had been raising pigs that originally belonged to Pala and others of his village but were to be slaughtered for the feast. Once the rift occurred, Bilo let it be known that Pala and the others might just as well come up to his village and cook and eat their pigs.

And so it was that a fight among teenage boys had reverberations that threatened to disrupt a feast being prepared by several villages. It is in fact the *repercussions* which are most at issue in the disentangling discourse. The narrative accounts related by Pala and Bilo are concerned essentially with how people responded to the fight incident and what those responses imply about their relations with one another. By describing events in a certain way and imputing feelings and motives of a certain sort, each speaker constructs a moral reading of the episode. The focal point for their readings is the evaluation of relations with one another.

Both Pala and Bilo are concerned with rationalizing actions that are morally problematic. Pala must speak to his taking the boys to court and Bilo to his threat to withdraw from community activities. In doing so, both construe their motives in a way that highlights their concern with valued, close relations threatened or damaged in some way by this incident. These concerns are stated explicitly but are also implicitly connected with the intentions and purposes of actors by talk about the way they *felt* in response to certain events and the way they pursued particular courses of action.

Pala weaves talk of emotion into the early part of his narrative (ll. 34–42), framing his interpretation of the beating and its aftermath. Specifically, he says that he was sad (*di'a nagnafa*) for his son (ll. 34, 42), "who almost died." By speaking of sadness rather than anger, Pala draws attention to the nature of his relation with the transgressors rather than with the transgression itself. While sadness, like anger, is an emotion felt in response to a perceived offense, it, unlike anger, is an appropriate response in the context of close, enduring relations such as those of kinship. The contrast between these two emotions is more starkly drawn in terms of their expected outcomes. Whereas anger begets a desire for redress or retribution, sadness gives rise to an attempt at repairing the breached relation. Linking together these understandings

about sadness in the form of the generalized emotion schema
outlined previously gives the following chain of reasoning:

TRANSGRESSION
[1]   and   → DAMAGED RELATION → SAD → MORAL REPAIR
CLOSE RELATION

As a representation of shared understandings about the emotion *di'a nagnafa* 'sad', the above schema suggests that attributions of sadness entail an interpretation of events that, above all,
have damaged close relations, and perhaps have induced some attempt at repair, at revaluing those relations. These conjectures
about the implied meanings of sadness are borne out in more
overt remarks that Pala makes about his relationship to the offenders at this same point in the narrative. Immediately following
his talk of feeling sad about the beating, he goes on to describe
his relation with the attackers and others in their village, Molana,
as one of diffuse solidarity.

Pala's characterization of social relationships draws upon two
powerful idioms of community: kinship ("Bilo's children are my
children") and shame. The kinship metaphor, which occurs
throughout Pala's narrative (ll. 35, 55, 62, 74, 82), is commonly
used to signify enduring social ties marked by mutual interest and
reciprocity. To buttress this characterization, Pala talks about the
absence of shame (*mamaja*) in his interactions with the people of
Molana. Shame in this society and many others is a marker of social distance and relations characterized by avoidance and formality. Talk of shame often indicates a failure of social definition
in which appropriate distance has not been observed (cf. Epstein
1984; Fajans 1985). When shame is evoked in face-to-face situations with the other, the breach of distance is typically resolved by
withdrawal or avoidance. Stringing together these propositions
yields the following prototypic shame schema:[9]

DISTANCE VIOLATION
[2]   and   ⟶ SHAME ⟶ AVOIDANCE
DISTANT RELATION

By negating shame in his encounters with the Molana people,
Pala implies that his relations with them are of the familiar sort

unencumbered by distance-maintaining rules of etiquette or avoidance:

NOT SHAME ⟶ NOT DISTANT (i.e., CLOSE) RELATION

He does this by stating that he is accustomed to going into people's houses to help himself to leftover food; and does so without shame.[10] The entering-a-house-for-food scenario is a common metonym for notions of community and solidarity. (As evidence of its stereotypic usage, this scenario is used by two other speakers elsewhere in the transcript [ll. 261, 364].) In Pala's narrative, the helping-oneself-to-food scene exemplifies familiar behavior that would certainly evoke shame in the context of more distant relations. Since it does *not* in this case evoke such an emotion, the listener is led to infer that the presupposition of social distance does not hold.

If all Pala was trying to accomplish in his narrative was to reestablish his close relations with Bilo and others, this sort of talk might be sufficient. Yet, he must also give an account of his actions taking Bilo's son and others to court. It is here that presupposed knowledge about emotion as *motive* mediating prior events and subsequent actions comes into play. Having asserted that he reacted to his son's beating with sadness, Pala may then draw upon the prototypic sadness schema to construct an interpretation of his subsequent actions. The sadness scenario would imply that his actions taking the boys to court were an attempt at *repair* rather than *retribution.*

Having outlined my overall assessment of what Pala and Bilo are up to in their narratives, I would now like to look more closely at *how* they work to accomplish their interpretive and pragmatic objectives. I do this by examining several passages from the disentangling narratives. The analysis focuses on talk of emotions in an attempt to tease out processes of inference by which interlocutors construct moral accounts. By locating statements about emotion and action in the context of generalized schemata, each attribution may be seen as a partial "filling-in" or *instantiation* of more general models. Insofar as cultural understanding is structured in terms of prototypic event-emotion-response scenarios, instantiation of the emotion portion of a scenario may lead listeners

to a specific interpretation of events leading to or following from
that emotion. By saying that she or he responded with a particular emotion to certain events, the speaker implicitly characterizes those events as specific instances of the general class of
events known to evoke that emotion. Thus, when Pala asserts that
the beating of his son made him sad he implies that the beating
constitutes damage to close relations—the sort of thing that
evokes sadness in this context.[11] The images of kinship and absence of shame reinforce Pala's assertion that he acted out of sadness by calling attention to the close relations that others had
presumably damaged. In the passage below, talk of shame occurs
between attributions of sadness, thus underscoring the notion of
close relations embedded in the sadness schema.

(My examination of the cultural significance of emotion talk is
facilitated by notational conventions used to diagram processes of
inference. Specifically, numbered sentences from the transcript
[see appendix] are listed along the left side of the page with emotion attributions underscored. The unspoken implications of these
attributions [or at least some of the possible implications] are
then indicated alongside in a propositional notation.[12] In this
notation, a hypothesized cultural premise or schema is given in
CAPITAL letters, and the spoken attribution or assertion that in-
stantiates part of that schema is given underneath in quotes [" "].
In this manner, the implicational significance of an emotion attribution may be represented as an inference which completes the
instantiation of the schema. Adopting a standard format for syl-
logistic reasoning, the inferred instantiation is depicted below a
horizontal line as follows:

GENERAL SCHEMA
attributed emotion
inference

Instantiation is represented in the samples below with an
"equals" sign, =, which may be read as shorthand for "is an instance of.")

034 Because of that (the beating)   DAMAGE CLOSE RELATION → SAD
     I was *sad* for my son.   "beating → sad"
                                        beating = damage close relation

035 They (my son and attackers)
    are all really children. . . .

038 Bilo's children are my children.   "Kinship = close relation"

039 The children of other men of
    Molana are also like mine.

040 Since I am not *ashamed* in   DISTANCE VIOLATION → SHAME
    these places, when passing   "entering house → not shame"
    by I can just go and reach   entering house ≠ distance violation
    for food in their baskets. . . .

041 (I am) not *ashamed*,   DISTANT RELATION → SHAME
    they are all my children,   "not shame"
    to my thinking.   not distant relation (i.e., close relation)

042 (I was) *sad* about my child   DAMAGE CLOSE RELATION → SAD
    who almost died, that is what   "beating → sad"
    I was *sad* about.   beating = damage close relation

Even though Pala's talk of sadness up to this point is cast in a reactive mode (how he responded to the beating), the attribution sets up later inferences about his subsequent actions taking the boys to court. Talk of sadness would imply that this act was one aimed at moral repair rather than retribution. The fact that both anger and sadness could plausibly be said to follow from the same event involving transgression creates the possibility of ambiguity as to which aspects of the event participants are attending to. It is just this ambiguity which Pala and others in disentangling are manipulating in their talk of sadness as a response and as a motive (see below).

Immediately after the passage quoted above, Pala raises the matter of how and why he went to court over the incident. He describes his participation in the court procedure and the issuance of fines as motivated by an interest in seeing that the boys be led to repent (*tughuhehe*: literally, 'change their minds'). He further rationalizes that participation by saying that he arranged for the fines to be lowered from a potential $30 to $5 and $3 because the attackers are "my boys, like my children." (Even the $5 and $3 fines were a stiff penalty in cash-poor Santa Isabel in 1975 when many adult men had difficulty raising the annual $11 tax.)

Pala then turns his narrative to Bilo's threats to return Pala's pigs and to leave his village before the scheduled feast. He describes this sort of response as sticking up for the boys who had misbehaved, rather than trying to teach them, which would be the way for Pala and Bilo to help each other (l. 099). Pala says ironically that these were his "wrong thoughts" (l. 100). He then brings up the topic of the pigs being raised by Bilo and says that since those pigs were taken up to Bilo's village as piglets they must now belong to him and the other chiefs of his village.

Prior to the closing coda (ll. 130–33), Pala concludes his narrative by asserting that he would have preferred dealing with the matter of the fight in the "way of togetherness, the way of discussion" (l. 127), but that once the police intervened, that was not possible. In this way, Pala brings his point of view in line with the avowed goals of disentangling to reassert solidarity in significant interpersonal relations.

Bilo's narrative follows directly. In many respects it mirrors the structure of Pala's account. Bilo also opens by distancing himself from the actual fight involving his son. He then addresses the act of reporting, referring to the man (Mark) who reported the matter to the district constable, noting that this action bypassed village discussions, which would have been the best way of handling the affair. Following this, Bilo agrees with Pala's account of his threats to leave the island prior to the planned feast, but goes on to rationalize these actions by describing the way in which Pala and Mark bypassed village-based solutions in favor of the police and court. He describes this use of the court with ironic references to getting "burned" in the "live fire" (l. 179). With these events as a backdrop, he refers again to his talk of leaving, characterizing it as a response of *sadness* (l. 182) to the actions of those who went to the police. So, just as Pala was sad about his metaphorical children beating up his son, Bilo is sad in response to the fact that his relations "burned" him and his son in court, rather than work things out as would be done in the customary ways of being "sympathetic" and "talking well" (l. 163) before trying more severe measures. Both attributions of sadness point to a prior undervaluation of significant social relations and, if not an attempt, at least a desire for revaluation.

The examples considered so far begin to illustrate the functional beauty of disentangling as a predefined social occasion that leads people to rhetorically transform problematic events and relations. In this situation, where there is little place for talk of anger that leads to retribution, people are able to characterize troublesome reactions as sadness and its implied desire for reconciliation. Disentangling—as cultural model and as social situation—creates a context in which A'ara speakers construct a social reality that stands in opposition to social division and isolation. Those who understand this seem to recognize the importance of bringing minor conflicts into this setting so that they may be dealt with accordingly.

Many of the remarks that conclude this episode reiterate the value placed on resolving conflict by "gathering together" and "talking" in order to "straighten things out." In a short statement at the end of the episode (ll. 258–63), Pala's wife refers briefly to having talked with her son Rubin about not going up to the feast in Bilo's village. In a reported dialogue with Rubin, she describes telling him that they would be ashamed to go into houses to eat and drink with residents of Bilo's village after what had happened. Her statement draws upon the same idiom of shame used by Pala in his remark cited earlier, only with opposite effect. Whereas Pala asserted that he felt close to the people whose children had beat up his son, evidenced by the fact that he could easily go into their houses and help himself to food without being ashamed, his wife's attribution of shame implies that the events in question had *distanced* her relations with Bilo and others of his village—creating a "boundary" where none had existed before. Both attributions, of shame and the absence of shame, depend upon the same propositional schema outlined above for their effect:

260 "All right, Rubin, you and I will just
     stay here when the time comes
     to gather at the Holo feast.
261 What houses would we go inside
     to eat and drink?
262 We two would be really   DISTANCE VIOLATION → SHAME
     ashamed to go inside   "entering → shame"
     with them.   entering = distance violation
263 So it is appropriate for us   SHAME → AVOIDANCE
     to just stay (here). . . ."   "shame → stay here"
                                      stay here = avoidance

As can be seen in the speaker's final utterance (l. 263), the shame schema provides a frame for interpreting her stated intention to stay away from the planned feast. Those actions are thus construed as avoidance in the face of anticipated shame—an appropriate response to strained relations—rather than as a hostile gesture or some other possible construal.

The above passage is a good example of the way in which interpersonal conflict is seen as straining or altering relations such that opportunities for shame are created where none had existed before. The acrimonious events had the effect of inserting social distance between people such that shame is anticipated for situations requiring their co-presence. To a large degree, then, shame is a matter of social definition, which may change over time as social relations are actively manipulated. The second case gives a more extensive example of this kind of contextualization and manipulation of shame.

Case 2

The second case, beginning at line 283 of the appendix, follows case 1 and consists primarily of one long narrative by Tom, one of the principals. Tom's narrative is then followed by a series of shorter statements. Several others who figure prominently in the story were not present at the meeting (a fact noted prior to the first narration as participants in the meeting attempt to evoke disentangling from these people before realizing they are absent). Relations among the key actors in this case are diagrammed in Figure 2.

Similar to the preceding episode, the narrative account in this case is concerned primarily with the way a set of people responded to the transgressions of two young people who had been having an endogamous extramarital affair, rather than with the transgression itself. Once discovered, the mother of the young woman apparently told the young man to "never set foot" in their village (Paka) again. The young man then went off in a rage and at some point cut himself with his bushknife. Tom, the young man's older brother, later encountered him in the bush, elicited this story, and led him back up to their village. Tom then decided to return to Paka to see the people there and retrieve his brother's

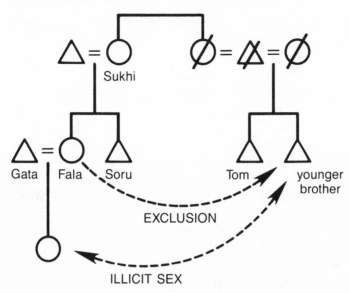

FIGURE 2. Relations among principals in case 2

bag. Along the way he encountered the young woman's father, Gata, and talked with him about what had occurred prior to his brother's injury. The father told him that his wife, Fala, had told Tom's brother not to set foot in their village again. Tom then proceeded to Paka, where he found Fala's mother, Sukhi, and apparently said that her group should not come up to his village, Holo, if they were going to talk in such a way to his brother. This encounter was followed by a period of uncertainty as to who, if anyone, from Paka would participate in preparations for the planned Christmas feast to be held at Holo. As in the first case, an initial transgression reverberated throughout the social order, igniting conflict between others related to the two offenders.

Tom's narrative consists largely of a chronological retelling of his involvement in the events following his brother's self-inflicted injury, making extensive use of reported speech to give the account immediacy and validity. He punctuates his retelling of these events by describing his feelings during the episode. Here again, it is the emotions of shame and sadness which emerge in the account, serving to reinforce and amplify the speaker's interpretations through inference. Like the two prior narratives, Tom begins by distancing himself from the illicit affair and his brother's self-inflicted injury. He then proceeds to retell the sequence of events leading to his first encounter with the young woman's father, Gata. In this retelling, Tom twice emphasizes his younger brother's responsibility for his own injury (ll. 293, 303). However, following this, he shifts focus to Fala's rejection of his brother, twice quoting her utterance, "Don't set foot in Paka again!" (ll. 316, 322). Much like Pala's use of the kinship idiom in case 1, Tom proceeds to build his interpretation of the significance of this rejection by characterizing his relationship with Fala as "like another mother" (l. 319). (As indicated by Figure 2, Tom and Fala are related as half-cousins. As a more elderly woman, Tom refers to Fala as "mother.")

In this narrative, as in the previous one, metaphors of kinship and images of food sharing are invoked to assert close relations with the others involved in the entanglement. For example, Tom describes his conversation with Fala's husband in which he learned of Fala's exclusion of his brother as follows:

319 "So, all right, (she) is just like another mother to me.
320 You married her, but she was already (just like) my mother.
321 There is water, there is food, there is sweet potato there (for me to share).
322 'Don't set foot in Paka!', my younger brother!"

Having established his mother/son-like relation with the woman Fala, Tom asserts that her banishment of his younger brother made him ashamed with her and, most immediately, with her husband who reported the act of exclusion to Tom. Like the last example of shame noted in case 1, Tom's statements imply that the act of exclusion created social distance in an otherwise close relationship, making shame possible. He characterizes his relations with Fala in terms of the same scenario of entering a house for food described above.[13] The juxtaposition of this characterization and the attribution of shame induced by Fala's rejection calls attention to her act as one that damaged or distanced valued relations. This implication is then further reaffirmed by the attribution of sadness—just that emotion which would be expected in response to a transgression that damages close relations:

333 It was the "Don't set foot in   DISTANCE VIOLATION → SHAME
Paka" that made me *ashamed*   "Fala's remark → shame"
with him.   Fala's remark = distance violation

334 This man is like our father,
we two (Tom and younger
brother) would go inside
(their) house, these sweet   CLOSE RELATIONS
potatoes were our food,
these houses, these beds. . . .

335 These feelings were probably
with him (T's younger brother)

336 Because of this I was *sad.* . . . DAMAGE CLOSE RELATION → SAD
"Fala's remark → sad"
Fala's remark = damage close relation

340 I was just *ashamed* from those DISTANCE VIOLATION → SHAME
ways, from the way, "Don't set   "Fala's remark → shame"
foot here."   Fala's remark = distance violation

341 (So) I came to the old woman
(Sukhi) up there.

As in the narratives discussed previously, Tom's talk of shame and sadness creates a framework for rationalizing his own actions. Most problematic is his telling Fala's group (through a conversation with her mother, Soru) not to bother coming up to his village for the Christmas feast. The attribution of shame provides a motive for Tom's hasty words: they were an awkward attempt at withdrawal and avoidance in the face of social distance created by conflict (specifically, by Fala's rejection of his brother). As Tom goes on with his narrative, he focuses more directly on his feelings and motives prior to making those remarks to Fala's mother. Similar to the passage analyzed in case 1, talk of shame is embedded between attributions of sadness. In this case, however, the emotion talk is oriented more toward establishing the type of response than characterizing antecedent events.

I have argued that much disentangling discourse is concerned with the transformation of anger to a more desired reality. In the passage below, the anger-retribution schema can be seen to be lurking just behind the scenes. In fact, the speaker, Tom, poses the anger scenario as an alternative interpretation of his hasty words to Soru so that he can explicitly reject it from consideration (ll.

356–58) (see Quinn [1987] for a similar example).[14] Whether this strategy works, of course, is questionable. But it is not so much his ability to persuade his audience of the truth value of his assertions as it is his attempt to rhetorically transform anger into sadness and/or shame that constitutes a successful disentangling performance.

354 It's just that when my real   SAD → REPAIR DAMAGED RELATION
    father said that I was *sad* and   "sad → Tom's remark"
    came and talked to the old   Tom's remark=repair damaged relation
    woman up here.

355 I was just *ashamed* is all.   SHAME → AVOIDANCE
                                        "shame → Tom's remark"
                                        Tom's remark = avoidance

356 It was not (I didn't mean),
    "You all don't come back up.

357 Don't set food in *my* village,   ANGER → RETRIBUTION
    you all."   "T's remark ≠ retribution"
                                            not anger

358 I didn't (mean) that.

359 That was just from my   SAD → REPAIR DAMAGED RELATION
    sadness, my own shame.   "sad → Tom's remark"
                                    Tom's remark=repair damaged relation

360 Now I'm in front of my mothers
    and sisters (in the village Paka).

361 These houses should be   CLOSE RELATIONS
    for coming inside.

362 These houses are for me to get a drink.

363 These houses should be for   DAMAGE CLOSE RELATION → SAD
    taking a rest, so when my   "Fala's remark → sad"
    father said that, I was *sad*   Fala's remark = damaged relation
    about it.

In this passage, both attributions of sadness and shame contribute to an emerging interpretation of Tom's response to his brother's rejection. In line 354, sadness is the emotion that links Tom's reaction to the exclusion of his brother with his own confrontation with Fala's group—an emotion that follows from a concern for valued relations and is supposed to lead to efforts at moral repair. Although Tom's statements in the above passage emphasize the types of action that *follow* from sadness (and shame), he also reminds his listeners about the *source* of those emotions in disrupted social relations by reiterating images of kinship and food sharing (ll. 360–63). These images foreground the social ties that are an essential element of the interpretation, which replaces a possibly angry confrontation with an awkward withdrawal motivated by shame and sadness.

After Tom concludes his narrative with a standard disentangling closing (ll. 370–74), several others speak to the aftermath of this incident, which threatened preparations for the Christmas feast. One of the most vocal speakers is Nina, sister of the chief, Frederick, in a neighboring village who was organizing the feast. In lines 404–43 she talks about her discussion with other women in Paka village who, because of this incident, were not preparing for the feast and refers to a conversation she had with Tom when he returned to Paka and spoke with Fala's mother. As she describes their conversation, she uses the inclusive plural pronoun 'we' (*tahati*) throughout, attributing shame to herself, Tom, and others as a collectivity. She goes on to underscore their collective agency by referring to them as "just one family," such that the two young people involved in the affair are "our own children" whose actions are also "our own ways." With this identification established, she attributes shame to "we adults" (inclusive) (l. 44).

Nina's contribution to the discussion exemplifies a more overtly political use of shame and, indeed, of the disentangling occasion as a whole. While her brother did not attend this meeting, Nina's remarks promote his interests. As the primary sponsor of the feast threatened by the conflicts discussed here, he had a greater investment than others in preventing rifts that might have spoiled the event. And so Nina reminds people that they share a collective interest in participating in the feast. Beyond simply celebrating Christmas, Nina's brother had promoted the event as a way for people living along the coast to reassert their common origins and attachments to land in the interior valley where the feast was to be held. Nina reviewed this rationale by referring to the shared concerns of people who are not landowners in the areas where they currently reside (l. 441). Since the need to cooperate in preparations for the upcoming feast created the occasion for disentangling in the first place, it is not surprising that someone would invoke the feast as a rationale for cooperation. (Although Nina herself notes that her drift from remarking on Tom's conflict to commenting on the rationale for the feast amounts to a topic shift away from matters to be disentangled [1. 443].)

To make her case, Nina speaks to the collective identity and interrelatedness of those threatened by conflict. By attributing shame to the inclusive "we," she implies that everyone is affected by the incident and presumably shares in the difficult task of closing rifts created by the transgressions of "our own children." She uses irony to drive this point home by asserting that "Our lives are separate" (1. 420) and characterizes the attitudes of Fala and Sukhi, who refused to prepare for the feast, by noting their use of the exclusive pronoun "we (but not you)" (1. 421). Nina's statements illustrate the multiple uses to which disentangling meetings may be put and provide an appropriate reminder that the analysis offered here has only touched on a few of the possible agendas that may be pursued by people as they talk about past events through the discourse of disentangling.

Conclusion

In this essay I have been concerned with giving an account of the A'ara activity of "disentangling" such that it may be understood in its own terms. This has involved paying attention to how disentangling is constructed in terms of local cultural understanding, forms of discourse, and interactive practices. Noting that talk about emotions is an important element of disentangling, I have attempted to specify what is said, what is implied, and what is done when people speak of their emotional responses to events. The analysis suggests that people use emotion talk to give problematic events a desired interpretation while at the same time fulfilling the avowed goals of disentangling.

As a general strategy, the analysis pursues emotional meaning by examining specific attributions in context and asking what must be known or inferred to give them an appropriate "reading." This requires postulating implicit cultural understandings about the kinds of events that elicit particular emotions and the sorts of responses likely to follow from them. Representing these understandings in terms of propositional schemata gives an explicit account of the way emotion attributions in the disentangling context give rise to inferred meaning and contribute to an emergent interpretation of events. The schemata proposed here should be regarded as working hypotheses. Alternative analyses are possible, especially with the limited data presented. However, the schematic structures are constrained by the definition and organization of the disentangling situation. A critical methodological question is, "How can the constraints on practical reasoning be discovered and brought to bear on the organization of the conceptual model?" One of the virtues of this type of model-building is that each schema may be revised or refined as it is put to the test of explicating additional occurrences of emotion talk.[15]

This approach to the analysis of cultural understanding and discourse has implications for problems of translation and explication. Examining the situated uses of emotion talk shows it to obtain meaning from several levels of linguistic, cultural, and social practice. Positing underlying schematic structures is one way of capturing implicit understandings which emerge from specific usages. Analysis of how such schemata give rise to inference requires a discourse context that in turn obtains significance from wider social and cultural contexts. The attempt to represent emotion concepts in terms of a series of embedded contexts, ranging across local models of social process, definitions of disentangling, and specific narrative accounts gives some sense of the poverty of meaning rendered by word-for-word translations such as glossing the A'ara term *di'a nagnafa* with the single English word *sad*. While both may pertain to the loss or rupture of significant relations (the reason for my choice of this gloss in the first place), the kinds of relational dilemma that are the heart of the former are more marginal to the cultural universe of most English speakers (see Rosaldo 1980 and Sweetser 1987 for different but compatible approaches to word definition as cultural knowledge structure).

Finally, the analysis of cultural understandings *of* emotion raises questions about the role of these understandings as models *for* experience. It was stated at the outset that disentangling does not involve catharsis in any obvious way indicated by immediate displays of emotion (Scheff 1979). There are few nonverbal indications that the occasion is concerned with personal feelings about conflicted events. And yet that is precisely the concern of disentangling. I have suggested in this study that disentangling provides A'ara speakers with a culturally constituted means of dealing with the dilemma of anger among kin in a society that both proscribes its expression and sees its suppression as dangerous to self and other. On the other hand, disentangling works to transform divisive angry events into solidarity-engendering sad ones. Secondly, and more ironically, the practice of disentangling facilitates the *indirect* promotion of moral claims that could readily exacerbate lingering conflicts if expressed overtly. Through the rhetoric of emotion talk and its unspoken moral entailments speakers are able to give public accounts of contested events without evoking direct challenges or angry confrontation.

Although this must remain at the level of conjecture in the absence of additional psychological data, I surmise that the therapeutic effects offered by disentangling follow from the rhetorical transformation of anger-arousing events to events giving rise to sadness and shame—the emotions associated with social solidarity gone awry (see White 1990). By giving a certain interpretation to problematic events, actors create a world that organizes their experience along the lines of a more ideal cultural model. Felt anger (which may have subsided greatly by the time a disentangling meeting is convened) may in this way be altered by reconstruing the events that evoked it. Although this baldly functionalist interpretation is not strictly in line with local views of the therapeutic effects of disentangling, it nonetheless suggests a means by which disentangling discourse may transform personal experience as well as social reality.

Notes

Acknowledgements. Research for this study was carried out in Santa Isabel in 1975–76 supported by a Foreign Area Fellowship from the Social Science Research Council and a grant (#3021) from the Wenner-Gren Foundation, which also supported follow-up work (grant #4248) during two months in 1984. Francis Kokhonigita, a friend and informant who has since passed away, gave invaluable assistance at all stages of data collection and provided the keys to many of the doors that have opened since. The paper has evolved over the course of several presentations and revisions. It was first presented at the 1979 meetings of the American Anthropological Association. Comments on that paper by Ron Casson, Janet Keller, Catherine Lutz, and Michelle Rosaldo were helpful in revising and reframing the analysis. An expanded and revised version was given at the 1983 Pitzer Conference. The participants and discussants at that occasion provided probing questions and comments, as have members of the Department of Anthropology at the University of California, San Diego, where the paper was presented most recently. I am especially grateful to Edwin Hutchins, Karen Ito, John Kirkpatrick, Naomi Quinn, Melford Spiro, Karen Watson-Gegeo, and Jane Wellenkamp for their close reading of the manuscript. The remaining inadequacies are, of course, my own.

1. I choose the terms *personal* and *social* rather than *private* and *public* in order to avoid the connotation that emotional experience is uniquely private, and hence divorced from the very sorts of public, moral negotiation with which this essay is concerned. As Irvine (1979) has noted, the public/private opposition is often construed as a dichotomy, parallel with other dichotomized notions such as individual/society or personality/culture. Rather than presume the separation of these domains, I wish to explore some of the ways people themselves manipulate understandings of personal experience and social reality. As Rosaldo (1984:146) has written: "There is a good deal of variability in the ways that people think about the opposition between public and private, inner life and outer deed, and that these differences prove related, on the one hand, to conceptions of such things as bodies, souls, relationships and role and, on the other, to the life of feeling."

2. In addition to the comparison of disentangling and Holy Communion service, there is an analogy between disentangling and Anglican confession. Unlike the former, the latter *does* involve divulging transgressions in an act of verbal expiation. An important difference, of course, is that disentangling is ideally done in the presence of those with whom one is entangled. In both cases sheer participation signifies good standing in the moral community. I was told by more than one informant that the confessional provided an alternative way of fulfilling the cultural "requirement" of divulging transgressions without the sorts of public revelation that could lead to further entanglements. At least one priest I talked with saw his role in taking confession as providing such an alternative to customary disentangling. For this and other reasons, the practice of disentangling as a large community event appears to be on the wane. Indeed, in discussions with the retired bishop of Santa Isabel (from a neighboring language group), I learned that he has discouraged this sort of public meeting (see White n.d.).

There is today a kind of continuum of moral events in which priests play a major role, ranging from confession to family disentanglings (which may be convened by a priest) to the less common village meetings (where a priest may sit in as listener and facilitator). I take the participation of priests in the latter type of meeting to follow primarily from their role as representatives of the moral order rather than as mediators of the spirit world, although both roles are probably relevant.

3. A'ara speakers talk routinely about feelings (*nagnafa,* also 'heart'), thoughts *(gaoghatho)* and actions *(puhi)* as the basic elements of social experience (see White 1985a for discussion and appendix, 11. 304, 393 for examples). Both thoughts and feelings are referred to as personal motives or causes of behavior. While feelings are generally more reactive and expressive of attitudes toward persons and events, thoughts tend to be planful, concerned with meanings, beliefs, and intentions. Yet there is no sharp distinction between thought and feeling, and the two terms are used interchangeably in some contexts (cf. Lutz 1985).

4. Glossing emotion words with English terms raises important translation issues. Obviously, the use of English glosses assumes some overlap in meaning, but at the same time simplifies and distorts understanding in those areas where the two languages diverge. Since much of this study is concerned directly with representing the meanings of A'ara emotion words glossed as 'angry,' 'sad,' 'shame,' the adequacy or inadequacy of these translations should become clearer as the analysis progresses.

5. The semantic and evaluative ambiguity of the term 'tangled' is apparent in the results of a lexical study I have done with a number of core A'ara emotion terms. Analysis of judgments of similarity among fifteen commonly used emotion terms shows the term *fifiri* to mediate two very different clusters of words (one with 'angry' and 'disgusted' and the other with 'love' and 'compassion').

6. The use of an inalienable possessive form in this term implies that anger *must* be attributed to someone to be verbalized. The A'ara term *di'a tagna* is correctly translated not as a noun ('anger') but as a stative verb ('be angry') modifying a particular person's feeling state. Given the obligatory possessive construction, the A'ara emotion *di'a tagna* '(he is) angry' is not easily discussed as a disembodied abstraction.

7. The two tape-recorded sessions were transcribed in their entirety by a local assistant who had been present at the meetings. I then checked the transcripts and reviewed their contents with him to fill in gaps in my translation and knowledge of the events discussed. Given the amount of presupposed knowledge in the meeting narratives, this "ex-

pansion" is an essential part of the analysis. The portion of the transcript analyzed in this study is given in the appendix. This begins with
the opening remarks for one of the recorded meetings and continues
uninterrupted over the two distinct cases taken up here.

8. For the purposes of this essay, I have simplified the notation of
propositions by leaving out any indication of relations among the actors
involved (i.e., who is transgressing against whom, who experiences
anger, and so on). While most emotion attributions are made from the
perspective of the speaker, they may also be used to indicate an identification with others. For lack of space, this aspect of emotion talk is
not taken up here (but see White 1979b and Lutz 1987).

9. To facilitate a compact representation, this schema oversimplifies
the A'ara understanding of shame by indicating both DISTANCE VIOLA-
TION and DISTANT RELATION as separate, conjoined propositions about
antecedent events. However, the quality of the relation involved (DIS-
TANT) is *presupposed* by the characterization of an action as a DISTANCE
VIOLATION. The implications of shame talk for social relations would be
more accurately represented as an additional layer of inference, with
DISTANT RELATION a precondition for DISTANCE VIOLATION. For present
purposes only one layer of inference is indicated (see White 1979b for
more discussion on this point).

10. This image relies on the understanding that people customarily
place leftover potatoes in a hanging basket inside the house. Not only is
the exchange of food *the* central symbol of reciprocity (cf. Fajans 1985),
but easy movement across house boundaries is usually reserved for
members of immediate or extended families.

11. According to the canons of deductive logic, this type of inference
(given A $\longrightarrow$ B, reasoning from the consequent [B] to antecedent [A]) is
not a strong, necessary inference. Noting, however, that such moves are
characteristic of commonsense reasoning, mathematicians and others
have legitimized them as probabilistic or *plausible* reasoning (see
Hutchins 1980:56 for examples and discussion). This is the most common form of inference noted in the examples discussed here. An exception in the first passage analyzed here is Pala's use of negation to
disclaim an emotion (shame) and thus make a strong inference negating its antecedent—a logical move graced with the Latin name *modus
tollens*.

12. As in any formalism applied to the unruly realities of natural
discourse, applying a propositional notation has both virtues and liabilities. The use of capital letters and other diagrammatic conveniences
is helpful to the extent that it clarifies the structure of the hypothesized
model and permits readers more readily to assess its adequacy in eluci-
dating cultural significance. But these conventions are a liability to the

extent that they connote a final or authoritative reading of the transcript, ruling out possible alternatives. While formal notations inevitably do suggest such claims, they may also have the opposite effect: allowing readers to more readily assess a model's limitations. I am indebted to Edwin Hutchins for a critique of the analyses proposed in this paper. He gave particularly helpful advice on the propositional notation, although he might not agree with the format finally adopted.

13. In this instance, the scenario is stated with conditional past tense markers (from the perspective of the narration, fixed at the time of the events), indicating that the relations signified are contingent on their continuing acknowledgement by participants. Tom's narrative implies that Fala's exclusion of his brother constitutes a failure of such acknowledgement, thus creating shame in encounters where none would be expected if conditions for the scenario still held.

14. In comments on an earlier draft of this paper, Naomi Quinn first directed my attention to this example of a rhetorical strategy rejecting an (angry) emotion attribution, even as the emotion and its associated schema are left unstated.

15. For example, in the course of analyzing and re-analyzing the discourse segments discussed in this study, I have significantly revised some of the interpretations offered in an earlier paper (1979b). Since I did not then grasp the relational and reciprocal quality of A'ara shame, I attempted to specify the meaning of Tom's shame in case 2 in terms of the Eurocentric notion that shame concerns an exposure of responsibility for wrongdoing. The revised shame schema given here can be shown to fit this as well as other occurrences of shame talk in the transcript.

References

Bailey, F. G.
  1983 The Tactical Uses of Passion: An Essay on Power, Reason and Reality. Ithaca, NY: Cornell University Press.

D'Andrade, Roy G.
  1987 A Folk Model of the Mind. In Cultural Models in Language and Thought. D. Holland and N. Quinn, eds. Cambridge: Cambridge University Press.

Epstein, A. L.
  1984 The Experience of Shame in Melanesia: An Essay in the Anthropology of Affect. Occasional Paper No. 40. London: Royal Anthropological Institute of Great Britain and Ireland.

Fajans, Jane
  1985 The Person in Social Context: The Social Character of Baining
        "Psychology." *In* Person, Self and Experience: Exploring Pacific
        Ethnopsychologies. G. White and J. Kirkpatrick, eds. Berkeley:
        University of California Press.

Harris, Grace
  1978 Casting Out Anger: Religion Among the Taita of Kenya. Cam-
        bridge: Cambridge University Press.

Hochschild, A. R.
  1979 Emotion Work, Feeling Rules and Social Structure. American
        Journal of Sociology 85:551–75.

Holland, Dorothy, and Naomi Quinn, eds.
  1987 Cultural Models in Language and Thought. Cambridge: Cam-
        bridge University Press.

Hutchins, Edwin
  1980 Culture and Inference: A Trobriand Case Study. Cambridge,
        MA: Harvard University Press.
  1973 An Analysis of Interpretations of On-going Behavior. Unpub-
        lished ms. Department of Anthropology, University of Califor-
        nia, San Diego.

Irvine, Judith T.
  1982 Language and Affect: Some Cross-Cultural Issues. *In* Contem-
        porary Perceptions of Language: Interdisciplinary Dimensions.
        H. Byrnes, ed. Washington, D.C.: Georgetown University Press.

Ito, Karen L.
  1985 *Hoʻoponopono*, "To Make Right": Hawaiian Conflict Resolution
        and Metaphor in the Construction of a Family Therapy. Cul-
        ture, Medicine and Psychiatry 9:201–17.

Kirkpatrick, John, and Geoffrey White
  1985 Exploring Ethnopsychologies. *In* Person, Self and Experience:
        Exploring Pacific Ethnopsychologies. G. White and J. Kirk-
        patrick, eds. Berkeley: University of California Press.

Labov, William, and David Fanshel
  1977 Therapeutic Discourse: Psychotherapy as Conversation. New
        York: Academic Press.

Lakoff, George, and Mark Johnson
  1980 Metaphors We Live By. Chicago: University of Chicago Press.

Lakoff, George, and Zoltán Kövecses
1987 The Conceptualization of Anger in American English. *In* Cultural Models in Language and Thought. D. Holland and N. Quinn, eds. Cambridge: Cambridge University Press.

Levy, Robert
1984 Emotions, Knowing and Culture. *In* Culture Theory: Essays on Mind, Self and Emotion. R. Shweder and R. LeVine, eds. Cambridge: Cambridge University Press.

Lutz, Catherine
1985 Ethnopsychology Compared to What?: Explaining Behavior and Consciousness Among the Ifaluk. *In* Person, Self and Experience: Exploring Pacific Ethnopsychologies. G. White and J. Kirkpatrick, eds. Berkeley: University of California Press.

1987 Goals, Events and Understanding in Ifaluk Emotion Theory. *In* Cultural Models in Language and Thought. D. Holland and N. Quinn, eds. Cambridge: Cambridge University Press.

1988 Unnatural Emotions. Chicago: University of Chicago Press.

Lutz, Catherine, and Geoffrey M. White
1986 The Anthropology of Emotions. Annual Review of Anthropology. B. Siegel, ed. Palo Alto: Annual Reviews, Inc. Pp. 405–36.

Myers, Fred R.
1979 Emotions and the Self: A Theory of Personhood and Political Order Among Pintupi Aborigines. Ethos 7:343–70.

Needham, Rodney
1976 Skulls and Causality. Man (n.s.) 11:71–88.

Pande, S. K.
1968 The Mystique of "Western" Psychotherapy: An Eastern Interpretation. Journal of Nervous and Mental Disease 146:425–32.

Poole, Fitz John Porter
1985 The Surfaces and Depths of Bimin-Kuskusmin Experiences of "Anger": Toward a Theory of Culture and Emotion in the Constitution of Self. Paper given at the 84th Annual Meeting of the American Anthropological Association, Washington, D.C.

Quinn, Naomi
1987 Convergent Evidence for a Cultural Model of American Marriage. *In* Cultural Models in Language and Thought. D. Holland and N. Quinn, eds. Cambridge: Cambridge University Press.

Quinn, Naomi, and Dorothy Holland
1987   Culture and Cognition. *In* Cultural Models in Language and Thought. D. Holland and N. Quinn, eds. Cambridge: Cambridge University Press.

Rosaldo, Michelle Z.
1980   Knowledge and Passion: Ilongot Notions of Self and Social Life. Cambridge: Cambridge University Press.
1984   Toward an Anthropology of Self and Feeling. *In* Culture Theory: Essays on Mind, Self and Emotion. R. Shweder and R. LeVine, eds. Cambridge: Cambridge University Press.

Scheff, Thomas J.
1979   Catharsis in Healing, Ritual and Drama. Berkeley: University of California Press.

Schieffelin, Edward
1985   Anger, Grief and Shame: Toward a Kaluli Ethnopsychology. *In* Person, Self and Experience: Exploring Pacific Ethnopsychologies. G. White and J. Kirkpatrick, eds. Berkeley: University of California Press.

Sweetser, Eve
1987   The Definition of "Lie": An Examination of the Folk Theories Underlying a Semantic Prototype. *In* Cultural Models in Language and Thought. D. Holland and N. Quinn, eds. Cambridge: Cambridge University Press.

Turner, Roy
1972   Some Formal Properties of Therapy Talk. *In* Studies in Social Interaction. D. Sudnow, ed. New York: Free Press.

Turner, Victor
1964   An Ndembu Doctor in Practice. *In* Magic, Faith and Healing. A. Kiev, ed. New York: Free Press.

Tyler, Stephen
1978   The Said and the Unsaid: Mind, Meaning and Culture. New York: Academic Press.

White, Geoffrey M.
1979a War, Peace and Piety in Santa Isabel, Solomon Islands. *In* The Pacification of Melanesia. M. Rodman and M. Cooper, eds. Ann Arbor: University of Michigan Press.
1979b Some Social Uses of Emotion Language: A Melanesian Example. Paper given at the 78th Annual Meetings of the Ameri-

can Anthropological Association. Cincinnati, Ohio.

1980 Social Images and Social Change in a Melanesian Society. American Ethnologist 7:352–70.

1985a Premises and Purposes in a Solomon Islands Ethnopsychology. In Person, Self and Experience: Exploring Pacific Ethnopsychologies. G. White and J. Kirkpatrick, eds. Berkeley: University of California Press.

1985b "Bad Ways" "and Bad Talk": Interpretations of Interpersonal Conflict in a Melanesian Society. In Directions in Cognitive Anthropology. J. Dougherty, ed. Urbana: University of Illinois Press.

1988 Symbols of Solidarity in the Christianization of Santa Isabel, Solomon Islands. In Culture and Christianity: The Dialectics of Transformation. G. Saunders, ed. Westport, CT: Greenwood Press.

1990 Moral Discourse and the Rhetoric of Emotions. In Language and the Politics of Emotion. C. Lutz and L. Abu-Lughod, eds. Cambridge: Cambridge University Press.

n.d. Rhetoric, Reality and Resolving Conflicts: Disentangling in a Solomon Islands Society. In Conflict Resolution: Cross-Cultural Perspectives. K. Avruch and P. Black, eds. Westport, CT: Greenwood Press (in press).

White, Geoffrey M., Francis Kokhonigita, and Hugo Pulomana

1988 Cheke Holo Dictionary. Pacific Linguistics Series C, No. 97. Canberra: A.N.U. Research School of Pacific Studies.

Appendix

This appendix gives a portion of the transcript of the disentangling meeting held at "Paka." Specifically, the transcript represents about one hour of continuous talk encompassing the two cases discussed here. Each case occupied about thirty minutes of the three-hour meeting. The transcript presents only English translation, but a vernacular version with interlinear translation is available from the author upon request. The speakers are all adult residents of Paka, with a few from neighboring villages.

Symbols: parenthetical notations, ( ), are used either to expand upon elliptical phrasings or to give additional locating information. The vernacular distinction between exclusive and inclusive pronouns (the "we" of "we, but not you" as opposed to "we, you and I") is indicated with the notations "(excl.)" and "(incl.)" respectively.

ARNON

001 Go ahead and disentangle at this time because it is nearly time for one group to go out (fishing).

002 It's only how many days (away) already?

BASI

003 Maybe Bilo and Pala should disentangle.

004 In order to go to the work, the hunting, (that) would be good.

CHAKU

005 The man who died at Mosu didn't follow the doctrine, collections, didn't stay in the Church (just) followed his own ways.

006 And then he went pig hunting and died.

007 (They) just accused Fada, (saying that) Fada made sorcery, is what they said about that.

008 That's what is strong (hot) with the Church: collection, prayer and disentangling before going out fishing, pig hunting and so on.

DOFU

009 There are always things that bite in the ocean and forest.

PALA

010 "Perhaps they (two) should disentangle," you all say.

011 But for myself, that sort thing that happened is already finished for me myself.

012 But perhaps for my older brother Bilo it is still with him.

013 But I will go through that story again about our (the two of us) going to court.

014 For you all and my older brother Bilo to know, "Ah! That's how it was."

015 I myself have simply finished with that already.

016 I have not a single thought about that which is gone, already finished.

017 All right, that incident that we all know about is the way of all the young (small) men.

018 When the three young men fought, they were still mine, not someone else's.

019 My boy also came to play.

020 I didn't know about them, didn't see them.

021 I don't know about their way, game, the wrestling of the young men.

022 But they themselves at Kolobanga did these kinds of things.

023 I didn't hear a thing here.

024 Because Rubin was there at Kolobanga.

025 So this kind of behavior ended up in that wrestling (fight).

026 I didn't know about it, when the report about the actions of the young men went in (to the police).

027 Maybe (I was) still here when they themselves or other young men who had watched told stories (about it) all over.

028 Maybe (it was) from that that (the story) leaked out to the Police.

029 Maybe they (the Police) came and got the story about the incident from Rubin.

030 I still didn't know about it.

031 It was from that that I heard about it.

032 "Your boy was choked by them until he almost died, man."

033 The other young men came and gathered and talked to Rubin," was the news that reached me here.

034 Because of that I was sad for my son (Rubin).

035 They are all really children.

036 What were they thinking when those young men choked him?

037 They are just like one man, just like one man, these boys are.

038 Bilo's children are my children.

039 The children of other men of Molana are also like mine.

040 Since I am not ashamed of these places, when passing by I can just go and reach for food in their baskets at those places.

041 (I am) not ashamed, they are all my children, to my thinking.

042 (I was) sad about my child who almost died, that is what I was sad about.

043 It was when they came to take Rubin before (I understood), "So the police have taken (them) because of the fight the young men had."

044 Because of that I thought, "Oh, that behavior will get them in prison."

045 The police pursued it until they got all the young men of Molana.

046 So then the three young men and Rubin had already gotten their papers (summons) before the police talked to Kapra (the court clerk).

047 The police said, "Man, the father of Rubin here should go to court because these boys are all still young; so it's up to his (Rubin's) father to allow them to pay a fine or to work in prison, it's up to the father of the boy who almost died, that's the way of this court," Tole (a policeman) said to Kapra.

048 Because of that (I thought) "I will go to court," I thought and ended up in the middle of our (excl.) court.

049 So then, we (excl.) went to the court in Buala.

050 I (was there because) Tole first said, "They (two) should go in order to listen to the talk and stories," Tole said, before I went.

051 "(We) want you two to go listen to the talk when the court day arrives, man" said Tole and Kulu.

052 Because of that they (two) said first, "So this is the way, man, it's up to you."

053 "But, this is already in the middle of the way of killing someone (has become attempted murder).

054 The money (fine) for this has gone very high," Tole said to me when that happened, because Tole was already a real friend of mine.

055 Tole was very much a partner of mine, I like him and so I first spoke to Tole, "All right, for this behavior, if (they go to) court (they) shouldn't have fines or prison, because some of these boys are simply my boys, man, like my children.

056 So if (they) go and end up with a fine or prison (sentence) then just leave part of it for these three boys to change their minds.

057 These (fines) can't become very heavy, big, high money.

058 I want (you to) just mark it so that these three boys will repent,"
I first said to Tole.

059 "All right, this is up to you, so on the court day just come and
say that," Tole said.

060 All right, when the court day arrived, we (excl.) went and the
young men made their statements, the witnesses did also, and
then Rubin went ahead and spoke.

061 Then those three boys said, "That's true."

062 The three boys of mine just nodded (agreement).

063 "All right, do you (all) still have more questions?" they said.

064 Then "No, they have nothing more to say.

065 (What has been said) is true," is what I said about that.

066 Because of that they began asking me, "All right, this is true but
it's still up to you," Tole said to me.

067 I would talk and they would talk.

068 "All right, if prison, then two months" they said at the end of it.

069 "If fine, then thirty dollars.

070 This is the way, man, because for striking a person the fine is
thirty dollars and prison is two months, but it's up to you to
release them from the fine and prison," he said.

071 So then I said, "All right, that's what I said to this man (Tole).

072 Not prison, but this thing is simply for you all to decide (mark)
them, because these men are still children.

073 (The fine) shouldn't reach thirty dollars," I said.

074 "Because these men are still just my children, man, I don't want
to raise it to thirty dollars," I said and they did it.

075 They first looked in their own book, and (found out) if such is
the case then, according to their book (the fine) shoud reach so
many dollars.

076 Then they lowered (it) in order that the three would repent, as I
said.

077 They moved it lower and revealed (the fine:) "five dollars for the
oldest (biggest)" they said.

078 Then the youngest got three dollars, and the other got three dollars, that's what they decided.

079 Since it was supposed to be thirty dollars they asked me, "Is this
all right?"

080 "That should follow what you (all) have already set."

081 "Five dollars and three dollars," I said to that.

082 I was just thinking about those children, my own.

083 Just make it enough for the three boys to repent about hitting people was all I wanted, to lower (the fine) to five and three dollars for those three boys.

084 So it was thirty dollars for them to pay.

085 That's how this went until (it was) finished, the thought (meaning) of it.

086 Then when we (excl.) were finished in court, you, older brother Bilo, probably heard that the mothers and fathers of the other children weren't called.

087 So you, Bilo, probably asserted "All right, if he is going to fine my child, if that is the case they should come up in order to cook their pigs because my brother here can't be at this feast they are planning.

088 This was their way, they were to come up from the coast to do this we (excl.) said.

089 All right, if that is the case, they should just come up and cook their pigs" was some talk.

090 Other talk (we heard was:) "I myself (Bilo) am going to run away to Yandina, I can't stay here when they come up and we (excl.) see each other at the feast" was some other talk.

091 And so these two thoughts came out to us (excl.).

092 One thought that came to me about that was this.

093 My older brother shouldn't stick up for those three boys because if I get in trouble then Bilo could go report to the police.

094 That trouble had already happened so I could go and do that.

095 That is the way of the present.

096 It shouldn't be that when they do something (wrong) then Pala here will not respond.

097 Whatever wrongdoing our (excl.) boys do then I will teach them.

098 Whatever wrongdoing my boys do to Bilo's boys then Bilo will teach (them).

099 So helping each other will make life better.

100 These were my wrong thoughts.

101 But he wanted to go, to run away, my older brother (Bilo).

102 All right, those one or two pigs which were sent up were just infants when we (excl.) sent them.

103 So it was their hard work, their feed, pig pen that belonged to the chiefs of Holo.

104 So they already owned these pigs.

105 I didn't own them, nor anyone (else).

106 They owned them.

107 The truth of it is that we (excl.) simply should not go up to the feast.

108 Just these (thoughts) here were my few bad feelings.

109 Because these pigs were small, simply nursing on their mothers when we (excl.) took them up.

110 And so they own them, the chiefs of Holo, because of their hard work, their feeding, pen, building a house, all the big things they were always doing for the pigs.

111 Then they were theirs, because (they were) just infants when we took them up.

112 We didn't own (them).

113 So in order for us (excl.) to go up and eat and cook the pigs was really nothing whatsoever.

114 It is all right that we (excl.) who sent the pigs up simply are not at the feast.

115 If that is their way until (we) reach the time (for the feast) then maybe we should believe it and not come up to that feast.

116 Maybe that was simply the truth of it.

117 So these were just the thoughts heard coming from my older brother Bilo's talk.

118 That's what I (thought) about that.

119 These were the thoughts with me.

120 So that these pigs were their hard work, their feeding, building a pig pen; the chiefs up in the bush already owned them.

121 For me, I (wondered if) I should go up to (see) them (the chiefs) or not.

122 So if that is the way it was until it reached time (for the feast), the chiefs of the bush should cook and eat (the pigs) so that way would reach women and children, good or bad.

123 So that was the kind of talk of my older brother Bilo or whoever, their talk, their own talk.

124 Those were the thoughts which came to me, two strands of talk which came down from my older brother Bilo, or whoever talked like that.

125 So that was the way I was thinking.

126 If when the boys did that, you, older brother Bilo, had acted, and

James Muno (catechist of Molana) had done so, had just come straight to me (and said) "The boys have done this, made it difficult for us (excl.), man."

127 If they three had just done that at the start of it, the news of the wrestling, maybe we (excl.) could have just finished it in the way of togetherness, the way of discussion, but when the police came, we (excl.) were finished, no way could that be.

128 That one thought was with me but those thoughts followed this.

129 They were already late.

130 That was my (thinking) about that, chiefs.

131 So now I am talking to you, older brother Bilo, in order that they (my thoughts) be revealed, beginning the work of hunting pig and fishing.

132 That's why I have (talked) to that, I have finished these kinds of thoughts.

133 So, whether falsehoods or truths, these come down to you older brother Bilo, this talk that I have made today.

BILO

134 All right, I will talk to that.

135 I was unaware of those things (the fight) that happened.

136 (It was) their way, (their) game, their own misbehavior.

137 We (excl.) didn't know, "Those men go and do things on New Years; they go and do those things." We didn't know about that.

138 We (excl.) had our work that we were supposed to be doing.

139 We didn't know about it there in Molana.

140 "We went and did this," those boys said, (but) we (excl.) still didn't know.

141 It was when Pakri came and told about them that (we realized) "Oh! So that's what they did."

142 We (excl.) still didn't know about the man (Pala or Mark) who went to talk to Pakri.

143 So we (excl.) didn't know those few things.

144 That happened before I started to have some thoughts about that.

145 "Oh! So the boys have gone and done that" was all (I heard).

146 So, in my thoughts about these things we (incl.) ourselves should have handled them first.

147 We should take care of them ourselves (incl.) before saying, "O.K., this way is bad, it is appropriate for that place over there (government court)."

148 (But) first running by in order to do that (report) is what actually happened.

149 That (other) kind of thinking could simply have happened also.

150 Chiefs, men for doing these things, for deciding these ways for us (incl.) are still here.

151 So that we ourselves (incl.) do those things, go to the bottom of it before (saying), "Oh, all right this fits that place (court)"; (that) would have been the best way.

152 This is what I was thinking and told to my brother-in-law, Mark, when we (excl.) had a meeting there at Kolobanga.

153 But you (Pala) were not (seen) there.

154 And the ideas you talked about concerning the pig, those are true.

155 I said those things.

156 "All right, this way, the way of that place (court) is on the rise, this way of fining done there in court is rising.

157 So I can't stay because of this.

158 I will go out.

159 If I am here and they (two, Pala and Mark) come, (I will think) 'That is the man who fined his child, the two who did this to me'.

160 If I see the two of them then I would (think), 'There are those two who did these things to me.'

161 If I don't want that, maybe I should leave.

162 This is the present (modern) kind, the modern way, the modern life.

163 The way before would have been to be sympathetic with a person, to (talk) well before going and doing something.

164 Probably (acting) like that before going and doing something (drastic) was the way before.

165 That is still the best way, which my open eyes didn't see, which my ears didn't hear even though I was listening."

166 That's what I was thinking when I went to talk to you.

167 "That would have been the best (way) for this."

168 (But) maybe these thoughts are bad.

169 "This is what my ears listen for, this is what my eyes are open for, is what is good to me."

170 That's what I was thinking.

171 But for me it was too late.

172 John (a policeman) told me "You are supposed to go to the police at Buala, man.

173 They said you're supposed to go," John said to me but (I said), "I have no thoughts, nothing to do with that, man.

174 The boys' actions are again (a problem) for us older men.

175 I don't want that incident to be a problem for us (excl.) older men.

176 Their behavior, all the boys we (excl.) should be able to teach them, (but) that is now too late.

177 So, you two (Pala and Mark) go right by, you two did that first, you two went right into the live fire (court)."

178 It seems that is what was happening.

179 I said to John there at Pakana, "This is just like something that is first burned in the fire."

180 While the Mother's Union women were selling things he (the policeman) said those things to me.

181 Then I did (say) those things that you, Pala, are talking about.

182 So those were the words that I spoke, the words which you speak about, all right, they sent the pigs to me, but I was here and heard about that behavior (the reporting), then I was sad.

183 "Maybe I should go out, go away" that's what I said when we (excl.) had our meeting there at Kolobanga, which you (Pala) were not at.

184 Those were the things we (excl.) did (said).

185 I went ahead and directed those (words) at my brother-in-law, Mark, but he was just quiet, he didn't say or do anything about them.

186 That's all I did when I said those things.

187 That's what that behavior was.

188 These here are the only feelings with me, they are simply finished.

189 No (further) talk, no thoughts about them after these.

190 In order to disentangle these actions, to make them better, these things, those bad things are finished.

191 Those are the thoughts with me.

DOFU

192 The two of them are finished.

193 All right, very good.

BILO

194   Since Pala simply didn't appear at that place (for the other meet-
      ing), maybe the two of them should disentangle.

195   "Maybe they haven't asked," Mark said earlier today. "The two of
      them should disentangle their feelings, because Pala didn't show
      up at our (incl.) meeting."

196   So, "Oh, ask the two of them to disentangle, because they still
      haven't done that from before.

197   They haven't seen each other, maybe their feelings are not yet
      disentangled," that's what was said, that they haven't yet done
      this.

PALA

198   I came down, you all, for the meeting.

199   I went to work at Nuha and when I came back up, they had al-
      ready gone down to disentangle.

200   "Oh! Probably just missed being there to talk back and forth."

BASI

201   So, it's gone all right, you two.

PALA

202   Those things you said, older brother Bilo, about not listening
      and not discussing are like that.

203   Nowadays it's like this.

204   The police simply look for talk and actions among us (incl.)
      people.

205   Even if the village chief didn't know something, it goes outside,
      and they (police) take the man.

206   They have already come and taken (him) to go to court, to the
      prison (iron house).

207   These days the police don't ask questions, don't whatever.

208   The village chief and men aren't involved.

209   They themselves (the police) just hear something and simply fol-
      low the talk to those people, go to the village and just ask ques-
      tions and keep going.

210   Because someone starts that talk.

211   It is not until however many people go to court that (they say),
      "Well, we (excl.) did these things, did these, sure."

212   That's all the police do.

213 It's not up to the village chiefs to send (anyone) to court while the police haven't come.

214 But nowadays they simply take (someone) from the path of the talk.

215 "These things, these things were like so, was hit like so."

216 That's all (they) listen for ( ).

NORU

217 You two are going to other talk.

218 Someone else go ahead, quickly.

PESI

219 On the day when we (excl.) had the mortuary ceremony, I was mad at Mark, at Mark who just went and reported that.

220 When I went to Molana, I thought, "He is wrong not to search forward and backward (before going to the police)," but kept quiet.

221 You all should have done that first.

222 It was Mark who first reported to them.

223 He didn't go to school (church), sure.

224 He just went to Molana about that matter.

225 But I thought it was still their matter, but he didn't search.

226 If the children had gathered together, if the big men had gathered, maybe simply that would have fit them, you all.

227 He himself was wrong, was mistaken, to me, but (I) kept quiet.

228 So if Mark had just simply done that at Molana, that would be the generous way.

229 I thought he should have gathered together the children, men and women to question them about what happened.

230 It might have been like Bilo said.

231 But no, Mark went there and (reported), that's what brought them (the police).

232 Those thoughts came to me.

233 "Well! Search backward and forward, just think about the sadness of Rubin's injury," I thought but was quiet with him (Mark).

234 You two (Pala and Mark) should have first done that, that's all I have (to say).

GAHE

235 You two are both mistaken with each other.

PESI

236 Yes, both mistaken with each other.

GAHE

237 I was still there working when they (boys) fought.

238 I saw them to the west.

239 Then when I reached Molana, I thought, "How should (we) correct their behavior?"

240 I thought that the boys should go talk to their mothers and fathers and Rubin's father should work it out with (my) father (an elder regional chief).

PESI

241 But maybe because it was New Year's ( ) they did that, was all that I thought.

GAHE

242 I thought this but didn't let my thoughts out all over the place.

243 I had seen them, but I didn't say, "I saw such and such," and I didn't inform people like the police.

244 "They (police) know about it, they themselves (Mark) already went."

245 Since that was the case, I didn't want to talk (about it) all over the place.

246 That's all, it's finished.

MANY

247 Yes.

BASI

248 These things are said just in order to disentangle.

249 Disentangle in order to end these things.

250 Someone else go ahead who has their rubbish talk.

251 Those things were finished before, but they were talking about them in order to disentangle their (two) feelings in case there were some bad (feelings) remaining.

CHAKU

252 Go ahead, Ghata and Fala.

UNIDENTIFIED SPEAKER

253 (I) don't see Fala here.

PRIS

254 You others go ahead.

255 "We (excl.) are like so, we (excl.) are like so" just like that you all, then go and finish.

256 Just like that, other rubbish ways.

CHAKU

257 That's their own business, but maybe I'll just finish what they're always talking about.

LIDA

258 I'll (talk) about Rubin.

259 When they said "You're child is (hurt)" then I (thought) "All right, this is their way to just choke a person to death," is what I thought when I heard that.

260 "All right Rubin, you and I will just stay here when the time comes to gather at the Holo feast."

261 What houses would we two (incl.) go inside to eat and drink?

262 We two (incl.) would be really ashamed to go inside with them.

263 "So it is appropriate for us (incl.) to just stay (here)," that's what I did (said).

UNIDENTIFIED SPEAKER

264 That's all right (that you say), "I did that."

265 Its simply straight (correct) that you talk about those things.

DOFU

266 To do that in order to think as one is good, those ways are powerful (mana), are straight.

DEBI

267 That (affair) was not just one.

268 Just one way comes from following them and disentangling.

EDI

269 You (go ahead and) open it up.

DEBI

270 Someone should go ahead (so we can) simply hear them.

271 Tom and Fala, go with that, just like that is all.

PRIS

272 That's good.

DEBI

273 Maybe they're a bit indignant *(gogodo)*, they went to the bush or wherever.

UNIDENTIFIED SPEAKER

274 Go ahead with those things.

DEBI

275 But they didn't come to do them.

UNIDENTIFIED SPEAKER

276 Because that is just like a Christmas gathering for all of us (incl.).

BASI

277 The chief said that all the villages are going up there.

278 How come they aren't?

279 It's wrong to act indignant.

DEBI

280 Otherwise we (incl.) won't want to go up.

281 Then the shrines will make us (incl.) sick and cold, make me sick.

BASI

282 So maybe go ahead with this.

TOM

283 I will tell a story about that for you all to hear.

284 He (my brother) hadn't said "I've been doing these things."

285 I hadn't heard anything until the day came when I went up (to the bush) ( ).

286 And then I went up there and saw him (my younger brother).

287 "Who hit you?" I asked him.

288 "Just myself," he said to me.

289 "You did this in order to die?

290 You thought 'I'm supposed to die,' but without pain?

291 Because of that you will remember.

292 So with this pain, man, now you understand ( ) how we two (incl.) are," I said to him.

293 "I'm always talking about these things just like I'm steering the two of us.

294 I'm still the man in front, and you are the man behind watching.

295 That's how I am, man.

296 And then you go astray and find pain yourself" is what I said to him.

297 "But now you go (back) up (to our village) with me.

298 I don't want you to stay here and follow your own thoughts.

299 Death wants us but that is for all of us (incl.).

300 Probably we all (incl.) will cry remembering our bodies.

301 That's how it is, man, but now let's go (back) up to our village."

302 So we two went up.

303 "It wasn't someone else who struck you, just you yourself.

304 Your own way, your own thoughts, your own feelings, that's simply straight," I said about that.

305 So I went up and we two reached Holo (our village).

306 "You take my bag, I'm going back to see them ( )" so (I) came down here to Molana.

307 We went down and reached there (but) I didn't have many thoughts or plans about that.

308 I came to the source of the Beagilo River and found Gata.

309 There one thought came to me.

310 "Have you heard what your younger brother did, man?" He said to me.

311 "Yes, I heard but it's all right (straight), it seems to me, man," I said to him.

312 "That's still straight" I said to him about that.

313 "It's his own doing that he struck himself, this is all it is."

314 (But) I didn't hear the real straight (story): "This is what led to that affair," I said to him.

315 He then began to tell the story about how it started to me.

316 Then he spoke up about "Don't step foot again in Paka."

317 "Who said this, man?" I asked him.

318 "Fala!"

319 "So! All right, (she) is just like another mother to me.

320 You married her, but she was already (just like) my mother.

321 There is water, there is food, there is sweet potato there (for me to share).

322 Don't set foot in Paka, my younger brother!

323 He did wrong (things) before (they started) thinking like this, so all right" I said, but my thoughts became all confused (tied up) about that.

324 And then he started talking about another matter.

325 "Even though I was angry, was fighting and was hitting when we were all there, they (his daughter and Tom's brother) were doing wrong" he said to me.

326 "I don't see you doing things like he has done," he said to me.

327 "How is that?" I asked him.

328 "If my children and wife were home then he would come in and eat."

329 If he saw me then he wouldn't come in with me (there).

330 "That may be why I was hitting my children and my wife before."

331 In my thinking, I didn't believe that.

332 I thought that was simply his way of behaving.

333 It was the (statement) "Don't set foot in Paka" that made me ashamed with him.

334 This man is like our (excl.) father, we two (excl.) would go inside the house, these sweet potatoes were our food, these houses, these beds. "Sleep, eat, you all:" our (excl.) mother would look after us, she who married our (excl.) father.

335 These feelings were probably with him (younger brother).

336 Because of this I was sad.

337 Then (I thought) "All right, well o.k., he has done wrong, he did those things.

338 It's not appropriate for him to set foot here."

339 I was just ashamed from those ways, from the way "Don't set foot here."

340 I was simply ashamed.

341 (So) I came to the old woman (Sukhi) up there.

342 "What's the matter?" (she said).

343 "Nothing, I simply came to get his bag."

344 "Oh! I already found his bag and already put it in Nani's house" she said.

345 "Yes, all right, I'm looking for his knife which he left in his bag, that's why I came looking," I said to the woman.

346 So then the woman said "You've come here, but are you going back up (to your village in the bush)?"

347 "Yes, I was beginning to go up."

348 "Where did this man (your son) go?" I asked about Soru.

349 "(He was) going west" she said.

350 "Oh! I wanted to see him, to come tell him my thoughts, but missed finding him on the road, so I'm going to tell them to you, then it would be good if you talk to him."

351 "These are the thoughts I was thinking about the behavior of my younger brother.

352 I wondered if I should go reveal them or not," I said to the old woman.

353 This is simply my thinking, (I was) not really thinking about actually going anywhere to another mother of mine, other friends of mine anywhere else.

354 It's just that when my real father said that I was sad and came and talked to the old woman up here.

355 I was just ashamed is all.

356 It was not (I didn't mean), "You all don't come back up.

357 Don't set foot up in my (village), you all."

358 I didn't (want?) that.

359 That was just from my own sadness, my shame.

360 Now I'm in front of my mothers and sisters.

361 These houses should be for coming inside.

362 These houses are for me to get a drink.

363 These houses should be for taking a rest, so when my father said (spilled) that, I was sad about it.

364 I've already talked to Soru and this business is finished.

365 I didn't really say these things to him.

366 I have really been disentangling with him in this.

367 We (incl.) are not asking about these things, are not doing this for my younger brother.

368 He's already done those things, the injury, but that's his own way, his own death, his own pain.

369 We (incl.) can't ask him about that, is all I say.

370 This is just like the two of us (excl.) disentangling when I talk, so after this I will not think again about that.

371 So, in order to have one straight thought, Soru and I raise this talk again in order to disentangle for you all to hear again, I'm talking about this, just like saying this a last time.

372 That is all the feeling with me, was simply my acting in shame.

373 Gata was supposed to be here, then he still would say "Yes, I said those things to him."

374 So to me, it was not bad for him to talk, but when he did say these things, "Oh! So this is what our father here has done to us (excl.)," I did those things.

DOFU

375 Yes, (it's) untangled, straight, just enough.

BILO

376 These things were already disentangled, you and Soru.

377 It's fine now.

SORU

378 The two of us have already done that but (some said we) should go ahead again.

379 In my thinking, that's already finished.

DEBI

380 We (excl.) haven't heard about those things.

381 Maybe those things were because of that, and that, according to Noru and Mark.

VURA

382 It's finished for you two yourselves, (it's) simply all right.

ARNON

383 When those things were said, I just (thought) "man!"

384 (I) simply heard that the two of them should not appear back here, (but) not "Don't come back here! (ever)"

385 The straight way is for us (excl.) simply not to go up to that affair, that feast that is going to be made.

386 Something like that would be proper (straight).

387 (We) are supposed to gather together there with the two of them (Tom and brother).

388 This bypasses "Don't step foot here (Paka) again."

389 (But) for us (excl.) here the proper (straight) way is not to go back up.

390 That's what I said when I heard about that.

391 (I was) waiting for them (Soru et al.) to say that and write up (to Tom's village), but only to not go up, that was the proper way.

392 That is what I (thought).

393 And then you two (Tom and Soru) already knew that and quick-

ly told us (so that) hearing that was like there was no longer any action, thought or feeling which was drawn out (long).

394 It was already finished, already better, already straight with the two of them.

395 It was also like that with my feeling, like I no longer saw that.

396 (I) had already said "No, the straight (way) is for Soru and I to not go up (to the feast)."

397 That's all that was with me.

398 I just said that the day after you (Tom) said those things, that's all there was to that.

NINA

399 We women felt this way about that incident.

400 Fala and old Sukhi here were talking about that and I heard them.

401 But I didn't know that Soru had already straightened that out with them.

402 I was just talking about making mats and just heard that.

MIFI

403 Maybe this man (Tom) hadn't yet talked to them (Soru et al.) (was still) looking for them with the old woman (Sukhi).

NINA

404 But I was just talking with Tom here on the day when Tom came and went to talk to them (Soru et al.) about those things.

405 "All right, Tom, doing those things makes it difficult for us.

406 We (incl.) are all ashamed, and it makes it difficult for us (incl.)" I said.

407 "These ways, our (incl.) own ways, our (incl.) own children, we (incl.) are just one family.

408 We (excl.) should be there at the feast.

409 And then you all are there.

410 These things that the children are doing are making it difficult for us (incl.), Tom.

411 But we (incl.) adults are uncertain and ashamed of them (the illicit pair) so then we (incl.) may just not talk.

412 It will be their own ignorance, until they kill themselves.

413 But it's as if there is no reason (basis) for that big incident in which he slashes himself.

414 That's his own death," I said to Tom.

415 In order for this to go straight, then it would be good if we (incl.) do not make (talk like) "If that is the case, then like this, if that is the case, then like this," for one mind and feeling.

416 That's what I was (thinking) when I said those things to you (Tom), "So don't you follow those ways, but if anyone was hit, maybe (he) should go to court.

417 Those ways would simply be straight for the two of them (the illicit pair)."

418 That's what I said to you, Tom.

419 But then there was the matter of the feast which Frederik is making, which would be for us (incl.) family.

420 (But) our (incl.) lives are separate.

421 And then I heard those two (Fala and Sukhi) saying "We (excl.) here."

422 "Having done those things, then Tom comes down and talks like that, then who will go up and stay, go inside those houses for going in and staying, eating?" they (two: Fala and Sukhi) said to me.

423 "Yes, that's true but it would simply be better if we (incl.) would just disentangle and straighten out those things to be of one mind.

424 Let them (the illicit pair) go and these things will be done later" I said to those two (Fala and Sukhi).

425 And then one day a little while ago old Sukhi came and (said) "If these are the things that they (Tom and brother) are still doing, how can I make mats?" she said to me.

426 And then this day came and (I) said, "Are you making mats?"

427 "I just have work here and am not making a mat" she said.

428 "Everyone is making mats, everyone is making things for that day (feast)" I said.

429 "Maybe not these" she said.

430 "Well! Why not?" I answered.

431 "That feast is for all of us (incl.) to gather together," I said.

432 "What about Sukhi and all?"

433 "They are not."

434 "All right, I'm going."

435 It's Frederik who organized these (plans) and we (excl.) women are supposed to make those things, so I'm going.

436 It's still difficult for me and these children.

437 "I'm not (saying) 'All you children go, not me.' I'm still making them" I said answering old Sukhi.

438 So then other people went and talked among themselves.

439 "All right, you all (say) No! No!, what are we (incl.) people here going to do?

440 We (incl.) are supposed to have Christmas there.

441 It's their (other land owners) place that we (incl.) are living in, you all."

442 These (thoughts) here I have now disentangled, my children.

443 I have gone over to other (topics of) talk.

Ho'oponopono: A Hawaiian Method of Solving Interpersonal Problems

Stephen T. Boggs and Malcolm Naea Chun

AS IS NOW FAIRLY well known, persons of Polynesian ancestry in Hawai'i today engage in a practice known as _ho'oponopono_ in which families reputedly come together to discuss interpersonal problems under the guidance of a leader (Pukui, Haertig, and Lee 1972; Shook 1986). A recent survey (Alu Like 1976) of households containing persons of self-defined Hawaiian ancestry reported more than one-third engaging in practices so labeled; even more among those with a higher percentage of Hawaiian ancestry. The purposes of this study are to describe and analyze the practice as an example of talk about conflict; to infer the principles of Hawaiian social structure that underlie it; and to suggest that these principles were present in a puzzling event that occurred early in the nineteenth century.

Such an effort encounters several problems. Unedited transcripts of spontaneous speaking in sessions of _ho'oponopono_, such as White and Watson-Gegeo and Gegeo present (this volume) are lacking. Second, accounts of what constitutes ho'oponopono vary among different observers, making it even unclear as to what the term refers. We attempt to solve the first problem by following a transcript of a staged event (Shook and Paglinawan n.d.), showing in the analysis that it slips beyond the bounds of a performance. The second problem is approached by examining the nature of the variation that occurs in the accounts of different observers. We suggest that common elements exist that may have given rise to differing practices and terminology under known historical circumstances.

The study begins with a brief review of published sources and supplemental data available to the authors, indicating the variations found in what is referred to as _ho'oponopono_. Common elements are then abstracted. Principal variations are found to include truncation and ritualization of the practice and indirect-ness of reference to interpersonal problems. Analysis of the staged event then illustrates the levels involved in an instance of family ho'oponopono: talk about past conflict and the reex-periencing of past events and of the feelings thereby generated. We argue that on this occasion actual behavior not in accord with the rules prescribing appropriate talk by the participants resulted from the participants' involvement in the feelings generated. Prin-ciples of social structure underlying *ho'oponopono* are inferred by analyzing this enactment and by examining the role of this type of speech event in the speech economy (Hymes 1974) of contem-porary Hawaiian culture. A historic event occurring in 1830–31 is then presented in order to show that these principles help us to understand what took place then.

The most general current meaning of the term *ho'oponopono* is to 'set things right' (Pukui, Haertig, and Lee 1972:60). As an in-teractional event, *ho'oponopono* was traditionally practiced in order to resolve interpersonal problems or to prevent their wor-sening. It might also be used to prevent illness or the complica-tions of childbirth (Pukui, Haertig, and Lee 1979:17). "Setting things right" is meant in a spiritual, not simply physical or inter-personal sense. The belief was that setting things right spiritually led directly to physical healing.

The most comprehensive published account of *ho'oponopono* comes from the efforts of Mary Kawena Pukui and the Hawaiian Culture Committee, part of the Queen Liliu'okalani Children's Center, consisting of Betty A. Rocha, William Apaka, Jr., Marian C. Haertig, Grace C. Oness, and Richard Paglinawan (Pukui, Haer-tig, and Lee 1972:60–72). Working under the guidance of Mrs. Pukui, the Committee has codified what it believes to be the authentic elements of the traditional practice of *ho'oponopono* in the context of physical and psychological healing. Aiona (cited in Ito 1983, 1985) earlier described the practice in a Hawaiian church. Peterson (1975) and Ito (1983, 1985) also studied the practices of Hawaiian churches, while the latter generalizes also on the basis of noninstitutional practices in South Kona and Honolulu. Mays (1973) surveyed practices that had functions similar to those of *ho'oponopono* in several places on O'ahu. Infor-mation from all of these sources is synthesized in the following description, along with some observations by the authors, which are based upon our own participation in the practice in several families and participation in a meeting of a civic association in which ho'oponopono was practiced on one occasion to resolve a serious loss of solidarity.

Variation in the practices reported by these sources appears so great that one hesitates to offer a definitive characterization. Pukui, Haertig, and Lee (loc. cit.) portray it as an extended session or sessions involving many phases, including a thorough inquiry into the causes of the problem, expression of feelings by all concerned, apology, and forgiveness. Shook and Paglinawan (n.d.), whose illustration we use here, follow this model. The churches, on the other hand, have a much more ritualized and truncated version, focused upon a set of prayers accompanied by the interpretation of randomly selected Bible verses (wehe 'ōlelo 'to explain the word')(Peterson 1975:205, 215–16; Ito 1983:24). Pukui, Haertig, and Lee (1972:62, 70) do not consider this practice (which they term wehe i ka Paipala 'to open the Bible') as an integral part of ho'oponopono, but rather as a practice that can be performed separately. Similarly, the church members studied by Peterson consider an extended inquiry into the causes of a problem a separable part of ho'oponopono.

Along with the different characterizations, different terms are also applied to related practices. Take mahiki, for example. According to the church members studied by Peterson (1975:215), the pule mahiki is a prayer "to rebuke all of the evil that will be brought up during the curing"; while in the church studied by Ito (1983:24) one of the leaders of the ho'oponopono session is called "the Rebuker." Pukui, Haertig, and Lee (1972:75–76) use the term mahiki alone to refer simply to an extended inquiry.

According to Pukui and Elbert (1971), this word may be used in either sense: to exorcise or to "pry, peel off." Pukui, Haertig, and Lee (1972:75–76) use the word in both senses when stating: "Think of peeling an onion. You peel off one layer and throw it away, so you can go on and peel off the next layer. That's mahiki (emphasis added)." This is a secular interpretation. One can reconcile the differences by considering traditional belief about healing. In traditional healing, a concept of contest was often involved: the curer had to combat the power of another who was

causing the illness. Chun (1986:23) states that "illness in traditional Hawaiian society was generally thought to be induced . . .
by magic or sorcery. . . . The means to correct or to heal this type
of illness was to counter it through chants, prayers, and medi-
cines so as to restore an ill person to physical, mental, and spiritual health to regain the lost *mana*" (see also Gutmanis 1976). In
the course of *mahiki*, therefore, the power of a sorcerer might be
encountered. Hence the need for prayer to rebuke.

Another example. According to Pukui, Haertig, and Lee
(1972:78, 62), *kūkulu kumuhana* may mean either "pooling of
strengths . . . for a shared purpose" or "statement of the problem
to be solved" in *ho'oponopono*. The church members cited above
(Peterson 1975) are calling upon both meanings when they term
the inquiry into the cause of problems *kumuhana*.

It is our educated guess that in these and other examples that
could be cited, cognate meanings associated with similar practices have evolved into different terminological usages. It is also
likely that the term *ho'oponopono* was used at different levels of
generality: to refer to a single activity or a whole range of associated activities. Frequently in ritual a part may stand for the
whole, and this is particularly likely when a practice has been
highly routinized or partly forgotten. One must remember that
ho'oponopono was a highly confidential matter by nature and was
also looked down upon for over a century by missionaries and
Christianized Hawaiians (see Pukui's experience in writing about
it; Pukui, Haertig, and Lee 1972:vii). Add to all of these influences that *ho'oponopono* was not written about until the latter
twentieth century, and one can see how easily a variety of associated practices could come to be given different labels while actually referring to the same custom as it developed and changed
over the years.[1]

Why is all of this important? We believe that it is useful to look
at the variety of meanings in this way because by looking at the
total assemblage we can infer the principles that may have been
common to all. We can then inquire into how people may have reacted to changing societal circumstances while maintaining these
principles. As far as the formalized versions of *ho'oponopono* are
concerned, we believe that the following principles were basic:
(1) discovering the cause of trouble; (2) curing or preventing

physical illness, depression, or anxiety by means of (1); (3) resolving interpersonal problems (compare White, this volume);
and (4) untangling or freeing agents from transgressions against
spirits and gods as well as humans.

All of the accounts reviewed include some reference to all of
these functions, or to activities that are known to have had such
functions in the past. For example, under (1) we have Bible selection and interpretation, questioning, and the interpretation of
dreams and "signs" (hō'ailona) (Ito 1983:26). In the church
studied by Ito, discovering the cause of the trouble was the sole
stated purpose of ho'oponopono, although other implicit functions
are apparent. One or more of these is always present in any practice termed ho'oponopono, or included within it.[2] Under (4) we
find apology and forgiveness among those involved or prayers
asking forgiveness from the supernatural, the latter even in the
secular version (Shook and Paglinawan n.d.: lines 75–76, see
appendix). Indeed, in contrast to the other studies of "disentangling" events in this volume, some kind of apology and forgiveness is considered an essential element in all forms of Hawaiian
ho'oponopono (cf. Ito 1983:25–26).

Informal practices are even more varied. Hawaiians are observed to refer to any of the activities covered in (1) through (4)
as ho'oponopono (Ito 1985; Mays 1973; Boggs field notes), "coming together" (Mays 1973), or " 'ohana" or " 'ohana time" (Boggs
field notes). The latter usage reflects the preference for restricting
participation in healing sessions to family members. Variations of
particular theoretical interest include the degree of participation
by everyone but the leader and the directness and specificity of
discussion of problems, which are apparently related in part to
ritualization. These variations are discussed below in connection
with participation and the content of talk about conflict and in
the conclusions.

Social Structure of Ho'oponopono Sessions

The social structure of ho'oponopono is regulated by rules as to
who participates and the statuses, attributes, and roles of participants within the session. Except for the leader, participants are
members of an immediate family, usually those currently or

formerly residing in the same household (as in Kwara'ae counseling; see Watson-Gegeo and Gegeo, this volume). The leader will most often be related to the participants, or at least known to one of them from previous encounters (see Peterson 1975:212). There is definite sentiment that only members of the immediate family should take part. Two reasons seem to account for this. First, as in Kwara'ae counseling, the matters discussed are confidential and shame would be felt if they were discussed openly with outsiders. Second, persons must be both available and willing to participate. Nonmembers of the family, such as in-marrying spouses of a different ethnic background and relatives with whom ties may already have been severed because of past conflict, are unlikely to be asked to participate. (For an instance of the latter, see Peterson 1975:207, 209. Pukui, Haertig, and Lee 1972:70, note 1, and Mays 1973 report the difficulty of involving spouses who are not Hawaiian.)

It is worth noting that as in Kwara'ae counseling, Hawaiian children as well as adults were supposed to attend *ho'oponopono* sessions and to participate as well as they could, even though they might not understand or be interested, since they were expected to learn by observation (Pukui, Haertig, and Lee 1972:70, note 2). This provides additional insight into why non-Hawaiian spouses are often not included. It may be because of their actual or assumed unwillingness rather than inability to understand, since children also may not understand. Willingness to participate is an extremely important attribute of participants, as will become clear below.

Ho'oponopono, then, is primarily conceived as involving a group, except as practiced in the churches referred to, where the focus is upon the individual seeking help. Peterson (1975:220) notes that even in this case at least three persons actually participated: the leader, a "helper," and those involved in the problem if available and willing to participate. Ito (1983:24) reports that three persons took part in addition to the one seeking help: a "Visioner," "Prophesier," and "Rebuker."

The leader in any case may be a member of the family—an "elder" (*hānau mua*) or "head" (*haku*)—or a recognized "healer" (*ho'ōla*) or "specialist" (*kahuna*). Significantly, Pukui, Haertig, and Lee (1979:233) note that one reason for the decline in family *ho'oponopono* is the absence of elders or heads of multigenerational families in Hawai'i. This is certainly true of most of the families known to us, who lack a head capable of calling the entire family together for *ho'oponopono*. A parent can of course conduct *ho'oponopono* with children, but where the problem affects both parents, as is usually the case, one parent does not have the status required to serve as leader. This is undoubtedly one reason why non-family members, outside healers, or church elders are called upon.[3]

A stand-in may take part because of the unavailability or unwillingness of another who is involved with the problem. In one case described by Pukui, Haertig, and Lee, the stand-in is a spouse (1972:70, note 1).

The leader, whoever he or she is, must be regarded as senior or superior to everyone else taking part. The reasons for this requirement derive from Hawaiian society and culture. People are not, and in the past were not, accustomed to elevating age peers into leadership positions. In the past, leaders were either chiefs (*ali'i*) with unquestioned power (compare Samoa; Duranti, this volume) or family elders (*hānau mua*). There were no other leaders at a family level and no means for elevating them (for further description of traditional social structure, see Boggs 1985:ch. 2). Nor has any means for elevating leaders evolved during recent times. Leadership remains a profound problem in contemporary Hawaiian movements.

A traditional reason why leaders had recognized status was their *mana*, or personal power and effectiveness. *Mana* and leadership or superiority of any kind are essentially equivalent in Hawaiian culture. Leaders are those who are effective, whose families and enterprises prosper. It is natural in *ho'oponopono* for persons who are anxious or afraid to turn to those who are seen to be possessed of attributes that make them effective. In order to be effective in untangling human emotions, a leader had to have tact, sensitivity, verbal ability, and an intuitive sense of group dynamics. Furthermore, if the causes of illness included the supernatural, other kinds of knowledge were needed as well. Hence the church elder, specialist (*kahuna*), or healer (*ho'ōla*) is called to lead *ho'oponopono*.

The role of the leader included the following in all of the accounts. First, the leader initiates and/or directs the session or sessions (cf. Ito 1983:26). In *ho'oponopono* within a family, one of the vital roles of the leader is to determine when *ho'oponopono* is needed. (In the church described by Peterson, however, *ho'oponopono* was usually initiated by someone seeking help. Compare Ito 1985.) But whoever initiates the session, the leader clearly directs it. She or he instructs and initiates various phases of the process, deciding when to move on from one phase to another. For instance, periods of silence and quiet reflection (*ho'omalu*) can be called for when calm is needed or someone may not be trying hard enough to understand (Pukui, Haertig, and Lee 1972:77). Questioning may alternate with testimony or volunteered narrative. All of this and more is, ideally, orchestrated by the leader. As can be surmised, *ho'oponopono* in any form other than a ritual, perhaps, would be impossible without a skilled leader whose authority is accepted.

Second, the leader acts as specialist in conducting the ritual, such as opening prayers, interpretation of passages from the Bible or dreams, and, most importantly, lecturing others as to proper values and behavior (for churches, see Ito 1983:24–25 and Peterson 1975:220 ff.). It would be clearly inappropriate for anyone other than the leader to engage in any of these actions.[4]

Finally, and likewise extremely important, the leader acts as a mediator. Participants should address their feelings and other remarks to the leader, not to one another. This is said to be done to avoid confrontation and consequent escalation of the conflict. Again, the need for someone who is "above the fray," that is, of superior acknowledged status, is obvious. This role of the leader is reminiscent of the ancient tradition of *pu'uhonua*: a place or person of great *mana* to which anyone could flee when under sentence of death (Pukui, Haertig, and Lee 1979:216).

The role of participants other than the leader is detailed in the following section, where we describe the forms of talk used by leader and other participants to enact the relationships that compose *ho'oponopono*. One question, however, must be addressed beforehand. This is how much participation is required or expected of participants other than the leader. As we shall see, this question goes to the heart of variations in the actual practice of *ho'oponopono*.

Pukui, Haertig, and Lee (1972:61–62) set a standard of extensive participation by nearly everyone present. Other sources, including our observations, indicate that there is great variability in the amount of participation. For example, in some sessions we have observed, only one or two participants other than the leader spoke at any length. Particularly in sessions with children, views and feelings may be attributed by the leader to others, who themselves say very little. Whether such limited participation is considered true ho'oponopono or not, it has a high probability of occurring in Hawaiian culture because of the ingrained obedience and respect accorded to the leader. Only if a leader sets aside her or his status outside the session to some extent will most Hawaiians, child or adult, speak volubly. (For more on this, see Boggs 1985:ch. 5.) Apoliona (1979) has suggested that some setting aside of status was in fact a necessary ingredient of ho'oponopono. It is not stressed in the accounts cited, however.

If people do not participate extensively, one consequence will be that communication about problems will become more general or indirect and not focused upon particular problems. An analogy would be group confession in church, where individuals do not get to specifics, except in their own minds. Mays (1973:45) analyzes sessions that do not focus upon specific problems. Describing the testimony that participants give, he writes: "Each person may choose an incident or recount a situation in which the role values or actual function as he sees them are elucidated." Usually in such instances, he states, there is role malfunctioning that must be corrected. But rather than confront the person, testimony is used to suggest indirectly what is wrong and "to work [the person] back into the right frame of mind." The significance of this feature is pointed up in the conclusion.

Limited participation, if ritualized, might result in sessions consisting primarily of spiritual messages, such as Bible readings and prayers. This is just what is termed ho'oponopono proper by the members of the churches described by Peterson (1975) and Ito (1983). Chun participated as a child in family ho'oponopono in which the lighting of candles, prayers, and other ritual are recalled as the most prominent features. We return to the significance of this ritualization in the conclusions. The suggestion here is that, in practice, ho'oponopono may involve a range of participation from near monologue on the part of the leader to fairly equal participation by all, or at least by those most involved with the problem. It is likely that this range of participation correlates with the extent to which details of past events are aired.

Talk About Conflict

Talk about interpersonal conflict or its consequences occurs in a typical session, although by no means is all of the talk concerned with social transgression. Other violations, now or in the past, could be violation of *kapu*, offending ancient spirits, or simply failure of *aloha* (see Peterson 1975:204, 215). In the remainder of this study, however, we shall focus upon talk about interpersonal transgression and its consequences: bad feelings, strained relationships, misfortune, illness, and the like.

Talk about conflict is significant for a number of reasons. First, it serves as a means whereby more serious conflict is avoided (see the historic case cited below). Second, the content of talk about conflict makes relatively explicit the theory of sentiments and the metaphor of relationships that the people hold (Ito 1985). Third, talk in *ho'oponopono* reinstates by reenactment the social relationships that are to be maintained ideally in the culture. In order to demonstrate this latter point, we will examine a specific session, pointing to the way in which particular forms of talk and their sequencing among participants function to enact relationships that Hawaiians regard as ideal. But first we will consider the content of the talk that occurs in *ho'oponopono* and some of its general attributes. This will be followed by discussion of specific types of speech acts and their functions in the *ho'oponopono* context, and, at a higher level of organization, consideration of the sequencing of such acts in *ho'oponopono*. All of the points will be illustrated in a text of a family *ho'oponopono* session conducted as a demonstration of the approach taught by Mary Kawena Pukui (Shook and Paglinawan n.d.; see appendix). Although the session started as a demonstration, the family had actually experienced the problems mentioned, and as they explored them, their behavior became increasingly spontaneous. The session therefore serves as a rich and moving example of one variety of *ho'oponopono*, even though the parents, who are both social workers, are not representative in that respect of Hawaiians in general.

Some Attributes of Ho'oponopono Talk

The referential content of talk about conflict includes the description or expression of bad feelings, "transgressions against others" (hewa), and the events related thereto. This content is determined by the theory that "enduring interpersonal conflict" (hukihuki) is an outgrowth of transgressions which create bad feelings, leading to entanglements (hihia) which continue and spread (Pukui, Haertig, and Lee 1972:71–72). As Ito (1983) interprets it, the theory is based upon the metaphor of entanglement, which suggests that the solution is to "loosen" or "release" (kala) and "cut" (oki) the entanglement. For instance, in the ho'oponopono session analyzed below, a daughter expresses her feeling that her mother does not listen to her, so the daughter argues back about particular tasks (see section V in transcript; appendix). During the session, the mother realizes that she has reacted to such behavior in the past by "digging in on the kids" when they do something wrong—all of the kids, not just the daughter (section T). The arguments spread to other family members, thus making ho'oponopono necessary. The solution is reached when all become aware of what they have done and mutually "apologize" (mihi) and "forgive," (kala).

While feelings and events related to them can be described and discussed by all participants in a ho'oponopono session, some topics are reserved to the leader. These include explicit references to proper behavior and the sanctions and "forgiveness" (kala) of the supernatural. The role of the leader as mediator with the supernatural is clearly indicated by this distribution of topics among participants. Thus, the leader is a mediator between participants and the supernatural as well as between participants.

The one essential attribute of talk about conflict is that it be sincere (oia'i'o) (Pukui, Haertig, and Lee 1972:62,72–73). Such talk is referred to as "talk from the na'au [the guts]." Sincere talk thus implies emotional truth, as well as outward expression of inward feeling. Involvement has to be signaled, either verbally or in body language. Everyone must remain involved. Any sign of lack of involvement may be reproved by the leader, as in the following interaction between the father and his elementary school-aged son:

M   (Mr. Kealoha speaks sharply to Kekumu who has been slouching and not paying much attention to the discussion. He reminds Kekumu that they are working on a family problem and that Kekumu is a part of that problem and needs to be involved. He agrees and straightens up.)

Another attribute, related to sincerity, is mutual understanding. There must be a meeting of minds, or, as Hawaiians would say, a sharing of *mana'o* 'thought, will' (a contrast with the Managalase; see McKellin, this volume). This is also what Mays (1973) refers to as "working the person back into the right frame of mind." One notices in the example below how regularly the leader requests confirmation of an interpretation.

Speech Acts and Functions

Certain forms of speech are used to accomplish particular functions in the course of a *ho'oponopono* session. It is the differential use of these forms by the leader and participants and their sequencing which constitute the social structure of talk in the *ho'oponopono* session. The leader is the only one who conducts prayer, questions others, reprimands, instructs and interprets, and initiates the various phases of the talk (as in Kwara'ae counseling). Leaders and other participant are allowed to complain, express feeling, and recount past events. The only speech acts exchanged by participants other than the leader (although initiated by her or him) are confession, apology, or request for forgiveness, and acceptance of the latter. Let us begin with those acts reserved for the leader. Prayer is illustrated below. The most ubiquitous form used by the leader is a question. While most questions appear to elicit information, the function of which is to enable the leader to interpret some behavior or its consequence, some questions appear to function as challenges to the addressee to reflect, look deeper, and the like. An example of the former kind:

16   Mr. Kealoha: What did you do after she shouted?
17   Kili: I snapped back at her. . . .
18   Mr. Kealoha: But you did get back at her in a nasty way and
      created further *hihia* for the entanglement.

An example of the latter is given in line 32 below. Occasionally, a question will simply invite the addressee to express feelings, or a viewpoint, as in the following:

(Mr. Kealoha asks Kalau if she wants to share her thoughts.)
65   Kalau: No, I think Mom said it all!
66   Mr. Kealoha: Well, what is this problem between you and Mommie?

Overall, however, one has the impression that *ho'oponopono* resembles an interrogation (compare the *pancayat*; Brenneis, this volume). The less the response of the addressee, the more this appears to be so. In an extreme case questions and minimal replies alternate with lectures by the leader. Lectures may in fact consist of a series of questions, as in lines 28–33, shown below:

28   Mr. Kealoha: Is that normally the way you talk to each other?
29   Kalau: When I'm mad at her, yeah.
30   Mr. Kealoha: And then you argue back and forth?
31   Kalau: Yeah.
32   Mr. Kealoha: But that doesn't make for resolution . . . am I correct?
33   Kalau: Yeah.

Reprimands are issued only by the leader, as illustrated earlier. It would be seen as a breakdown of the process if other participants were to reprimand one another, since this would violate the sequencing rule, as noted below. The leader's authority to reprimand derives from status (being "above the fray") and her or his role as mediator with the supernatural. Thus reprimands from the leader do not provoke reprisal, as they would coming from other participants.

Only leaders have the right to interpret the statements of other participants or directly comment upon their behavior. Interpreting is a form of mediation, like orientation, evaluation, and reprimand. (For a full discussion of this in narrative, see Watson 1975 and Boggs 1985:ch. 7.) It seems appropriate, therefore, for the leader as mediator to have the exclusive right to interpret directly. Other participants may interpret their own behavior, but in this case, our hunch is that the leader would have the last say (see further discussion below).

As noted earlier, only leaders instruct and initiate, as illustrated in the following:

C (Mr. Kealoha asks Mrs. Kealoha to begin with her side. She begins . . .)

Later:

35 Mr. Kealoha: In *ho'oponopono*, we need to look at ourselves.
36 Can you look at yourself and see how you contributed to the problem?

Initiation is frequently done with formal statements that frame the interaction expected. See, for instance:

A (Mr. Kealoha is the leader for the session. He first reminds them that they are there because of the things that had been going on at the breakfast table.)
01 Mr. Kealoha: I think we need to resolve some of the differences that we have among ourselves, O.K.?
02 Are you folks ready for this?
03 Others: Yeah.
B (They all join hands and bow their heads.)

Turning to acts which both leader and other participants perform, there are complaints, as follows:

C (. . . today she [Mrs. Kealoha] feels "disgusted" at Kalau's attitude and behavior. It further upsets her to see Kalau taking her anger out on her sisters and brother during breakfast.)

And there are expressions of feeling:

J   ... Kalau says that she "exploded" at Kili because she felt that
     Kili was defending Mom.

and reports or narratives:

E   (... Kili admits that when she heard Mom and Kalau arguing in
     the kitchen, "curiosity got the best of me," and she entered the
     kitchen.)

These forms of speech enable the leader to analyze and interpret the "entanglement" (hihia) that made the ho'oponopono
necessary. As noted above, this working through constitutes
mahiki 'extended inquiry', as the term is used by Pukui, Haertig,
and Lee (1972).

One kind of narrative, not illustrated in this case, is a testi-
monial based upon a personal experience (see Mays above and
compare A'ara disentangling; White, this volume).

Confession and apology or request for forgiveness from one
another (mihi) are offered typically only by participants other
than the leader. But these are usually initiated by the leader when
the time is right:

38   Mr. Kealoha: Now, are you folks ready to undo this with each
     other?
39   Kili and Kalau: Yeah.
40   Mr. Kealoha: Are you ready to mihi?
41   Kili and Kalau: Yeah.
42   Mr. Kealoha: Are you sure now?
43   Kili and Kalau: Yeah.
44   Mr. Kealoha: (Speaking to Kili) Are you sure you understand
     what mihi is in terms of your interference with her?
45   Kalau: Yeah.

Wisdom is required to determine when this should happen. A premature apology, like an insincere one, would constitute a miscar-
riage of the process. Indeed, one reason for continuing ho'oponopono
at a later time may be the leader's sense that one or more participants is not ready for a sincere apology. One disadvantage of
ritualized ho'oponopono may be the absence of sincere apologies.

Forgiveness (*kala*) is the reciprocal of apology and has to be given by the person to whom the request for forgiveness is given. Line 49 is *mihi*. The answer "yes" is *kala*.

49   Kili: Kalau, do you forgive me for putting my nose where it's not supposed to belong?

50   Kalau: Yes. Will you forgive me for snapping at you, because my anger was misplaced—it belonged to somebody else.

51   And for giving you a double dosage at the table? (She wipes a tear from her cheek.)

52   Kili: Yeah. And me, for also barking at you—do you forgive me?

53   Kalau: Yeah. Do you forgive me too?

54   Kili: Yeah.

P   (Both girls move across the circle towards one another and embrace. As they hug, they both cry and laugh a bit, then return to their places.)

It is metaphorically significant that these are the only speech acts that may be exchanged by participants other than the leader. The leader is not required to mediate mutual forgiveness among the participants.

It is otherwise with the supernatural. As mediator, the leader *is* required to untie the bonds of transgressions against the supernatural by means of a final prayer:

74   ... And dear Lord, we thank Thee for the opportunity for the *'ohana*, the family, to be here and to ask forgiveness one from the other, to release and let go, never more to come.

75   And we ask of you that as we hurt one another among ourselves, that we also hurt You, and we ask your forgiveness.

76   Please forgive us.

77   Please release and set into the depths of the ocean our *pilikia*, never more to rise.

78   All this we ask in Thy Holy name. Amen.

This action is part of the leader's mediating role and is retained in even the most truncated form of ho'oponopono (Peterson 1975, loc. cit.).[5]

Sequencing

Rules of sequencing concern who speaks in what order and which speech acts appropriately follow one another. The most important rule of speaker rights is that only one person speaks at a time, as illustrated by the following:
Kili has been telling her story.

F   (At this point, Mrs. Kealoha begins to protest and Mr. Kealoha reminds her, with gestures and words, not to interrupt, that she's "had her chance" and that in *ho'oponopono* "everyone has the chance to talk in peace and others listen.")

Invocation of this rule at this point allows the leader to continue to focus on Kili's motivation, in order to interpret it, as shown below in section G and lines 14–15.

A number of rules of speech-act sequencing are illustrated in the example text. Instruction is frequently followed by a directive, both spoken by the leader, to which the addressee gives assent, as in:

35   Mr. Kealoha: In *ho'oponopono*, we need to look at ourselves.
36   Can you look at yourself and see how you contributed to the problem?
37   Kalau: Yeah.

Such an exchange also helps to frame *ho'oponopono* as an event in which attention is refocused from a particular content to a way of talking about it, and thus regarding it.

Requests for information are succeeded by replies, which may be elaborated in the form of reports or narratives. The replies often lead to a complaint or justification of the speaker's behavior by the speaker, which in turn produces an interpretation by the leader, coupled with a request for confirmation, which in turn yields an acceptance. The latter part of such a sequence is illustrated in the following:

Kili, after being interrupted, proceeds with her narrative:

G   (Kili admits that she had been *maha'oi* ('bold, inquisitive') and yet protests, "but she didn't have to shout at me!" Mr. Kealoha asks her to explain more about the shouting episode, which Kili proceeds to do. Mr. Kealoha then paraphrases and summarizes Kili's account.)

14   Mr. Kealoha: So you recognize that the timing you went in was probably not correct?

15   Kili: Yeah.

In sessions attended by Boggs, sequences like the above have been shortened to descriptions of the child's behavior by the parent/leader, often in the form of questions, which simultaneously served as interpretations, to which the child answered only, "yeah." This is one form of lecture, as illustrated above (lines 28–33).

A single sequence of question/report ... interpretation ... may lead immediately to another directed toward the same participant. This is one form of the type of extended inquiry (*mahiki*) in *ho'oponopono* which has been referred to as "peeling the layers of an onion" (Pukui, Haertig, and Lee 1972:67). Another sequence with the same function occurs when the turn shifts from one participant to another about whom a complaint has been made or implied. If a participant interprets her or his own behavior, it is likely to be followed by a question from the leader, producing a report, etc., as in the following:

J   (... Kalau says that she "exploded" at Kili because she felt that Kili was defending Mom.)

24   Mr. Kealoha: You felt your sister was ganging up on you?

25   Kalau: Yeah.

26   Mr. Kealoha: So what did you say to her?

27   Kalau: "Get out of the kitchen!"

Finally, apology and forgiveness constitute a sequence, as already discussed.

It is apparent that the repetition of these structured formats, along with the sequencing of participants' turns, makes it possible for each participant to anticipate when he or she is likely to be called upon and to some extent to know what to say. This in turn allows time to rehearse what to say. And it provides a lot of information about how the leader is likely to respond to what one says. All of this must be helpful when persons are upset and uncertain.

This type of analysis of the sequential structure of the event makes it possible to formulate interesting hypotheses when the structure appears to be violated. Consider, for instance, sections M–N, where Mr. K. invites Mrs. K. to comment on Kalau's story. Instead of doing so, Mrs. K., following an interruption, issues a directive of her own: that they clear up the *hihia* between Kalau and Kili first (section N). This is a departure from the rule that only leaders initiate and issue directives. The directive should be Mr. K.'s as leader. Why did this exception occur? It might be because Mrs. K. is also a leader and slipped into the role unthinkingly. But consider what happens when the same topic—Mrs. K.'s relationship with Kalau—is next broached:

S   (The atmosphere in the session becomes quiet and serious,
      since it is now time to attend to the major problem between
      Mrs. Kealoha and Kalau.)

It is now Mrs. K.'s turn, everyone else having been attended to. A report or narrative would be expected at this point. Instead, "Mrs. K. starts to speak, but then quietly begins to cry" (section S). This is followed by another break in the structure as Mr. K. and Kekumu interpose an interpretation of Mrs. K.'s behavior:

60   Mr. Kealoha: Mommie needs to pull herself together because she
      feels . . .
61   Kekumu: Sad!
62   Mr. Kealoha: But also so that she can say things in a way that
      doesn't create more *pilikia* (trouble), O.K.?

This is surely not Kekumu's prerogative! What is going on here?

It subsequently becomes apparent that Mrs. K. is more upset about her relationship to Kalau than she had realized. Thus:

T   (. . . She says that while listening today she realized that Kalau has a hard time talking to her. Also in reflection on past problems, she realized that she often "digs in on" the kids when they do something wrong and that this might be hard for Kalau.)

We suggest that this may account in part for her departure from the role accorded her as a nonleader. That is, she may have started to portray the role of mother in a demonstration, but as she became aware of her actual relationship with Kalau ("while listening today . . .") reality took over. In attempting to deal with this conjuncture, she departed from the role of mother in the demonstration and took over the leader role temporarily, perhaps in order to have greater control over the unfolding problem.

This portion of the session illustrates our earlier emphasis upon variation. There is form and structure: it is possible to determine, as we have done, who is acting as leader at any given point and overall. Likewise, there is variation: a temporary shift in leadership is noted, which departs from a general rule. This variation we find to be revealing, as it coincides with the one participant's realization of feelings that have become implicated in an attempt to role play.[6] This interpretation likewise reinforces the view that *ho'oponopono* operates on several levels: that of talk about events, past events as reexperienced, and feelings generated by both. We shall see this dramatically illustrated in a historical event described below.

Ho'oponopono and Other Speech Events Compared

Hymes's (1974) concept of "speech economy" directs attention to the distribution of particular linguistic codes and modes of speech within a speech community. In the present case, it leads us to examine when and under what circumstances particular speech events would occur in Hawaiian culture. There are several speech events in Hawaiian culture that resemble *ho'oponopono* in some respects while contrasting with it in other respects. One traditional form, called *ho'opāpā*, allowed for maximal competition and verbal conflict between rivals. Another form, still very much in evidence, called "talk-story" promotes solidarity among equals. The disciplining of children resembles *ho'oponopono* in that it reestablishes hierarchy; but does so in a stern and threatening way, which is not supposed to characterize the latter. By comparing the structure of these speech events and the circumstances in which they occur, we can better understand the unique function of *ho'oponopono* in Hawaiian social structure.

Ho'opāpā was a traditional verbal contest in which speakers matched wits using a variety of genres: word play, riddles, taunts, and proverbs intended to insult. The motivation for these contests could vary from entertainment to deadly serious conflict in which property and even life were wagered (Luomala 1979; Beckwith 1970:455; Pukui, Haertig, and Lee 1979:218–19). Contests pitted rivals who were striving for superiority. The entertainment function remains today among adults, although the riddles and proverbs are rarely heard. Verbal competition, especially sex joking, word play, and nursery rhymes, is ubiquitous among children of about the same age. Children often compete with the intention of hurting, exactly as in *ho'opāpā* in the past among adults (see Watson-Gegeo and Boggs 1977 and Boggs 1985:ch. 6).

There is maximal contrast between *ho'opāpā* and *ho'oponopono* in each of the features just described. *Ho'oponopono* is structured to prevent participants from addressing or attacking one another, as we have seen. Its major purpose is to overcome conflict and bad feelings, not to exacerbate them. To accomplish both purposes all communications (except apology and forgiveness) are confined to the leader and a single participant: a relationship that is clearly hierarchical. This is because nowhere in Hawaiian culture is there any provision for a subordinate to compete with a superior. Hence restricting communication in this way rules out competition or conflict altogether.

Talk-story is another event. It consists of narratives of personal experience, banter, joking, and word play of a friendly sort intended to suggest sentiments and feelings which can then be shared (see Boggs 1985:11 and ch. 7, Watson 1975; Watson-Gegeo and Boggs 1977). It resembles *ho'oponopono* in the exchange of personal narratives and the function of building a mood of shared experience. But talk-story is a direct exchange of turns among participants, not mediated by one leader; and stories, jokes, and word play are often jointly performed, unlike *ho'oponopono*. The latter is hierarchically organized, whereas talk-story is a metaphor for egalitarian relations. One purpose of *ho'oponopono*, however, is to restore friendly egalitarian relations. Mays (1973) in fact describes families trying to set things right by holding family parties, hoping that talk-story will restore proper relations. When this fails they may move on to *ho'oponopono*.

Chun has noted how meetings conducted in bureaucratic settings in which non-Hawaiians are present frequently resemble *ho'oponopono* in some of the features discussed. Thus, one leader presides, and everyone addresses others through this acknowledged leader. Contentious matters are not raised directly by others. Indeed, those likely to be estranged by the matters to be discussed may arrange in advance for someone else to represent their interests. Instead of direct expressions of conflicting views, there are long presentations of thought (*mana'o*), the content of which is already known to the Hawaiians present. These features are absent or minimized when only Hawaiians are present. The latter meetings are likely to resemble either talk-story (as described above), outright verbal conflict, or some combination. To put it in status terms: meetings involving "outsiders" are formalized, following some of the rules of *ho'oponopono*; those involving "insiders" are informal, egalitarian, and competitive. This is much in keeping with Polynesian practice of insisting upon formality of talk and ritual when strangers (or those who have been estranged) meet. We return to the central role of talk in Polynesian cultures in our conclusion.

The speech event that most resembles *ho'oponopono* in its structure is that attending the disciplining of a child. When a parent has become angry after a child's long delay in obeying a command, a confrontation occurs. During confrontation a parent specifies the command that was violated, questions the child to elicit evidence that the command was violated, and announces a judgment. This is followed immediately by a physical punishment or a scolding, or some other punishment is announced. During this confrontation, the child is expected to be absolutely still with downcast eyes, to answer questions minimally, and under no circumstances to "talk back" (Boggs 1985:ch. 5). The similarities with *ho'oponopono* are several: (1) the adult or leader initiates, not the other, (2) questions are directed to the child or other which must be answered, (3) the answer provides the basis for a judgment, and (4) communication is strictly dyadic. Obviously there are important differences as well. In *ho'oponopono* there is no immediate punishment or scolding, nor should there be any anger on the leader's part. The leader is not punishing the others, but helping them. However, if we look at the context in which *ho'oponopono* takes place, it is clear that one purpose is to avoid (further) supernatural sanctions. Another difference in *ho'opono-pono* is that the participants are not expected to answer minimally but to express themselves at length and with feeling, which would be absolutely unacceptable during punishment of a child. These differences amount to this: in *ho'oponopono* a superior by means of questions helps a subordinate to express feelings that result in the avoidance of (further) punishment, instead of eliciting evidence that leads to punishment.

Considering all of these speech events and the relationships in which they occur it is perhaps not farfetched to draw the following picture of their interrelationship. When relationships among peers—adults or children—have reached a point of serious conflict such that the relationships cannot be restored by talking story or other informal means, it is appropriate for a superior to call everyone into a formal session in which hierarchy is firmly reestablished. This event, *ho'oponopono*, is cast as a helping event and combines some of the features of talking story—specifically, its mood of shared feeling and sincerity. Reconciliation is achieved in this way and punishment for all from a supernatural source is thereby avoided.

We wish to stress that we see *ho'oponopono* as a restructuring event, not simply as one that promoted solidarity. Indeed one could argue that solidarity is promoted in part by reestablishing everyone's proper relationship in a hierarchy (cf. Duranti, this volume).

A Historical Case: The Pahikaua War

A series of events known as the Pahikaua War, which unfolded in Hawai'i in 1830–31 (Kamakau 1961:297–305), dramatically illustrates the function that *ho'oponopono* is supposed to have had within the social structure at a time when, we believe, it had probably not been codified. A conflict between rival factions had broken out over control of the kingdom. A council that resembled *ho'oponopono* was called in order to restore (or establish) hierarchy and prevent an escalation of conflict. But a crucial rule of *ho'oponopono* was not followed, and hierarchy had to be established another way. To understand the story, some circumstances and background are necessary.

Ka'ahumanu, *kuhina nui* ('chief minister') after the death of Kamehameha the Great, together with her siblings (hereafter referred to as Ka'ahumanu *ma*), whose lands were in East Maui and Northwest Hawai'i, were trying to consolidate their power over Boki and his siblings (Boki *ma*), who were based in Central and West Maui. Boki had already been sent to O'ahu as governor there. At the time the story opens, Boki had disappeared on a voyage of ostensible conquest to the South Seas. Kuini Liliha (referred to as Liliha), Boki's widow and granddaughter of the most honored of Kamehameha's war leaders, had been appointed guardian of the young king Kauikeouli. The contending groups were first cousins (grandchildren of Kekaulike and Haalou), and both were in the line of "political chiefs," that is war leaders, as distinguished from the "sacred chiefs" Liholiho (Kamehameha II) and Kauikeouli (Kamehameha III).

In pursuit of their goal, Ka'ahumanu *ma* took the young king away from Liliha on the pretext that the latter had led him astray by giving him liquor. Liliha appeared to Ka'ahumanu *ma* to be in rebellion, for she had ceded some of the king's lands to "Abner" Paki.[7] However, Ka'ahumanu *ma* did not accuse Liliha publicly of rebellion. Instead, they chose the charge of moral turpitude, since religion was the field upon which political struggle focused after the overthrow of the *kapu* and the native gods (see Chun n.d. for evidence that supports this interpretation).

The events relevant to *ho'oponopono* began when members of the "church party," that is to say, Ka'ahumanu *ma*, rebuked Liliha. Privately, and then publicly, the latter admitted her own drinking (she had been caught drunk by members of the church party), but Liliha denied that she was responsible for giving liquor to the young king, explaining that foreigners had done so. Liliha apologized (*mihi*) and "promised to do right" (Kamakau 1961:300). Subsequently, a council of chiefs was held on O'ahu which functioned in some respects like a *ho'oponopono* session. Liliha repeated her confession and denial. "At these words both natives and foreigners shed tears" (Kamakau loc. cit.). We take this to mean that the people had accepted her *mihi*, since this is customary behavior at such a point.

Then, however, Kahiehiemalie, younger sister of Ka'ahumanu and wife of Liliha's father, Ulumahiehie Hoapili (Hoapili), violated the rules. Instead of accepting Liliha's sincere apology, Kahiehiemalie made reference metaphorically to Liliha and Boki as "getting out of line" in the past and being punished for it and threatened Liliha not to do it again. The crowd, mostly O'ahu supporters of Boki, reacted to this with anger and subsequently began preparations for war, stockpiling arms and threatening to "cut off Ka'ahumanu's head." Thus the Pahikaua War began.

It can be seen in this event how powerful words are. To reply to a sincere *mihi* with rebuke and a threat is to *oki* (cut) the relationship; and it was so interpreted. Back in Lahaina, Ka'ahumanu's followers had no doubt about the consequences of Kahiehiemalie's words. When someone suggested going to O'ahu, Naihe and Kuakini (Ka'ahumanu's brother) said, "You cannot get to O'ahu; they will shoot you down as the British did. And it is not their fault. We sent you to O'ahu to speak the word of God . . . but you condemned and insulted them and hurt their feelings." Ka'ahumanu and her followers were even prepared to retire to the island of Hawai'i, for when the relationship was severed everyone knew that a war to the finish would ensue. The situation was clearly out of control.

Ho'oponopono in such circumstances was out of the question and was not attempted. But the purpose that it would serve—namely, to restore hierarchy—could still be achieved. The council decided to send Hoapili, Liliha's father, to O'ahu, "since there was some chance of his being spared" (Kamakau 1961:302). He went and was spared. This turned the tables, for in sparing her father, Liliha surrendered in the Hawaiian view. Thus, her followers told her in advance, "if he [Hoapili] lives we shall be poor in this world." Soon after, Ka'ahumanu's followers took over the fort in Honolulu and stripped Liliha and her followers, including Paki, of all their lands, leaving them "destitute" (Kamakau 1961:303). Thus was hierarchy reimposed. Boki *ma* were completely vanquished.

We see in this story the operation of those principles that we have inferred to underlie the use of *ho'oponopono*. Relationships had become entangled. At a council meeting a sincere effort to *mihi* was made. In violation of the principles of *ho'oponopono*, the *mihi* was rebuffed. The situation thereupon got out of control. Hierarchy was then reestablished by sending a father to confront his daughter, who led the opposing faction. All of this happened according to principles of Hawaiian social structure which were still in effect at the time. *Ho'oponopono*, we think, may have codified these principles at a later time.

Conclusion

Talk is both expression and enactment of social structure. Within the speech event known in Hawai'i as *ho'oponopono*, talk is structured in such a way that hierarchy is reestablished in the relationship between leader and other participants. This is done while allowing participants, including the leader, to express bad feelings, so as to overcome conflict. Conflict is overcome by mutual apology and forgiveness. *Ho'oponopono* is the only event in the speech economy that performs such a function, although there are other means for restoring hierarchy in dyadic relationships, such as disciplining of children. We have seen that similar principles of social structure operated at the level of family relations and in chiefly politics.

The emphasis upon talk as a way to resolve conflict in *ho'oponopono* reflects the importance of talk in Polynesian cultures generally. For instance, in Aotearoa (New Zealand) formal oratory and ritual are used to establish or reestablish relationships when visitors approach the *marae* (meeting ground). Chun, who has participated in such ceremonies, had a difficult time reconciling the Maori concept of *mihi*, which is part of the greeting ceremony, *whaikōrero*, with the Hawaiian concept of *mihi* as apology. To *mihi* in the Maori ceremony is to recite genealogy and legendary events related thereto for the purpose of establishing relationships between visiting and host groups. The more elaborate the oratory on each side, the greater the prestige accorded to both parties (see Salmond 1974). While this is quite different from repenting or apologizing, both function to reestablish, or establish, solidarity. Moreover, both ritual and formal talk are used for this purpose.

In this discussion we have also been concerned with the different forms in which *ho'oponopono* is practiced today. One of the principal variations concerns the relative emphasis upon spontaneous talk versus ritual talk. This relates to the emphasis upon psychology in recent interpretations of *ho'oponopono* (cf. Pukui, Haertig, and Lee 1972) and to the feature of indirectness, raised in connection with ritualization in discussing Mays's (1973) study and also observed in meetings within bureaucratic settings. In conclusion, we wish to consider the possible historical significance of this variation.

If an occasion is formal, which *ho'oponopono* is, then ritual is bound to play an important part. Just how much a part is at issue. In retrospect, we place particular emphasis upon the fact that family elders, the natural leaders of *ho'oponopono*, are no longer present in most families. How might they have functioned in the past? Chun believes that as soon as people became aware that something was wrong—an unproclaimed presence of tension, a sense of something amiss—the *haku* or elder would immediately react to determine what had happened and who was involved. Simultaneously, attempts would be made to resolve the problem. Pukui, Haertig, and Lee (1979:228) report that elders in the past would conduct a series of dyadic meetings with those who might be involved in a problem without necessarily bringing all of them together, in the same way that Kwara'ae elders investigate conflicts before calling a counseling session (Watson-Gegeo and Gegeo this volume). If this is what happened, then the function of *ho'oponopono*, if and when a session was called, would be less to discover what had happened and more to ratify collectively a resolution already negotiated (compare, e.g., the *pancayat*; Brenneis, this volume). A lot of talk would thus not be required, and ritual would be foremost. Moreover, under these circumstances, the bulk of talk would appropriately consist of lecture, and perhaps some testimonials of the kind described by Mays.

Given the changes of the past century, however, specifically the absence of the *haku* (head) and the dispersal of nuclear families and their members throughout the state and nation, changes in *ho'oponopono* would have to occur. For one, *ho'oponopono* would be necessary more often as a means of obtaining information about possible family troubles and also for negotiating resolutions on the spot. Stand-ins would also be necessary, as well as leaders who were not family members, as we have noted earlier. In addition, given the emphasis upon psychotherapy in recent decades, those more in touch with such concepts would be inclined to see and to emphasize the therapeutic value of talk (cf. Pukui, Haertig, and Lee 1972). Those less influenced by psychology, such as the church members studied by Peterson and Ito, would cling more to the ritual component of *ho'oponopono*. The selecting of Bible passages would be functional in all forms of *ho'oponopono* as a legitimizing device. More recently it would function also as diagnosis in the absence of sufficient information about participants' daily lives. Whether or not such changes as we have imagined really took place, this view reconciles the variations discussed above in the emphasis placed upon psychology, in ritual versus spontaneous talk, and in indirectness, insofar as it is associated with ritualization.

Extensive similarities among *ho'oponopono*, Kwara'ae counseling, and A'ara disentangling suggest they may have a common source. All three are based upon the metaphor of entanglement: bad thoughts and feelings (e.g., hurt, anger [Hawaiian], sadness, shame [A'ara]) are believed to cause illness, accident, or failure of joint enterprise. Accordingly, all are practiced as treatment and preventively. They all function as therapy and as a form of conflict resolution, but are viewed as a single phenomenon—at least we believe that the therapeutic interpretation of *ho'oponopono* is recent and syncretic. The description of Kwara'ae counseling sessions is particularly like *ho'oponopono* sessions that the authors have attended: a monologue by the leader, participants silent and inward/downward looking, the importance of heavy silences, the leader imputing feelings to individual participants. In addition, the Hawaiian "unpeeling" the layers of entanglement resembles Kwara'ae *'ini te'ete'e sulia*.

Differences among the practices, seen against this background of similarities, suggest some possible causal relations among certain features. The directness of evaluation by the leader in the Hawaiian and Kwara'ae practices contrasts with the absence of a leader and the "indirect, narrative style of moral discourse" by the participants which, according to White, functions to "maintain a certain degree of ambiguity in the definition of the situation" in disentangling. It is plausible to suppose that the *mana*, or charisma, possessed by Hawaiian and Kwara'ae leaders enables them to act in this way and get away with it, so to speak. Indirectness of reference to particular behavior is manifest in some of the "testimony" described by Mays in certain cases in Hawai'i. Following the same line of reasoning, this may be due to the absence of a family elder to lead such lessons.

We have stressed in the analysis of *ho'oponopono* the interactive devices that express and enact the social structure, rather than the cultural knowledge of social and moral reasoning presupposed by the content of the talk itself. This is undoubtedly a difference in theoretical interest rather than in the nature of the phenomena themselves. For example, the idea that bad feelings presuppose, and lead to, social conflict/transgression/breaking of solidarity among kinsfolk, more broadly, that certain events give rise to emotions that in turn produce action responses, is behind the Hawaiian concept of *hihia*, which has been mentioned above and is easily observable in the family session analyzed.

By their role in counseling, Kwara'ae elders enact custom (*falafala*). In a comparable way, *ho'oponopono* both expresses and re-enacts fundamental principles of the social structure, at both family and community levels. Watson-Gegeo and Gegeo suggest that the retention of counseling has enabled the Kwara'ae to keep the core values of the culture alive. In like manner, the variations that we have described in *ho'oponopono*, and its continued practice, suggest the continuing vitality of Hawaiian culture and social structure.

Notes

1. Ito (1985) cites Malo (1951:95), who states that a ceremony called *ho'omana* functioned in the early nineteenth century to prepare the way for treatment, much as *ho'oponopono* is often used today. See also the historical case cited below.

2. Boggs has data which indicate that other types of curing also alternately use questioning, dreams, signs, and Biblical passages.

3. Mays (1973) has noted the tendency for extended families undergoing a structural crisis to organize themselves as a Hawaiian church.

4. The sole exception we noted occurs in the church *ho'oponopono*, where on the third day the "patient" (*nāwaliwali*) is allowed to offer the closing prayer. This exception is significant, for *ho'oponopono* is used here in part as a means of teaching church members how to conduct these sessions (Peterson 1975:222).

5. Mays (1973:44) states flatly that confession does not occur in family sessions called to correct role malfunction. He argues that the problems of self-presentation are so formidable for a person regarded as a miscreant by the others that confession would be unbearable and hence is not called for. However, it is well attested in a number of accounts, even under these conditions, for example, Mahelona (1976). Some form of apology and forgiveness, even if formal and collective, would seem to be required by the very logic of *ho'oponopono* as analyzed here.

6. I am indebted to Karen Watson-Gegeo for calling attention to the generalization about variation here.

7. Paki was a cousin of Kina'u, who was herself married to a brother of Boki. He had loyalties to both parties. Traditional land tenure was in flux at this time. It is unclear to us whether Liliha had the right to cede this land. But it does not matter: Ka'ahumanu chose to regard it as rebellion (Kamakau 1961:298).

References

Aiona, Darrow

1959   The Hawaiian Church of the Living God: An Episode in the Hawaiians' Quest for Social Identity. M.A. thesis, University of Hawaii.

Alu Like, Inc.

1976   Social and Economic Patterns of Hawaiians. *In* Needs Assessment Survey. Honolulu: Alu Like, Inc.

Apoliona, Haunani

1979   Lecture to Anthropology 486, February 13. University of Hawaii at Manoa.

Beckwith, Martha Warren

1970   Hawaiian Mythology. Honolulu: University of Hawai'i Press (orig. 1940).

Boggs, Stephen T.

1985   Speaking, Relating, and Learning: A Study of Hawaiian Children at Home and at School. Norwood, N.J.: Ablex.

Chun, Malcolm Naea
n.d.   The Arrival of Missionaries and Tahitians. Unpub. ms.
1986   Hawaiian Medicine Book: He Buke La'au Lapa'au. Honolulu: Bess Press.

Gutmanis, June
1976   Kahuna La'au Lapa'au. Honolulu: Honolulu Publishing Company.

Hymes, Dell
1974   Ways of Speaking. In Explorations in the Ethnography of Speaking. R. Bauman and J. Sherzer, eds. London: Cambridge University Press.

Ito, Karen L.
1983   *Ho'oponopono* and the Ties that Bind: An Examination of Hawaiian Metaphoric Frames, Conflict Resolution and Indigenous Therapy. Paper presented at Conference on Talk and Social Inference, Pitzer College, Claremont, CA.
1985   *Ho'oponopono*, "To Make Right": Hawaiian Conflict Resolution and Metaphor in the Construction of a Family Therapy. Culture, Medicine and Psychiatry 9:201-17.

Kamakau, S. M.
1961   Ruling Chiefs of Hawaii. Honolulu: Kamehameha Schools Press.

Luomala, Katharine
1979   Hawaiian Oral Arts. Lecture at the Kamehameha Schools, March 15, Honolulu.

Mahelona, John
1976   *Ho'onoho*. Paper prepared for Anthropology 486, University of Hawaii at Manoa, spring semester.

Malo, David
1951   Hawaiian Antiquities. N. B. Emerson, Trans. Second Edition. Bernice P. Bishop Museum Special Publication 2. (First ed. 1898).

Mays, Michael P.
1973   Coming Together: A Conflict Resolution Theme in Hawaiian-American Families. Honolulu: Governor's Office, State of Hawaii, 299 Task Force Report.

Peterson, John
1975   Status and Conflict: An Ethnographic Study of an Independent Hawaiian Church. Doctoral dissertation, University of Hawaii.

Pukui, M. K., and S. H. Elbert

1971 Hawaiian Dictionary. Honolulu: University of Hawaii Press.

Pukui, M. K., E. E. Haertig, and C. A. Lee

1972 Nana I Ke Kumu (Look to the Source), Vol. 1. Honolulu: Hui Hanai, Queen Liliuokalani Children's Center.

1979 Nana I Ke Kumu (Look to the Source), Vol. 2. Honolulu: Hui Hanai, Queen Liliuokalani Children's Center.

Salmond, Ann

1974 Rituals of Encounter Among the Maori: Sociolinguistic Study of a Scene. *In* Explorations in the Ethnography of Speaking. R. Bauman and J. Sherzer, eds. London: Cambridge University Press.

Shook, E. Victoria

1986 *Ho'oponopono*: Contemporary Uses of a Hawaiian Problem-Solving Process. Honolulu: University of Hawaii Press.

Shook, Vicky, and Lynette Paglinawan

n.d. Instructional Guide to Accompany Two Videotapes Entitled 'Ho'oponopono—A Lecture by Lynette Paglinawan' and 'Ho'oponopono with the Kealoha Family.' Honolulu: Pacific Basin Family and Children Center.

Watson, Karen Ann

1975 Transferable Communicative Routines: Strategies and Group Identity in Two Speech Events. Language in Society, 4:53–72.

Watson-Gegeo, Karen Ann, and Stephen T. Boggs

1977 From Verbal Play to Talk-Story: The Role of Routines in Speech Events Among Hawaiian Children. *In* Child Discourse. S. Ervin-Tripp and C. Mitchell-Kernan, eds. New York: Academic Press.

Appendix

(The following is quoted from Shook and Paglinawan, n.d.:31–40. Paraphrases of the transcript are as made in the source. Minor editing, lettering of paraphrases and numbering of utterances are added so that parts of the transcript can be cited in the text. We are indebted to the authors for permission to use the material here.)

In this section of the guide an abbreviated account of the videotape is presented. Emphasis is placed on giving examples from the dialogue and interaction patterns to illustrate some of the distinctive features of *ho'oponopono.* Other parts of the videotaped session are summarized. The case includes members of the Kealoha (pseudonym) family:

Mr. Kealoha
Mrs. Kealoha
Kalau (teenaged daughter)
Kili (teenaged daughter)
Ka'ai'ai (younger teen daughter)
Kekumu (elementary school-aged son)

Setting for the Problem

The problem emerges on a Sunday morning during a debate among family members about who is to cook breakfast. Based on his understanding of an earlier agreement, Mr. Kealoha tells Kalau it is her turn to cook. Kalau becomes angry, since she cooked the day before. She says she will do it but that it is unfair. Once in the kitchen, Kalau noisily bangs the dishes around and is visibly angry. When Kili and Mrs. Kealoha come into the kitchen, Kalau speaks sharply to each of them and they in turn argue back. Later at the breakfast table, with the whole family gathered, the tension mounts. Kili calls Kalau a "grump." Kalau scolds Kekumu for using his hands to eat, rather than using a spoon. Ka'ai'ai and Kalau exchange sharp remarks and looks. Finally, Mr. Kealoha intervenes, questioning what is going on. Frustrated, he suggests, "Well, it's about time we stop it for now and after breakfast we'll do *ho'oponopono,* O.K.?" The family members nod or grumble agreement and quietly finish breakfast.

The Ho'oponopono Session

A   (The family gathers in the formal living room. Each are seated on the floor and form a circle. Mr. Kealoha is the leader for the session. He first reminds them that they are there because of the things that had been going on at the breakfast table.)

01   Mr. Kealoha: I think we need to resolve some of the differences that we have among ourselves. O.K.?

02   Are you folks ready for this?

03   Others: Yeah.

B   (They all join hands and bow their heads.)

04   Mr. Kealoha: Let's join our hands and pray.

05   Dear Heavenly Father, Creator of heaven and earth and to his

only son, Jesu Cristo, . . . Dear Lord, we thank thee for this opportunity to get together as an 'ohana, as a family.

06   It was obvious during this morning that many things were happening to our family.

07   People were getting at one another and things weren't right.

08   As you know, we need to restore harmony within our family in
order for us to continue on.

09   Dear Lord, as we get together in this ho'oponopono, give us the
strength and wisdom and understanding to be able to lay the
problems out and identify what the problems are.

10   Give us also the understanding and the know-how to be able to
discuss things freely without hurting one another, and to say
things in a way that makes for understanding.

11   And, dear Lord, give us the opportunity so that as one is talking
about the problem . . . that the others will sit quietly and listen
with an open ear, so that they can understand as to how the
other one person perceives what is happening.

12   And, dear Lord, after we've identified it all, may we be able to
open our hearts to one another, to forgive each other, so that we
can then carry on.

13   Always, we ask in Thy holy name, Amen.

C   (The family members drop their held hands and raise their
heads. Mr. Kealoha asks Mrs. Kealoha to begin with her side. She
begins, "As I saw it this morning," and continues to describe her
understanding of the cooking agreement. Originally, she says
that she was pleased with the arrangement, but today she feels
"disgusted" at Kalau's attitude and behavior. It further upsets her
to see Kalau taking her anger out on her sisters and brother
during breakfast.)

D   (Mr. Kealoha asks Mrs. Kealoha for clarification about the actual
agreement, "Was everyone there?" She recalls that they were although Kili had gone in and out of the room during the discussions.)

E   (Mr. Kealoha then turns to Kili to discern her involvement. Kili
admits that when she heard Mom and Kalau arguing in the
kitchen, "curiosity got the best of me," and she entered the
kitchen.)

F   (At this point, Mrs. Kealoha begins to protest and Mr. Kealoha
reminds her, with gestures and words, not to interrupt, that
she's "had her chance" and that in ho'oponopono "everyone has

the chance to talk in peace and the others listen.")

G   (Kili admits that she had been *maha'oi* (bold, inquisitive) and yet
      protests, "but she didn't have to shout at me!" Mr. Kealoha asks
      her to explain more about the shouting episode, which Kili
      proceeds to do. Mr. Kealoha then paraphrases and summarizes
      Kili's account.)

14   Mr. Kealoha: So you recognize that the timing you went in was
      probably not correct?

15   Kili: Yeah.

H   (Mr. Kealoha again paraphrases, this time recognizing that Kili's
      motives had been inquisitive and that she nevertheless did not
      like Kalau shouting at her.)

16   Mr. Kealoha: What did you do after she shouted?

17   Kili: I snapped back at her . . .

18   Mr. Kealoha: But you did get back at her in a nasty way and
      created further *hihia* for the entanglement.

19   Kili: Yeah.

I   (Mr. Kealoha then attempts to corroborate the account by asking
      Mrs. Kealoha who had been present. She says that she actually
      asked Kili to come into the kitchen twice, once to set the table
      and later to ask her opinion about the terms of the cooking
      agreement. She also says that she does recall that Kili had
      seemed overeager to get involved.)

20   Mr. Kealoha: *Maha'oi?*

21   Mrs. Kealoha: Yes.

22   Mr. Kealoha: (to Kili) Did Mommie state this correctly?

23   Kili: Yeah.

J   (Kalau now has her opportunity to share. She describes the
      events of the morning and admits that she was upset at Mom
      when Kili came into the kitchen. Kalau says that she "exploded"
      at Kili because she felt that Kili was defending Mom.)

24   Mr. Kealoha: You felt your sister was ganging up on you?

25   Kalau: Yeah.

26   Mr. Kealoha: So what did you say to her?

27   Kalau: "Get out of the kitchen!"

28   Mr. Kealoha: Is that normally the way you talk to each other?

29   Kalau: When I'm mad at her, yeah.

30   Mr. Kealoha: And then you argue back and forth?

31   Kalau: Yeah.

32 Mr. Kealoha: But that doesn't make for resolution . . . am I correct?

33 Kalau: Yeah.

K (Mr. Kealoha then asks Kalau to explain more about what occurred at the breakfast table. Kalau complies and admits that she had snapped at the others "for revenge," and she laughs.)

34 Mr. Kealoha: Is that all? What about you and Mommie?

L (Kalau turns toward Mrs. Kealoha and gives her a dirty look and says, "Oh." Mr. Kealoha reminds Kalau to look at and speak to him. Kalau explains that she knew Mom was disgusted with her and that she was angry in return. Mr. Kealoha asks Kalau to examine her actions at the time.)

35 Mr. Kealoha: In *ho'oponopono*, we need to look at ourselves.

36 Can you look at yourself and see how you contributed to the problem?

37 Kalau: Yeah.

M (The discussion goes on to reveal a basic misunderstanding about the cooking agreement. Kalau thought the agreement was that she was to cook one day out of the weekend. Since she had cooked the day before, she believed that she had fulfilled her responsibilities. Mr. Kealoha then asks Kili if she had gone in and out of the room when the decision was being made. She says that she had because "I didn't want to stay and listen." Mr. Kealoha admonishes Kili that this behavior wasn't very wise since a decision had been made that affected her. He then paraphrases Kalau's story thus far and turns to Mrs. Kealoha for comments. She begins but is interrupted when Mr. Kealoha speaks sharply to Kekumu who has been slouching and not paying much attention to the discussion. He reminds Kekumu that they are working on a family problem and that Kekumu is a part of that problem and needs to be involved. He agrees and straightens up.)

N (Mrs. Kealoha defers discussing her side of the problems with Kalau because she thinks it's important to clear up the *hihia* between Kili and Kalau first. Mr. Kealoha then summarizes this *hihia*, as it was discussed earlier.)

38 Mr. Kealoha: Now, are you folks ready to undo this with each other?

39 Kili and Kalau: Yeah.

40 Mr. Kealoha: Are you ready to *mihi*?

41 Kili and Kalau: Yeah.

42 Mr. Kealoha: Are you sure now?

43 Kili and Kalau: Yeah.

44 Mr. Kealoha: (Speaking to Kili) Are you sure you understand what *mihi* is in terms of your interference with her?

45 Kalau: Yeah.

46 Mr. Kealoha: O.K., can we start with Kili-Kili first?

47 Kili, are you ready to *mihi*?

48 Kili: Yeah.

O   (At this point, Kalau and Kili face and speak directly to one another. Mrs. Kealoha, seated next to Kalau, pats her leg reassuringly during the *mihi*. Both girls are a bit teary as they speak.)

49 Kili: Kalau, do you forgive me for putting my nose where it's not supposed to belong?

50 Kalau: Yes. Will you forgive me for snapping at you, because my anger was misplaced—it belonged to somebody else.

51 And, for giving you a double dosage at the table? (She wipes a tear from her cheek.)

52 Kili: Yeah. And me, for also barking at you—do you forgive me?

53 Kalau: Yeah. Do you forgive me too?

54 Kili: Yeah.

P   (Both girls move across the circle towards one another and embrace. As they hug, they both cry and laugh a bit, then return to their places.)

Q   (Mr. Kealoha turns to Kekumu next to clear up the difficulties between him and Kalau. Kekumu says he was angry at Kalau for snapping at him when he used his fingers instead of a spoon to eat. "She uses her fingers sometimes too!" Mr. Kealoha interprets that perhaps Kekumu objected, not so much to what Kalau had said, but to the way she said it. He also suggests that Kalau may have misdirected her anger. Mr. Kealoha asks Kalau for her side and she agrees that she did bark at Kekumu and recognizes that he didn't like it.)

55 Mr. Kealoha: What are you going to do about it?

56 Kalau: Ask him for forgiveness.

57 Mr. Kealoha: Are you ready for that?

58 Kalau: Yeah.

R   (Mr. Kealoha asks Kekumu if he is ready and he says he is. Kalau asks Kekumu for his forgiveness for her barking. Kekumu forgives her, they lean towards one another and hug.)

S   (A very similar, short discussion follows up to unravel the *hihia* between Kalau and Kaʻaiʻai. The problem was caused by Kalau misplacing her anger and speaking sharply to Kaʻaiʻai. Since Kaʻaiʻai responded in kind at the table, both had to ask each other for forgiveness. The atmosphere in the session becomes quiet and serious, since it is now time to attend to the major problem between Mrs. Kealoha and Kalau. Mrs. Kealoha starts to speak but then quietly begins to cry.)

59 Mrs. Kealoha: Let me pull myself together.

60 Mr. Kealoha: Mommie needs to pull herself together because she feels . . .

61 Kekumu: Sad!

62 Mr. Kealoha: But also so that she can say things in a way that doesn't create more *pilikia* (trouble), O.K.?

T (Kleenexes are passed around to Kalau, Kili, and Mom, then Mrs. Kealoha begins to speak. She says that while listening today she realized that Kalau has a hard time talking to her. Also, in reflection on past problems, she realized that she often "digs in on" the kids when they do something wrong and that this might be hard for Kalau. She says that although Kili had been going in and out of the room during the agreement, it is the parent's responsibility.)

63 Mrs. Kealoha: And Kalau, I didn't check it out with you. . . . And this *pilikia* might have been avoided.

64 I have contributed to my failure—to not follow through to make sure that the communication was clearly understood.

U (Mr. Kealoha then paraphrases to Kalau two major points: Mom gets after her when she thinks Kalau has done something wrong, and Mom didn't check out the agreement because she assumed it was understood. Mr. Kealoha asks Kalau if she wants to share her thoughts.)

65 Kalau: No, I think Mom said it all!

66 Mr. Kealoha: Well, what is this problem between you and Mommie?

V (Kalau explains that Mrs. Kealoha doesn't listen to her and that they argue back and forth. Mr. Kealoha suggests that perhaps when Kalau argues back that Mrs. Kealoha also feels that Kalau has not heard what she had to say. Kalau agrees and Mr. Kealoha goes on to remind her about the importance of keeping "our big mouth shut" and listening to one another. He instructs her further.)

67   Mr. Kealoha: After listening, and you still have a point to make, say it.

68   But not in a hostile way, but in a way that makes for better understanding . . . do you understand?

69   Kalau: Yeah.

W   (Mr. Kealoha asks if there are any further problems. Kalau makes an aside about a cramp in her leg from sitting too long. Everyone laughs, dispelling the tension. Mr. Kealoha then reminds the family that after *mihi* and *kala* there is *oki*. "Problems are laid to rest, not to be brought up again." He also reminds them that when they hurt one another, they hurt and disrupt the harmonious relationship with "the powers that be" and must ask forgiveness of them also.)

70   Mr. Kealoha: Are you folks ready for that?

71   Family: Yes.

X   (They all bow their heads.)

72   Mr. Kealoha: Dear heavenly Father, Creator of heaven and earth and to his only son, Jesu Cristo, we thank Thee for this opportunity in this *ho'oponopono* to work out our family problems and difficulties; to identify the *hihia*—all the personal entanglements one with the other, to help us to discuss it in a way that does not create further hurts, but in a way that will lead to resolution of our problems.

73   We also thank Thee for giving us the opportunity to listen so that we can understand how we ourselves have impacted on others, to examine ourselves, and in the communication one with the other, to be able to understand that possibly we may have contributed to the problems ourselves, whether by commission or whether by omission.

74   And dear Lord, we thank Thee for the opportunity for the *'ohana*, the family, to be here and to ask for forgiveness one from the other, to release and let go, never more to come.

75   And we ask of you that as we hurt one another among ourselves, that we also hurt You, and we ask for your forgiveness.

76   Please forgive us.

77   Please release and set into the depths of the ocean our *pilikia*, never more to rise.

78   All this we ask in Thy Holy name. Amen.

Y   (The family members hug and kiss each other and rise.)

Shaping the Mind and Straightening Out Conflicts: The Discourse of Kwara'ae Family Counseling

Karen Ann Watson-Gegeo and David W. Gegeo

IN HIS ESSAY, "Ethos, World View, and the Analysis of Sacred Symbols," Clifford Geertz argues that religious symbols, dramatized in rituals and myths, fuse ethos (behavior, personality, affect) and eidos (world view), making social values appear to be objective (1973:126–27, 131). In this essay we examine *fa'amanata'anga*, a set of social contexts and speech activities among the Kwara'ae (Malaita, Solomon Islands) in which personal problems and social conflicts are examined and resolved or managed through discussion and evaluation of individual actions in cultural and social terms, and instruction on skills, knowledge, and behavior is undertaken. In the course of dealing with everyday problems, these contexts and the interaction that goes on in them accomplish the fusing of ethos and eidos as a *social* rather than *religious* activity.

Fa'amanata'anga is the general term for the teaching of knowledge and abstract skills (from the verb *fa'amanata* 'teach', literally 'cause to think' or 'shape the mind'). In its narrower sense, *fa'amanata'anga* refers to counseling in which intellectual instruction, therapeutic talk, and social conflict resolution occur simultaneously, serially, or independently.[1] From a Western perspective, intellectual/skill instruction, therapy, and conflict resolution are often regarded as separate activities undertaken by different specialists—for example, the school teacher, the licensed psychotherapist or counselor, and the civil or criminal court official. But in Kwara'ae, teaching, counseling, and conflict resolution are extensions of each other by virtue of the *kula* ('part', see below) framework underlying the Kwara'ae theory of the self and social relationships. This framework provides cultural grounds for the fusion of ethos and eidos.

The term *fa'amanata'anga* applies both to contexts in which counseling occurs and to the speech activities (Levinson 1978,

Gumperz 1982) that constitute them. The initiation of *fa'amana-ta'anga* redefines an ongoing context as a counseling context until further notice, and any other speech activity under way is ended or postponed until counseling is formally terminated. Counseling activities therefore take precedence over other activities, and counseling contexts may be nested in other contexts. An important example is the occurrence of counseling in *ala'anga* sessions. *Ala'anga* (n., 'speaking, speech, meeting'; from v. *ala'a* 'speak') is a general term covering talk (including *fa'amana-ta'anga*), from private conversation to village meetings. In its narrower sense, *ala'anga* refers to relatively formal to very formal meetings[2] held to plan group undertakings, clarify issues, or resolve disputes (Watson-Gegeo and Gegeo 1979; compare *nag-kiariien* on Tanna, Vanuatu; and Lindstrom, this volume, and 1984). Counseling often plays an important role in village meetings and always occurs in association with dispute resolution (Watson-Gegeo and Gegeo 1987).

As with Hawaiian *ho'oponopono* (Boggs and Chun, this volume), Kwara'ae conflict resolution or "disentangling" (the A'ara term; White, this volume) is a process involving a continuum or spectrum of contexts and speech activities, varying along dimensions of private–public, small group–large group, relative formality, and characteristics of speech style. As attempts to mediate an ongoing interpersonal conflict, some of these contexts and activities are called *fa'amanata'anga*, and others are called *ala'anga* or *mitingi* (from Solomon Islands Pijin). Many conflicts are settled before arriving at the group-level *fa'amanata'anga* sessions which are the focus of this paper. Thus, some *fa'amanata'anga* sessions are meant to resolve conflicts, while others emphasize group reintegration or reaffirm group understandings of cultural meanings and social expectations. Long before a dispute reaches the stage of group *fa'amanata'anga* or *ala'anga* sessions, therefore, a great deal of negotiation and mediation will often have gone on between individuals and within much smaller groups.

Interactions and events that are called *fa'amanata'anga*, then, vary from private conversations to group sessions. Counseling begins in infancy, with simple counseling moments with children as young as eighteen months in some families. In these early counseling interactions negatively and positively sanctioned behaviors are discussed, lessons in cultural knowledge offered, and child–child disputes resolved (Watson-Gegeo and Gegeo 1986b, 1988). Regular counseling sessions begin in early childhood, become increasingly elaborate and formal,[3] and continue throughout life as group meetings held to resolve interpersonal problems or communicate knowledge within the family, the extended family, and the descent group. *Fa'amanata'anga* in the form of dyadic counseling, teaching, and advice-giving also continues throughout life. As we will show, ultimately it is in the discourse itself that the distinction between *fa'amanata'anga* and other forms of talk is made.

In this study we examine Kwara'ae adult family counseling aimed at resolving interpersonal problems, as illustrated by one session led by Dalea, a respected elder, in which the topic is a dispute between a young unmarried man and his married brother and sister-in-law. We examine characteristics of discourse organization and style in counseling sessions, the kinds of cultural meanings assigned and inferred in talk, the way emotions and behavior are treated and evaluated, and what constitutes "resolution" for the Kwara'ae in terms of social relationships and personal feelings.

A number of theoretical assumptions underlie the analysis. With Bateson we assume that "mind" is not coterminous with individual or self, being instead an information system encompassing the human being and (in this case) the social environment (1972:319–20; 1980:127–41). This assumption is in keeping with the Kwara'ae theory of the self (see below) and with "shaping the mind" as an evolving social process across the life span. With Vygotsky (1962; see also Leont'ev 1969), we assume—as do the Kwara'ae—that speech shapes thought and action. Vygotsky argued that higher mental functions appear first on the interpsychological (social) plane and later are internalized on the intrapsychological (individual) plane (Wertsch 1979; see also Dore 1985). Similarly, the counselor as socializer hopes to negotiate, guide, and shape the internalization of socially significant ways of thinking that will result in changed behavior. "Negotiate" is far from being an empty term here, for counselors model and persuade; they do not compel.

Bakhtin argued that utterances are *dialogic*, for "all discourse is in dialogue with prior discourses on the same subject, as well as with discourses yet to come, whose reactions it foresees and anticipates" (Todorov 1984:x). The ultimate dialogic relationship is that linking counseling discourse with the evolution of *falafala* (tradition, culture), the system of intersubjective understandings distilled from centuries of thinking, talking, and acting (see conclusion). Because discourse in a counseling session is in dialogue with all other cultural, especially counseling, discourses, interpretation of any utterance must be made in the context of previous and anticipated counseling sessions on the same or related issues. Memorable counselors and counseling moments known through personal observation or oral history also influence the rhetorical forms and interpretive procedures realized in a given session.

Finally, with the Kwara'ae we assume that the social takes precedence over the personal. In interpreting utterances, therefore, we focus on social meanings and relationships, together with their implications for handling conflict, rather than on subjective or personal meanings.

Data, Methods, and Ethics

Background ethnographic and linguistic data for this paper were collected in 1978, 1979, 1981, and 1984 in connection with our research on Kwara'ae discourse and socialization. We taperecorded and observed *fa'amanata'anga* in nine families, in sessions with children ranging from eighteen months old through teenage. We also recorded, observed, and took accounts of *fa'amanata'anga* in *ala'anga* events in three villages, including village dispute-settling meetings, marriage-planning meetings, and descent-group district-level counseling meetings. Eight adult counseling sessions were recorded, and several others observed. The session examined here, which we attended and taperecorded in 1981, was transcribed by Gegeo. Naturally occurring informal discussions with participants about the events that led up to this session, their thoughts and feelings during the session, and the leader's strategic choices in approach were used in interpreting the transcript. Gegeo's knowledge as a member of the culture is also important to the analysis.

In contrast to brief, situational counseling of infants and

children, on the one hand, and openly public counseling meetings at the village level, on the other, family counseling sessions dealing with conflict and relationships are *ābu* (tabu, forbidden, sacred) and are therefore closed to outsiders. Counseling is never initiated when outsiders to the family are present and is always instantly terminated if visitors arrive. Would-be visitors who, on approaching a house, hear or suspect counseling to be going on inside are expected to withdraw quietly and never to repeat or discuss what they overheard, whether about adults or children. Given these cultural prohibitions, we need to clarify here how we obtained the recording and our rationale for making it public.

On the evening that Dalea counseled his sons, we were gathered with members of his family for dinner, which we were tape-recording with a hidden recorder, as part of our study of Kwara'ae children's acquisition of communicative competence. The children's parents knew about the recorder, but Dalea did not. The recorder was running when counseling unexpectedly began. Afterwards we informed the principal parties in the session that it had been recorded. This family knew that we had already tape-recorded counseling of children in the other families in our sample. Each of those recordings had been voluntarily made by the sample family in our absence, rather than solicited by us. At first we were surprised that the families were so willing to record counseling, given that they understood we would not only listen to the recordings, but also transcribe, analyze, and possibly make them public through written reports (preserving their anonymity as far as possible). In time, however, all of the Kwara'ae families with whom we worked expressed to us the important role they believed counseling to have in children's learning.

We would hesitate to make a transcription of adult family counseling public if we did not feel its social importance justified it. *Fa'amanata'anga* is a central activity in Kwara'ae social organization, and central to understanding Kwara'ae teaching-learning and problem-solving processes. As mentioned earlier, we will also argue that *fa'amanata'anga* fuses ethos and eidos in Kwara'ae culture. We selected the Dalea example for analysis because his counseling style is highly regarded and imitated in several West Kwara'ae villages.

The Kwara'ae: Social Organization and Discourse

The Kwara'ae occupy a large cross-section of north-central Malaita, the most densely populated of the five major islands (another is Santa Isabel; see White, this volume) in the Solomons. One of ten to thirteen languages and dialects spoken on North Malaita (Tryon and Hackman 1973), Kwara'ae—with an estimated twenty thousand speakers—is the language with the largest number of speakers in the Solomon Islands. Although some villages in the mountainous interior still follow the traditional religion of ancestor-worship, most West Kwara'ae are Christian. Our work has been primarily among members of the Church of Melanesia (Anglican) and secondarily the South Seas Evangelical Church. (The Roman Catholic church also claims a large following in West Kwara'ae.)

The West Kwara'ae are subsistence gardeners currently experiencing the pressures of rapid social change. Exposure to Western ideas is great because of the location in West Kwara'ae of the island's urban center of Auki, together with the main airfield serving it, heavy logging by multinational corporations, and sporadic government attempts at major development projects. Some West Kwara'ae men have found jobs in Malaita's wage-labor economy, and some work on other islands before marriage, returning with new ideas and behaviors. Nevertheless, Anglicans and Catholics, especially, strongly adhere to *falafala* (tradition, culture, or *kastom* in Solomon Islands Pijin) in values, worldview, and interactional style. Like *moumou* (tradition) on Tobi island in Micronesia (Black 1983), *falafala* is constituted of all cultural ways of thinking, believing, and doing, whether mundane, moral, or sacred, and thus is coterminous with Kwara'ae culture. The West Kwara'ae are concerned that their children know *falafala* and learn to speak Kwara'ae well.

In contrast to the matrilineal A'ara, the Kwara'ae are patrilineal and virilocal. Since the breakdown of the paramount chiefdom system perhaps as long as two hundred years ago, traditional leadership has been vested in men and women called *gwaunga'i* (elder; literally, 'headness'). Since independence in 1978, the national government has mandated that villages be governed by an elected village committee and chief. In practice, decisions in small villages are still made as they were traditionally, by open discussion resulting in consensus among adult members in a village *ala'anga*.[4] *Gwaunga'i* men and women, however, are particularly influential in decision making, for they are heads of their families and of the community social order. Their influence is partly a manifestation of the numinous or charismatic (*'abainuinu*) quality that, like Tikopia (Firth 1979) or Tobi (Black 1983) chiefs, they project. Criteria for *gwaunga'i* rank, which is potentially open to everyone, include growing older (at least to late middle age), having one child marry, and demonstrating cultural skills and appropriate behavior. *Gwaunga'i*-hood itself is achieved through a consensual process whereby, over a period of several years, one becomes increasingly recognized as *gwaunga'i*-like and finally *gwaunga'i*.

Beyond specializing in at least one area of *falafala*, a *gwaunga'i*'s life and being are expected to embody the eight key or "ultimate values" (Firth 1964:174) that form the basis of *falafala*, the family, and the whole person. These eight values (easily elicited from adults) are regarded as equal, with all other values subsumed under them. They are: (1) *alafe'anga*, love, including obligations to kin as well as feelings of affection; (2) *aroaro'anga*, peace, peaceful behavior; (3) *babato'o'anga*, emotional and behavioral stability and maturity, dependability, settling down in one place peacefully; (4) *enoeno'anga*, humility, delicacy, adaptability, gracefulness, tranquility, gentleness; (5) *fangale'a'anga*, giving, sharing, and receiving, as well as etiquette and manners (lit., 'eat good'); (6) *kwaigwale'e'anga*, welcoming, comforting, hospitality, (lit., 'bring to one's bosom to comfort'); (7) *kwaisare'e'anga*, feeding someone without expectation of return; and (8) *mamana'anga*, honesty, truthfulness, and power (both charisma and the power to make things happen). Allusion to one or more of the key values is frequent in conversation and counseling, whether judging the behavior of infants or adults or weighing a course of action.[5] While they are cultural ideals, therefore, these values permeate everyday life.

A crucial *gwaunga'i* skill is fluency in *ala'anga lalifu*, the formal level of Kwara'ae. Kwara'ae social contexts and speech activities are classified as either important (*'inoto'a, lalifu*) or unimportant (*kakabara, kwalabasa*). Unimportant contexts are clearly mundane, but important ones are not necessarily sacred. Unimportant contexts embrace everyday life, including polite and ordinary conversations. Such contexts and speech activities are associated with *ala'anga kwalabasa* (speech "vine-like"), the level of discourse we call "low rhetoric." *Kwalabasa* suggests a root that goes down into the ground for a distance and then suddenly splits into many lesser, wandering roots, without bearing fruit. Of speech it implies ideas that go every which way, making no significant point; such speech is without weight (*sasala*, 'light'). Important contexts and speech activities, including meetings, oratory at feasts, counseling, dispute settling, poetry, storytelling, and serious discussions of politics, religion, tradition, marriage, and the like, evoke *ala'anga lalifu* (speech "importantly rooted"), or "high rhetoric." *Lali* is a taproot, the main root anchoring a plant, and *fu* means publicly known; hence, speech that carries important sociocultural meaning. High rhetoric is characterized by special vocabulary and pronouns, very abstract phrasing, complex syntactical forms, special intonation contours, a set of graceful, somewhat stylized gestures, and other discourse features. Talk about the eight key values always takes place in high rhetoric, even when addressing language-acquiring infants (Watson-Gegeo and Gegeo 1986a,b). *Lalifu* speech is said to be *fafakulu* 'heavy'.

The exercise of *gwaunga'i* leadership depends on the requirements of a given social context. An important example is participation structure in speech events (Philips 1972). An *ala'anga* held to resolve a minor village conflict is usually characterized by unstructured turn-taking. The leading *gwaunga'i*—who may or may not convene or "run" the meeting—characteristically sits at the back or in a darkened corner, speaking with dignity but no fanfare after others have had their (at least initial) say. In contrast, *fa'amanata'anga* sessions among adults or at the village level are controlled by *gwaunga'i*, who do virtually all of the speaking. Across all the contexts on the *fa'amanata'anga–ala'anga* continuum, however, there is always a leader, whether an elected chief or the local ranking *gwaunga'i*. Unlike A'ara disentangling meetings, even a very informal Kwara'ae dispute-settling meeting has a leader who monitors the progress of the meeting, putting in a crucial interpretation or point here, refocusing the talk there.

This leader (usually a man) may sit at the back or out of the limelight, but his role is recognized. If he does not speak, eventually someone will gently say, for example, *Arai' kwa, 'ok manat ha'uat?* (Sir, what do you think?). The leader does not nominate speakers in small village meetings, but he usually opens the meeting with a statement of (at least) the first topic to be addressed and closes it with a summary and perhaps brief counseling of the village. However, in the very structured village meetings that constitute a traditional court, the *gwaunga'i* called in to resolve the case controls the floor and questions witnesses.

The leadership role played by *gwaunga'i* is one instance of the principle of seniority fundamental to Kwara'ae social organization. Within the patrilineal descent group and extended family, families are hierarchically ranked as senior or junior to each other. Within the extended and nuclear family, adults are senior in rank to children, and older siblings (and classificatory siblings) senior to younger. The oldest son is the head of his sibling group through life, and one senior *gwaunga'i* male will become the head or *ara'i* of the descent group. The principle of seniority is always potentially and sometimes actually at variance with another important Kwara'ae social organizational principle, egalitarianism. The Kwara'ae highly respect individual autonomy and initiative, hence the open participation structure at most village meetings. Nevertheless, the welfare and concerns of the social group take precedence over those of the individual, and the larger social group is organized by seniority. Elsewhere we have argued that interactional strategies based on the key cultural values help to mediate between egalitarianism and seniority (Watson-Gegeo and Gegeo 1986b). *Fa'amanata'anga* itself can be viewed as one set of such strategies. Interactional strategies also reflect Kwara'ae personality theory, to which we now turn.

The *Kula* Framework:
Person, Relations, and Conflict

The Kwara'ae conceive of the person as constructed of physical, emotional, spiritual, intellectual, and behavioral characteristics much as a mosaic is constructed of small tiles. "Mosaic" seems an appropriate rendering of the implied Kwara'ae "container" metaphor (Lakoff and Johnson 1980) because it emphasizes both the aesthetic quality that the Kwara'ae notion of self includes and the visual way in which the self is discussed. (A Kwara'ae metaphor sometimes used is a "wasp's nest of many chambers.") Each "tile" in the mosaic of the person is called *kula*, n. 'part, point, or place'. A variety of terms describe the relationship between the self and its parts. A *kula* may be *rora* 'wrong' in the sense of *firu* 'entangled'. Or it may be *'a'a* 'deformed', or *'iribolo* 'not fitting', in the sense of what *falafala* 'tradition, culture' expects. When one or more *kulas* are so described, the person is *kakabara/kwalabasa*, meaning 'incomplete' in this context; or more seriously, *korenga'a* 'half' as opposed to *ali'afu* 'complete'.

Imbalances in one's personal mosaic of *kulas* have social meaning because of their effect on social relationships; for the person is regarded as only one *kula* in a concentric circle of *kulas* beginning with the individual, moving to the nuclear and then extended family, to the village, descent group, tribe, and finally the whole society and beyond. Incorrect, inappropriate, or nonfunctioning *kulas* in the individual result in various kinds of inappropriate social behavior. Because all of the levels of *kula* are interdependent, every act of an individual has the potential of affecting and involving all of the relationships connected in the mosaic. It is in this sense that relations become *firu* 'entangled' and need to be *fa'asaga* 'straightened out'.[6] More specifically, what is entangled are thoughts, feelings, relationships, and possibly hidden wrongdoing.

With the A'ara (White, this volume) and Hawaiians (Ito 1985), the Kwara'ae believe that hidden, intense negative feelings such as anger or hidden conflicts and wrongdoing will come out in a physical manifestation in some way, often as serious illness, misfortune (e.g., lack of pregnancy or an unusual accident), or failure of individual or group projects. An innocent child rather than a responsible adult may be the victim, a belief also found among Hawaiians (Ito 1985). The focus in "straightening out" contexts, however, is usually on the *kulas* of thought and relationships rather than the *kula* of feelings. Kwara'ae culture downplays emotions. Unlike A'ara, there is no Kwara'ae approximate gloss for "emotion." Strong negative feelings such as anger are expected to be displaced or suppressed more than expressed. The behavioral ideal is for one's presentation of self, at least, to be infused with a quiet happiness and serenity reflected in the key cultural values of *aroaro'anga* 'peace', *enoeno'anga* 'humility and gentleness', and *babato'o'anga* 'stability'. In a Melanesian parallel to Western cognitive therapy (Beck 1976, Ellis 1971), the Kwara'ae believe that straight thinking leads to correct behavior and appropriate feelings. In this belief we see part of the rationale for why the term *fa'amanata'anga*, 'teaching' or intellectual instruction, is linked to therapeutic counseling and conflict resolution and why all of these take place together in *fa'amanata'anga* sessions. By emphasizing the interdependence of *kulas* within one level and across levels, the *kula* framework guides the counselor toward a holistic approach to personal and social issues, reflected in the multiple functions a counseling session may address.

Serious misfortune or illness copresent with suspected hidden conflicts is attributed by Kwara'ae Christians to a displeased God, in contrast with A'ara Christians, who do not see spiritual mediation as necessary (White, this volume). But often Christians privately concur with the traditional belief that ancestral spirits signal their displeasure at conflict through illness or misfortune. One alternative is to call in a traditional healer to detect and treat the cause of the problem. Healers are also called in when other techniques of problem solving have failed. Often healers *fa'amanata* their patients about behavior, life-style, and relationships after the healing ceremony is over.

In contrast, counseling sessions focused on conflict or relationships seek to solve a problem that might reach the village meeting stage or lead to serious illness if not treated early. *Fa'amanata'anga* may have either preventive or therapeutic goals (as in A'ara disentangling: White, this volume), or both may occur in the same session. Prevention aims to resolve conflict within the family before it becomes openly public, perhaps spreading to other families and resulting in a village-level dispute-settling meeting where resolution involves significant social shame and possibly an imposed fine. The therapeutic goal is aimed at changing an individual's behavior, but the context assumed for that behavior is his or her social relationships. Unlike the Western psychotherapist, who may advise a client to end an "unhealthy" relationship, the Kwara'ae counselor assumes that social relation-

ships—which are almost always based on blood or marriage—
cannot be terminated. No matter how bad their condition, they
must be repaired.

Our use of "framework" follows Bateson (1972) and Goffman
(1974). As the belief system and model for all cultural behavior,
falafala constitutes the Kwara'ae "framework of frameworks"
(Goffman 1974:27). The kula system for psyche and person is one
of the frameworks within falafala. Among interactional frameworks, fa'amanata'anga is a "primary frame" (ibid.). We turn now
to the way counseling sessions are constructed.

Counseling Sessions:
Frame and Format

An important dimension running through counseling as a cultural activity is the public/private dichotomy affecting counseling
contexts and (as we shall see) argumentation within them. Counseling on abstract knowledge or generalized strategies for preventing socially disruptive events may be open to adults outside
the family but within the descent group, who are allowed to sit
in for instruction along with family members. But counseling is
strictly private when it involves intrafamily disputes or tensions.
If possible, all family members will be present, including children. Parties in the conflict may request counseling, or a senior
family member—who is likely to investigate the dispute carefully
beforehand—may initiate counseling on his or her own. The
gwaunga'i counselor may notify everyone to gather for a family
meeting at a particular time and place or may wait for an occasion on which the whole family is together for some other purpose and begin counseling without prior announcement. As a
result, adults come to most family gatherings knowing that counseling could occur, but not necessarily expecting it. In some
families fa'amanata'anga sessions take place weekly or monthly,
in others only when triggered by a recognized family problem or
request for teaching.

Typically counseling takes place after dinner in the evening,
when everyone has had a good meal shared with humor and
demonstrations of alafe'anga (love). Seated informally on the
benches of the kitchen or main room, family members share betel

and tobacco and engage in joking and light conversation. Perhaps waiting for a lull and perhaps not, the counselor frames counseling by suddenly code-switching to high rhetoric, speaking with the grave tone of voice and facial expression that accompany serious speech in Kwara'ae. The leader's voice is usually slightly louder than the ongoing conversation for the first counseling utterance, which is further marked by a pronounced terminal fall and imperative stresses. By taking the form of an abrupt statement addressed to the target individual(s), whether by name or reference to the issue in dispute, the counselor's opening statement also sets the topic.

The first counseling utterance instantly triggers a dramatic shift in behavioral and affective characteristics of the gathering. Everyone falls silent, eyes lowered to the floor or focused in midspace, facial expression serious or affectively blank. In these ways all but the youngest children signal that they have taken on the role definition of audience and listener. Participation structure is thus radically altered. Counseling may be spoken as a monologue by one counselor, as in the example by Dalea (a widower) analyzed below. The counselor may question disputing parties if facts or motivations in the conflict are unclear. Sometimes counseling is carried out by two or more senior persons (e.g., a mother and father), who may alternate stretches of speech on the same or related topics. This contrasts with Hawaiian *ho'oponopono*, where the leader does not share primary speaking rights with another (Boggs and Chun, this volume). A third participant structure is cospeaking, in which two counselors construct one lesson together, interweaving their utterances to offer and corroborate propositions, ask and answer rhetorical questions, and mediate each other's utterances through elaboration, summary, emphasis, repetition, or recapitulation. Cospeaking is most commonly found in counseling sessions with children or adolescents. *Falafala* can also be seen as a party in the discussion, for interpersonal behavior is constantly measured against what *falafala* expects, and expressions such as "*Falafala* says . . ." or "in the eyes of *falafala*" are often used. In another sense, however, *falafala* speaks through the counselor. Listeners are to understand that the counselor's statements of social rules or behavioral evaluations framed by "This is what I say to you" kinds of expressions are spoken as *falafala*, not as an individual or as a parent.

Whatever the participation structure, the counselor controls the conversational floor, and may or may not temporarily relinquish it to others. All listeners, including persons who are not a part of the conflict, are expected to be occupied in the activity of reflectively examining their personal and interpersonal *kula* systems and asking themselves, "How does this (what the counselor is saying) relate to my *kulas*?" The lowered eyes and affectively blank facial expression, therefore, are not only signs of respect for the seniority and knowledge of the counselor or for *falafala* speaking through him or her. These signals also express a meditatively inward focus in which all listeners, the troubled and untroubled alike, are joined.

After the opening there follows a statement and development of the problem through narration and examples, including an account of how the issue came to the counselor's attention. Evidence is presented, and through a series of if–then possible outcomes, the counselor analyzes the seriousness of the conflict should it continue to grow worse. As in the *mahiki* stage of *ho'oponopono* (Boggs and Chun, this volume), related problems are raised, discussed, and analyzed as the counselor follows out the lines of entanglement one by one. This process is called *'ini te'ete'e sulia* 'inch with the fingers along it', a gardening metaphor for how, in a tangle of potato vines, the end of a particular vine is located by feeling along it with the fingers; or alternatively, *didi sulia* 'chip according to a design', a metaphor from making stone tools in earlier times that implies the careful chipping away with arguments one by one until a final conclusion is reached. The counselor speaks quietly, gently, and calmly, qualities of speaking which characterize *falafala* and are associated with high rhetoric. This manner of speaking enacts the key values of *aroaro'anga* 'peace', *enoeno'anga* 'humility, delicacy', *babato'o'anga* 'stability', and *alafe'anga* 'love'.

The Kwara'ae counselor's license to control the speaking floor, lecturing other adults and even another *gwaunga'i* on occasion, would seem remarkable to the Managalase (McKellin, this volume) or to the Fiji Indian community, where overt attempts to influence the opinions or actions of others is a violation of equality (Brenneis, this volume). Although a *gwaunga'i*'s words carry more weight than others, based in rank and seniority, no one has the right to dominate a village meeting in the way that Samoan chiefs and their orators dominate a *fono* (Duranti, this volume), or a Kwara'ae counselor may choose to dominate counseling. The counselor's stance is therefore context-specific to *fa'amanata'anga* (wherever it occurs). Given the importance of egalitarianism in Kwara'ae, how does the counselor get away with taking such an authoritarian stance? The notion that *falafala* speaks through the counselor may help downplay the stance of one individual telling another what to think and do. Counselors also use a variety of interactional strategies to mitigate the sharpness of their words (Labov and Fanschel 1977), as we shall see.

To terminate the session, the counselor may summarize what was said, then code-switch back to low rhetoric, perhaps joking or mildly teasing the targeted individual(s). Code-switching signals a return to ordinary conversational behavior and participation structures. The counselor may initiate handshaking all around (an innovation since Western contact) to mark the resolution of the conflict and a return to normal relationships. With the counseling session over, the family usually shares another meal or a cup of tea or milo (a chocolate drink), as well as new rounds of betel and tobacco. The counselor or an elder sibling may propose a new joint venture or raise for discussion a family project everyone is interested in pursuing. Counseling frequently ends, therefore, by reintegrating the targeted individual(s) into the larger family unit through discussion and then performance of some physical group task, such as building a new enclosure for pigs or chickens. Thus, although counseling is primarily a rite of intensification, from the standpoint of the targeted individual its organization includes separation, liminality (with instruction), and reincorporation found in rites of passage (Van Gennep 1960; Chapple and Coon 1942).

Dalea's Counseling:
Discourse Organization and Cultural Inference

A widower, Dalea is a *gwaunga'i* of a senior-ranking family living in a small inland village of West Kwara'ae. His very large family of married and unmarried children live in a series of households located, by happenstance, in widely separated parts of the village. At the time of the recording, Sale and Sama, Dalea's nineteen-year-old twin sons, had joined the household of their eldest brother, Robin, who will become head of the family upon his father's death. Robin's household included his wife, Mere, and several young children (see Figure 1). But from time to time tension would build between the twins and Robin's family, usually around the quality of Mere's cooking and the twins' work responsibilities in the household. For some weeks prior to Dalea's counseling, Sale had refused to eat at home, going instead to the nearby houses of close relatives, whose gardens he now worked in rather than Robin and Mere's gardens. Sama had stopped showing up for work in Robin's household, too. Robin tried counseling his brothers himself, but when this failed, Dalea was informed of the conflict and asked to intervene.

Dalea investigated the complaints against his youngest sons by talking to other members of the family. He then planned his counseling for an anticipated whole family dinner at the house he shares with a married son and an unmarried daughter. The family did not know that counseling was about to take place, although Robin, Mere, and the others involved in bringing the conflict to Dalea recognized the setting as appropriate for it.

Dinner had ended, and the adults were joking, singing, and lightly teasing each other as they smoked, chewed betel, and babysat sleepy infants and young children. In the midst of this pleasant interaction (in which the twins were full participants), Dalea abruptly said:[7]

001 *Aia' (.)   nauk   oga (.)*   All right (.) I want (.) to say
    all right 1sg+sm   want   a little something to Sale//
    saea   tai' ru   huan
    say+om   lim thing for+3sg,poss
    sa (.) Sael//
    art,m Sale

002 *Nauk   rongoa   na   fa'a–*   I heard a report
    1sg+sm   hear+om   art caus+   about you, Sale//
    rongoa'   sulio'   Sael//
    hear+nom   about+2sg,om   Sale

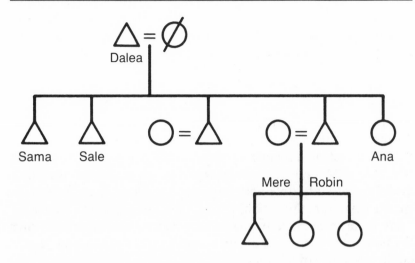

FIGURE 1. Partial kin chart of Dalea family

Dalea's opening sentences were slightly louder than the ongoing talk, with a terminal rise and slow pacing. The intonation contours, stresses, and pitch were those of high rhetoric expression (see Watson-Gegeo and Gegeo 1986a for a discussion of intonation contours in high and low rhetoric), and the wording of 001 was similar to the opening of formal oratory. Before Dalea had completed his first sentence, the room had fallen silent; the only sounds (which we have edited out) were those of women shushing the younger children. Everyone else assumed the deportment correct in counseling contexts—eyes lowered, faces serious but affectively blank. Dalea then continued his introduction, speaking rapidly, quietly, and in a low pitch as he stated the problem:

003 *Ne' noa' 'aesi–/ noa'*   That you have not–/
      that not 2sg+neg–/ not   you have not (.)
      'aesi (.) 'aes hang   you're not eating
      2sg+neg 2sg+neg eat   at the house of the one born
      na' luam ai nao'omu   before you (= your elder
      perf house one before+2sg,poss   sibling) these days lately//
      san aos ne' ki
      inside+3sg,poss day here,e pl
      mai'//
      hither

004 *Aos ne'*   *ki 'aok*   *rarah*   These days you avoid
    day here,e pl 2sg+sm avoid   Robin's house//
    'ain na (.) *luam* *sa*   *Robin//*
    with art   house art,m Robin

These sentences complete the opening of the session by introducing the first issue Dalea will address in the conflict, Sale's refusal to eat at his elder brother's house (returned to in lines 027, 072, 182, and 212). Already Dalea has used one mitigating device to soften his talk with Sale. In 001, *ta'i ru* limits the talk to "just a little something," but *ta'i* also implies focusing on a single thing. In a sense, then, *ta'i ru* is a mitigating way of emphasizing the talk of the session as distinct from ordinary talk, using *ru* as a euphemism for counseling.

Having reframed the family gathering as a counseling session, and stated the first problem to be addressed in summary form, Dalea goes on to explain how he learned of the dispute:

005 *Ne' 'i   Mere ka*   This is what Mere
    that art,f Mere sm   reported to Ana
    ha'rongoa   'i   Ana/
    caus+hear+om art,f Ana

006 *Ne' 'i   Ana ka ha'rong   nau/* And Ana reported to me/
    that art,f Ana sm caus+hear   1sg

007 *Halhal   ne'eir di' ba*   Behavior like that
    behavior there,e like that,p   is rather bad/
    ni   tai' ta'a   nai/
    3sg lim bad   there

008 *Ne' nai tai' saea   huaum//* This is what I say to you//
    that 1sg lim say+om for+2sg,poss

These lines constitute an orientation to what will follow. They are spoken as one unit (broken into brief breath-groups), cohesively tied by terminal rises, the connective *ne'e* (that), and parallel phrasing; utterance 008 is marked by a pronounced terminal fall, signaling closure of the orientation. Prosodically,

Dalea's rendering of these lines closely resembles Kwara'ae poetry as well as the more poetic aspects of traditional oratory. In fact, both in witnessing a counseling session and in rehearing the tapes later, one is struck by the aesthetic quality of counseling performances.

Turning to the inferential work for Sale in interpreting these lines, Dalea here reports that he learned of the conflict through a chain of women. Sale is to infer several things from this. First, a female channel of communication is appropriate because the issue of Sale's refusal to eat at Robin's house is a female issue. Women are the food providers in Kwara'ae culture; rejecting food from a sister-in-law damages her and the whole family's reputation in the larger village. Second, Sale is to infer that he should not get angry at Mere, for it is his sister Ana, not Mere who reported his behavior to Dalea. It is far less inappropriate for Sale to be angry and argumentive toward his biological sister than toward his sister-in-law. Third, Mere, Ana, and Dalea's talking about the conflict means that there is widespread concern in the family, suggesting that villagers—especially other women—are noticing the incident and talking about it, a point Dalea will soon directly address. In several ways, then, the channel of communication through women is culturally significant. In lines 007–008, Dalea evaluates Sale's behavior as bad, again softening the evaluation with *ta'i*. Sale is to infer that "bad" refers to *falafala*'s evaluation and that Dalea speaks as *falafala* in line 008.

Then Dalea begins a new phase of the session, putting forth propositions from *falafala* on several issues of concern in Sale's behavior and the possible social consequences of it. Each proposition is elaborated with corollaries and then applied to the issues under consideration. We will examine some of these propositions. Dalea's first two propositions introduce the ideas of source and seniority, both of which become major themes in the session:

009 *Luam kamu ne'*   Your-all house is your-all
    house 2plh   here,e   house = Your house is
    luam kamu na'//   the house of all of you//
    house 2plh   perf

010 *Luam ai na'omu*   *ne'*   The house of the one born
house one before+2sg,poss that   before you when we– we
di' ba   kail–   moved down here like this/
like that,p 1pl,ex

kail 'iud mai' 'uri/
2pl,ex move hither thus

011 *Aeo' na' ne' hain*   (But) you yourself are
2sg+e perf that with+3sg   already staying with Robin//
sa   Robin//
art,m Robin

012 *Aes'   rarah lau' 'ain*   Don't instead avoid the
2sg+neg avoid again with   house that belongs
luam– luam kamu≠   to you all≠
house– house 2plh

013 *Ao na' hain   ai*   You should be with the one
2sg perf with+3sg one   born before you//
nao'um//
before+2sg,poss

Line 009 is an argument from the cultural premise of one's home as source, *fuli*: a person without a home is said to have no roots or source and is like a wandering cloud soon blown apart by the wind. The principle of source, which entails family unity and cooperation, is returned to several times in the session (lines 026, 052, 115, 129, 139, 143, 190). The counselor's prosodic patterns are important in setting the emotional tone of the discourse and shaping the interpretations made by listeners. For example, line 009 is spoken with a rise on the first three words, mirrored by a fall on the final three words; its parallel prosodic structure is thus reflected in its intonation contour, carried out in an emphatic, chant-like style reminiscent of *kana* (traditional chanted narrative) or story-telling, as a statement of cultural significance.[8] The counselor's grammatical, lexical, logical, and prosodic choices converge in dramatic, persuasive effects: counseling talk is "heavy words" and "important silences" (*fata'a fafakulu ki* = word heavy pl; *aroaro'anga 'inoto'a* = peaceful, quiet + nom important). In fact, counseling talk exhibits features of both impressive and persuasive speech (Arno 1986; Firth 1975), making use of a variety of rhetorical strategies.

Dalea then narrates the history of how Sale came to be living at Robin's house (lines 010–011); the perfective *na'a* in 009 (which can be glossed as "now") grammatically points back to that history. Lines 012 and 013 combine a directive with an intensified repetition of the point made in line 009, that Sale should live with his elder brother, a reference to the seniority rule. In lines 014–017 (see appendix), Dalea explains what the rule implies, using an if-then form of argumentation. Specifically, Sale is to work for his brother in gardening and other tasks appropriate for a male. These lines are also spoken in rhythmical, parallel phrases with pronounced rise-fall patterns, typical of how items are listed in high rhetoric talk. A subsidiary argument is introduced in 016, when Dalea gives as explanation for why Sale should work for his brother that Robin and Mere have several very small children.

In line 018, Dalea summarizes the argument with an evaluation, and a part-to-whole contrast, before moving onto the next issue he will discuss:

018 *Kual 'unair ki ne' noa'//*   Those kulas no (= those
     part thus,p pl that no   parts of your behavior,
                                        don't)//

019 *Si   ne' noa' kul 'is*   Because we also don't want
     because that not 1plh neg   some women talking about
     oga long ne' al'ang   Mere as in the past//
     want also that speak+nom

     an   ti (.) kin   ne'
     of + 3sg,poss some woman that

     ka ala' an   'i   Mere
     sm talk of+3sg,poss art,f Mere

     'ubain//
     that,p

020 *Noa' nais   oga   halhal*   No, I don't want that
     no   1sg+neg want behavior   kind of behavior//
     'unair//
     thus,p

021 *Si   leleak–≠ kul   'is*   Because continuing–≠ we
    because rpl+go   1pl,in neg   also don't want some
    oga   long ne' (.) ti   women saying, "Goodness!
    want also that   some   Mere, isn't she giving any
    kin   ka 'uri≠ "Se (.) 'i   food to this child or is she
    woman sm thus emph art,f   denying food to this
    Mere 'uri   ma noa' kais (.)   child, is this maybe why
    Mere thus and not sm+neg   he doesn't stay still
    kwaetkwaet go' ta   hang   down there at their house?"
    rpl+give   int some food

    huan   ngeal ne'e   tak
    for+3sg,poss child here,e maybe

    nin   kaisi– (.) kais   tua
    this here sm+neg   sm+neg stay

    hu'ba   luam kia re?"
    dnthfr house 3pl emph

022 *Ai'   kual ne'eir   noa'*   Eh, that kula I also don't
    emph part there,e not   want want, Sale//
    nais   oga long nai
    1sg+neg want also there
    kwal   Sael//
    emph Sale

Dalea raises the third issue, gossip and family reputation (returned to in 088, 112–14, and 163), as a persuasive argument for
why Sale must change his behavior. All are aware of Mere's
awkward position of an in-marrying woman seen by other village
women as incompetent in running a household. That she arrived
poorly trained from her own family's household and that she has
been slow to learn how to garden and cook properly have been
the frequent topics of village gossip since she joined Robin's
family four years ago. Like the Nukulaelae (Besnier, this volume), the Kwara'ae have a predilection for identifying improper
conduct of others, and gossip is a strong method of social control
in Kwara'ae society, where indirection characterizes social interaction across nuclear family lines. Sale's behavior is compound-
ing the gossip because his rejection of Mere's hospitality and role
as food-giver undercuts her status in the family and draws public
attention to her private failings.

Dalea strengthens his argument by emphasizing (in 018 and again in 021) that the whole family (implied in the high rhetoric pronoun *kulu*, we all inclusive) does not want gossip to develop. Sale is to make the following inferences about the impact on the family of the chain of events that gossip about Mere can set off. If Sale continues his behavior, the village will begin to gossip about Dalea and Robin, as well, from the standpoint of "Why aren't they doing something about Sale's behavior?" As a senior ranking family and the source of leadership *(gwalona)* in the village, Dalea's family would suffer shame if villagers laughed at them behind their backs or went around to other villages saying, "This *gwaun-ga'i* and his senior family are supposed to be people of *falafala*, but see how they behave"—especially since family harmony and loving behavior are strengths for which the Dalea family is known throughout West Kwara'ae. Dalea is very concerned that Robin's future role as village and descent group leader is jeopardized by Sale's behavior.

Although not directly addressed, the family also knows that, given Mere's vulnerable position, Dalea *must* counsel Sale as he is now doing. If he does not, his own relationship with his daughter-in-law will suffer, and she may report it to her biological family. In this way, larger and larger circles of people—social *kula* circles—beyond Dalea's family will become involved in gossip and in the dispute. Eventually Robin may be forced to bring the matter to a village *ala'anga* to ask for compensation from the gossipers, assuming he has not already been brought to an *ala'anga* himself by Mere's parents demanding compensation for not protecting their daughter's social reputation. This scenario is implied; the opposite scenario of Mere happy with her in-laws is given in lines 083–086 and 162–63.

To make his argument more persuasive, Dalea enacts the kind of talk that might be expected from gossiping women (line 021). As in A'ara disentangling and Hawaiian *ho'oponopono* (Boggs and Chun, this volume), narrative and quoted speech are frequent devices in counseling used for dramatic effect as well as presenting evidence. The quoted speech is rendered in a high-pitch register with the breathy, excited voice quality and rapid sequencing imitative of gossiping interactions among women. Beyond reflecting in a mirror-image fashion the key cultural values of *kwaisa-*

re'e'anga (feeding each other) and *fangale'a'anga* (sharing), this strip of gossip illustrates how gossip distorts the real situation. Rather than as a woman whose cooking doesn't please him, here Mere is made to appear as a selfish woman denying food to Sale, who is culturally defined as an orphan by virtue of his mother's death. Treatment of orphans in an extended family is a favorite topic of gossip; Dalea wants to make sure that the conflict between Sale and Mere is not read in this light. Indeed, once the gossip reaches this degree of seriousness, Robin will have to take the perpetrators to court. Dalea intends Sale to think about how his actions can be thusly construed, for people outside the family will regard his behavior as symbolic of what is going on internally in the family. Dalea's evaluation (in 022) includes the emphatic *kwala*, a direct term of address implying affection but also surprise. It is an ambiguous and therefore subtle or mitigating way to express amazement at his son's behavior.

Then Dalea changes his strategy to clarify what he is asking of Sale through contrast. "We aren't forbidding you from eating" at other houses, he says, listing some of those Sale has been visiting—all close relatives with whom, according to *falafala*, he should share some meals and work tasks. "But your-all house is the first house, is the source (*fuli*) inside which you must eat" (025–027)—giving a direct statement of the cultural premise of source. Now Dalea's arguments recycle to Sale's avoidance of Robin's house, his unavailability for work, and Robin's need for help due to having children—adding the intensifying point that the children are often ill. Sale should "stay still" (030)—invoking with this phrase the key cultural value of *babato'o'anga* 'stability'. Talk in counseling (and in *ho'oponopono*) often recycles to take up the same arguments again, each time in a slightly different way. In lines 030–032, Dalea returns to the work that Sale should do for Robin (as he will again later), this time using quotatives to give reality and immediacy to the discussion. Dalea portrays the kinds of requests Robin makes of Sale; later he will do the same regarding Mere, and suggest the kind of replies Sale should give. Spread out across the session, then, is an implicit lesson on appropriate requests and replies between elder and younger siblings.

Although the principle of seniority has already been introduced, it is stated in the form of a cultural rule in line 035:

035 *Ai   na'oka   ne'*   Our older sibling is our
     one before+1plh,in,poss here,e   older sibling, friend/
     ai   na'ok   na'
     one before+1plh,in,poss perf
     ngwaed//
     friend

036 *Noa' kisi (.)   'i   tae'ean noa'*   We shouldn't (.) today we
     not 1plh,in+neg loc today   not   shouldn't (.) follow in the
     kisi   ma–   footsteps– as the saying
     1plh,in+neg and–   goes, "follow in the footsteps
     adai'≠ad'aekwanga   (of people different)
     follow footsteps   from us"//
     di' ba   saea   ba   "Adai'
     like that,p say+om that,p follow
     'aekwang na' hais   kia"//
     footsteps perf from 1plh

To mark its importance, line 035 is given the same parallel phrasing and rise-fall, sing-song intonation contour earlier given to the source principle in line 009; notice that later "Your sister-in-law is your sister-in-law, friend" (line 067) is exactly parallel to 035. Dalea returns several times (lines 066–068, 106, 131–32, 186, 193, 210) to elaborate this rule and explain its meaning for Sale's future. To prepare for those later elaborations, he cites a Kwara'ae traditional saying that one should not follow people whose values differ from those of *kia*, the high rhetoric (true plural) "we all" which includes one's *fu'ingwae*, clan or tribe. Dalea complains that "Any person comes along and you just follow him" (037), pointing to Sale's proclivity to form friendships with questionable characters of his own age outside his descent line. Not associating with questionable characters is a very frequent topic in counseling children and adolescents in all the families we recorded. Parents fear their children getting into the kinds of trouble, such as stealing, that would result in a court case and paying compensation. Lines 035 and 036 are examples of what Brenneis calls "text-centered indirection" where the expression is formulaic and the meaning "mysterious"; the audience must work to make the expression fit the situation (Brenneis 1986).

After reemphasizing that Sale and his brothers should be one (039–040), that Sale should live with Robin, and that he should work for Robin and Mere (using quotatives; 041–042), Dalea closes this cycle of counseling with a direct statement of cultural values as linked to the principles of source and seniority. Sale should be doing the work that Robin and Mere ask of him because:

043 *Ne'ria' ne' (.) ro'oing-*   That is (.) obedience, it is (.)
  that th that be obedi-   the source of the family//
  ru'angai na' ne' di'ia ba
  ent+nom perf that like that,p
  ni (.) gwaloan   tua'//
  3sg source+3sg,poss family

044 *Gwaloan   tua'a*   The source of the family
  source+3sg,poss family   inside the family is
  san   tua'ai   obedience or peace//
  inside+3sg,poss family
  na' (.) ro'oingru– 'ang (.)
  perf be obedient+nom
  nam aroaro'ang//
  or peaceful+nom

045 *Ne' ru le'ai ne'//*   It is a good thing//
  that thing good that

These lines are spoken more slowly and emphatically than those which preceded them. They are cohesively tied back to earlier arguments with *ne'eri'a* (that there). *Gwalona*, the high rhetoric word for source, is a sacred term. *Fuli* refers to source as foundation, base, position, or responsibility. But *gwalona* (derived from *gwau*, head) means source of all the persons, relationships, and material goods in a family or kin line; these, in turn, are seen as extensions of the head, their source. Obedience, a value subsumed under the ultimate cultural value of *aroaro'anga* 'peace', is here metaphorically referred to as the *gwalona* of the family. This, then, is a very strong statement about the importance of seniority and, specifically, the younger brother's relationship to his eldest brother and sister-in-law. In line 045, this kind of obedience is explicitly evaluated as "good" from the perspective of *falafala*.

Having set up the proper relationship between Sale and Mere, in the next segment Dalea again uses contrast by returning to the impact of Sale's behavior on his sister-in-law:

046 *Ai' 'aok   hat   'uhunia'*   Then you say things down
     then 2sg+sm speak that dnth   there about your sister-in-
     ru   ne'e   luam'a   law when she (.) she is the
     thing here,e sister-in-law   one who misses you at
     'oe ne' di' bain   home, and she is ashamed
     2sg that like that,df,p   (of that)//
     nia (.) nia lia   talhio'
     3sg   3sg look not find+2sg,om
     san   lumai dia' ba
     inside+3sg,poss house like that,p
     nia 'ek//
     3sg ashamed

047 *'Ek   long≠*   Also ashamed ≠
     ashamed also

048 *Nia≠ 'uri "Se   ngeal ne'e   sais* She says, "Good heavens,
     3sg   thus emph child here,e do   why is this child behaving
     lau' 'uri 'ita re?"//   like that?"
     again thus why emph

049 *Ai'   ka lulua   lal*   And she is searching for the
     then sm search+om rather   cause of what you're
     mantai'ngwae tae   huin//   thinking//
     idea   what that dnth

Dalea here raises a fourth issue regarding Sale's behavior: the family strongly suspects that Sale himself is gossiping about Mere at the homes where he now eats and works, based on bits of gossip reported to Ana and Mere. Dalea continues the comparison, contrasting Sale's gossiping about Mere with her caring for him as his surrogate mother (directly addressed in lines 078–079, and 212) implied by *lia talafi* (missing, caring for). Mere's feelings are also given expression in 048, when Dalea putatively quotes her anxious thoughts about Sale, giving them an elevated pitch with voice tension suggesting stress, worry, and irritation. Counselors express the feelings participants are known or suspected to have, along with those culturally expected in given situations. In high rhetoric, some emotion terms are subsumed under others (much like groups of values are subsumed under the ultimate values). Here, all of the feelings Mere may have are subsumed under shame (returned to in line 160), the culturally expected emotion for her in this situation. The grouping of emotions in high rhetoric discourse parallels Lutz (1987) and White's (this volume) analyses of the relation between attributions of emotion and inferred rule violations. Mere (but also Robin and Dalea) is to feel shame because Sale's wrongdoing indicates an undervaluing of the significant position she occupies in the family's social relations, both internal and external. But feelings of anxiety and anger are also nonverbally expressed for her in Dalea's voice. Here again we see the importance of prosody as a way of setting tone and indirectly referring to emotions.

Dalea also expresses the counterarguments and therefore implicitly the feelings that Sale is having as he listens to the counseling, especially in lines 092–094 and 192–97. He points out that because the twins were adopted by different families after their mother's death, he recognizes they do not share the specific values and behavioral expectations characterizing interactions in the larger nuclear family. As a result, they resist conforming to family expectations, arguing "Hey, these people did not raise me" (line 192). Dalea counters this attitude by narrating how the twins' older sister Ana wept when the adopting adults came to ask for them. She had not wanted to give them up, even though she was herself a child. Although Dalea is arguing against the position taken by Sale, his addressing it shows that his counseling does take into consideration Sale's personal history and known feelings and as such constitutes a form of mitigation. This counseling episode was one of many occasions on which Dalea and his older sons expressed direct or indirect empathy for the twins and regret that they had allowed the adoptions.

Dalea also addresses the disrespect Sale sometimes feels toward Robin, using Sale's social future as an effective argument against it:

123 *Saean   aos ma‘ ‘oe*   When your father dies Robin
     inside+3sg,poss day father 2sg   will be the source (=
     mae– mae ni   huil   go‘   responsible for anything
     die die   3sg source int   you do)//
     an   sa   Robin//
     of+3sg,poss art,m Robin

124 *'Aes– ‘aes   lia ‘uri*   You cannot just follow
     2sg+neg 2sg+neg look thus   anybody (and when
     hais ‘ai ro‘oi'ngwae go‘   something happens, expect
     from 2sg follow   int   then to help you)//
     kwau   leleleak–//
     thither rpl+go

125 *Ai: ni   ‘aot hu//*   Eh, it's difficult//
     emph 3sg hard dnth

126 *Ro"oingwae‘angai di‘ ba*   If you just keep following
     follow+nom   if that,p   people until something
     ‘aok   saisais (.) ‘aok–   happens, they will say, "Let
     2sg+sm rpl+do   2sg+sm   his elder brother
     leleak   rui huli   kiar   (help him)"//
     rpl+go   thing happen 3pl
     ‘uri "Ae   ai nao‘oan"//
     thus emph one before+3sg,poss

127 *Lisia (.) hoi'tain*   See (.) that's how they will
     see+om turn+tran+3sg,poss   turn it around//
     na‘ mai‘   nai//
     perf hither there

128 *Ai‘   Mere na‘   ma*   All right, Mere and Robin
     all right Mere perf and   will be the ones to talk on

art,m Robin there 3pl   speak   these things (= responsible
sa   Robin nai   kiar hat   for what has to be done)//
suil   ru   'uri//
along thing thus

129 Ai'   'unair tama   All right, for this reason, as
     all right thus,p rather   you are entering young
     'aok   eatngia   'aok   manhood, (put) your
     2sg+sm begin+om 2sg+sm   source at home//
     'alaok   go' 'aoko   huil
     bachelor int 2sg+sm source

     na' san   luam kamu//
     perf inside+3sg,poss house 2plh

Dalea here traces out the effects of not building close ties with
one's elder brothers. As long as his father is alive, Sale can count
on him to handle court cases and pay compensation if he gets
into trouble. Once his father has died, however, he will have to
rely on Robin and Mere. But more importantly, "something happening" and Sale's beginning of the 'alako'anga stage of adulthood (lines 126, 129) refer to Sale approaching marriageable
age. When the time comes for marriage, he will have to depend
on his elder brother (who is socially qualified, now that he himself is married) to arrange the marriage and pay the brideprice.
Mere will also play an important role in that event, since her
own family will have to contribute to the brideprice, and she herself will lead the contingent of women who bring the bride back
to the village, welcome her, and help her settle in. Whatever
promises his friends may make now, they will be unwilling to invest the resources and time that Robin will invest to make Sale's
marriage a reality. The effort Sale puts into Robin and Mere's
gardens and children now will be handsomely repaid on the
event of his marriage. Respect toward and willingness to work
for an elder brother and sister-in-law are therefore not merely
their due by virtue of seniority or convenience, but an investment
on the part of younger siblings in their own future. This relationship between elder and younger sibling is kwairokisi'anga,
reciprocity.
     Dalea wraps up his counseling of Sale by linking what he has

said to ultimate values in Kwara'ae culture, then giving a standard closing:

240 *Mal'iontoa"angai   ta'a//*   Making yourself important
    make important+nom bad   is bad//

241 *Mal'iontoa"angai   ta'a//*   Making yourself important
    make important+nom bad   is bad//

242 *Bolhain   'ae ionion (.) ko*   Fitting (it should be that)
    fit with+3sg 2sg humble   sm   you are humble, that you
    rong hata' (.)   noa' 'aes   obey, that you not take
    hear speech+nom not   2sg+neg   advice as a personal attack,
    lausim (.) 'aes   lau   that you not be quick to
    grab   2sg+neg again   anger (at what) the one
    baulbalua (.) –   ai   born before you
    quick to anger+adj. one   says to you//
    na'omu- na'omu   saea
    before+2sg,poss say+om
    huaum//
    for+2sg,poss

243 *Si   ru   ne'eir Ana*   Because Ana reported that
    because thing there,e Ana   thing to me, I said "Oh, I
    ha'rong nan   'ain   will speak to him about it
    report   that th,df with   this evening"//
    nauku   "O:: nai saea
    1sg+sm Oh 1sg say+om
    huan   tae'ean sau'hail
    for+3sg,poss today   evening
    nan"//
    that th,df

244 *Ai'   lea' nin   kul*   All right, it's good that we
    all right good this here 1pl,in   gather here like this, (and)
    hiuk   mai' 'uri nai tai' (.)   I report just a little on
    gather hither thus 1sg lim   those *kulas* to you//
    ha'rong 'ain   kual
    report   with part
    ne'eir   ki huaum   nai/
    that th,df pl for+2sg,poss there

245 *Sui   ne' Sael//*   That's all, Sale//
    compl that Sale

246 *Kual 'oe nai//*   That's your kula//
    part 2sg there

Pride is strongly discouraged in Kwara'ae culture, and in its place humility (*enoeno'anga*), obedience, and being slow to anger are emphasized. Dalea also stresses that Sale not take the advice of his father and older siblings as a personal attack as it concerns the goal of the larger group. Even from early infancy caregiving parents and siblings orient children to the needs and concerns of the social group and away from their own feelings (Watson-Gegeo and Gegeo 1986a,b). An infant who readily cries when it is scolded raises concern among its caregivers that it is *lausimi* (overly sensitive, taking criticism as a personal attack), and efforts are made to train it out of this tendency through joking and teasing. Sale and Sama's sensitivity to criticism from their father and elder siblings is regarded as the result of their being reared elsewhere. Statements of key cultural values, as in lines 240–42, are structural markers for the end of a cycle of arguments and constitute a summary of the lesson when they occur at the end of a session. Dalea terminates his counseling of Sale with reference again to the *kula* concept; his words up to now were Sale's *kula*.

Dalea went on to counsel two other sons individually. Finally, he counseled the whole group about the need to start a new family project to earn money for the children's school fees. The session closed by a handshake all round. As Ana and Mere brought in hot milo and biscuits, Dalea and his sons gathered around a table to begin plans for enlarging the pig enclosure (to raise pigs to sell), amid light teasing and joking about the late hour.

Subsequent to the session, Dalea and his sons built the new pig enclosure, as planned. When we returned to the village in 1984, we learned that tensions between Sale and Mere were gradually lessening, but were still the focus of Dalea's counseling from time to time. When we returned again in 1987, the twins and an older brother were living in another house they had built for themselves at the far end of the village. Despite the distance between the two houses, Sale still continued to be part of Robin and

Mere's household. He ate his meals there, worked in Mere's garden, and helped with babysitting and household chores. His relationship with Mere was now very relaxed and warm. Sale, Mere, Robin, and Robin and Sale's older sister Ana emphasized the importance of Dalea's counseling to the change in Sale and Mere's relationship.

Fa'amanata'anga as Therapeutic Counseling

We now compare *fa'amanata'anga* and Western psychotherapy, with the caveat that there is little consensus among Western therapists on the elements of psychotherapy.[9] We will discuss the focus on ongoing problems, motivations to change and the change process, the handling of emotions and hidden motives, and the use of rewards.

Fa'amanata'anga sessions aimed at therapeutic resolution of problems are usually concerned with ongoing interpersonal problems in the family, as in *ho'oponopono* and much like family therapy in the West. The foregoing counseling of Sale by Dalea was one of a series of sessions dealing with the conflict between Sale and Mere that we learned about or witnessed over the period of 1978–84. The proscription that participants should never refer to the topic again once it is dealt with in a counseling session (akin to the privacy sanctions in Western therapy), therefore, is a social fiction perhaps aimed at reducing the counselee's embarrassment, as well as giving participants time to think about their actions and repair relationships on their own.

Like Western therapists, Kwara'ae counselors do not expect one session to necessarily have a permanent effect. *Fa'amanata'anga* is seen as a lifelong process because interpersonal problems and conflicts arise, are temporarily resolved, but come up again. Or, alternatively, one set of relational problems is resolved, but another set develops and must be addressed. Even the most respected *gwaunga'i* may be counseled by another and is expected to respond with the humility and openness required of everyone else.

What, then, is seen as motivating change in individuals and relationships? Like psychotherapists and also like Hawaiians (see Ito 1985; Boggs and Chun, this volume), the Kwara'ae believe that self-examination is important in motivating people to change their behavior. Kwara'ae self-examination, however, emphasizes social relations, invoking public shame and damage to the family reputation to motivate change. This point is reflected in the concern with relations external to the family even when internal relations are being discussed (as in Dalea's counseling). We will return to the issue of personal motives later. First we examine the role of the leader in inducing or motivating change.

Like the Western therapist, the Kwara'ae counselor's interpretations and explanations may help the counselee perceive experiences in meaningful ways (John Paul Brady quoted in Goldfried 1980:273). This includes challenging the counselee's ideas and behavior (Gerard Egan, quoted in Goldfried 1980:274), as Dalea does. Second, the Kwara'ae counselor gives feedback to the counselee by commenting on his or her behavior, albeit in a very different participation structure from Western psychotherapy. The *gwaunga'i* faces the same hazards in doing this that the therapist faces—personal biases, incorrect identification or interpretation of the patient's thinking, emotions, or behavior, and the possibility that the patient may become defensive or angry (John Paul Brady and Gerald C. Davison, quoted in Goldfried 1980:280). On the positive side, both the therapist and the *gwaunga'i* are in "a unique, socially sanctioned position to tell clients things other people are not likely to directly address" (Davison, ibid.). In Kwara'ae where indirection is preferred in ordinary talk, this point may be even more pronounced than in the West.

Third, like the therapist, the Kwara'ae counselor is a catalyst to change, providing the context (in the counseling session itself) and the "inviting pointing" direction to the changes needed (Walter Kempler, quoted in Goldfried 1980:289). Role modeling is an essential part of the process (Arnold A. Lazarus, quoted in Goldfried 1980:289). Indeed, the Kwara'ae counselor not only teaches but poses himself or herself as a model for dealing with conflict by counseling in a way that reflects *babato'o'anga* (stability), *aroaro'anga* (peace), and *enoeno'anga* (humility, gentleness).

Finally, language, cognition, and awareness are seen by psychotherapists as essential in inducing change. Here language goes beyond experience by allowing for a more abstract consideration of events (Davison ibid.:293). Certainly Dalea's coun-

seling illustrates the application of socially and culturally important abstract concepts and ideas to behavior. And as we have
seen, *fa'amanata'anga* is concerned with cognition, with how the
counselee and other participants think about their behavior and
the social world.

But what about personal awareness of the kind important to
Western psychotherapists, especially hidden individual motives
and feelings? For Trobriand Islanders (Hutchins, this volume)
and the Managalase (McKellin, this volume), motivations are
irrelevant, only consequences as socially viewed count. Similarly,
fa'amanata'anga focuses on social relations and external behavior
more than on the hidden feelings and motives of the individual
psyche. Yet the Kwara'ae do not take the extreme position of the
Trobriand Islanders or Managalase. The Western psychotherapist
wants to straighten out the individual; the Kwara'ae counselor
wants to straighten out *both* the individual *and* social relations.
Although depth probing by a counselor would be seen as potentially damaging to the counselee and as overstepping the rights of
status or seniority on the part of the counselor, the Kwara'ae are
interested in motives. The distinction is when and how motives
are taken into consideration. People do a lot of speculating about
the motives of others privately, examining behavioral episodes in
careful detail for what they reveal of attitudes, emotions, and hidden problems (compare the A'ara, White, this volume). Counselors have these in mind, which is one reason counseling
discourse includes digressions and mitigations. The hypothetical
scenarios and scripts offered by counselors follow from their
firsthand understanding of the participants' motives of in a conflict, for the counselor nearly always is a member of the family
who has observed the disputing individuals daily, investigated the
conflict quietly beforehand, and is centrally located in the web of
talk that knits an extended family together. The counselor's
knowledge of counselees, therefore, is very different from at least
the therapist's beginning knowledge of a client. Indeed, in a
marked contrast with Western therapy, a good Kwara'ae counselor
is one who can interpret the counselee's thoughts without asking
a lot of questions. If the counselor makes a mistake, there will be
corrective feedback later, and the counselee always has the option
of ignoring the counselor's advice.

The counselor's handling of emotions is parallel to the handling of underlying motives. Because particular emotions are culturally associated with particular actions, emotions are rarely discussed at length in counseling. (However, young children are allowed some expression of feelings when being counseled, and their counselors teach them cultural interpretations of emotions in terms of causes and consequences.) In Dalea's counseling session, everyone understood that Sale and Mere were angry with each other. The focus was on actions resulting from that anger. In another counseling session Dalea might make suggestions to Sale for ways to release anger. Yet though implied rather than directly referred to in the counseling, emotions are very much in the counselor's awareness, for the counselor carefully watches the face and body of the target individuals, looking for signs of tension and emotion. Dalea's mitigations and attention to counterarguments Sale might raise are ways of publicly recognizing Sale's feelings so as to head off a possible emotional outburst. Emotions may be invoked on behalf of the wronged individuals, as when Dalea speaks of Mere's shame. Mere is to go away from the session with a sense of catharsis, having had her feelings openly expressed through the counselor. In fact, the Kwara'ae recognize that dealing with the dispute together as a family releases tension for everyone.[10]

But emotional catharsis is a secondary goal of a counseling session rather than the primary goal as in *ho'oponopono*. Because the Kwara'ae believe that right thinking leads to right feelings, it is the shape of thinking (perspectives, reasoning) that is central to the counselor's persuasive effort rather than feelings. In fact, *fa'amanata'anga* sessions are a major cultural strategy used by parents to teach children forms of reasoning, through modeling and direct instruction (Watson-Gegeo and Gegeo 1988). *Fa'amanata'anga* therefore contrasts with A'ara "disentangling" and Hawaiian *ho'oponopono*, in which feelings are the central focus, as in several forms of Western psychotherapy. Instead the Kwara'ae counselor is concerned with setting out the rationale for the way relationships are to be thought about and persuading the counselee to act accordingly. The extensive use of logical argumentation (largely absent from *ho'oponopono*) coincides with this relative emphasis on thought over feeling.[11]

Both psychotherapy and Kwara'ae counseling use rewards to induce and reinforce change. The Kwara'ae counselor may end a session with inviting the target individual to participate with him or her in a special outing or as did Dalea, a new but previously discussed joint family venture. Reward efforts are aimed at reintegrating the targeted individual into the larger social group. But the structure of a family counseling session itself often reflects the aim of reintegration by the leader counseling several individuals one by one (as Dalea did), as well as by the traditional joking and sharing of food at the end.

Finally, Western psychotherapy and *fa'amanata'anga* start from contrasting ontological bases—the former from a theory of the individual emphasizing subjectivity and levels of consciousness, the latter from a social framework emphasizing intersubjectivity, social relationships, and the role of interaction in shaping thought and action. Western therapy is a business: practitioners take formal training in schools, work out of offices, meet their clients in preset appointment times, maintain a professional distance, and charge fees for their services. Their assumptions about appropriate behavior and values, the world view they represent to their clients, is white middle-class in orientation, whatever the client's background. Their focus is on helping the client to become a normal, functioning person through bringing to the fore private, subjective elements of the personality. Existential questions are peripheral to this aim.

In contrast, Kwara'ae counseling is undertaken by those closest to the person(s) in difficulty, near kin whose own social fate is entangled in the problems addressed by the session. Respecting personal autonomy, the counselor does not seek to ferret out the secrets of the unconscious or other highly personal aspects of thought. Instead the focus is on changing the way the counselee thinks about relationships and acts on those thoughts. Existential questions are at the heart of the counselor's intervention, for counseling talk defines for persons where they are located in the Kwara'ae sociocultural universe. *Fa'amanata'anga* is also a primary instructional context for the transfer and analysis of cultural knowledge.

Conclusion

Fa'amanata'anga sessions are deeply spiritual experiences for the participants. The meditative stance of listeners, reinforced by the nighttime context of most sessions, may play an important role in accomplishing intrapsychological change. Outside the dimly lit house it is uniformly dark, the silence broken by an occasional cricket's chirrup. The darkness, the silence, and the surrounding walls of the dwelling emphasize the unity and safety of those sitting together inside. Faces are hardly distinguishable in the shadowy interior of the building. Staring into mid-space, listeners hear and reflect with little to distract them from the counselor's alternation of talk with reflective silence. Marked linguistically and by its relative "scarcity" (Arno 1976, Weiner 1984) vis-à-vis ordinary talk, the characteristics of high rhetoric talk single it out for attention, give it "weight," and help imbue it with formative power. Reflective silences are said to clear the mind as if approximating a prebirth condition, so that "bad seeds" may be uprooted and new ones planted. "Important silences" are therefore on equal footing with "heavy words" (compare ho'omalu in Hawaiian ho'oponopono, Boggs and Chun, this volume).

An alternative expression for "important silences," one possibly significant to the shaping of mind and intersubjective understanding, is gwagwa rorongo (black + rpl = 'nothing'; hear + repl = sound), equivalent to "dead silence" in English. Gwagwa rorongo is absolutely still, to the point of nothing or emptiness, and it includes a visual correlate: one sees either pitch darkness or pure white light behind one's partially closed eyelids, but no other color or image. Such an experience suggests a channeling of consciousness similar to Eastern forms of meditation.[12] This level of concentration both responds to and creates the deeply spiritual, sacred quality of the counseling session.

Duranti (this volume) suggests that Samoans redefine their social order over the course of several fono through negotiation and interpretive processes. The same may be said of Kwara'ae village-level ala'anga sessions, in which decisions are arrived at by consensus, and shifts in policy and interpretation are negotiated. In their ongoing dialogue with prior and current discourses, *fa'ama-nata'anga* activities also redefine the social order and are a major vehicle through which the concepts and rules embodied in *falafala* are defined, adapted, reinterpreted, and transmitted from one generation to another.

In fact, as a marked, sacred context, *fa'amanata'anga* is metaphorical for *falafala* in that it is an enactment of *falafala*. We can see this in the leader's stance of speaking as *falafala*. Brenneis's taxonomy of forms of indirection is useful here in understanding the social meaning of counseling. He would describe *fa'amanata'anga* as an example of *event-centered indirection*, where "the event's occurrence in itself is a meaningful message, in fact perhaps the most important message being conveyed" (1986:344). For instance, the construction of a public communicative context among the Fiji Indians is itself meaningful because it fuses emotional experience with discourse message (Brenneis, this volume and ibid.). Taking Brenneis's argument one step further, we maintain that *fa'amanata'anga* fuses ethos with eidos.

It is important to recognize that this fusion takes place as a social rather than religious activity. There are elements of the sacred in *fa'amanata'anga*, as there are in any activity in which *falafala* plays a prominent role. But *fa'amanata'anga* is not a religious activity, and indeed, religion is only one *kula* within *falafala*. Traditionally in family counseling, the ancestors were rarely mentioned; today in Christian families, God may be invoked but if so, only as another argument for changing behavior. *Fa'amanata'anga* deals with everyday needs and problems—with "this life," "this world," and "our cultural behavior," as the counselor often phrases it. Rather than on the vertical relationship of human being to ancestral spirits/Christian God, then, the emphasis is on horizontal relationships among human beings. It is in these horizontal relationships that *falafala* (eidos) is to be fused with behavior and personality (ethos). It is in the working out of social relations that the fusion becomes complete.

Not surprisingly, correct performance is a critical factor in *fa'amanata'anga* sessions. The leader's language must have weight (*fafakulu*), that is, be spoken in well-formed high rhetoric, carry important social meaning, and properly argue propositions with reference to *falafala*. The leader must thoroughly understand and be able to make the links between *falafala* and human nature (as the Kwara'ae see it), ordinary experience, and everyday life. Points and responses must be timed for effect, and the speaker must have good control of paralinguistic and prosodic features of spoken language. An understanding of the situation and individuals involved is a fundamental requirement, as well as skill in putting across points without losing control of the session. A leader who is incompetent in speaking or pushes the targeted individuals too far loses the stance of speaking as *falafala* and will be seen speaking only for himself or herself, or nagging. The counseling session may then blow up in an outburst of emotions, creating a deeper entanglement for everyone. Resolution of the conflict, change in individual behavior, and the fusing of ethos and eidos are therefore tied to the leader's performance.

Finally, we think that one reason the Kwara'ae have been able to maintain their cultural identity in the face of Christianization and modernization is the way they have conceived of tradition and the role played by *fa'amanata'anga* in supporting tradition. It would seem that Christian Kwara'ae substituted Christianity for the *kula* of ancestor worship in *falafala*. All other *kulas* of *falafala* have gone on as before, with pragmatic updating from time to time as has probably always been the case. Meanwhile, counseling continues to support the notion that *falafala* is alive and applicable to today's problems and that the social values it embodies are objective.

Notes

Acknowledgements. We deeply appreciate the trust extended to us by the Kwara'ae families who allowed us to witness or record counseling sessions. This study was partially supported by grants from the National Institute of Mental Health (1978–79), the Milton Fund (1978–79), the Spencer Foundation (1978–82, 1983–84), and the National Science Foundation (1984–86). We are grateful to participants of the Pitzer Conference (including Susan Philips, Andrew Pawley, and Bambi Schieffelin, who came as observers) for their comments; to Geraldine Fasnacht for introducing us to the cognitive therapy literature; and to Stephen T. Boggs, Geoffrey White, and Robert Blust for insightful comments on an earlier draft.

1. Our use of the English "counsel, counseling" to gloss *fa'amanata*,

fa'amanata'anga is in the *Webster's New World Dictionary* sense of "to give advice to, advise; to urge the acceptance of (an action, plan, etc.); recommend." As an English gloss, "counsel" is in keeping with the tone and spirit of the original Kwara'ae. That "counseling" is ambiguous in English, subject to interpretation as both "advising" and "therapy"— whether individual or group—is fortuitous given *fa'amanata'anga*'s many functions. Two other Kwara'ae terms also mean "teach." *Fa'atala-ma'i'anga*, which is *not* used to refer to counseling sessions, implies teaching in the sense of the acquisition of skills. *Fa'amanata* can be applied to the teaching of only those skills (such as language learning) seen to involve "shaping the mind," but not to direct instruction in physical skills such as canoe-building or mat-weaving. The third term for "teach," occasionally used as a synonym for *fa'amanata'anga*, is *fa'anaunau'anga*, teaching someone to perform fearlessly, a term reflecting the cultural importance, for example, of public speaking skills in Kwara'ae (see below in text).

2. Irvine's essay on the problems of "formality/informality" as an analytical term has been useful to us in sorting out the characteristics of meetings and language we call "formal." For example, all *ala'anga* (meetings) are formal to some degree, in particular with reference to a central situational focus, the invoking of positional identities (Irvine 1979: 778–79), and features of context. *Ala'anga* also requires speech in high rhetoric, the formal level of Kwara'ae (see below in text and note 3).

3. By "increasingly . . . formal" we mean that as a child grows older its parents increase the structuring of *fa'amanata'anga* sessions in the direction of adult sessions. More specifically, this structuring affects features of context, turn-taking, and listening behavior. It also involves three aspects of formality discussed by Irvine (1979): emergence of a central situational focus, increased code structuring, and increased code consistency. The emergence of a central focus allows counseling sessions to increase in length from the counseling moments of infancy to the one- to two-hour sessions common in middle childhood through adolescence. Increased code structuring and consistency (through co-occurrence rules; see Ervin-Tripp 1972) refer, in this case, to the way high rhetoric (see below, in text) is spoken in counseling sessions. For infants and young children, counseling takes place in high rhetoric of simplified syntax and vocabulary and mixed with low-rhetoric expressions.

4. Drawing on the work of political scientists, Lindstrom (1984) makes a distinction between "found" (the collective will discovered through talk) and "negotiated" (compromise among individual desires) consensus in dispute settling on Tanna (Vanuatu) (see also Lindstrom,

this volume). Both consensus types occur in Kwara'ae dispute settling, depending on the issue involved. The Tanna have little means to enforce decisions reached by consensus. Lindstrom comments that Tanna meetings succeed in generating a single version of the disputed issue, but that once enunciated, this consensus may last "only as long as the particular context" of its generation (ibid.:39 and this volume). In contrast, the Kwara'ae back up their decisions with the threat of enforcement (usually in the form of fines) from an *ala'anga* convened as a traditional court, or by taking the issue to the provincial *kastom* court in Auki; like Americans, the Kwara'ae are quick to litigate.

5. Several of the societies described in this volume appear to adhere to similar "ultimate" values (such as sharing) and similar cultural premises (such as seniority and placing concerns of the social group over those of the individual). To clarify the social and cultural meanings of these values and premises, it is important to situate them in typifications of actual behavior in the respective societies. As Kirkpatrick suggests, a fruitful way to conceptualize differences between societies is in terms of expectations for "normality," recognizing that "ultimate" values constitute cultural assumptions of the minimum conditions for social (group) life (Kirkpatrick 1984). For example, the A'ara have a strong sense of group identity, follow their leaders willingly and enthusiastically, and are generally compliant toward authority. In contrast, outsiders and other Solomon Islanders regard Malaitans as truculent, assertive, and independent, as resistant to leadership, and as having held out long against pacification by the British. They are therefore much less compliant toward leaders than the A'ara and hesitant to join group endeavors unless leaders are above reproach. These characteristics are recognized and criticized by the Kwara'ae themselves. Counseling sessions mediate conflicting social organizational principles and thus nearly always include an emphasis on or at least allusion to unity and interdependence while at the same time elaborating what it means to be a "complete person" (not depending on others, being able to make decisions for oneself).

6. A metaphorical synonym for *firu* is *garo'a* (adj. 'spidery'), that is, "like a spider's web." *Firu* and *rodo'a* (adj. 'dark') are contrasted with *madakola'a* (adj. 'clear/light'). Similarly, issues are said to be *'ere* (adj. 'crooked') vs. *saga* (adj. 'straight'). *Saga* has the high rhetoric meaning of being in accord with *falafala*. Besides "straightening out" an issue, one can also *fa'amadakola'a* ('clear or clear up') it. A nonfunctioning or wrong *kula* may be referred to as black or dark.

7. Breath groups are marked by /, and those ending in a terminal fall by //. Pauses are marked by (.), and self-interruptions by —. Bound morphemes are joined with +. Grammatical and other abbreviations

used in the transcript are: art = article; caus = causative prefix; compl = completive; df = definite; dnth = down there; dnthfr = down there far; e = emphatic; emph = emphatic expression; ex = exclusive; f = feminine; in = inclusive; int = intensifier; lim = limiter; loc = locative; m = masculine; neg = negative; nom = nominalizer; om = object marker; p = past; perf = perfective; pl = plural or pluralizer; plh = plural high-rhetoric pronoun; poss = possessive; rpl = reduplicative; sg = singular; sm = subject marker; th = there. Kwara'ae words in the text of the paper are represented in their underlying form, but in transcripts or quotations are represented as speakers actually said them. Spoken Kwara'ae is affected by regular metathesis, which Pawley convincingly argues is actually the cumulative effect of anticipatory vowel copying and vowel reduction (including partial devoicing and deletion; see Pawley 1982); other processes, such as the habitual substitution of an aspirated *h* for the fricative *f*, and various kinds of contraction are also common in spoken or phonetic Kwara'ae. The orthography used in this paper was designed by Gegeo in 1976 for a dictionary of Kwara'ae he is compiling and was subsequently used in Gary Simons's 1977 Kwara'ae word list.

8. Boggs (personal communication) notes that as one of the earliest learned aspects of discourse, prosody—like the early routines shared by caregivers and infants (see Watson-Gegeo and Gegeo 1986a)—carries important emotional memory. This point coincides with the early induction of children into counseling at eighteen months in some Kwara'ae households, where children are taught to respond to what Bateson calls "categories of contextual organization of behavior" (1980) through nonverbal (silence, lowered eyes, grave facial expression) and prosodic (grave voice quality, intonation contours) cues well before they can decode high-rhetoric speech.

9. In preparing this section we have drawn on Parsons's (1951) discussion of the four elements of Western psychoanalysis (support, permissiveness, denial or reciprocity, and manipulation of rewards), which Gibbs (1967) later used to analyze the Kpelle moot as a therapeutic encounter, and the contributions of thirteen leaders in different psychotherapeutic "schools" to a (1980) special issue on "Psychotherapy Process: Some Views on Effective Principles of Psychotherapy" of the journal *Cognitive Therapy and Research*.

10. In keeping with the *kula* framework, culpability for intrafamily conflicts is seen as resting in all the participants to the conflict. The reason Sale is the target in Dalea's counseling has to do with the degree of magnitude of Sale's culturally inappropriate behavior toward his sister-in-law. Mere's contribution to the conflict is well recognized, as is the fact that tensions exist between Mere and the other members of the

family. Hence, when Dalea finished his counseling of Sale, he told the others, "You see me saying this to Sale, but it also applies to all of you."

11. The fusion of thought and feelings in the Hawaiian conception of self is shown in the rhetoric of conflict resolution, where logical argumentation is accompanied by appeals to emotions and relationships (Boggs and Chun, this volume; Ito 1985). Appeals to feelings and relationships are also important in *fa'amanata'anga*, as we have seen. However, in contrast to Hawaiians, the Kwara'e always speak of actions and the motivations for them as being under the control of the mind; as mentioned earlier, strong negative emotions are supposed to be suppressed, and counseling sessions focus on thought over feelings.

12. In Eastern meditation, such visual experiences are characteristic of *pratyahara*, the channeling of consciousness during an intermediate state in which the mind is open to internal and external suggestion (Mishra 1959:66–70). *Gwagwa rorongo* is also the term used in precontact times to describe an empty village after its inhabitants had been destroyed by a raid. This term focuses on the point at which death and life come face to face (compare darkness and light behind the eyelids, above in text)—both are seen as simultaneously immanent at that juncture. For the Kwara'ae, life and death are each a form of existence, parallel to the ordinary human conception of light and dark as realities— that is, darkness is not merely the absence of light, but has a "presence" of its own; death is not merely the absence of life, but has an animated existence of its own.

References

Arno, Andrew

1976 Joking, Avoidance and Authority: Verbal Performances as an Object of Exchange in Fiji. Journal of the Polynesian Society 85:71–86.

1986 Impressive Speeches and Persuasive Talk: Traditional Patterns of Political Communication in Fiji's Lau Group from the Perspective of Pacific Ideal Types. Oceania 56(2):124–37.

Bateson, Gregory

1972 A Theory of Play and Fantasy. *In* Steps to an Ecology of Mind. New York: Ballantine.

1980 Mind and Nature: A Necessary Unity. New York: Bantam.

Beck, Aaron

1976 Cognitive Therapy and the Emotional Disorders. New York: International Universities Press.

Black, Peter W.
1983 Conflict, Morality and Power in a Western Caroline Society. Journal of the Polynesian Society 92:7–30.

Brenneis, Donald
1986 Shared Territory: Audience, Indirection and Meaning. In The Audience as Co-Author. A Duranti and D. Brenneis, eds. Special of Text 6(3):339–47.

Chapple, Eliot D., and Carleton S. Coon
1942 Principles of Anthropology. New York: Holt.

Dore, John
1985 The Origin and Structure of Linguistic Mentation. Unpublished ms.

Ellis, Albert
1971 Growth Through Reason: Verbatim Cases in Rational-Emotive Therapy. Palo Alto: Science and Behavior.

Ervin-Tripp, Susan
1972 On Sociolinguistic Rules: Alternation and Co-occurrence. In Directions in Sociolinguistics: The Ethnography of Communication. John J. Gumperz and Dell Hymes, eds. New York: Holt, Rinehart and Winston.

Firth, Raymond
1964 Essays on Social Organization and Values. London: University of London, Athlone.
1975 Speech-making and Authority in Tikopia. In Political Language and Oratory in Traditional Society. Maurice Bloch, ed. New York: Academic Press.
1979 The Sacredness of Tikopia Chiefs. In Politics and Leadership: A Comparative Perspective. W. Shack and P. Cohen, eds. Oxford: Clarendon Press.

Geertz, Clifford
1973 Interpretation of Cultures. New York: Basic Books.

Gibbs, James L., Jr.
1967 The Kpelle Moot. In Law and Warfare: Studies in the Anthropology of Conflict. Paul Bohannan, ed. Garden City, NY: Natural History Press.

Goffman, Erving
1974 Frame Analysis: An Essay on the Organization of Experience. Cambridge, MA: Harvard University Press.

Goldfried, Marvin R., ed.

1980 Psychotherapy Process: Some Views on Effective Principles of Psychotherapy. Special Issue of Cognitive Therapy and Research 4(3):269–306.

Gumperz, John J.

1982 Discourse Strategies. Cambridge: Cambridge University Press.

Irvine, Judith T.

1979 Formality and Informality in Communicative Events. American Anthropologist 81(4):773–90.

Ito, Karen L.

1985 Ho'oponopono, 'To Make Right': Hawaiian Conflict Resolution and Metaphor in the Construction of a Family Therapy. Culture, Medicine and Psychiatry 9:201–17.

Kirkpatrick, John

1984 'Gentle' Persons and Violent Moments in the Marquesas Islands. Paper presented at the American Anthropological Association Meetings, Denver, November.

Labov, William, and David Fanschel

1977 Therapeutic Discourse: Psychotherapy as Conversation. New York: Academic Press.

Lakoff, George, and Mark Johnson

1980 Metaphors We Live By. Chicago: University of Chicago Press.

Leont'ev, A. A.

1969 Yazk, Rech; Rechevaya Deyatel 'Nost' (Language, Speech, and Speech Activity). Moscow: Izdatel 'stvo Prosvesh-chenis.

Levinson, S. C.

1978 Activity Types and Language. Pragmatics Microfiche 3:3–3 D1-G5.

Lindstrom, Lamont

1984 The Power of Witnessing on Tanna, Vanuatu. Paper presented at the American Anthropological Association Meetings, Denver, November.

Lutz, Catherine

1987 Goals, Events and Understanding in Ifaluk Emotion Theory. In Cultural Models in Language and Thought. D. Holland and N. Quinn, eds. Cambridge: Cambridge University Press.

Mishra, Rammurti
1959 Fundamentals of Yoga. New York: Lancer.

Parsons, Talcott
1951 The Social System. Glencoe, IL: The Free Press.

Pawley, Andrew
1982 Kwara'ae 'Metathesis' as a Gradual Sound Change. Unpublished manuscript.

Philips, Susan U.
1972 Participant Structures and Communicative Competence: Warm Springs Children in Community and Classroom. In C. B. Cazden, V. P. John, and D. Hymes, eds., Functions of Language in the Classroom. New York: Teachers College.

Todorov, Tzvetan
1984 Mikhail Bakhtin: The Dialogical Principle. Translated by Wlad Godzich. Minneapolis: University of Minnesota Press.

Tryon, D. T., and B. D. Hackman
1973 Solomon Islands Languages: An Internal Classification. Pacific Linguistics Series C, No. 72. Canberra: Australian National University.

Van Gennep, Arnold
1960 The Rites of Passage. Chicago: University of Chicago Press.

Vygotsky, Lev Semenovich
1962 Thought and Language. Cambridge, MA: MIT Press.

Watson-Gegeo, Karen Ann, and David Welchman Gegeo
1979 Ala'anga: Settling a Dispute in Kwara'ae. Paper presented at the Northeastern Anthropological Association Meetings, New England College, Henniker, New Hampshire.
1986a Calling Out and Repeating Routines in Kwara'ae Children's Language Socialization. In B. B. Schieffelin and E. Ochs, eds., Language Socialization Across Cultures. London: Cambridge University Press.
1986b The Social World of Kwara'ae Children: Acquisition of Language and Values. In J. Cook-Gumperz, W. Corsaro, and Jurgen Streeck, eds., Children's Worlds and Children's Language. The Hague: Mouton.
1987 Strategic Alternatives and Contextual Variation in Kwara'ae Dispute Settling. Presented at the International Pragmatics Association Meeting. 17–22 August, Antwerp, Belgium.

1988 'Heavy Words' and 'Important Silences': The Social Transfer of
      Cognitive Skills in Kwara'ae. To appear in Apprenticeship in
      Thinking. Alison Adams and Vera John-Steiner, eds.

Weiner, Annette
1984 From Words to Objects to Magic: "Hard Words" and the Boun-
      daries of Social Interaction. *In* Dangerous Words: Language
      and Politics in the Pacific. D. L. Brenneis and F. R. Myers, eds.
      New York: New York University Press.

Wertsch, James V.
1979 From Social Interaction to Higher Psychological Processes: A
      Clarification and Application of Vygotsky's Theory. Human
      Development 22:1–22.

Appendix

The speaker is Dalea, father of Robin (c. 33 years, eldest son), Sale and
Sama (twin brothers c. 19 years), and Ana (c. 37 years). Others
present include Mere (c. 28 years, Robin's wife), and other married
and unmarried sons of Dalea (with their families). Background talk
of/to infants edited out. Full text (in Kwara'ae and English) is available
from the authors.

001 All right, I want to say a little something to Sale.

002 I heard a report about you, Sale.

003 That you're not eating at the house of the one born before you
     these days lately.

004 These days you avoid Robin's house.

005 This what Mere reported to Ana.

006 And Ana reported to me.

007 Behavior like that is rather bad.

008 This is what I say to you.

009 Your-all house is your-all house (your house is the house of all of
     you).

010 The house of the one born before you when we (excl.)—we
     moved down here like this.

011 (But) you yourself are already staying with Robin.

012 Don't instead avoid the house that belongs to you all.

013 You should be with the one born before you.

014 If on a day if he sees things in the gardens.

015 (That) need doing in the gardens, you go do them.

016 Because he has children.

017 Some cutting brush and hoeing and. . . .

018 That *kula*(part; = refusing to work), no.

019 Because we also don't want some women talking about Mere as in the past.

020 No, I don't want that kind of behavior.

021 Because continuing— we also don't want some women saying, "Goodness! Mere, isn't she giving any food to this child or is she denying food to this child, is this maybe why he doesn't stay still down there at their house?"

022 Eh, that kula (kind of thing) I also don't want, Sale.

023 If we moved down here like this, you now are living with the one born before you.

024 You go— we are not forbidding you from eating at (other) houses.

025 Houses like Rutu's house and Tomo's and/ (Rutu = widow of Sale's classificatory father; Tomo = her married son, Sale's classificatory brother). We aren't forbidding you from them.

026 But your-all house is the first house is the source.

027 Inside which you must eat food.

028 Right now as in the past you are instead avoiding the person born before you (and) you are not stable (always wandering, never available).

029 His family (Robin's) is not good (= has illness).

030 You (should) stay still you— Robin wants to say something to you in the family, he says, "You go hoe this thing."

031 Or "Go cut the brush in front of the potato garden, brother Sale."

032 Like that.

033 Because you are a (young) person, you don't have to work until night down there, you just have to work a little while.

034 Because Ana just reported it to me yesterday and I wanted to talk to you a little bit today because today your coming down here made it easy for us to talk.

035 Our older sibling is our older sibling, friend.

036 We shouldn't (.)— today we shouldn't follow in the footsteps— as the saying goes, "follow in the footsteps (of people different) from us."

037 Any person comes along and you just follow him, any person

comes along and you just follow him /

038 No, you're an adult now.

039 Fitting (it should be that) you and your older siblings are one.

040 You-all are you-all (= you all should be one).

041 That house up there (is where you should be now that) we have come down here (.) you should be with Robin.

042 If whatever Robin needs and asks you to do or your sister-in-law Mere says, "Go and bring water (in this container), Sale," or "Go do this thing, Sale."

043 That is (.) obedience (and) it is (.) the *gwalona* (source) of the family.

044 The *gwalona* (source) of the family inside the family is (.) obedience (.) or *aroaro'anga* (peace).

045 It is a good thing.

046 Then you say things down there about your sister-in-law when she (.) she is the one who misses you at home, and she is ashamed (of your absence).

047 Also ashamed/

048 She says, "Good heavens, why is this child behaving like that?"

049 And she is searching for the cause of what you're thinking.

050 All right that *kula* I don't want these days from you all.

051 From Sama and yourself.

052– Dalea reemphasizes the family as being of one *fuli* (source) and
082 repeats how Sale should respond when asked by Robin or Mere to work, and that evening meals must be taken together "even if you all starve." Sale's refusal to listen to his sister-in-law because of pride *(mala'inoto'a)* and thinking he's grown up *(mala'alako)* is evaluated "That's bad behavior" (065–066). Dalea emphasizes "Your sister-in-law is your sister-in-law, friend" (067). Sale should treat his brother Robin as a *gwaunga'i* now that Robin has married (068) and not joke about his brother. Dalea again emphasizes respecting Mere and helping her, because Robin "is important to you" (074) and "Your sister-in-law is also like your mother" (fills that role; 078–079). Sale should obey his sister-in-law's requests.

083 Your obeying your sister-in-law like this, she is very happy because of it, too.

084 Even her life is happy, too.

085 "Oh children, I married into this family here and I am very happy, I say some little thing and these children go do it right

away" (= the kinds of things Mere will report to others, including her biological family).

086 All right, on that side I want you to do accordingly.

087– Dalea repeats Mere's missing Sale and being in pain over village
092 gossip about her. If he is too full to eat, Sale should politely refuse the food (Dalea demonstrates), which "is good" (090). But refusing food when he hasn't eaten, "that *kula* is bad" (092).

093 Because I know that Sama and you, yes, you two in the past, you two grew up in different families.

094 Okay, therefore I don't— I don't condemn you as bad, rather.

095 All right, don't think— don't think like this, "Oh, I'm adult now, I don't obey anything, any married woman or any man."

096 No (.) when it comes to the day that something happens to you, your older brother is the one, friend.

097 Or the day when something happens to you, your sister-in-law is the one, friend.

098 That's the *kula* (= the point to think about).

099– Dalea repeats Sale should be "willing" to work for Robin and
121 Mere, stresses the difficulties they face with several young children, and how Sale should support them "with obedience and peace" (111). He again emphasizes he doesn't want gossip about Mere, and how home should be the source, *fuli*) for all the siblings. He repeats he's not forbidding Sale from eating at other relatives' homes, but Robin's must be the first house:

122 Because your older brother is just like your father.

123 When your father dies, Robin will be the source (of anything you do).

124 You cannot just follow anybody (and when something happens, expect them to help you.)

125 Hey, that's difficult.

126 If you just keep following people until something happens, they will say, "Let his elder brother (help him)."

127 See (.) that's how they'll turn it around.

128 All right, Mere and Robin will be the ones to talk on these things (responsible for what has to be done).

129 All right, for this reason, as you are entering young manhood, (put) your source at home.

130– Reemphasizing the point of 129, Dalea recycles to how Sale
185 should work at home, not resist obeying Mere, how much work there is to do, how he should respond to requests to help, that it

is all right to work for other relatives, too ("that's good . . . willingness is good," 155–57). The first thing, however, is "obeying
what your father says" (158). He again repeats Ana's reporting
of the story to him, and Mere's missing Sale and being
ashamed— that *kula* I don't want (160). "I want Mere to be
happy in our family, I want all of us to be happy" (162). He emphasizes Robin's rightful role as family leader, and how if "something happens" others will not help them, they must "return to
your elder brother" (171), whether they steal or anything else.
Therefore obedience is very important.

186   All right, that is the way I talk, toothlessly lisping, but if you follow it, perhaps one day you will arrive at a good *kula* (position
in life).

187   You will arrive at a very good *kula*.

188   All right my talking may not (seem important) until someday
when you're grown up, you will see it (realize it), and then you
will say, "Hey people, the things my father told me were very
good."

189   You will then think back and say, "People, if I had followed my
own mind— I did (as) I thought, I would be a person in bad circumstances today."

190– Dalea again emphasizes making Robin and Mere the source.
192

193   You (think) "Hey, I am not— these people did not raise me."

194   Oh, they begged me (to let them keep you), friend.

195   Ana cried with her two eyes.

196   She cried (when) they (a group of relatives) came to ask for
(adopt) you, (and) Ana said, "But I do not fear feeding children,
I don't fear feeding these children."

197   They asked for you and you left with them, and for you to say,
"Hey I did not grow up in this family."

198   Oh no, my friend.

199– Dalea emphasizes Robin being grown up and as the source; for
239   Sale to obey and work for him; that Dalea is not forbidding Sale
from going to other relatives' houses but Robin comes first; that
the sister-in-law is like the mother, and the elder brother like the
father; that obedience now will lead to being a good man later;
that avoiding his brother's house is a bad *kula*; that Sale should
be respectful to his siblings; that he should not wander about
but work in the garden; obey his sister-in-law "because your

food is down there" (236), and babysit for her. His refusal to babysit, "that *kula*, don't" (239).

240 Making yourself important is bad.

241 Making yourself important is bad.

242 Fitting (it should be that) you are humble (*enoeno*), that you obey (*rongo fata'a* = hear words), that you not take advice as a personal attack (*lausimi*), that you not be quick to anger (*balubalu'a*) (at what) the one born before you says to you.

243 Because Ana reported that thing to me, I said, "Oh, I will speak to him about it this evening."

244 All right, it's good that we gather here like this (and) I report just a little on those *kulas* to you.

245 That's all, Sale.

246 That's your *kula*.

Dramatic Gestures: The Fiji Indian
Pancayat As Therapeutic Event

Donald Brenneis

THIS STUDY analyzes the *pancayat,* a public event for the mediation of disputes in Bhatgaon, a Fiji Indian community. Although
pancayats are held quite infrequently, they are regarded by Bhatgaon villagers as the definitive Indian occasion for the amicable
settlement of conflict.[1] The *pancayat* (literally "council of five")
has a long history in India as both a conflict-managing and
decision-making institution but has assumed a very different form
in Fiji, as will be evident below.[2] How the *pancayat* "works" in
Bhatgaon depends in large part, I will argue, on several Indian aesthetic and psychological notions introduced to and reinterpreted
in the Fijian context. These underlying notions differentiate the
construction and implications of *pancayat* from, on the one hand,
Western notions of therapeutic events and, on the other, from
some of the traditional theories of emotions and therapy suggested
for the Pacific by Lutz (1982), Ito (1985), White (1979, this volume), and others in this volume.

   Gibbs's article, "The Kpelle Moot" (1963), is important here in
two respects. First, it is a *locus classicus* for the description and interpretation of moots and other public mediation occasions, of
considerable importance in the development of legal anthropology. Second, it provides a clear if general statement of an important Western theory of therapeutic events. Drawing upon
Parsons's (1951) characterization, Gibbs cites four elements of
Western psychotherapy: support, permissiveness, denial of reciprocity, and manipulation of rewards (1963: 284; see also
Watson-Gegeo and Gegeo, this volume). Gibbs argues that these
four elements are also present in the Kpelle moot or house
palaver, a public discussion and resolution of conflict primarily
within households or between neighbors. The moot is supportive;
it is culturally defined as a valued and beneficial event. One can

discuss a wide range of events and issues within the moot and be very emotionally expressive without fear of revenge or anger in response. Finally, the audience for the moot provides not only a sympathetic hearing but real rewards as well; reaching accord is a warrant of full participation in the life of the local community.

Perhaps central to a consideration of the theory of therapeutic talk implicit in Gibbs's model are his second and third elements, the permissiveness or "anything goes" quality of moot discourse and the safety from angry response which makes it possible.[3] "Permissiveness in the therapeutic setting (and in the moot)," he argues (1963:285), "results in catharsis, in a high degree of stimulation of feelings in the participants, and an equally high tendency to verbalize those feelings." Apart from those etiological insights which the session might afford, *how* those insights are reached, that is, in apparently unrestrained expression, is central to the therapeutic experience. As Labov and Fanshel (1977) note, "It had been observed many times that the [therapeutic] interview is simultaneously a diagnostic device and the method of therapy." While empirical studies of both therapeutic conversation and mediation sessions demonstrate that this freewheeling quality is often more appearance than fact—that successful events involve careful if indirect guidance—the underlying notion that catharsis, a purging or cleansing of troubling emotions through their identification and expression, is a critical element remains central in many Western theories.

The term *catharsis* is at present primarily used in psychological contexts, but its first major use, apart from the literal meaning of cleansing or purification, is by Aristotle in the *Poetics*. Although it is unclear exactly what Aristotle *meant* by the term, he argues that catharsis is a critical aesthetic element in tragedy. As literature professors rather than classicists generally understand the term, "Aristotle appears to wish to put the emotions of fear and pity into his audience, to 'cleanse.' A real emotional transformation, a real experience is intended" (Gerow 1974:133). Drama works through the catalyzing and purging of strong emotions in the individual spectator. Therapy, by analogy, works in part through the similar processes of expression and cleansing, although the emotions are located in oneself rather than in a play. Aesthetic and therapeutic models are closely intertwined.

Whether Gibbs's discussion accurately reflects what the Kpelle themselves saw in the moot, his article remains a fair characterization of a Western model of therapy. It also reflects a usually unspoken premise shared by many legal anthropologists. This is the notion that a wide range of conflict management events—from the Eskimo song duel to an American's "day in court"—are effective in large part because they afford individuals positively sanctioned opportunities for emotional expression and release. What is striking about the *pancayat* is that, in regard to emotional expression, it is very unlike the Kpelle moot or even the less cathartic emotion talk in A'ara "disentangling" (White, this volume). The *pancayat* seems concerned not with emotion but with questions of fact and is highly decorous, restrained, and subject to very narrow relevance rules (compare Trobriand land litigation, Hutchins, this volume). The *pancayat* is, however, considered by Fiji Indians to be a very powerful occasion for social mending, for repairing damaged interpersonal relations and restoring amity. The central questions addressed in this paper are, first, what the salient features of *pancayat* as communicative events are and how they are related to conditions of Indian life in Fiji; and, second, how the *pancayat* "works," how it effects the therapeutic results claimed for it.

My answer to the first question, that of the relationship between social and communicative forms, is methodologically rather straightforward, although fairly complicated in its details. The discussion is rooted firmly in the ethnography of speaking tradition and follows directly my earlier considerations of other discourse genres in Bhatgaon (see, for example, Brenneis 1978, 1984; Myers and Brenneis 1984).

The second question is much more problematic, as it raises a range of theoretical and methodological issues. One problem is a definitional one: how is therapy to be defined, and for whom or what is it intended? As will become evident in the discussion below, the problem to be remedied is located neither in an individual nor in the relationship between conflicting parties alone. The *pancayat* must affect a broader village public as well as those immediately involved; disputants and audience alike must be satisfied. A practical resolution alone is insufficient. As one man declared during the *pancayat* described below, "The political work is finished; religious work is remaining." In this "religious work" are entwined ethics, aesthetics, and ethnopsychology.

As ethnopsychological enterprise, the *pancayat* stands in marked contrast to those characteristic features suggested by Gibbs. In fact, the *pancayat's* effects on individuals do not figure greatly in villagers' discussions. However they may actually perceive their world, Bhatgaon villagers rarely talk about it in terms of a personal self.[4] The *pancayat* is said to lead not to the stimulation and release of individual feelings but to a shared experience of some sort. These local theories rest upon an ultimately dramatic model, one drawn from Sanskritic poetics rather than those of Aristotle.

To claim that villagers share these ideas is not to imply that their theories are clearly or systematically articulated. They are, rather, what I would call "partial theories," drawing upon orally transmitted beliefs, the semantic resources and constraints of Fiji Hindi, and local interpretations of classical Hindu notions introduced to Fiji in published religious texts. Further, they are most fully expressed not in ordinary discourse but in ethnographic interviews, a kind of event often leading to greater clarity and coherence than observations of everyday village life might suggest. This study draws upon field notes, interview data, and my own interpretations, tested and refined through continuing discussions with my village colleagues. The final product, however, remains my responsibility.

After a brief discussion of the historic and contemporary situation of Bhatgaon, I describe in detail one *pancayat* and the events leading to it in "The Case of the Purported Profanities." I then examine salient social and communicative features of Bhatgaon as a community and move to the characteristics of the *pancayat* as a speech event. In the final section I explore Fiji Indian emotional notions and their implications for an understanding of how the *pancayat* works.

Bhatgaon: A Fiji Indian Community

Bhatgaon is a rural village of 671 Hindi-speaking Fiji Indians located on the northern side of Vanua Levu, the second largest island in the Republic of Fiji. The villagers are the descendants of

north Indians who came to Fiji between 1879 and 1919 as inden-
tured plantation workers. Bhatgaon was established in the early
1900s and now includes ninety households. There has been little
migration to or from the village for the past twenty years. Most
families lease rice land from the government of Fiji, and, although they may work as seasonal cane cutters or in other outside jobs, most men consider themselves rice farmers. Rice and
vegetables are raised primarily for family use, although surplus
produce may be sold to middlemen. Leaseholds are generally
small, and rice farming does not afford Bhatgaon villagers the
same opportunities for wealth available in sugar cane raising
areas.

The following account, "The Cast of the Purported Profanities,"
both exemplifies *pancayat* procedures and gives some of the
flavor of troubled social relations in Bhatgaon.

The Case of the Purported Profanities

Amka and his married son Arun lease nine acres of land in a relatively new subdivision. Amka had applied for two acres adjacent
to this fields and had begun to clear the area in March, 1972,
before his lease was approved. In mid-March the government
surveyors came and laid out boundaries for the new leases; the
two acres Amka had cleared were to be rented to Satish and
Jeshwan, two other farmers.

One day soon after the surveyors' visit Amka was walking to
his nine-acre plot when he encountered the wives of Jeshwan and
his younger brother working in Jeshwan's new field. He told
them to stop working there, as he had not yet accepted the surveyors' decision. Jeshwan's wife subsequently claimed that he had
sworn at them as well; she and Amka had a long-standing dispute
from the days when they had lived in adjacent households and
had quarreled about Amka's dogs, which frequently entered her
compound. A few days later, Amka also stopped the wife of
Surend, Satish's son, from working in the new field. The rumor
that Amka had sworn at her as well spread rapidly.

Allegations of Amka's insults became widespread. Such charges
are taken seriously, as profanity to women is viewed in Bhatgaon
as an *adharmik* offense, that is, one "against religion" (Brenneis

1980). Such behavior also raises more practical concerns; Fiji Indian communities are village-exogamous, and few parents would
want their daughters to marry into a community where women
were not safe from such verbal assaults. Although the three
women were the targets of Amka's alleged oaths, from a local perspective the injured parties were their male affines—husbands or
father-in-law—as men are considered responsible for protecting
female relatives from attack, whether physical or verbal.

Satish, as the senior and most widely respected male related to
any of the women and the one closest to Amka in age, was seen
as the primary injured party. As Amka and Satish were both *arya
samajis* and respected men, several leaders of that reform Hindu
association became concerned. After individual discussions with
Amka, Satish, and Surend, they called a *pancayat*, which met
several days later on the edge of Satish's new field.

Satish, his son Surend, and Birendra, a friend of Surend, were
waiting when Amka and seven other association members joined
them. Surend and Birendra were both in their late thirties and
shared a reputation for hot-headedness; the *pancayat* committee
was particularly concerned that they not be aroused. Everyone
walked through the disputed field and agreed that Amka had put
considerable effort into clearing the land. Then they sat together
on a hillside overlooking the land. Satish began by speaking of
his own difficulties with the government, which had given him
this acre but had given some of his older fields to two other villagers. Then Satish said that the *pancayat* had not been called to
deal with the land issue, as the surveyors' decision was final.

Amka then stood and agreed with Satish that, "The political
work is finished; religious work is remaining." The *pancayat*
members then began to discuss the alleged profanities. They had
arranged that Jeshwan's brother's wife, Rina Devi, would be waiting at Satish's house to serve as a witness. They avoided notifying
Jeshwan's wife as all knew of her antipathy toward Amka and
doubted she would be willing to alter her story. It would have
been impossible to construct a satisfactory account of the incident
had she persisted; the *pancayat* does not provide the opportunity
to judge between competing accounts. Rina Devi was called. She
stood fifteen feet away from the men with her young son as she
swore to tell the truth. When Prakash, a *pancayat* member, asked

her about the incident, she responded that Amka had said that it
was not yet their land, but that he had not insulted them. Amka
agreed with her testimony when questioned, admitting that he
might have been somewhat short-tempered. At this point,
Surend's friend Birendra unexpectedly entered the discussion by
claiming that three years earlier Amka had sworn at him for tying
his bullocks in Amka's field, where they ate some rice. The other
men were dumbfounded at this accusation, as they had heard
nothing about it in the past three years. When no one responded
to his complaint, Birendra walked away angrily. As Rina Devi had
been called as a test witness, everyone seemed satisfied that
Amka had probably not sworn at Jeshwan's wife either. At this
point, Amka's son Arun jokingly commented that when he had
seen the witness arrive he had thought that the *pancayat* members had intended to embarrass his father. Amka had known
beforehand of the witness and had agreed to her testifying, as he
knew it would exonerate him, but he had not told Arun. Satish
was angered by Arun's comment and claimed to have known
nothing of the witness. Surend then spoke for the first time and
was furious, displaying the temper for which he was well known.
He shouted that there was no conspiracy against Amka, but that
Arun could have it that way if he so desired. Surend then called
his wife, Amka's third alleged victim, from the house. She also
testified on oath that, although Amka had said that the land was
not theirs, he had not sworn at her. She returned to the house,
and Surend sat down apart from the others. His father, Satish,
made a brief speech, quoting a Fiji Indian political leader on the
virtues of reasoned discussion of disputes. One of the *pancayat*
members then assured Surend that Arun had only been joking,
and Arun apologized for his comment. Surend and Arun then
shook hands, and the *pancayat* ended without further comment.

The Politics of Equality in Bhatgaon

Among Bhatgaon males, an overt egalitarian ideology prevails.
Although ancestral caste appears to influence marriage choice to
some extent (Brenneis 1974:25), it has few daily consequences.
As one villager said, *Gaon me sab barabba hei* (In the village all
are equal). This public ideology is manifest in such practices as

sitting together on the floor during religious events and equal opportunity to speak. The roots of this egalitarian outlook lie in the conditions of immigration and indenture (for a detailed discussion of the development of egalitarian ideology in Fiji, see Brenneis 1979). In Bhatgaon this ideology is reinforced by the relative similarity in wealth throughout the village.

Such egalitarianism, however, is problematic in several important respects. First, not every villager is a potential equal. Gender is a crucial dimension, for men do not consider women their equals. Men and women are both politically active in Bhatgaon, but they take part in very different ways and in different settings. Men are the performers in such public political events as religious speechmaking and insult singing (Brenneis 1978; Brenneis and Padarath 1975). As the case above demonstrated, the conflicts engendering *pancayat* are defined as being between men, even if women are the immediately affected parties. Women may speak in *pancayat* as witnesses, but men organize and run the events (compare Tanna, Lindstrom, this volume). Women's political participation generally occurs in less public settings, as does much male politicking through *talanoa* 'gossip'.

Age also makes a difference. Adolescent boys are accorded less respect than older, married men. As there are no formal criteria or ceremonies to mark the transition from adolescence to social adulthood, disagreements about how one should be treated are common and often lead to serious conflicts between males of different ages. Even after adolescence, age remains an important factor. Thus, Amka and Satish, not Amka and Surend, were treated as the principal parties in the case above.

A second problematic aspect of Bhatgaon egalitarianism is the delicate balance between people who should be equals. One of the hallmarks of such an egalitarian community is that individual autonomy is highly prized. Equals are those who mutually respect each other's freedom of action. As among the Managalase (McKellin, this volume), attempting too overtly to influence the opinions or actions of another is a violation of this equality. Further, individual reputation is central to one's actual social standing. A man's *nam* (name or reputation) is subject to constant renegotiation through his own words and deeds and through those of others. Reputation management is a constant concern in disputes, for conflict often arises from apparent insult, as that to Satish implied by Amka's alleged profanities. The remedy lies in the public rebalancing of one's reputation with that of one's opponent.

A number of men are recognized as *bada admi* 'big men' because of their past participation in village affairs, religious leadership, education, or other personal accomplishment. Both Amka and Satish were considered *bada admi*. They also gain respect through the successful management of the disputes of others. This status is always under stress, however, as obtrusive attempts to assert authority or to intervene in others' problems abuse the autonomy of other men. Successful big men do not exercise their informal power ostentatiously. Continued effectiveness as a respected advisor depends upon an overt reluctance to assume leadership. Even when requested to intervene in a dispute, big men are often unwilling because they fear both being identified with one party's interests and being considered too eager to display power. The willing exercise of authority leads rapidly to its decline.

There is a police station three miles away, but there are no formal social control agencies within Bhatgaon itself. The village has a representative on the district advisory council. He is not, however, empowered to regulate affairs within Bhatgaon. With the decline of caste as an organizational feature of Fiji Indian life, such bodies as caste councils are not available for conflict management. Conflict in Bhatgaon remains largely dyadic, the concern of the contending parties alone, yet as long as the disputes are dyadic, the chances of a settlement are slim. The face-to-face negotiation of a serious dispute is usually impossible, as open accusation or criticism of another is taken as a grievous insult. The offended party might well express his displeasure through clandestine mischief. While such vandalism would not be praised, other villagers would interpret it as the natural result of direct confrontation and would not intervene. Only a *kara admi* 'hard man' would risk such revenge through direct discussion. Most villagers resort to less confrontational strategies. It is difficult to enlist third parties in the management of a conflict, but such triadic participation is crucial. The recruitment of others, not as partisans but as intermediaries and mediators, is a central goal of disputants. Compelling their interest and involvement is therefore a major end in dispute discourse. Not surprisingly, avoidance remains the most common means of managing conflict.

Central to an understanding of conflict discourse in Bhatgaon is a consideration of the sociology of knowledge in the community. As in any society, both what people talk about and how they talk about it are to some extent informed by what they know, what they expect others to know, and what they and others should know. However, just as local organization and social values were transformed during immigration, indenture, and post-plantation life, expectations concerning the social distribution of knowledge were also dramatically altered from those characteristic of north Indian villages.

The radical leveling of Indian immigrant society in Fiji had obvious implications for the allocation of knowledge in Bhatgaon. While in north India the differential distribution of knowledge had both reflected and sustained a system of ranked but interdependent caste groups, in Fiji the groups were at best ill-defined, and the division of labor in part responsible for the division of knowledge no longer existed. Secular knowledge became, in effect, open to all.

In Bhatgaon there was a corresponding democratization of sacred knowledge as well. The reformist *arya samaj* sect has as a central tenet the notion of *sikca* 'instruction'. Members are expected to educate both themselves and others in religious practice and understanding. The stated purpose of most types of public communication, from hymn singing to the *pancayat*, is mental and spiritual improvement. Although reform Hindus are a minority in Bhatgaon, their stress on instruction has had a considerable effect on orthodox Hindu villagers.

The generally egalitarian nature of social life in Bhatgaon has a counterpart in the relatively equal opportunity of all villagers to pursue knowledge, both sacred and secular. The sacred has become shared knowledge, in most cases no longer the property of a particular group. It is important to note that in this community where egalitarian ideals are stressed, continuing evidence of one's membership in a community of peers is necessary. One must not only feel membership but be able publicly to display it. Apparent exclusion from that community is taken very seriously, and knowledge continues to define one's social identity, albeit in ways quite different from those characteristic of India.

A crucial way of demonstrating one's membership is through sharing in what is "common knowledge" in the community— what "everyone" knows. Although sacred and technical knowledge can be included in this, they are relatively unchanging. The real action lies in the dynamics of everyday life, for which familiarity with local events and personalities is necessary. No one, however, knows everything, and some villagers are considerably better informed than are others. This differential participation in common knowledge lies at the root of political talk in Bhatgaon.

Talk in Bhatgaon

A consideration of the *pancayat*—or of any other particular type of verbal event—requires a brief consideration of the larger speech economy of the village. The general features of male speaking in Bhatgaon derive in large part from its character as an acephalous, egalitarian community in which individuals are concerned both with their own reputations and freedom of action and with maintaining those of others, particularly of men with whom they are on good terms. One's enemies present a more complex situation. Their reputations are tempting targets, but too overt or successful an attack might lead to immediate revenge or preclude future reconciliation, as the insult would· be too grievous to remedy.

These broad features of life in Bhatgaon underlie a speech economy the salient feature of which is indirection.[5] One rarely says exactly what one means. Instead, in a variety of public and private performance genres, speakers must resort to metaphor, irony, double entendre, and other subtle devices to signal that they mean more than they have said, as do the Managalase (McKellin, this volume). Such indirection is particularly marked in situations where overt criticism or comment would be improvident or improper. In Bhatgaon public occasions recurrently pose the same dilemma: one must both act and avoid the appearance of such action. The perils of direct confrontation and of direct leadership in the village have fostered oblique and highly allusive speech. Understanding political discourse in Bhatgaon therefore requires both the interpretation of texts in themselves and the unraveling of well-veiled intentions. In such genres as *parbacan* 'religious speeches', such oblique reference is particularly marked. *Parbacan* are oratorical performances with ostensibly religious content given at weekly services. Their contents are not ambiguous in themselves. Thus, it is easy for the Hindi-speaking outsider familiar with Hinduism to follow a discussion of, for example, the fidelity of Sita, the wife of the epic hero Ram. The relationship between such a text and its intended function, however, remains quite opaque. The audience knows that some speakers have no hidden agenda while others are using *parbacan* for political ends. Such indirection both precludes revenge and pricks the curiosity of others who feel they should understand what is really going on. A successful *parbacan* compels the interest and involvement of potential third parties.

A second important feature of men's talk in Bhatgaon is that the culturally ascribed purpose of most genres of public, generally accessible performance is *sikca* 'instruction'. Whatever intentions speakers might have, their texts must focus on such topics as moral and spiritual improvement, and their apparent motives must be didactic (compare Kwara'ae counseling, Watson-Gegeo and Gegeo, this volume). Such genres as *parbacan* work politically by joining sacred teaching with covert secular interests. The political implications of *pancayats* are most overt. They provide authoritative and licit public explanations—though not evaluations—of particular incidents. Villagers can refer to these authoritative accounts in later discussions without fear of revenge.

Private conversation, whether gossip or not, is not limited by this concern for instruction. Topics of conversation may range from national politics to the weather, the selection of topic depending upon participants and their shared interests rather than on generic requirements. Most conversation is neutrally evaluated and seen as not offering the same scope for instruction as speechmaking. Gossip, however, is negatively evaluated as worthless. The activities discussed in gossip are themselves considered worthless or wasteful. What could one possibly learn from such talk, especially given its potential dangers? Despite these negative associations, gossip is a popular activity from which villagers take considerable pleasure.

Talk is evaluated not solely in terms of topic, however. Artfulness, fluency, and wit are highly praised along dimensions specific to each genre. Speechmakers, for example, should display a good knowledge of standard Fiji Hindi, a large Sanskritic vocabulary, and a knack for apposite parables. While gossip is thought to be worthless in itself, men who excel in it are much appreciated.

Finally, genres of verbal activity in Bhatgaon are linked together not only in terms of the expressive repertoire of the village but in an inferential web as well. Given the indirect nature of most public communication, a crucial question is how one learns the background information in terms of which these oblique references can be interpreted. The *pancayat* plays a critical role in village background information.

The *Pancayat*: Constructing Public Knowledge

A *pancayat* is usually convened by the elected officers of a religious association after considerable prodding from disputing members of the group. *Pancayats* involve quite direct talk about specific events and personalities. Allegations which in most contexts would lead to revenge are discussed at length and without repercussions. Given the nature of political life in Bhatgaon, the *pancayat* poses interesting questions: What makes such direct performances possible? What are their implications for the future relationships of the contending parties? And why do participants claim to find them satisfying experiences? These questions can partially be answered by outlining the process by which *pancayats* are arranged, their participants, the formal organization of the session as a communicative event, the contents of testimony, and the effects of the sessions. The *pancayat* must then be located within the broader context of local theories of "therapy."

Pancayat sessions are planned and convened by elected officers of the disputants' religious association. These officers meet as the *antarang samiti* 'confidential committee' and very deliberately discuss the case, choose appropriate witnesses to summon, and otherwise prepare for the session. Often committee members will interview witnesses clandestinely before the session is held. While they are concerned that factual evidence will be presented, they also want to manage the presentation of the evidence in such a way that neither party will be completely vanquished. Reinstating the good reputations of both disputants is a central goal. In the above case, only Jeshwan's wife, the original accuser who was not called as a witness, was not vindicated; from the male point of view, women's reputations are more expendable. Committee members are also concerned with the public evaluation of their own behavior. They must not appear to be too eager or to dominate the proceedings. The successful management of others' conflicts requires at least the appearance of reluctance; the committee remains as far backstage as possible.

The *pancayat* itself is held on neutral ground. Both parties attend along with their supporters, the witnesses, and the committee members. The session is often the first public occasion since the beginning of the dispute to be attended by both disputants. Such joint participation is important in itself.

The *pancayat* audience presents a complex picture. Discourse in the *pancayat* chiefly takes the form of testimony under oath, and various deities compose an important secondary audience insuring the truthfulness of eyewitnesses' accounts. The committee members also play an important role in asking questions and maintaining fairly close control over the issues that witnesses can pursue. The primary audience for the event, however, is not present. This audience includes coreligionists and the village as a whole, and it is from this audience that the *pancayat* derives a great deal of its effectiveness. Before the session is held, an individual villager's knowledge of the case comes through private and frequently factional lines. Such knowledge is unauthorized; it can be discussed with close and trusted friends but cannot be drawn upon in public talk. As in Tanna (Lindstrom, this volume) and the Trobriands (Hutchins, this volume), through *pancayat* testimony an official and definitive account of events crucial to the development of a dispute is publicly constructed. It becomes the basis for later discussion and a new baseline against which the subsequent behavior of the disputants can be measured. It also lets everyone know what happened between the parties and answers those critical questions raised obliquely in *parbacan* (religious speeches).

The interrogative form of *pancayat* proceedings is another factor in their success. Members of the committee interview a series of witnesses, each of whom has sworn to give truthful testimony. Such oaths are taken quite seriously, although personal animosity can at times interfere, as was feared in the case discussed above. In marked contrast to American courtrooms, there is no adversarial questioning. Only the committee can ask questions, and they ask only those questions to which they already know the answers. Women, who rarely figure in other public events, are called as frequently as men, although the disputes are construed as being between men, even if through their female kin.

The question-answer format has two features of critical importance for the sessions' success. First, questions compel answers (Cf. Goody 1978). An unanswered question is an interactional vacuum, and especially in public contexts, response is necessary. It is likely, furthermore, that the style and degree of directness of an answer are patterned on the same qualities of the question (see Conley et al. 1978 for some suggestive findings in this area). The direct questions put by committee members draw forth terse but equally direct answers.

A second important feature of the question-answer format is suggested by the work of Keenan, Schieffelin, and Platt (1978). In interpreting its extensive use by mothers in speaking with very young children, they suggest that the question-answer pair be considered a single propositional unit. By answering the question—whether verbally or nonverbally—the infant completes the idea begun by its mother. If this notion is applied to the *pancayat*, the committee member's question and the witness's answer compose a single proposition. No one is solely responsible for any claims. Such evasion of personal accountability and the concomitant shared resolution of contention fit well in the acephalous and egalitarian context of Bhatgaon. The public narrative is constructed through the propositions collaboratively stated by questioner and witness. The committee is not presenting an account of its own but is contributing to its composition.

The orchestration of *pancayats* as events is a delicate job. The appropriate witnesses must be located and their accounts compared and checked. The planning involved, however, cannot be evident to the disputants or the neutrality of the committee might be challenged. Witnesses and audience alike must be carefully controlled. The perils posed by extraneous issues are clear in the case above. In contrast to the Kpelle moot, the *pancayat* by no means involves a full airing of grievances, since potential hostile responses are not denied but carefully avoided. *Pancayat* testimony is confined to a particular incident from which the dispute is considered to stem. The committee has a clear prospective interest in future relationships between the disputants, but a constrained, unemotional, and retrospective focus is the most effective way of insuring a successful outcome.

A final crucial feature of *pancayats* is the manner in which they end. After the last witness there is no summing up, no discussion, and no decision by the committee. The disputants are not embarrassed by any directly suggested solution, and the committee members do not overstep their roles. Testimony establishes a single and noncontradictory account of crucial events. These publicly accomplished facts are seen to stand on their own. The disputants usually shake hands without much conversation, serving as both a public statement of the resumption of amicable relations between them and a signal that the session is over. The participants may linger, but they talk about other subjects. It is important to understand that no consensus is articulated as authoritative, and no decision is made. A cooperative and binding account of a contested incident is accomplished, and interested villagers are left to draw their own conclusions and interpretations. Everyone's autonomy is maintained.

Dramatic Gestures

In the preceding section I explored the *pancayat* as a shared social occasion, an event in which communicative form, political flexibility, and concern for the values of individual autonomy and reputation are closely interwoven. In this section my focus remains on the *pancayat* as communicative event, but I am more concerned with questions raised by the striking contrasts between its features and those suggested by Gibbs for therapeutic talk. The *pancayat* is clearly a supportive context, one in which the reward of respectful treatment as a worthy social equal is critical. It is not, however, an event in which just any kind of talk is permitted, in terms of either content or style. Further, there is no denial of reciprocity in that speakers are still accountable for the conduct of their talk and not sheltered from anger or revenge should they go beyond acceptable limits. These two elements are critical for the cathartic quality of much therapeutic talk. In their absence, how does the *pancayat* work as a psychologically satisfying event for those involved?

Any valid measure of "psychological satisfaction" was beyond both my intent and my ability when I went to the field. It was clear, however, that many villagers valued the *pancayat* for reasons quite apart from its role in developing a public narrative. One reason was clearly its association with archaic Hindu institutions, a very important quality for *arya samajis* in particular. Further, the *pancayat* was often discussed in aesthetic terms: how well staged was a particular *pancayat*, how well did it hang together, how well spoken were its participants? In short, the *pancayat* as a whole fits Bauman's definition of verbal performance (1977:11), "involving on the part of the performer(s) an assumption of responsibility to an audience for the way in which communication is carried out, above and beyond its referential content." A *pancayat* is more than its topic, for aesthetic pleasure, or pleasure expressed in aesthetic terms, is central to it. In the preceding section I discussed in detail some of the nonreferential features of the *pancayat*, especially the basic organizational fact that it is coperformance, an event relying upon cooperation and the coordination of numerous people's efforts. In this section I will concentrate on some aspects of local aesthetic theory and its confluence with notions of personal experience and emotion. While these ideas are not elaborated or associated in very systematic ways with each other, they provide a missing link between social action and individual satisfaction in the *pancayat*.

There are two salient features in Bhatgaon villagers' discussion of emotion and expressiveness. First, the word in local Hindi for emotion or feelings—*bhaw*—is the same as that for gesture or display. Second, none of the feelings glossed by *bhaw* seem to be individually experienced ones, at least as people spoke of them. *Bhaw*, "feelings," are not viewed as internal states.

A distinctive element here is the explicit link between the language of emotion and expressiveness and theories of performance. It is indeed very difficult to separate ethnopsychological from aesthetic notions; in articulating the bases of their enjoyment or appreciation of particular events, villagers also articulate their sense of self and experience.

The Hindi word *bhaw* derives etymologically from the Sanskrit *bhava*. *Bhava* is linked with a second Sanskrit term, *rasa*, in the central theory of classical Hindu poetics, usually known as *rasa-bhava* theory. *Rasa* refers to "moods," or, among more poetic translators, "flavors," impersonal, universal sentiments. *Bhava* is usually translated as "feelings," individualized, experienced, situationally specific. The role of drama, and of artistic endeavor more broadly, is to provide the opportunity for audiences to share in the experience of the nonindividualized, universal moods.

> In a play, what the actor acts is not the central mood of love or grief. He acts out the conditions that excite that mood and the responses that follow from it. . . . The Indian theorists spell this out in great detail, prescribing for each of the *rasas* the correlative consequents, the kinds of dramatis personae, the gestures and scenery and kinds of diction, thus analyzing content into forms. The feelings of an individual are based on personal, accidental, incommunicable experience. Only when they are ordered, depersonalized and rendered communicable by prescriptions do they participate in *rasa*. . . . *Rasa* is a depersonalized condition of the self, an imaginary system of relations. (Ramanujan 1974:128)

In contrast to usual Western notions of the locus of emotion being in the individual and to those regionally Pacific ideas of "emotion words . . . as statements about the relationship between a person and an event" (Lutz 1982:113), *rasa-bhava* theory seems to locate mood in events themselves. The nonindividualized mood—*rasa*—is more highly valued than the personal and inexpressible feeling associated with it. Performers are not "expressing" themselves in any way; they are rather helping construct a shared emotional experience for the audience.

Specific *rasas* are integrally linked with specific kinds of interpersonal arrangements, often redundantly encoded through costume, makeup, gesture, and setting as well. The example of Hindi films might be helpful here. They are full of what most Westerners see as stock characters and a predictable range of stock scenes, more like a series of tableaux than a drama in the Western sense. These elements, however, are seen by Indian audiences as conventionally engendering particular responses shared by the audience as a whole.

While the term *rasa* is not heard in Bhatgaon, it is clear that *bhaw* is related in more than etymological ways to the dramaturgic and psychological notion of *bhava*.[6] *Bhaw* is used most frequently in compound constructions in religious discourse, as in *prembhaw* ('love' + *bhaw*), which carries the multidimensional meaning of a situation of interpersonal amity, the display of the mutually respectful and amiable demeanor which embodies this amity, and the experience of that state. *Prembhaw* is definitively associated with the weekly meetings of religious associations and linked through that event with such performance genres as *parbacan* and hymn singing. Moral didacticism—the willingness to teach and be taught—is a critical component of *prembhaw*. Clearly defined turns, a focus on moral or spiritual improvement—on the "message"—and the willingness to attend to what an individual is saying are among other features encoding *prembhaw* and enabling its experience.

The *pancayat* both instances and allows for the experience of *prembhaw*. Although organized differently from the religious meeting, the *pancayat* similarly demands cooperative coperformance. Strict turn-alternation, mutually respectful demeanor, and its clearly marked status as an event are social and individual gestures of amity. Strong emotion need not, indeed must not, be expressed in such a context. Central to its success is the participation of all present in a depersonalized, and hence less dangerous, experience of shared good will. Therefore such eruptions as those of participants not fully primed for their parts—as in Birendra's outburst over an alleged swear three years earlier—can be especially threatening. The accounts developed in the *pancayat*, and the means by which those narratives are cooperatively constructed, allow participants to join in an "imaginative system of relations" (Ramanujan 1974:128), one in which a shared sense of social stability and common purpose in a frequently tumultuous social world is possible.

My analysis here clearly relies on attention to very localized and particularistic materials. If Gibbs possibly erred in using Western theories to explicate the effectiveness of the Kpelle house palaver, does this paper go too far in the other direction, eschewing any cross-cultural applicability for the sake of providing a culturally rooted account? I would suggest that ethnographically rooted analyses can indeed have broader heuristic and substantive implications.

First, studies make it increasingly clear that the "political" and the "psychological" do not constitute easily definable, let alone clearly separate domains. Rather, sociopolitical features of life in particular communities interpenetrate cultural theories of personhood and experience. The Fiji Indian situation is a striking example of how closely entwined the two strands can be and of how rapidly they can change. Bhatgaon villagers are engaged in an ongoing process of interpreting and redefining cultural notions and applying them to new problems and situations. Their theories are "partial" because they are emergent, responding to a social world already dramatically transformed and still changing.

Second, Fiji Indian theories concerning conflict and its resolution proceed from somewhat different premises than those shared by many Western analysts. Scholarly treatments often, in effect, "psychologize" conflict, making social process—at least in its more disruptive aspects—sometimes seem to represent individual processes writ large. In such treatments, frustrations unexpressed lead to aggression, and individual aggressiveness leads to broader conflict.[7] Gibbs's arguments, and those of many other legal anthropologists as well, fall firmly within this tradition of psychodynamic analysis. Gibbs argues that the individual catharsis and release afforded by the moot help reduce the likelihood of future conflict and that personal therapy serves social ends as well.

In Bhatgaon, on the other hand, what we might consider psychological is made social. The internal self so critical to Gibbs's model is peripheral to the *pancayat*. Instead, "persons" are political actors, embodied in large part in their reputations, what others think and say of them. As political solution, the *pancayat* allows the public restoration of good names. The possibilities of shared sentiment critical to satisfaction with the event, however, are socially based and can only be socially experienced.

Notes

Acknowledgements. Ram Padarath has been a patient friend and invaluable colleague in working through a number of the ethnographic puzzles pursued in this paper. An earlier version was presented at the Pitzer College conference. I am indebted to fellow participants for their admonitions and encouragement. Geoff White and Karen Watson-Gegeo were particularly helpful in sustaining the general framework and goals while gently guiding our individual contributions. Wynne Furth, Roger Abrahams, Ronald Macaulay, and an anonymous reader for the Stanford University Press also provided valuable criticism.

1. During my thirteen months of fieldwork in 1971–72 I attended three *pancayats* and heard of only four others taking place during that time. An exhaustive survey of *pancayats* was impossible, but I am certain that I learned about almost all the more or less successful ones after they had taken place. Subsequent fieldwork in 1975, 1980, and 1984 indicates that *pancayats* have become even less common events. I was welcome at the three *pancayats* I attended but was asked not to bring the tape recorder in case something went wrong; only successful *pancayats* were to go on the record.

2. With Indian independence in 1947 village *pancayats* were reorganized or, in some cases, created from scratch by the national government for local-level development or as alternatives to formal courts. A wide range of village studies in India mention *pancayats*, at least in passing; for particularly useful discussion, see Baxi and Galanter (1979), Cohn (1959), Hayden (1984), and Mechievitz and Galanter (1982). The most thorough and revealing study of the communicative dimensions of a contemporary traditional *pancayat* in India has been Robert Hayden's work with the Nandiwallas of Maharashtra (1981). In a recent explicit comparison with the Fiji Indian *pancayat*, Hayden (1987) argues that the Indian *pancayat* is primarily concerned with questions of evaluation and response, in contrast to the "fact finding" central to the Fiji Indian event. The style and organization of the two kinds of *pancayats* as communicative events are strikingly different, the Nandiwalla version being exceptionally raucous and full of conversational overlap. These differences in part reflect the considerably more authoritative position of the Nandiwalla *pancayat*; its role is taken for granted, while the occurrence, let alone the effectiveness, of its Fiji Indian counterpart, relies on delicate negotiation.

3. Since Gibbs's article was published in 1963 a wide range of therapies not premised upon the idea of catharsis have become increas-

ingly salient in the United States (see Watson-Gegeo and Gegeo, this volume, for a discussion of cognitive therapy). This paper is concerned solely with contrasts between Fiji Indian practice and that model of therapy Gibbs presents.

4. The minimal role of the "self" in Fiji Indian ethnopsychology has a counterpart in the more general Hindu notion of "open" personhood (Marriott n.d.). The highly "concrete-relational," contextually specific person descriptions found by Shweder and Bourne (1984:172) in Orissa contrast strongly with the more abstract descriptions given by Americans and illustrate an apparent Oriya reluctance to think of the "self" as a consistent, rigidly bounded unit. See also Surya (1969) for a discussion of related difficulties he had in applying Western notions of "ego" in psychotherapeutic work with north Indians.

5. I have characterized several critical dimensions of "indirection" as communicative practice in a recent survey article (Brenneis 1987:504–5): "First, speakers 'mean' more or other than what they say. Meaning does not lie in the text alone; the literal message would be inadequate or misleading in itself. Second, indirection implies something about the speaker's stance vis-à-vis his or her message. Although worked out in many different ways, indirection usually allows the avoidance of full responsibility for what one has said. Third, listeners are not only allowed but compelled to draw their own conclusions. The audience is actively involved. Finally, indirection has a formal dimension. Formal features of the texts or aspects of the organization of the communicative event itself both make messages oblique and signal that more is going on than meets the ear. Indirection joins together form (how something is said or, beyond that, staged); function (both individual intentions and the audience's definition of what is taking place); and meaning (the overt and covert content of what is being said)."

6. There is a more direct link between Indian rural culture in Fiji and the literate Hindu great tradition than there might be for most mainland Indian villages as Hindu missionaries, both orthodox and reform, have been very active in Fiji, drawing upon and using a wide variety of textual materials which have subsequently been adopted by villagers. The reform *(Arya Samaj)* missionaries particularly took classical Hindu notions such as *bhava* as rhetorical focuses for their work.

7. One of the clearest discussions of the "psychologization" of conflict in Western scholarship is in Koch's (1974:5–7) concise essay on anthropological theories of warfare.

References

Bauman, Richard

1977   Verbal Art as Performance. *In* Verbal Art as Performance. Bauman, ed. Rowley: Newbury House.

Baxi, Upendra, and Marc Galanter

1979   *Panchayat* Justice: An Indian Experiment in Legal Access. *In* Access to Justice: Emerging Issues and Perspectives. Mauro Cappelletti and Bryant Garth, eds. Alphen aan den Rijn: Sijthoff and Noordhoff.

Brenneis, Donald

1974   Conflict and Communication in a Fiji Indian Community. Ph.D. dissertation. Department of Social Relations, Harvard University.

1978   The Matter of Talk: Political Performances in Bhatgaon. Language in Society 7:159–70.

1979   Conflict in Bhatgaon: The Search for a Third Party. *In* The Indo-Fijian Experience. Subramani, ed. St. Lucia: University of Queensland Press.

1980   Strategies of Offense Choice: Malice and Mischief in Bhatgaon. Canberra Anthropologist 3:28–42.

1984   Grog and Gossip in Bhatgaon: Style and Substance in Fiji Indian Conversation. American Ethnologist 11: 487–506.

1987   Talk and Transformation. Man (n.s.) 22:499–510.

Brenneis, Donald, and Ram Padarath

1975   About Those Scoundrels I'll Let Everyone Know: Challenge Singing in a Fiji Indian Community. Journal of American Folklore 88:283–91.

Cohn, Bernard

1959   Some Notes on Law and Change in North India. Economic Development and Social Change 8:79–93.

Conley, J., W. O'Barr, and E. Lind

1978   The Power of Language: Presentational Style in the Courtroom. Duke Law Journal 1375–99.

Gerow, Edwin

1974   Dramatic Criticism. *In* The Literatures of India: An Introduction. E. Dimock, Jr., et. al., eds. Chicago: University of Chicago Press.

Gibbs, James
1963 The Kpelle Moot: A Therapeutic Model for the Informal Settlement of Disputes. Africa 33:1–11.

Goody, Esther
1978 Towards a Theory of Questions. *In* Questions and Politeness: Strategies in Social Interaction. Goody, ed. Cambridge: Cambridge University Press.

Hayden, Robert M.
1981 "No One Is Stronger Than the Caste": Arguing Dispute Cases in an Indian Caste *Pancayat*. Ph.D. dissertation. Department of Anthropology, State University of New York at Buffalo.
1984 A Note on Caste *Panchayats* and Government Courts in India: Different Kinds of Stages for Different Kinds of Performances. Journal of Legal Pluralism and Unofficial Law 22:43–52.
1987 Turn-Taking, Overlap and the Task at Hand: Ordering Speaking Turns in Legal Settings. American Ethnologist 14:251–70.

Ito, Karen
1985 *Ho'oponopono*, "To Make Right": Hawaiian Conflict Resolution and Metaphor in the Construction of Family Therapy. Culture, Medicine and Psychiatry 9:201–17.

Keenan, E., B. Schieffelin, and M. Platt
1978 Questions of Immediate Concern. *In* Questions and Politeness: Strategies in Social Interaction. Goody, ed. Cambridge: Cambridge University Press.

Koch, Klaus-Friedrich
1974 The Anthropology of Warfare. Reading: Addison-Wesley.

Labov, William, and David Fanshel
1977 Therapeutic Discourse: Psychotherapy as Conversation. New York: Academic Press.

Lutz, Catherine
1982 The Domain of Emotion Words of Ifaluk. American Ethnologist 9:113–28.

Marriott, McKim
n.d. The Open Hindu Person and the Humane Sciences. Unpublished ms.

Meschievitz, Catherine, and Marc Galanter
1982 In Search of *Nyaya Panchayats*: The Politics of a Moribund In-

stitution. *In* The Politics of Informal Justice, volume 2. R. Abel, ed. New York: Academic Press.

Myers, Fred R., and Donald L. Brenneis

1984 Introduction: Language and Politics in the Pacific. *In* Dangerous Words: Language and Politics in the Pacific. D. L. Brenneis and F. R. Myers, eds. New York: New York University Press.

Parsons, Talcott

1951 The Social System. Glencoe, IL: The Free Press.

Ramanujan, A. K.

1974 Dramatic Criticism. *In* The Literatures of India: An Introduction. E. Dimock, Jr., et. al., eds. Chicago: University of Chicago Press.

Shweder, Richard A., and Edmund J. Bourne

1984 Does the Concept of the Person Vary Cross-Culturally? *In* Culture Theory: Essays on Mind, Self and Emotion. Richard A. Shweder and Robert A. LeVine, eds. Cambridge: Cambridge University Press.

Surya, N. C.

1969 Ego Structure in the Hindu Joint Family: Some Considerations. *In* Mental Health Research in Asia and the Pacific. W. Caudill and T.-Y. Lin, eds. Honolulu: East-West Center Press.

White, Geoffrey

1979 Some Social Uses of Emotion Language: A Melanesian Example. Paper read at the annual meeting of the American Anthropological Association. Cincinnati, Ohio.

PART III

CONFLICT, AMBIGUITY, AND THE RHETORIC OF INDIRECTION

Disentangling Indirectly: The Joking Debate in Fijian Social Control

Andrew Arno

DISENTANGLING is an appropriate term for the way Fijian villagers in Southern Lau use talk, in the context of culturally defined communication events, to deal with conflict (Arno 1980). To disentangle is to set something straight—something intricate, flexible, and multistranded, like a fishing net or a complex of ongoing social relationships. This is just what Fijians do as they go about the detailed work of discussing and evaluating one another's actions. Such talk is a commonplace of everyday life, crosscutting all sorts of activities and events, but the villagers who were my hosts in 1971 and 1972 on the island of Yanuyanu[1] (Lau group) did not explicitly use a term like disentangling to describe their own conflict-management discussions. Instead, the metaphorical resonance of the term for the observer of Fijian conflict discourse derives from the centrality of the concept of *dodonu*, straightness or propriety, in such talk. In serious public discussions, Fijians emphasize the goal of the conflict-management process—straightness—rather than the problem state of entanglement.

The word *dodonu* is used to describe things that are right, proper, and appropriate, such as correct social relationships. But it also refers to things that are physically straight: a good timber, a path, or a sailing course. The metaphor of entanglement is used to convey the notion of deceit in social relations, as found in the term *fereferea* 'intricately tangled'. Another term for entangling, *vakataotaka* 'tangled, snared', is used rhetorically by speakers in one of the debates I present in this study (Appendix A: 028, 042, 044, 047, 064), and that usage suggests the salience of the metaphor and draws its force from the idea that entanglement caused by inappropriate behavior can interfere with group activities, dragging social action to a halt (compare White, Boggs and Chun, and Watson-Gegeo and Gegeo, this volume).

Problems in social relationships can be talked about as entanglement, but Fijians do not extend the metaphor to conflict-
management discourse. The verbal processes by which they
pursue social correction are largely covert. In a sense, they prefer
not to say explicitly what they are doing when they "straighten"
relationships. Despite the value they place on social straightfor-
wardness, Lauans are unlikely to deal with social discord in the
open, controlled format of explicit group discussion, as do the
A'ara, for example (see White, this volume). The difference between the two styles (A'ara and Lauan) is dramatic. Unrestricted
and earnest discussion across lineage or subclan lines concerning
wrongdoing would be almost unthinkable in the Lauan village.
Certain modern communication events, such as meetings of the
cooperative societies, land-rights hearings, or island political
meetings, are specifically designed to produce open, public discussion, but when they touch on individual or group misconduct,
traditional rules of etiquette generally prevail and limit frank interchange.

The indirect style of conflict discourse prevalent in Lau, I will
argue, is related to the logic of traditional Fijian political structure and to traditional notions of individual psychology. Joking is
the preferred strategy for veiled or privileged public discussion of
misconduct, and it is within the general context of joking that
veiba 'debate' can be understood to function in social control.

Debating was a popular form of impromptu entertainment
among men engaged in informal kava drinking during the time I
lived on Yanuyanu. It is a verbal game—a well-defined, playful
form of interaction in which serious issues might nonetheless be
ventilated. In tone, a debate might vary from a measured and dignified exchange of arguments to a raucous, free-swinging verbal
brawl. Here I will contrast two debates that I recorded on Yanuyanu. In one the rather abstract issue of the impact of kava drinking on national development in Fiji is assessed in a measured way
that approaches the form of a serious discussion. The other debate is virtually a naked joking attack on the habits of a specific
individual. Comparison of the two clarifies the relationship between the social function of the particular debate and its specific
sociolinguistic form, which varies along such pragmatic lines as
code selection, tempo, turn taking, pitch register, and laughter.

Compared to the specific genre of *veiba*, joking is a pervasive, polymorphic pattern of interaction in Lau that is indicative of, and indeed constitutive of, specific social relationships (Arno 1976b). Among people in the appropriate social categories, joking can take a multitude of forms and vary in strength from weak and innocuous to painfully intense. The significance of joking in Lauan social control is that it invalidates anger and physical aggression as a response to allegations of wrongdoing.

I will argue that with respect to conflict issues *veiba* functions as a form of joking. As play (Bateson 1972), it disclaims serious intent and therefore provides a protective frame within which disagreements can be expressed publicly without provoking anger or shame. As the issue being debated moves closer to the dangerous zone of direct personal accusation, the joking dimension becomes more and more dominant, and sociolinguistic features of the debate signal the transition.

The question of precisely how a communication event such as a debate is related to politics and to individual psychology raises basic theoretical issues. Strathern (1982), in the context of New Guinea ethnography, comments critically on the general theoretical trend in political anthropology away from a structural-functional, systemic view that describes the normative and institutional framework of individual action toward an individual-centered, intention-oriented perspective in which actors' options and strategies are seen to generate political structures. In the anthropological study of language and society, a similar movement can be discerned. The theoretical situation is complex, however, because two disciplinary traditions are involved. From the point of view of linguistics, the ethnography of communication (e.g., Hymes 1962) represents a movement from the traditional language system focus, which is structural, to consideration of concrete situations of language use, which is actor oriented. Within anthropology, however, the ethnography of communication actually represented an extension of the existing structural-functional approach into a new area of ethnography. Ethnographers of communication were at first intent on showing that communication is not an autonomous system obedient to internal rules of grammar, but is instead governed by social rules and part of an encompassing sociocultural system. The seeds of the paradigm change had been sown, however, because sociolinguists working within the anthropological tradition remained sensitive to the intention of the individual speaker (e.g., Hymes 1972). Gumperz (1982) completes the cycle, so to speak, in developing a strategic, actor-focused approach to the integrated analysis of social and linguistic variables.

Gumperz's approach is especially useful in the analysis of modern urban societies because it deals with the essential, small-scale accommodations that people in complex, multiethnic social situations must make in negotiating an order sufficient to sustain their fleeting, highly contingent interactions. But Gumperzian "discourse strategy" analysis clearly does not replace Hymesian ethnography of communication. The negotiated miniorder of the specific interethnic conversation is constructed *from* relevant standardized prescriptive models of the sort that the ethnography of communication describes. In the analysis of politics, too, the focus on individual intentionality does not account for the larger structural forces that come into play (Strathern 1982). Giddens (1979) places the problem within the larger perspective of the social sciences as a whole, arguing that the reconciliation of structural and phenomenological approaches is a central problem in the development of general social theory (see also Myers and Brenneis 1984).

Studies of communication about conflict, such as those included in this volume, represent a valuable opportunity for exploring the gap in social theory between explanations of the powerful constraints on action imposed by existing social structure and explanations of the ultimately creative process whereby discrete social acts constitute that structure. Elements of the social order are explicitly at issue in communication events of this kind. In the disentangling process we observe the microevolutionary forces of communication at work, creating structure while simultaneously using it to express *ad hoc* strategy.

Disentangling events and processes represent clear instances of control communication (Arno 1985a). The *way* disentangling communication takes place in a particular sociocultural setting is directly related to the nature of the encompassing social process, and lines of causation run in both directions.

Disentangling and Social Structure

Social relationships in small groups of intimately interdependent people—the kinds of groups that characterize villages in Lau and elsewhere in the Pacific islands—constitute the basis for cooperation, stability, and predictability in everyday life. But in their richness and complexity, such relationships also inevitably include the darker shadings of resentment, jealousy, and fear that contribute to the psychological texture of social life and, as mechanisms of control, help to maintain the structural configuration of a group. This psychosociological chiaroscuro is maintained by a dynamic process of adjustment whereby the structurally useful (see Coser 1956) but overtly inhibiting and negatively evaluated dimensions of social relationships—such as anger, conflict, and rivalry—are themselves controlled and limited.

Talk that centers on how group members do—and ought to— treat one another is perhaps a universal mechanism in all kinds of groups for creating and maintaining a balance between evolving systems of action and expectation—a balance that translates into a group sense of propriety. Elsewhere I have argued that control communication, which includes forms of discourse such as disentangling sessions that explicitly locate conflict behavior in frameworks of explanation and evaluation, is related in form as well as in substantive content to structural communication, which is the nonreflective acting-out of social relationships in everyday life (Arno 1985a, 1985b). It follows that, while the generic communication event of a disentangling session may be universal, particular groups will vary in how such sessions are carried out, according to their own politico-psychological formations.

In an ideal type of egalitarian group, where one would expect standards of conduct to be general rather than tied closely to elaborate social status categories, individuals may be responsible for working out mutually satisfactory relationships within permitted frameworks. In this kind of situation, many choices and justifications are available in the process of shaping social relationships. Discretionary judgments must be allowed to individual actors, and straightforward negotiation aimed at consensus can predominate in public group discussions of the members' behavior. In broad terms, this is how I would read White's account of A'ara disentangling (this volume).

In southern Lau, however, social categories and standards for interaction across and within them are esteemed for their fixity, and elements of proper behavior are often precisely specified (compare Western Samoa, Duranti, this volume). Both particular social relationships, between individuals and groups, and the body of traditional custom are *tudei* (permanent, firmly fixed). The element of individual, mutual consent in determining the form of social relationships is characteristically subordinated to an ideal of conformity to an established pattern. For persons in given reciprocal relationship categories, there are certain proper and respectable ways to come and go, sit, talk, drink, eat, and dress (see Hocart 1929, Thompson 1940). The general tenor of each kind of relationship is also specified, and open, direct negotiation about such matters may therefore itself be a form of impropriety. Because a single, fixed standard is assumed, and that standard is invested with an almost reverential aura of respect for *i tovo vakavanua* 'customs of the land', allegations of failure to conform are highly charged. Under the circumstances, a person who is openly criticized is put at risk of being labeled bad or unrespectable, rather than simply in disagreement with other members of the group, as may be the case when a variety of standards are available for invocation. But although it is the public nature of criticism that makes it highly charged, it need not be—and in fact seldom is—very open by Western standards. Relatively private criticism of an individual's behavior, even though out of his hearing and that of his close patrilineal relatives, is a source of anxiety. I would argue that the covert nature of such talk encourages a heightened sensitivity to it among alleged wrongdoers.

This is not to suggest, of course, that Lauan social relationships actually are fixed or that negotiation about statuses and roles does not take place. Individual pairs of spouses, siblings, and parents and children, for example, evolve their own distinctive ways of realizing their relationships. But when conflict becomes recognized and talked about, people assume that a rigid code is being applied. This assumption then shapes the processes of adjustment and change that are used to straighten out relationships that have become entangled with confusion and dissatisfaction.

Because proper behavior among kin is not thought of as something negotiable, problems in relationships are considered reducible to bad behavior by one or both parties. Fijians argue that if people conform to proper standards of conduct conflict will not arise. When conflict does appear it is not viewed as an inherent part of the social system. Rather, someone is at fault. And fault is not offset or diluted by being distributed among the parties. A man might be severely criticized for speaking disrespectfully of his elder brother, for example, even though the elder brother himself might be regarded as virtually a criminal in his own right (Arno 1980:353). Furthermore, and perhaps consistent with the notion that the individual is not capable of creating new forms of *proper* behavior, blame for bad conduct is not just focused on the individual but is generalized to his or her patrilineal kin group. In this sense the kin group can be thought of as generating the behavior of its members.

Given its weight and importance, public criticism in the Lauan village must be handled carefully, and it is generally undertaken indirectly through joking. In turn, because everyone understands the reason for its use, this indirection reinforces the power of criticism. Indirection is carried to such extreme that the total process of social control, or adjusting relationships, is distributed to different segments of the community according to the positions of the relevant parties within the overall relationship system. To understand how the system works, and how joking and the specific genre of *veiba* fits into it, it is necessary to consider both the social structure and the communication system of the group.

Social Structure and Communication on Yanuyanu

The six hundred or so residents on Yanuyanu depend heavily on traditional subsistence agriculture and fishing, but they also produce copra and handicrafts for cash, which they need for school fees and nontraditional goods and services. They are linked to neighboring islands through marriage and traditional exchange networks that channel the flow of forms of wealth such as tapa, mats, carved wooden utensils, and canoes. Garden products and house timbers also form part of the exchange cycles, as do ritual items like kava, polished whales' teeth, and ceremonial performances (Arno 1976b). Yanuyanu island's traditional political organization is centralized in form but not in practice. Villagers belong to patrilineal descent groups that form the constituent elements of exclusive, land-owning subclans, *mataqali* (Arno 1979b:46; and see France 1969; Sahlins 1962). One of the subclans, and one descent group within it, owns the "paramount chief" title for the island and provides an incumbent for the position. Each of the other subclans also owns a title which is an essential part of the traditional island political organization (compare Samoan political organization, Duranti, this volume). Conceptually, the chief and the temporal and spiritual powers represented by the chiefly office are part of every discussion and decision regarding community matters. For example, the ideal of "chiefly" *(vakaturaga)* behavior is often invoked. Yet in matters of conflict management and dispute settlement, as in many other day-to-day economic and political functions of the community, the paramount chief seldom becomes directly involved. An incumbent chief may intervene in village affairs with great impact, but normally the patrilineal descent groups are the responsible units of negotiation and decision making.

The kinship system, which is of the two-section dravidian type (Groves 1963), provides the pervasive social framework within which interpersonal interaction is carried out. Relationships are generally talked about in reciprocal terms: *veitamani*, parent–child or father–child; *veitinani*, mother-child; *veitacini*, siblings of the same sex; *veiganeni*, cross-sex siblings; *veivugoni*, in-laws; *veitavaleni*, cross-cousins; and others. In each case a specific way of interacting is considered proper, and each way is, in essence, a pattern of message exchange. The relationship system, therefore, can be looked at as a prescriptive program for communication within the group. For example, to be in-laws is to practice mutual avoidance and exchange messages through third parties, while to be brother and sister is to avoid certain topics of conversation.

The kinds of communication patterns required by the relationship system can be distinguished from one another along lines of relative freedom and restriction (Arno 1976a). In some cases, restriction is almost total, and virtually no direct communication is allowed, while in other relationships almost any kind of message is allowed. The prescriptive patterns are also distinguished from one another in that they are either symmetrical or asymmetrical in the application of restrictions between the participants in an interaction. When restrictions are very strong and the prohibition is mutual, symmetrical avoidance is called for, as it is between parents-in-law and children-in-law. Brothers and sisters practice a partial form of symmetrical avoidance in that they must not, for example, make or hear sexual references in one another's presence.

The other symmetrical prescriptive pattern of communication among relatives is the almost total freedom from restraint allowed to cross-cousins. An important qualification of this freedom, however, is that it must not be exercised in a way that denies the symmetrical character of the interaction—as, for example, by attempting to give orders. Moreover, when messages go beyond the ordinary exchange of information and opinion to touch on sensitive, shame-producing topics, joking must be employed.

Asymmetrical communication takes place when restrictions are imposed on one party to the interaction but not the other. A parent, for example, is free to address criticism, advice, and orders to a child, but the child must not respond in kind. By definition, an order is a demand that cannot be answered except by compliance; there should be no "talking back," either in words or in failure to act.

As Bateson observed (1958), patterns and dynamics of message exchange actually constitute social relations. In this case, for example, the giving of orders *is* authority or the exertion of power. The prescriptive communication patterns in Lau, then, map onto the social groupings in such a way as to define their organizational character. Symmetrical patterns, both avoidance and joking, define relations between a person and his or her other section relatives, who belong to other subclans. Within the patrilineal subclans, however, asymmetrical or "authority" communication is enforced, which is to say that the subclan is hierarchical in character. Goffman (1979) makes a similar observation about the relation of communication to hierarchy in his assertion that asymmetrical rituals of interaction do not reflect social hierarchy so much as constitute it; "they are the shadow *and* the substance" (1979:6). Fishman (1978) makes the same point in discussing asymmetries in communication between men and women in American society.

What Hymes (1962) has called the total *means of speaking* in any community includes a set of recurring, rule-governed communication events that are defined by the transmission of recognized messages as a central focus. This set of communication events can be thought of as the group's *communication system*, which is the medium through which its social structure is expressed. By way of analogy, the group's language system produces sentences and larger units of discourse, while the expressions produced through the medium of the communication system are social processes, such as economics, politics, and religion (Arno 1983).

On Yanuyanu, communication system elements, each with its own range of settings, participants, topics, and linguistic features, include: *bose*, meetings; *veivosaki*, conversation or discussion; *veitalanoa*, anecdote exchange; *veileti*, argument; and *vakavulica*, "teaching" or scolding. As realized in concrete social occasions, such as informal kava-drinking sessions, these forms of talk constitute a medium through which the social process of disentangling or conflict management is expressed on the island.

Within each patrilineal descent group in the village, seniority, based on order of birth, determines the direction and character of communication flow. The junior of two patriline members must accept orders and criticism from the senior without argument or attempts as self justification. Within the social hierarchy thus created, the scope of communication processes aimed at disentangling—restoring the balance of negative and positive feelings among members—is quite narrow. Communication about conflict within the group tends to be congruent with, or in the structural idiom of, normal intragroup communication. An ongoing state of overt conflict, therefore, is generally signified by mutual avoidance rather than by confrontation, and a restoration of proper relations is brought about by the performance of a ritual apology, *i soro*, in which the junior relative reaffirms his or her subordinate role (Arno 1976a; and cf. Duranti, this volume).[2]

Communication about conflict among the subclans or lineages, however, presents a more complex pattern. While each person is locked into a hierarchical communication system within the lineage, he or she enjoys unrestricted, symmetrical, potentially joking relationships with cross-cousins in the other groups. When allegations of improper behavior by an individual are involved, reprimand, criticism, and scolding within the patriline represent an effective sanction in many cases. But the fact-finding and norm-application functions that are part of the conflict-management process (Arno 1980) are largely allocated to freely communicating groups of cross-cousins.

Shame, Conflict, and Communication

The Fijian folk psychology of conflict provides the motive force for managing entangled relationships through talk. The central concept energizing the process is that of *madua*, shame. The individual wrongdoer is assumed to feel shame vis-à-vis the injured party and the community as a whole, and furthermore, the entire subclan of the wrongdoer is also thought to suffer from a sense of shame because of the individual member's actions. The feeling of shame, itself psychologically uncomfortable—like a bone in the throat, as one informant put it—is expressed behaviorally in a raised level of inhibition in interaction between individuals affected. Even freely interacting cross-cousins may avoid one another to a degree if some improper behavior by one has caused an injury to the other. Only when the air has been cleared, by a ritual apology, for example, can normal relations be resumed. Even then, however, shame is not entirely eradicated. Egregious wrongdoing is never forgotten, even over several generations, and descendants of a notorious patrilineal ancestor will be taxed with his misdeeds if any present circumstances make them salient. This being the case, people are very sensitive to having themselves or their lineage relatives talked about adversely.

A person should not talk about, and more especially should not hear others talk about, the misconduct of patrilineal relatives. He or she can neither defend nor condemn such relatives, and the individual exposed to public comments of this kind is assumed to suffer intense shame—demonstrated by remaining silent and bowing one's head. To prevent such awkward social situations, etiquette prescribes punctilious avoidance of reference to a person's misconduct in front of the wrongdoer's lineage mates. But when one knows—through indirectly conveyed information—that one's relative is indeed being talked about in the village, even an overly lengthy pause in conversation or a momentary but slightly too abrupt silence when one joins a group already engaged in conversation assumes a painful subjective significance.

Shame, personally experienced and brought upon one's patriline, represents a direct sanction for serious misconduct. Perhaps a more effective sanction, however, is brought into play through the dynamics of the hierarchically organized patriline itself. Senior members of the group have no hesitancy in confronting their juniors and correcting their conduct through harsh reprimands (compare senior–junior relationships among Hawaiians; Boggs and Chun, this volume). The weight of this kind of sanction, as with shame, is largely psychological in nature. For many people, especially mature men, it is a powerful sanction, and it draws its strength from a built-in psychosocial conflict associated with Fijian social organization (Arno 1979a). Conflict between unequals—such as fathers and sons in Fijian society (see Williams 1982; Thompson 1940:61; Sahlins 1962:114)—is a structural fault line in hierarchical organizations that must be shored up on rational and emotional levels by ritual and ideology. The sensitivity of the relationship involved, with its deep-seated ambivalence, makes criticism from a senior to a junior male within the patriline especially highly charged psychologically.

As between men and women of the community, the same overall pattern of conflict communication is repeated in two scarcely overlapping systems. A woman takes orders from her seniors and communicates freely with her female cross cousins in the community. Outside the household, however, communication between men and women is limited, with the major links between male and female systems of talk in the village being those between husbands and wives. Married women are in a special structural position, different from that of men, with regard to the patrilines and their communication flows. A married woman is a member of her own patriline but outside the mainstream of its daily activities. In contrast, she is a central actor in all of the activities of the patriline of her husband and children, though not a formal member. She is of but not in the one group and in but not of the other.

From the male point of view, women who have either married in or married out of the patriline represent indirect links that can overcome formal restrictions on communication flow. Members can learn what is being said—especially in the way of adverse criticism—about their lineage mates even though they themselves would be excluded from such talk in order to avoid public shaming.

Both asymmetrical, hierarchically organized communication about conflict within the patriline, which provides the basis for important sanctions in social control, and indirect communication through married female members of the patriline, which lets people know what is being said about members of their group, are important components of the complex system of social control through talk in a Lauan village. But the equally essential and much more visible part of the process takes place in direct, symmetrical communication among cross-cousins of the wrongdoer as they discuss and evaluate his behavior, and in joking, which allows them to confront the accused and hear his side of the story. Although they are functionally parts of the same social process, and can only be understood in relation to one another, the reprimands, criticism, and "instruction" that flow from senior to junior within the patriline have a clear-cut social-control character, while joking—including the debating genre that is the focus of this paper—involves a far greater scope and flexibility for the adjustment of feelings and understanding (cf. the disentangling communication described among the A'ara by White, this volume).

Joking Contrasted with Serious, Formal Discussion

As a speech event, joking in Lau is best described as a sort of antithesis of formal, serious discussion. As Hocart (1929) observes, the most highly esteemed and respected forms of behavior in Lau are conceptualized as "chiefly" (*vakaturaga*). The ideal applies to speech involving serious, formal discussion as well as to other kinds of behavior. Chiefly behavior is not just the way chiefs act; any person can aspire to chiefly ways of comportment and expression and in so doing signify respect for the traditions of the land (compare *gwaunga'i* behavior and high rhetoric talk among the Kwara'ae described by Watson-Gegeo and Gegeo, this volume). Conversely, of course, persons of chiefly rank can be criticized for nonchiefly behavior. The *vakaturaga* ideal translates into everyday communication behavior in such a way as to preclude chatting aimlessly and carelessly. Keeping silent and allowing others to speak is said to indicate an attitude of mutual respect (*veidokai*), which is a basic element of chiefly behavior. Furthermore, sparing use of words is indicative of the value and power of verbal performance (Arno 1976b). For example, chiefs do not need to cajole or persuade people, and they are institutionally insulated from speech in formal, ceremonial contexts by the employment of the herald (*matanivanua*) (Arno 1985b). This basic attitude toward the social meaning of speech translates into certain pragmatic features of formal, *vakaturaga* discussion. The pace of such speech is relatively slow, almost halting in some cases. Pauses can be fairly frequent and long, formal openings and closings delineate turn-taking, and there is no overlapping of speakers or competition for the floor. The only interruptions of a speaker's turn are in the form of standardized responses from the audience that indicate assent or encouragement. The pitch register is even and low, and there is no laughter.

Williams (1982) felt that Fijian orators or heralds he heard in formal situations at chiefly courts in the nineteenth century were poor speakers. But perhaps the indications he cites, such as heralds seeming to falter, hissing through their teeth between phrases, and plucking at the mat or at stems of grass with their hands as they spoke, were conventional gestures indicating a ritualized reluctance to speak, out of respect for the chief who was being addressed.[3] A modern anecdote supporting this view of formal speech characteristics is provided by a Fijian communication scholar (Vusoniwailala 1980) who early in his career worked as a disc jockey for Radio Fiji. He and the other disc jockeys working on the Fijian-language segments of the programming listened to their foreign, English-language counterparts from American and Commonwealth stations on the air, and they began to conform to the accepted style. This meant that a fast-paced chatter had to be employed to fill every moment of air time, with few pauses between items. Early on, they met with criticism, especially from villagers living outside the urban area of Suva. People complained that the fast pace and lack of pauses was rude, indicated a lack of respect for the listeners, and would lead younger people into nonchiefly language habits.

Joking speech in Lau is almost an exact reversal of *vakaturaga* formal speech. It is fast, loud, competitive, and essentially abusive and nonrespectful. Lauans conceptualize joking, like ceremonial *vakaturaga* speech, as a public performance. Two cross-cousins alone together do not joke, but when others are present the two may joke "to show the others that they are cross-cousins." Joking in a small gathering is generally considered weak and unexciting, but as the size of the gathering increases so does the exhilaration of a good joke—one that skates the line between mortifying insult and welcome release of underlying social tension. In terms of pragmatics, this "public performance" aspect of joking is represented in relative loudness of enunciation. Especially in large groups, jokes sound as if they are being called out so that everyone can hear. In contrast, the content is something that must *not* be said, in normal non-joking circumstances.[4] In *vakaturaga* speech the ceremonial, ritual context of the speech enforces its public character, and volume and assertiveness are not necessary to make it so.

Two other features that characterize joking are the substantive character of the statement as a personal attack on the addressee—again a direct reversal of the *vakaturaga* emphasis on mutual respect among speakers—and the presence of laughter. These two aspects of joking are related. Laughter seems to be an assertion of perceived incongruity or inappropriateness. If the joking remark were to be interpreted literally without the joking frame, serious social disruption or even physical violence would be the expected result. Laughter, vigorous in proportion to the seriousness of the threat to relationships that would otherwise be implied, represents an immediate assertion of incongruity—"this statement is not what it seems"—before the alternative, nonjoking reaction can take place.

The debating game, *veiba*, is a form of joking by definition because in it people are playing at doing something that they are in fact not doing. Incongruity is built into the situation, just as seriousness and formality are built into the ceremonial situations in which real *vakaturaga* speech is required. In *veiba*, then, participants can pretend *vakaturaga* forms of talk, but they signal lack of serious intent by laughter or other indications short of laughter that point out the incongruity.

The Joking Debate, *Veiba*

In form, the *veiba* is similar to European-style debating; a general proposition or question is stated, and one or more persons take opposing sides on it. Speakers try to make persuasive arguments for their sides as well as to counter the arguments of the opposition. At times, in the course of the *veiba*, references may be made to contemporary, European-derived national institutions that feature debate. Such remarks serve to underline the playful, make-believe nature of the activity. For example, in the transcript of the debate about kava drinking and development presented here, one speaker says that the men on the other side are "another party" (A:006). In several other cases, I noted statements such as "We are the *Federation* here. They on that side are the *Alliance*" in playful, direct reference to the opposition and government political parties in Fiji. The radio news broadcasts, heard daily in the village, often featured long, blow-by-blow accounts in Fijian of debates in Parliament, and villagers enjoyed the give and take of verbal points being scored. Sometimes also the legal system is referred to by way of playful analogy in a *veiba*. In such cases, a third person in the group takes the role of referee or arbiter, calling himself a *turaga ni lewa*, the term for judge (Arno 1985b).

It seems unlikely that the village-level game of debating in groups is totally explainable as a recent, European-inspired institution, however. The play aspect of the situation lends itself to the pretense of acting out parliamentary and courtroom scenes, but the basic form of interaction—the trading back and forth of clever arguments and repartee between cross-cousins for the entertainment of the group, as well as the support provided one another by allies—is quite consistent with the pattern of traditional joking.

Debates can range from the innocuous, largely intellectualized displays of verbal skill represented here by the *yaqona* 'kava' debate to a very pointed joking attack that is only thinly disguised as debate. The transcript I have called Sakiusa v. Manu is of this latter kind. Comparison of the two brings out differences that help to define joking in its disentangling role. Both were debates, games, according to the participants' definitions of the situations, but Sakusa v. Manu is much more infused with joking spirit and motivation, as pragmatic differences between the two demonstrate.

Debate A: *Yaqona* and Development

While naturally occurring *veiba* are unplanned, spontaneous group responses to the composition of the gathering—who happens to be present together—in light of issues that are currently salient, the *yaqona* debate A (see Appendix) was planned. My friend and host Soko knew from many previous conversations that I was interested in *yaqona* drinking and its place in village life. He suggested that he would arrange a discussion about it so that I could record what people thought. In other words, I did not ask for an example of a debate to record; the form the discussion took derives from Soko's judgment about what would be an appropriate way to go about it.

The gathering took place one evening at Peni's house. *Yaqona* was prepared and served just as it would have been for any informal gathering. Soko had specifically requested that several men come and discuss something for the benefit of my research. Other men heard about it and came along to enjoy the event, making a total of about ten participants. All this is very much in line with ordinary *yaqona* drinking practice that is part of the daily routine on the island. The planned debate, then, became imbedded in a larger, informal social event that grew up around it.

The speakers in the debate are Soko, who sets the problem and makes the first argument; Peni, who speaks as an ally of Soko's; Cagi, who takes the other side of the question, and Sakiusa, who supports Cagi. Turanga also makes a brief statement on Cagi's side.[5] Because of the generalized, "safe" nature of the topic, relationships among the participants do not appear to have been particularly salient. Soko and Peni are related as remote in-laws, *veivugoni*. A very close relationship of this kind would have prevented their appearing together in this way, but under the circumstances no impediment was presented. Soko does refer to Peni using the honorific form "Tu-" as a prefix to his name (e.g.,

A:003, 007), which is unusual among Yanuyanu residents.

Soko's chief opponent in the *veiba* is Cagi, who is *veitacini*, parallel cousin, to Soko. In my research, I found that informal symmetrical interaction of the kind represented by this debate was not usually engaged in by *veitacini* on Yanuyanu (see Arno 1980). But here again the relationship is slightly remote—the two men share a father's father's father. Sakiusa has the expected cross-cousin, *vetavaleni* relationships with both Soko and Cagi.

On Yanuyanu the topic of *yaqona* drinking is not a particularly exciting or controversial one, although excessive *yaqona* drinking is routinely condemned. *Yaqona* has great traditional prestige, and there is no argument, really, about its inherent virtue. Beer (or home brew) drinking would have been a more controversial topic because there is more deeply felt disagreement about it in the community. Sakiusa, who in reality is notorious as an excessive drinker of home brew, follows up on a previous speaker's point to praise *yaqona* by contrasting it with beer. Beer is expensive and promotes rowdyism, he says, while *yaqona* is relatively cheap and provides "a type of gentle fun that suits our living in the Fijian village" (A:077). Given his personal history and reputation, this would be a ludicrous argument for Sakiusa to be making in earnest, but the "play" frame provided by the *veiba* makes it highly acceptable.

Debate B: Sakiusa v. Manu

The background of the second example is quite different from that of the first. Soko and Sakiusa, cross-cousins who are major participants in the first debate, became interested in my tape recorder and, without encouragement (just the contrary, given my limited battery supply), began to explore its possibilities for entertainment and local politics. One afternoon, while Soko, Sakiusa, and I sat talking and drinking *yaqona* in Soko's house, Master Manu, a teacher at the district school on the island, dropped in to join us. Sakiusa suggested, after a while, that he and Manu would engage in a debate and that I would record it.

The ostensible topic of the debate between Sakiusa and Manu is the "money life-style," *na bula vakailavo*, as opposed to the traditional kinship way of life, *na bula vakaveiwekani*, in Fijian villages. In the abstract, this is a serious topic, just as is that of "*yaqona* v. progress" taken up in the first debate. The application to Manu, however, is rather pointed, and this fact gives the debate its joking energy.

As a teacher at the government school on the island, Manu is a salaried person among people who live largely by subsistence farming. In terms of money, therefore, he is rich. Like most teachers, who are assigned to schools throughout the country during their careers, Manu is also an outsider, only weakly integrated into the local kinship regime. He is from a small island between Lau and the larger, more central islands of Moala and Totoya. In a journal I kept of overheard evaluative statements that villagers made about one another, Manu appears as a fairly frequent target of unfavorable comments from certain quarters, which is an indication of unsatisfactory relationships of the kind that might be the object of joking. Subsequent retelling of the debate, and playing the tape, seemed aimed at building consensus about his unacceptable behavior, and ultimately some kinds of informal sanctions might have been applied to correct him. As an outsider with a cash income, however, Manu enjoyed considerable immunity from the usual forms of pressure. In part, this may explain the vigor of the joking attack upon him.

Comparison of the Two Debates

In both cases, the fact of their being tape-recorded was significant to the participants. The novelty of taping and replaying was much remarked on, there being no other recorders on the island. Hearing oneself played back over a speaker was likened to being heard over the radio, an enjoyable fantasy, especially to those in this performance-oriented community who fancied themselves just as capable as the news readers and speakers they listened to over the air. Another important factor was that joking debates are almost as much enjoyed in the recounting on later occasions as in the events themselves. A recorded version was seen as an especially powerful way of exposing participants to post hoc criticism or praise.

The *yaqona* debate did not provide much interest in this regard, although many Fijians, from Yanuyanu and elsewhere, who

have heard the tape have remarked in some way on Turaga's
notably weak intervention in which he mentions the medical
benefits of *yaqona* (A:055–060). Both Soko and Sakiusa, however, often requested me to play the tape of the Sakiusa v.
Manu debate to people who had not heard the original. To them, it was
clear evidence of Manu's silliness and lack of judgment. Typically
Soko or Sakiusa would say to listeners: "Just listen to this. What a
truly silly (*lialia*) man. Andrew was sitting right there." They
were drawing attention to the statement by Manu during the debate to the effect that money was not manufactured by people
(*tamata*) but by Europeans (*kai palagi*), implying that *palagi* are
not people (B:033–036).

My presence in the debating session and in the village is also
incorporated into the *yaqona* debate, as when, for example, Cagi
points out the utility of *yaqona* in entertaining guests (A:104–5).
Broadly speaking, however, I do not think my presence or the fact
of tape recording altered the forms of the two events.

Differences in rhythm and style between the two debates are so
striking that anyone listening to the two tapes can easily differentiate between them without knowing what is being said. In terms
of pace and timing, the Sakiusa v. Manu debate is much more of a
rapid-fire exchange. In the *yaqona* debate a pause is usually observed between speakers, and each speaker opens his remarks
with a standard phrase (e.g., *vinaka vakalevu* 'thank you very
much') and also closes with one (e.g., *oya na levu ni noqu
vakasama* 'that is the extent of my thinking'). The *yaqona* debate
speeches are relatively long, with one or more complete arguments being stated, and there are few cases of overlapping speech
or contests for the floor. By comparison between the two, the
yaqona debate is slow, deliberate, and courteous. In general, as I
have argued, a measured, dignified pace is characteristic of chiefly *vakaturaga* behavior in interaction, and the *yaqona* debate
definitely evokes or refers to that style, although it is not literally
a *vakaturaga* event.

In the Sakiusa v. Manu debate, however, utterances are very
short and there is almost continual interruption of one speaker by
the other. They often overlap each other by talking at the same
time, and there is little or no space between turns. Formal openings and closings are also absent. Each speaker is hard-pressed to

complete his argument without the other rushing in to counter it. Overall, there is an escalating, headlong quality to the exchange. Although still recognizable as a debate—in that a broad issue is referred to, and the statements of each participant are arguments and answers that respond to one another—this one inclines heavily away from the *vakaturaga* standard.

The use of laughter is also very different between the two debates. Although the *yaqona* debate had a jovial, good-natured tone, and there was none of the grave dignity that a serious discussion would have evoked, little laughter was heard. Because it is a joking form, although a weak one, however, one would expect some laughter as an underlining of the fact that no serious state of disagreement is signified by the argument and contradiction. In a subtle way, this obligatory disclaimer is provided by Soko and Cagi in their closing arguments. Soko begins in apparent earnest, but almost at the end of his speech he pauses, half laughs, and says, "Or, what about it?" as if he really was not convinced by all that he himself had just said (A:094). In Cagi's final argument, he too laughs, apparently in spite of himself, when Soko clownishly supports the wrong side by saying "True!," "*Dina!*," when Cagi has emphatically stated that *yaqona* is good (A:109–10).

By contrast, in the Sakiusa v. Manu debate there is almost continual laughter. Manu's howling, infectious laughter is particularly striking, and Sakiusa finally comments on it by telling Manu that he is "using up the time in [his] laughing" (B:075). That Sakiusa is the more aggressive of the two, in that he is much closer to actually intending serious criticism, is perhaps indicated by his noticeably lower level of laughing. On the other hand, Manu's excesses in this dimension may have rendered Sakiusa's contributions superfluous.

Code selection is another aspect of difference between the two debates. The choice is between the local, Lauan dialect[6] and the standard Bauan, which is the "official" dialect used in the Fijian mass media and in everyday conversation on Yanuyanu. In the *yaqona* debate almost no feature of Lauan is present, except perhaps in the ways certain words might be pronounced. For example, a Lauan might say *raica* 'to see (it)', accenting the *i*, while a Bauan speaker might say *raica*, but a stronger assertion of

Lauan dialect would be to use the word *boka* instead of *raica*. In the Sakiusa v. Manu debate, Lauan words are used at times. Some Lauanisms, such as use of the word *yaba* for "mat" instead of the Bauan *ibe*, occur in Sakiusa v. Manu but do not appear in the *yaqona* debate in *either* form, but in other cases there is an overlap. For example, the Lauan *meca* is sometimes used in Sakiusa v. Manu in place of the Bauan *ka* for "thing," but only *ka* is used in the *yaqona* debate. Similarly, the Lauan *tawa* or *ta* is sometimes used in Sakiusa v. Manu for "not" instead of the Bauan *sega*, and *valata, make* is used in place of *cakava*. Another dialect feature more prominent in Sakiusa v. Manu is the use of the Lauan ending *-takina* instead of the Bauan *-taka*. For example, Sakiusa says *Au burogo kina!* 'I am selfish about it' (B:078) and then intensifies the point by saying, *Au bureitakina!* 'I refuse it! (B:079). The apparent intent of intensification is signaled in this case by heavy stress on and lengthening of the vowel *i* in *-takina*.

Fijians from other areas in Fiji who have heard the two debates have characterized Sakiusa v. Manu as having a "heavy Lauan dialect" in contrast to the *yaqona* debate. But it is interesting that when one examines the debate line by line it appears that one party uses Lauan much more than the other. Both men use some Lauan words, such as the locatives *i* or *i yei*, but it is Manu who introduces heavily Lauan phrases. For example, Manu says, "A *yaba e valata* tamata"—"a person makes a mat"; "e na kena soli na *meca i*"—"in giving this thing"; and "au kaya ga ni'u sega ni rawa ni solia na *meca* ni'u *tawa* bulia"—"I only say I cannot give a thing I cannot make" (B:033, 058, 045; I have italicized the Lauan words). It is Manu too who says, "au *ma ta'* kaya"—"I did not say so," in which he uses not only *tawa* but the verbal particle *ma* instead of the Bauan *a* (B:050). The standard Bauan phrase would have been *Au a sega ni kaya*. I never heard *ma* being used in any other context, and Capell (1968:129) records it as a dialect variation from Kadavu and Vanua Levu, not Lau.

Conclusion

I argue that the joking debate, *veiba*, on Yanuyanu provides a vehicle for the face-to-face discussion of differences of opinion and interpretation among villagers in a way that does not publicly label any person wrong or bad (cf. White, this volume). It is one part of a larger process that includes asymmetrical, authoritative communication within patrilines (Arno 1976a), nonconfrontative "gossip" or discussion of absent persons' conduct (Arno 1980), and the public, face-to-face confrontation demonstrated in joking.

The level of joking intensity within the *veiba* can vary according to the potential inherent in the topic for disruption of relationships. The *yaqona* debate was mild in form because there was little real disagreement, and no individual was in danger of being publicly shamed. In the Sakiusa v. Manu debate, however, Manu was being more or less directly attacked for seriously inappropriate behavior vis-à-vis his fellow island residents—namely, not sharing and being too fond of money. In this latter debate the joking dimension is much more evident.

By contrasting the two debates one can isolate the features of verbal communication that signal joking on Yanuyanu. The *yaqona* debate is relatively slow, measured, and courteous, with pauses and formal openings and closings to separate the participants' speeches. In Sakiusa v. Manu the pace is rapid-fire, and the speakers aggressively interrupt one another. Sakiusa v. Manu is also marked by raucous laughter, while the *yaqona* debate is jovial but sedate. In sum, the milder form of joking much more closely approximates the ideal of serious discussion, the *vakaturaga* style, in which slowness and formality represent caution and respect for those addressed, as though direct communication among equals about a serious topic were something potentially dangerous that must be carefully handled. Joking, on the other hand, is an explicit *reversal* of polite convention. The frame it erects around the exchange means "we are cross-cousins," "this is not a serious discussion," and "no one is allowed to become angry or to feel shame."

Code switching is also a revealing difference between the two debates. The *yaqona* debate not only does not include the local dialect but in one instance even includes the use of ceremonial, chiefly language, as when Cagi uses the term *kamunaga*, albeit incorrectly,[7] to mean *yaqona* (A:164). In Sakiusa v. Manu, however, the use of the local dialect is a prominent feature.

The meaning of local dialect use is probably best expressed by a review of the contexts in which it is normally used. Aside from joking, I noticed the use of Lauan language features in two situations. One was when adults addressed small children, and the other was when men in groups talked about fishing or turtle-hunting expeditions. The common thread of meaning may be the intimacy and solidarity of local, in-group activities as contrasted with more general concerns of serious, formal, national culture.

The use of the local dialect, therefore, conveys not only "we are cross-cousins" but also "we are intimates, united against outsiders," which further reduces the disruptive impact of public criticism. This interpretation is supported by Gumperz's observations about "we" and "they" codes in bilingual situations (1982:66) in which "we" codes invoke social solidarity. From this point of view, Manu's use of boisterous laughter and also of local dialect reflect his special sensitivity to the "joke" and his need to portray himself as an insider. The reason is that in fact he is *not* an insider, being from another island.[8]

In one sense, the *veiba* on Yanuyanu is entertainment. In an isolated village, this is not an unimportant function. However, as a form of joking or play, *veiba* claims not to be what it appears. That is, it is *not* an argument, it is *not* a serious confrontation among equals, and it is *not* related to intragroup conflict. But, at another level, it is all these things. Viewed in context of the other kinds of communication events that make up the communication system of the community, the *veiba* provides the ambiguity, subtlety, and indirection that paradoxically are necessary to reconstruct clear and straightforward (*dodonu*) relationships that have become entangled.

Notes

Acknowledgement. I would like to thank Kini Suschnigg and Titilia Barbour of the East-West Center's Pacific Islands Development Program for their invaluable help in transcribing the two debate transcripts. I would also like to thank Don Brenneis and Geoff White for their excellent suggestions for improving the sketchy first draft of this paper.

1. I have used *Yanuyanu*, "island" in Fijian, as a fictitious name for the field site out of respect for the privacy of the people whose conflict cases I have discussed in various articles, many of which I cite in this paper.

2. An interesting exception to this general practice took place during my field study when a subclan involved in an internal land dispute held what they referred to as a *veivakameautaki* 'a mutual clarification of facts' in an attempt to settle the controversy. Accounts of this closed family meeting, which I could not attend, indicate that facts— who planted which trees where—were the focus, rather than violations of duties. The parties were returning children of a family member who had left the island years before, on one side, and resident members of the group on the other. The meeting went smoothly, with emphasis on family integration and solidarity, but the issue was in no way resolved. The conflict continued.

3. While Williams derided Fijian characterization of this or that person as an eloquent speaker, he apparently was referring only to public speaking or oratory. Elsewhere, throughout his book, Williams provides numerous examples of Fijian verbal artistry and poetic sense of language use.

4. This incompatibility between *what* is said and *how* it is said embodies the defining characteristic of joking as incongruity.

5. Another statement is made by a person I have called Takila, "don't know." I find I cannot identify him from the sound of his voice, and my field notes on this gathering do not make definite identification possible.

6. For a discussion of Fijian "communalects," the term they prefer, see Pawley and Sayaba (1971) and Geraghty (1983), who deals with some features of Lauan.

7. *Kamunaga* is a ritual word for *tabua*, a polished whale's tooth, used in ceremonial presentations. On one occasion that I witnessed, the herald, *matanivanua*, for Yanuyanu carelessly used *kamunaga* for *yaqona* instead of *tabua*. This slip was ignored, except by some children nearby who laughed at the mistake.

8. The possible explanation of Manu's greater use of the local dialect as reflecting merely a personal lack of facility in Bauan is negated by the fact that, as a government employee and school teacher, Manu would have a better than average command of Bauan. Instead, it is probably Manu's marginal position that makes solidarity an issue.

References

Arno, Andrew

1976a Ritual Reconciliation and Village Conflict Management in Fiji. Oceania 47(1):49–65.

1976b Joking, Avoidance, and Authority: Verbal Performance as an

Object of Exchange in Fiji. Journal of the Polynesian Society 85(1):71–86.

1979a Conflict, Ritual, and Social Structure on Yanuyanu Island, Fiji. Bijdragen 135:1–17.

1979b A Grammar of Conflict: Informal Procedure on an Island in Lau, Fiji. In Patterns of Conflict Management: Comparative Studies in the Anthropology of Law. Klaus-Friedrich Koch, ed. Vol. IV. Boston, Sijthoff and Noordhoff.

1980 Fijian Gossip as Adjudication: A Communication Model of Informal Social Control. Journal of Anthropological Research 36(3):343–60.

1983 Ethnography in Communication Research: Expanding the Metaphorical Limits of a Discipline. In Communication Research and Cultural Values, 42–54. Wimal Dissanayake and Abdul Rahman Mohd Said, eds. Singapore: AMIC.

1985a Structural Communication and Control Communication: An Interactionist Perspective on Legal and Customary Procedures for Conflict Management. American Anthropologist 87(1):40–55.

1985b Impressive Speeches and Persuasive Talk: Traditional Patterns of Political Communication in Fiji's Lau Group from the Perspective of Pacific Ideal Types. Oceania 56(2):124–37.

Bateson, Gregory
1958 Naven: A Survey of the Problems Suggested by a Composite Picture of the Culture of a New Guinea Tribe Drawn from Three Points of View. 2nd Edition. Stanford University Press.

1972 Steps to an Ecology of Mind. New York: Ballantine Books.

Capell, A.
1968 A New Fijian Dictionary. Suva, Fiji: Government Printer (originally published 1941).

Coser, Lewis A.
1956 The Functions of Social Conflict. New York: The Free Press.

Fishman, P. M.
1978 Interaction: The Work Women Do. Social Problems 25(4):397–406.

France, Peter
1969 The Charter of the Land: Custom and Colonization in Fiji. New York: Oxford University Press.

Geraghty, Paul S.
1983 The History of the Fijian Languages. Oceanic Linguistics Special Publication No. 19. Honolulu: University of Hawaii Press.

Giddens, Anthony
1979 Central Problems in Social Theory. Berkeley: University of California Press.

Goffman, Erving
1979 Gender Advertisements. Cambridge: Harvard University Press.

Groves, M.
1963 The Nature of Fijian Society. Journal of the Polynesian Society 72:272–91.

Gumperz, John J.
1982 Discourse Strategies. New York: Cambridge University Press.

Hocart, A. M.
1929 Lau Island, Fiji. Bernice P. Bishop Museum Bulletin No. 62. Honolulu.

Hymes, Dell
1962 The Ethnography of Speaking. In Anthropology and Human Behavior. T. Gladwin and W. C. Sturtevant, eds. Anthropological Society of Washington.
1972 Models of the Interaction of Language and the Social Life. In Directions in Sociolinguistics: The Ethnography of Communication. J. J. Gumperz and D. Hymes, eds. New York: Holt, Rinehart and Winston.

Myers, Fred R., and Donald L. Brenneis
1984 Introduction: Language and Politics in the Pacific. In Dangerous Words: Language and Politics in the Pacific, 1–29. D L. Brenneis and F. R. Myers, eds. New York: New York University Press.

Pawley, A. K., and Timoci Sayaba
1971 Fijian Dialect Divisions: Eastern and Western. Journal of the Polynesian Society 80(4).

Sahlins, Marshall D.
1962 Moala: Culture and Nature on a Fijian Island. Ann Arbor: University of Michigan Press.

Strathern, Andrew, ed.
1982 Inequality in New Guinea Highlands Societies. Cambridge:

Cambridge University Press.

Thompson, Laura
1940   Southern Lau, Fiji: An Ethnography. Bernice P. Bishop Museum Bulletin No. 162. Honolulu.

Vusoniwailala, Lasarusa
1980   Personal Communication

Williams, Thomas
1982   Fiji and the Fijians Vol. 1. The Islands and their Inhabitants. Originally published in 1858. Reprinted by the Fiji Museum, Suva.

Appendix

Debate A: Yaqona and Development

SOKO

001   *Bula vinaka, Adriu.*
Greetings, Andrew.

002   *Keitou mai gunu yaqona tiko vei kemuni e na bogi ni kua.*
We are here drinking yaqona with you tonight.

003   *Keitou veitalanoataka tiko ikei ni . . . keirau vata'ei Tupeni, ni . . . keirau kaya tiko ni sa dua na ka ca na yaqona ni Viti.*
We are talking here about . . . Tupeni and I, about . . . we are saying that Fijian yaqona is a bad thing.

004   *E saga sara ni dua na ka vinaka e kauta mai vei keimami na i taukei.*
There is certainly not any good thing that it brings to us taukei.

005   *Kerea . . . kevaka e na la'ki rogo vakalevu na neitou i talanoa [ ] a tiko na ka oqo me ka ni veiba.*
I ask . . . if our talk will be widely heard . . . (we will make) this thing into debate.

006   *Ia, keirau i toto kei Peni e na tabana oqo, e ratou toka mai yasana kadua, e ratou e dua tale na pati, e ratou kaya ni uasivi na yaqona.*
Well, Peni and I are allies on this side here, they are on the other side, they are another party, they are saying that yaqona is excellent.

007   *Ia, keirau kei Tupeni, keirau kaya tiko e na bogi ni kua, neitou*

gunu yaqona tiko oqo, ni sa dua na ka sa veivakarusai na yaqona.
Well, Tupeni and I, we two are saying tonight, we (several) are
drinking yaqona here, that yaqona is a thing of mutual ruination.

008   *E sega sara ga ni dua na cakacaka keimami rawata kina na i
      taukei ni kemami kania vakalialia na yaqona e na veibogi.*
      There certainly is not any task we achieved, we taukei, through
      drinking yaqona like crazy every night.

009   *Au vakabauta kevaka e na vakalailaitaki sobu na [kena] gunuvi
      na yaqona e na bau rawa vakavinaka na toso ki liu ka vinakata
      tiko na matanitu.*
      I believe that if yaqona drinking could be curtailed, the move-
      ment forward that the government wants might well be ac-
      complished.

010   *Sa dri yani.*
      It rebounds away.

011   *Dou mai keri.*
      (To) you over there.

CAGI

012   *Ia, vinaka vakalevu, Soko.*
      Well, many thanks, Soko.

013   *Au sega ni duavata kei na i vakamacala sa vakamacalataka oti.*
      I am not in agreement with the argument that has been put for-
      ward.

014   *Ko i au e tukuna tiko ni sa dua na ka vinaka na noda
      vakayagataka na i taukei na yaqona.*
      I am saying that our use of yaqona by us taukei is a good thing.

015   *E da vakakila tiko na i taukei ni sa dua na ka yaga vei keda
      vakalevu na yaqona.*
      We taukei know that yaqona is a very useful thing to us.

016   *E da dau vakayagataka vakalevu sara e na vuqa na ka.*
      We use it a great deal for many things.

017   *Dua, kevaka e ra dau lako mai e so na noda liuliu vakamatanitu,
      ke e ra taukei se ra fulagi, e na da vakayagataka na yaqona me
      dau ka ni noda veiqaraqaravi vakavanua.*
      One, if some of our government leaders, whether they be taukei
      or visitors, come here, we always use yaqona as a thing for our
      traditional welcome.

018   *E sega ni la'ki vakayagataki kina, me vakayagataki kina vakasivia
      me rawa ni vakaleqa kina edua na nodra cakacaka, se e dua na
      noda cakacaka.*

It is not going to be used in this case, to be used to excess in it
so as to hinder some work of theirs, or some of our work.

019 *E na noqu vakila, e na kena dau vakayagataki vakavuqa e na*
nomudou tiko kina, au kila ni dau vakayagataki vakarauta ga me
rauta na soqo se na i tavi e ra lako mai kina.
In my understanding, in its being used frequently, with your participating, I know that it is being used properly, appropriately to
the meeting or to the task they came for.

020 *Dua tale, au kila ni sa dua na ka yaga vei keda na i taukei na*
yaqona kevaka e dua na cala, e dua na i taukei vua e dua na
wekana, sa rawa ni dau bulubulutaki se sorovi ga kina na nona
cudru e dua na wekana mai na yaqona.
Another thing, I know that yaqona is a useful thing to us taukei
if there is an injury, by a taukei to one of his relatives, his relative's anger can be erased by i soro or i bulubulu through yaqona.

021 *Sa rawa ni vakavuna me rau veivinakati tale ka guilecavi na cala*
e a cakava e dua vei rau.
It can be the cause that they like one another again and that the
wrong that one of them has done is forgotten.

022 *Sa i koya au tukuna kina ni sa dua na ka vinaka na noda*
vakayagataka na i taukei, ka dua na lewa matau e ra sa [ ] kina o
ira na tukada mai liu meda vakayagataka na i taukei na yaqona
me ka yaga vei keda.
It is for this that I say that our use of yaqona by us taukei is a
good thing, and it was a fitting decision that our forefathers before us made that we taukei use yaqona as something useful to us.

023 *Ia, au nuitaka tale ga ni tiko tale ga vei iratou na noqu i tokani e*
so na i vakamacala uasivi sara.
Well, I trust also that they, my allies, will also have some very excellent arguments.

024 *Sa dri.*
It rebounds.

PENI

025 *Vinaka.*
Good.

026 *Ko i au, au sega soti ni duavata toka kei na vakamacala sa oti*
toka ni tukuna tiko ni . . . ni vinaka na yaqona.
Myself, I don't exactly agree with the argument just finished that
is saying that . . . that yaqona is good.

027 *Au vakabauta ni sa dua na ka sa bau vakacacani keda vakalevu na*
i taukei oqo na yaqona.

I believe that yaqona is a thing that injures us taukei very much.

028 *Levu na veika vivinaka e sa rui vaka e vakataotaka e na levu ni gunuvi vakasivia na yaqona e da sa vakarautaka . . . e da sa vakayacora tiko na i taukei.*
A lot of good things are too sort of entangled in the amount of excessive yaqona drinking that we prepare . . . that we taukei carry out.

029 *Kevaka e beka me a dau gunuvi vakarauta, e kena la'ki beka me gunuvi vakarauta e na rairai vinaka cake vakalailai, e na kena sa mai sivia e na noda gunuvi tu e vakavuna sa levu na ka veivinavinaka e da sega ni rawata kina.*
If perhaps it could be drunk in a measured way, in its maybe being drunk in a measured way, it looks like being a little better (but) in its being drunk to excess is the reason for our not attaining many desired things.

030 *Oqori e vica na noqu [ ] lekaleka au sagata kina na kena ca dina na yaqona.*
There are a few of my short (thoughts) that I argue against (yaqona) that yaqona is truly bad.

SAKIUSA

031 (two start to speak at once, other stops) *tautauvata kei Cagi e na nona kaya tiko ni ka vinaka na yaqona.*
The same as Cagi in his saying that yaqona is good.

032 *E vuna datou sa gunu yaqona tiko e na bogi ni kua, ka e dau kena i vakarau vei keda na i taukei e na veiyakavi.*
Because we are drinking yaqona here tonight, and this is the custom among us taukei every evening.

033 *E dua na ka au kaya ni vinaka kina e na gunu yaqona ni Viti ni dau mai soqovata vakalewelevu, e da mai soli vakasama kina, levu na i talanoa yaga e caki sara e na dau rawata me na noda soqo ni . . ., vata vaka gunu yaqona.*
One reason I say that drinking Fijian yaqona is good is that many people meet together, we exchange thoughts, a lot of useful accounts are given in the accomplishment of our meetings to . . . to drink yaqona together.

034 *Ko au. . . . e na vanua oqo au kaya kina ni sa dua na ka yaga, ka vinaka na yaqona.*
I in this area, I say that yaqona is a useful thing, a good thing.

035 *Kevaka o la'ki taura mai na nodrau vosa na. . . . kaya tiko ni ca na yaqona—e rau kaya tiko ni . . . e vaka me rau la'ki kaya tale dina ni dua na vanua ni vinaka na gunu yaqona, kevaka e gunuvi*

vakarauta.
If you go take their (two) speech saying that yaqona is bad, . . .
they are saying that . . . it is as if they are truly again saying that
there is an area of good in yaqona, if it is drunk in proper
measure.

036 *Ia, au vakabauta ni sa tu ga na tamata me lewa nona gunu*
     yaqona, vakasivia se vakarauta se [ ].
     Well, I believe that the man exists who judges his own yaqona
     drinking, to excess or properly ( ).

037 *Ia, oya na yaga ni . . . na yaga ni yaqona, au kaya tiko, ni da sa*
     dau [ ] soli vakasama vinaka kina na i taukei.
     Well, there is the usefulness of . . . the usefulness of yaqona I am
     saying that we taukei exchange thoughts over it.

038 *Au nuitakina eso tale tiko ga na neitou [ ] e vo vei rau tiko oqo*
     tiko tale vei rau e so na vakasama vinaka e vinaka na yaqona.
     I hope that some of our remaining arguments to these two will
     enable them (two) to understand that yaqona is good.

039 *Oya na levu ni noqu vakasama . . . au tukuna rawa.*
     That is the extent of my thoughts . . . that I can tell.

SOKO

040 *Ia, oiau, sa. . . . rau vakamacala oti o irau na rua oqo . . . au taura*
     e dua na tala ni vosa ni noqu i to, au sa . . . au sega sara ga ni
     raica rawa e dua na ka me vinaka kina na yaqona.
     Well, I . . . . they have finished arguing, they two here . . . I take
     a phrase from my ally, I . . . I just cannot see any good thing in
     yaqona.

041 *E dina ni'u dau gunu yaqona vakalevu.*
     It is true that I am a heavy yaqona drinker.

042 *Me vaka e tukuna o Tupeni ni vakataotaka levu na veicakacaka*
     yaga e dodonu me vakayacori na gunu yaqona.
     As Tupeni said, drinking yaqona entangles many useful tasks
     that ought to be done.

043 *Kena i vakatautauvatataki, au raica e na so na gauna e dau*
     kacikaci ko Turaga ni Koro ena nodatou koro oqo ko Yanuyanu
     me la'ki vakayacori na tapi ni bili.
     For example, I see some times the Turaga ni Koro (Village Head-
     man) here in our village of Yanuyanu calls out that communal
     work will be done.

044 *Au a raica kina keimami taucoko na dau gunu yaqona, levu ga na*
     gauna ni vakatavako, ka'u raici lewe vica walega e ra sega ni dau
     gunu yaqona, e ra cakacaka sara tiko ga ena gauna ka sa

*vakalutuki tiko o ya ka sa vakataotaka, ka kaya tiko ko Tupeni, ni
levu na veicakacaka yaga e dodonu me toso ki liu, e sa vakaleqai
keimami na dau gunu yaqona.*

I have observed that all of us who are yaqona drinkers spend a
lot of time smoking, and I see only a few people, they who do
not drink yaqona, they just keep working during the time that
useful projects necessary to progress are felled, or entangled as
Tupeni is saying, hindered by us yaqona drinker.

045 *Au vakatautauvatataka na cakacaka levu e dau vakayacori e na
loma ni koro levu mada oqo o Korodua.*

I give as an example the big project that is carried out inside the
big village here, Korodua.

046 *Au raica votu kina na gu ni neimami Turaga ni Koro, ia, o ira
taucoko ga . . . o i keimami taucoko na dau gunu yaqona, e dua ga
na i ta . . . se tautauvata beka ni rawa ni kaya ni dua ga na vu
dua na toso, ka ra dau veiwaletaka vei keda na Idia.*

I see clearly in it the desire of our Turaga ni Koro, well, all of
them . . . all of us yaqona drinkers, only one chop . . . or maybe it
would be the same as saying one cough, one move, so that the Indians are always joking about us.

047 *E vaka sara ga kina na noqu raica, ka'u sa beitaka tu ga ni ka
vakataotaka na neimami toso ki liu nai taukei e dua vei ira oqo e
naba dua tiko na yaqona ni Viti.*

It is just that I observe, and I blame as among the things that en-
tangles the progress of us taukei, number one among them is
Fijian yaqona.

048 *Sa kena levu e ya, ni noqu vakacala tiko na yaqona ni Viti, e na
kena laukana vakasivia.*

That is the extent of my blaming Fijian yaqona, in its being
drunk to excess.

TAKILA

049 *Dua ga na noqu vosa lekaleka (cough by others) [ ] . . . na noqu i
tokani me vaka e datou tukuna tiko ni vinaka na yaqona se gunu
yaqona.*

One short speech by me ( ) my allies as we are saying that
yaqona, or drinking yaqona, is good.

050 *Na ka au tukuna kina ni vinaka na gunu yaqona, se vinaka na
yaqona, dua me vaka e dau lasavi se e dau [ ] sara vakalevu e na
veisoqo e bibi me vaka na soqo ni mate, se e dua na ka e dau
vauca vakalevu noda soqo na i taukei na yaqona.*

The thing I say is good about yaqona drinking, or yaqona, one, it
is as though it makes us very happy in the serious gatherings

such as funerals, or it is a thing, yaqona, that binds firmly
together our gatherings of us taukei.

051 *Dua tale, me vaka na yaqona ni Viti e vaka e dau vakaseyavutaka
na lasa ni na gunu bia, se e dua tale na veimataqali soqo e dau
caka kina na veitalanoa [ ] raica sa [ ] na yakavi ni kua ni sega
[ ] se e dua tale na ka me ca e na vanua.*
Another thing, it is as though the Fijian yaqona destroys the fun
of drinking beer, or another of the kinds of gatherings in which
(bad) discussions take place, look how in this evening there is
no (rowdy behavior) or some other kind of thing bad for the
community.

052 *Na ka ga e datou rogoca tiko, nodatou veimarautaki vaka, i taba
vata, se vakaveiwekani.*
The only thing we are listening to, we are amusing ourselves
taking sides or as relatives.

053 *Au kila ni levu na ka au na [ ] talega vakalailai noqu vosa ni
keitou.*
I know that many of the things I will ( ) also a little my speech
for our side.

054 *Sa rauta koya.*
That is enough.

TURAGA

055 *Vinaka vakelevu.*
Many thanks.

056 *[ ] neitou tokani ni vinaka tiko na . . . e vinaka na yaqona.*
( ) our side that it is good . . . that yaqona is good.

057 *Au tukuna ni vinaka na yaqona baleta na. . . . tukuna na
tabacakacaka ni vuniwai ni ka vinaka na gunu yaqona.*
I say that yaqona is good because. . . . the Public Health Department says that drinking yaqona is good.

058 *Ni e so na mate e dau tauvi keda e vakamatea kina na noda mate
na gunu yaqona.*
That some of the sicknesses that always afflict us . . . drinking
yaqona kills off our illness.

059 *E tukuna kina ni ka vinaka na gunu yaqona.*
That means that drinking yaqona is a good thing.

060 *Kena levu.*
That is all.

PENI

061 *Vinaka.*
Good.

062 *Au sega soti toka ni duavata kei na vakamacala sa [ ] Cagi,
tukuna tiko na kena vinaka na gunu yaqona.*
I am not exactly in accord with the clarification Cagi (offered)
telling the good of yaqona drinking.

063 *Au vakabauta ni da sa dui kila sara toka go oi keda vakataki keda
na kena ca vei keda e na noda gunuva vakasivia na yaqona.*
I believe that each of us knows well individually the evils to us
of excessive yaqona drinking.

064 *E tekuvu sara ga mai na noda dui cakacaka ga yadudua na kena
lakolako vaka dredre [ ] na veika vinaka e da vinakata me da
vakayacora, ia e sa vakataotaka tu e na levu ni yaqona e da
gunuva, e na noda yadra sivia kina, ka vuqa tale na veika e da
vakayacora na kena [ ] dau vinakata na gunu yaqona, e da la'ki
tiko vakaca kina e na noda veivalevale.*
It begins right with our individual work, it's making it difficult
going for us to achieve the many good things that we want to
do, well, they are entangled in the amount of our yaqona drinking, in our staying up too late, and many more things we do are
(hindered) by our desire to drink yaqona, we all start living
badly in our households.

065 *Vaka e levu na i lavo e la'ki vakayali kina na sau ni yaqona, ia e
sega soti ni dua na ka vinaka e kauta mai ki na noda matavuvale
na gunu yaqona.*
Much money is wasted in the price of yaqona. . . . well, there is
not much good that drinking yaqona brings to our families.

066 *E sa dui yaga ga vei keda yadudua.*
Its use affects each of us individually.

067 *E sega ni dua na kena vinaka e da raica kina.*
There is no good we see in it.

068 *E na noda vucevucesa ga, na noda yadra sivia, e kauta mai oqo na
yaqona.*
Our laziness, our staying up too late, yaqona brings here.

069 *Oqori e dua tale nai vakamacala lekaleka au saqata tiko kina ena
kena ca na yaqona.*
That is another short argument that I contest with yaqona's badness.

070 *E vaka na kena levu.*
That is about all.

SAKIUSA

071 *Au via vakuria vakalailai.*
I wish to add a little.

072 *Au via. . . . noqu saqata tiko ga . . . e na kena kainaki ni ca na yaqona.*
I wish . . . my contending . . . it's being said that yaqona is bad.

073 *Au nanuma. . . . kevaka e na tauri mai na nomudrau vosa, nomudrau kaya tiko ni ca na yaqona, e na vu ni kena [ ] na i lavo, ni da taura vata na gunu oqo sa [ ] mai vei keda na bia, kevaka e da taura vatakina na i voli ni yaqona, ni sa rui ka lailai, mai na ka e rawa ni saumi kina na bia, ni tiko kina mataqali marau vata e rau tiko kina.*
I think. . . . if their (two) speech is taken here, their saying that yaqona is bad, a source of (the loss of) money, that we compare this drink here (with the effect) beer has on us, if we compare the buying of yaqona, it just a small thing, compared to what we pay for beer, and the same pleasure is in both.

074 *Au kaya kina ni sa bau dua na ka kalougata ni ya duatani ga na meda yaqona na i taukei, se na yaqona ni Viti, ka kauti tiko vei keda vakamalua tiko me veiganiti kei na noda rawa i lavo na i taukei.*
For this, I say it is surely a blessed thing that our yaqona of us taukei is a different kind of thing, Fijian yaqona, that we can obtain easily, as is appropriate to our ability to earn money, us taukei.

075 *Ia, na gunu yaqona ni vavalagi, sa rauti ira toka na turaga ni vavalagi baleta ni levu tiko nodra i lavo.*
Well, drinking the yaqona of the palagi suits the palagi gentlemen because their amount of money is large.

076 *[ ] gunu yaqona vei keda na i taukei kena rui saumi lailai.*
Drinking yaqona among us taukei is very cheap.

077 *Ka mataqali lasa malumu ka veiganiti kei noda tu e na koro vaka Viti.*
And a type of gentle fun that suits our living in the Fijian village.

078 *Oya na ka au [ ] tale kina sa dua na ka vinaka na yaqona.*
That is the thing I (assert) again in that yaqona is a good thing.

079 *E dua na ka au rawa ni. . . . [ ] kevaka e dina na nomudrau vosa, e na nomudrau kaya ni ca na yaqona ni Viti, ia e daidai nomudrau gunu yaqona ni Viti vata tiko.*

One thing I can. . . . if it is true what you (two) say, your saying that yaqona is bad, well, your drinking yaqona together here is a lie.

080 *Au vakabauta ni ka e da vakayacora e ka vinaka vei keda.*
I believe that the thing we do is a good thing for us.

081 *Au sa sega ni duavata kei kemudrau e na nomudrau kaya tiko ni ka ca na yaqona.*
I am not in accord with you (two) in your saying that yaqona is a bad thing.

082 *Vinaka vakalevu.*
Thank you very much.

083 *[ ] neitou [ ] tale e dua na neitou tokani.*
( ) our ( ) again one of our allies.

SOKO

084 *Sa vinaka.*
Good.

085 *Sa yaco tiko na veileti oqo e na ka e baleta na yaqona.*
The dispute occurring here is about yaqona.

086 *Keirau kerea tiko ga me keirau kakua ni vakalewai kina, keitou tovola tiko oqo me keitou dui solia na neitou vakasama na ka e baleta na yaqona, ia keirau vakadinadintaka tale ga ni sa levu na i vakamacala e dou laki vakayacora mai me keirau leqa kina, ia keirau na sega ni druka rawa.*
We two are only asking that we are not blamed for it, we (several) are trying here for each of us to give his thoughts about yaqona, well, we two confirm yet again that you have brought many an argument to trouble us, well we two cannot be beaten.

087 *Keirau tukuna na neirau dui vakasama ni dua na ka e vakaberaberataka na noda toso oqo na gunu yaqona.*
We are each telling our (2) own thoughts that drinking yaqona is a thing that slows our (all) movement.

088 *Au vakabauta kevaka e vakayacori ga mai na ono na kaloko me la'ki tini koso en na walu se ciwa na kaloko e na bogi.*
I think that if it began at six o'clock it will go and finish off at eight or nine o'clock at night.

089 *Ia, kena ca ka'u lauraica ni sa dau levu noda lasa marau ni taukei, sa rawa ni toso sara tiko ga na gunu yaqona me la'ki yacova na siga rarama.*
Well, the bad I see is that a lot of our jolly fun of us taukei is

able to keep right on going drinking yaqona until day light.

090 *Na vanua oya keirau beitaka tiko keirau (cough) ni dua na ka e*
vakabera tiko na noda toso na gunu yaqona ni Viti.
This is the area we blame drinking yaqona as a thing that slows
our progress.

091 *Kevaka beka me ya tautauvata na lomada i da vakayalayalataka.*
If perhaps we were of even temperament we would limit it.

092 *E vaka e laurai votu sara vei ira e ra sega ni dau gunu yaqona, na*
nodra bula vakavuvale, e vakayacori sara kina vakavinaka na
veiqaravi, na nodra. . . . noda cakacaka vata vakavanua, vakoro, e
da raica votu sara e kea na nodra toso vinaka sara ga nodra
cakacaka, sega tale vakaoti noda. . . .
It would be as we see among those who do not drink yaqona,
their family life, in which they provide very well, ( ) their. . . .
our working together traditionally, by village, we see clearly
their very good progress in their work, ours not yet finished. . . .

093 *Ia, o keda na dau gunu yaqona, ni toso ga vakalailai, dua na i vivi*
tavako, ka da laʻki dabe toka.
We, we who drink yaqona we move a little, then a cigarette,
then we go sit down.

094 *Vaka me laʻki. . . . keirau kaya tiko ni ca na yaqona me laʻki*
vakamalumalutaki ira . . . vakamalumulumataka na cakacaka
vakoro, se vakavanua, e na loma ni dua koro, e na nodra
vakawelewele ka keirau beitakina toka oqo ni e na sa rui kania
vakasivia na yaqona ni Viti, ni da sa rui kania vakasivia, sega ni
dua na gauna ne da bau yalataki me vakalailaitaki kina. . . . se
vaka evei (near laugh). . . . au vakabauta ni rairai sa balavu
nodatou veileti ka sega ni macala se na vakadinadinataki rawa
mai vei.
As it goes to. . . . we two are saying that the evil of yaqona is to
go to weaken them. . . . weaken the working by village, or traditionally in the midst of a village, their laziness that we are blaming here, they too often drink Fijian yaqona to excess, that we
too often drink to excess, there is no time that we limit it or cur-
tail it in. . . . or what about it . . . I think it looks like our debate
is long, and it is not clear how it will be resolved.

CAGI

095 *IA, KOI au na kurivosatakina vakalailai [Vinaka: (Sakiusa)].*
Well, I will speak up again a little. (good)

096 *E na [veitokoni kedatou tiko] noqu i lewa.*
My judgment will support our group.

097 *Baleta au na sega tavakokotu na vanu drau beka tiko Peni kei
     Soko.*
     Because I will not ( ) the area Peni and Soko are doubting.

098 *O i au vakadinadinataka tiko ni sa dua na ka yaga na gunu
     yaqona . . . ka yaga na yaqona vei keda na i taukei.*
     I am confirming that drinking yaqona is a useful thing . . . a use-
     ful thing to us taukei.

099 *Drau la'ki kauta mai kemudrau . . . drau tukuna ni vakaberai
     keda na i taukei.*
     They two go and bring here their . . . they say that it slows us
     taukei.

100 *Ia, na vanua oqori sa dui tu ga vei keda na i taukei.*
     Well, that area there depends on each of us taukei.

101 *Koya sa na davudi, veitalia ni sega ni gugu yaqona sa na vucesa ga.*
     He that will be lazy, never mind if he doesn't drink yaqona, he
     will be lazy.

102 *Sa gunu yaqona se sega ni gunu yaqona, sa na vucesa ga.*
     Drinks yaqona or doesn't drink yaqona, he will be lazy anyway.

103 *Ia, o koya sa makutu, gunu yaqona se sega ni gunu yaqona, e na
     rawata na ka ni sa vakaciciva e na kena gauna sa dodonu me
     rauti koya.*
     Well, he who is assiduous, drink yaqona or not drink yaqona, he
     will achieve the object and run it in the time that has been al-
     lotted to it.

104 [*Vinaka, Vinaka: (Sakiusa)*]. *Ia, na ka munaga oqo na yaqona, e
     dua na kena yaga au raica kina, [oqori] sara ga, ni sa toka oqo o
     misita Adriu, oqo e dua na i lakolako vakayawa sara mai, e tou na
     rawa ni wilika ni nodatou vulagi tiko beka, ia oqo au sa vakatoka
     me dua na ka dokai [Turaga vuku tale: Sakiusa].*
     (Good, good.) Well, the treasure here (note: this is ritual lan-
     guage), the yaqona, one use I see for it, right here, here is Mr.
     Andrew, here a very long journey here, we shall perhaps be able
     to read about our visitor, well I assert that it is an honor (An edu-
     cated gentleman, too).

SAKIUSA

105 *. . . io . . . au vakabauta koi au ni ka dokai sara vei misita Adriu e
     na nodatou lako mai, tou sevusevu mai vua, tou mai . . . kauta
     mai na yaqona, tou mai gunu vata, tou veitalanoa, tou soli
     vakasama tiko vua me baleta na nona . . . na nona mai sasaga,
     sagati ga nona vuli.*
     Yes . . . I think myself that it is a true honor to Mr. Andrew that

we come here, we sevusevu here to him, we here . . . bring
yaqona here, we drink together, we exchange stories, we exchange thoughts with him about his . . . his quest . . . study.

106 *Ia, au vakabauta kina koi au ni sa dua na ka yaga se dua na
vulagi tale, mai vei sara beka e rawa ni lako mai e na nodatou
koro i Korodua se mai Kororua, tou na kauta yani kina na yaqona
me vakamatau ni nodra yaco mai ki na nodatou yanuyanu.*
Well, I think myself, it is a useful thing if another visitor comes—
from wherever it may be—he will be able to come here to our village, Korodua or to Kororua we will carry over the yaqona to
make proper their arrival here to our island.

107 *E rawa ni ra lesu e ra na la'ki talanoataka se e ra na mai marau e
na noda lako yani me da la'ki veitalanoa e na noda kauta yani na
yaqona.*
They can return and go and tell about how they were happy because of our coming over and our exchange of stories, in our
bringing yaqona.

108 *Au vakadinadinataka se tokoni iratou kina vakaukauwa na noqu i
toqo ni sa dua na ka yaga dina na yaqona.*
I confirm or support them strongly my allies here that yaqona is
a useful thing.

109 *[Dina!: (Soko)].*
(True!: interjected by Soko).

110 *Ka'u sa vaka (laughs) vakavinavinaka kina vakalevu vei iratou na
noqu i to en nodratou duavata kei au ena neitou tukuna tiko ni sa
ka yaga dina na yaqona.*
And I tha . . . thank very much for this my allies for their agreement with me in our saying that yaqona is truly a useful thing.

Debate B: Sakiusa v. Manu

Brackets are used to indicate interruptions.
SAKIUSA

001 *o Manu. . . . e bau dua na tamata. . . . e tukuna tiko vaka oqo o
Manu e vinaka sara vakalevu vei koya me. . . . sa rui ca na bula
vaka i lavo.*
Manu. . . . he is the kind of person . . . Manu is saying like this,
that he likes very much indeed. . . . that the money life is too bad.

002 *Ia, na . . . ia qo sa qai vunitaka na kena tapako vei na vugona, oqo
o Mo ni lako i tuba, eh?*

Well, the . . . well here he then hides his tobacco from his in-law,
Mo who was going past outside, eh?

MANU

003 *[uh . . .]*
(uh)

SAKIUSA

004 *Totolo sara oqori ni o sa vunia na kemu tapako baleta ni . . . ni na*
mai taura.
You hid your tobacco so very fast because he might take some.

MANU

005 *[Sega!]*
(No!)

006 *Ia e kena balebale ni na mai taura oqori, o sa vunitaka baleta ni o*
vakalusia na nomu. . . .
Well, the implication of that taking, you hid it because you
would lose your. . . .

MANU

007 *[E Sega.]*
(No.)

SAKIUSA

008 *. . . i lavo.*
. . . money.

MANU

009 *Sega, sega.*
No, no.

010 *Kakua ni tukuna mai vakaoqori.*
Do not talk like that.

011 *Au kaya va'qo: kevaka e vinakata a qou tapioke lako i cavuta . . .*
taya kena tapioke!
I say like this: if he wants my cassava, go pull . . . cut his cassava!

012 *Kevaka e vinakata a kawai, la'ki cavu a kawai.*
If he wants kawai, go pull up kawai.

013 *A meca taucoko e vinakata e rawa ni'u tea, ia me'u solia vua.*
All the things he wants, that I am able to plant, well I'll give to
him.

014 *Ia oqo e lako mai na sede!*
Well, here comes the cent!

015 *He he . . . sede tiko. . . .*
     (laughs) Heh heh, being a cent.

SAKIUSA

016 *Ia e kena balebale sa. . . .*
     Well, that means. . . .

MANU

017 *[Au ta' bulia a sede. Au sega ni bulia na sede.]*
     I can't make a cent. I cannot make a cent.

SAKIUSA

018 *. . . kena balebale oya ni sa toto sara ga vei iko na nomu i lavo.*
     . . . the meaning of that is that your money is very painful indeed
     to you.

MANU

019 *E toto . . . ni silini, ni a caka a kai palagi.*
     (laughs) It's painful . . . like a shilling, that the European makes.

SAKIUSA

020 *Ia, e vaka evei na veigauna sa oti. . . .*
     Well, what about in previous times. . . .

MANU

021 *[EH?]*
     (eh)

SAKIUSA

022 *. . . e vakaevei na veigauna sa oti.*
     . . . what about in previous times.

023 *Au nanuma . . . au nanuma ni qai mai toto. . . .*
     I think . . . I think that it has become painful. . . .

MANU

024 *[Na sede! (laughs)]*
     (The cent!)

SAKIUSA

025 *. . . walega e na vica na gauna i yei.*
     . . . only recently here.

MANU

026 (laughs) *Sega, sega!*
     No, no!

SAKIUSA

027 *E sega na noda i tovo nai taukei. . . . noda i tovo na i taukei e dau
     vaka yei.*
     It is not the custom of us taukei. . . . our custom as taukei is like
     this.

MANU

028 *[E tu ga na noda i tovo na i taukei.*
     (Our customs as taukei just keep on.

029 *E tu ga. . . . (laughs)]*
     They keep on. . . .)

SAKIUSA

030 *E dau so na noda i tovo na i taukei e dau vaka yei, e dau oti mada
     ga. . . . raica e na veigauna sa oti. . . .*
     Some of our customs as taukei are like this, it is perhaps
     finished. . . look at previous times. . . .

MANU

031 *[Sega]*
     (No!)

SAKIUSA

032 *. . . lako vei na vugomu ka kaya: "Au mai kauta mada. . . ."*
     . . . you go your in-law and say: "I will take this please. . . ."

MANU

033 *[Yaba, e valata a tamata]*
     (Mat a person makes)

SAKIUSA

034 *Wawa mada, wawa mada. . . .*
     Wait please, wait please

MANU

035 *[a gatu a valata a tamata.*
     (A sheet of tapa, a person makes.

036 *Koya i yei e ta' valata a tamata, e valata a kaipalagi. (laughs)]*
     This here isn't made by a person, a European makes it)

SAKIUSA

037 *. . . wawa mada, wawa mada.*
     . . . wait please, wait please.

038 *Raica.* . . .
     Look. . . .

MANU

039 *E valata a kaipalagi a sede.*
     The European makes the cent.

040 *E sega ni buli a sede e na dua na vanua i yei!*
     (laughs) The cent is not made any place here!

041 *Tukuna mada, vei e dua na vanua e buli tiko kina a sede e*
     Yanuyanu?
     Tell me please, where is there a place where the cent is made on
     Yanuyanu?

SAKIUSA

042 *Io e kena balebale ni sa rui toto sara vakalevu vei iko na sede?*
     Yes, is that why the cent is so very painful indeed to you?

MANU

043 *E sega ni toto vei au na sede.*
     The cent is not painful to me.

SAKIUSA

044 *[he. . . .]*
     (Heh. . . .)

MANU

045 *Au kaya ga ni'u sega ni rawa ni solia na meca ni'u tawa bulia!*
     (laughs) I am only saying that I cannot give something that I
     can't make!

SAKIUSA

046 *O Koya au kaya tiko kina.* . . . *o koya au kaya tiko kina . . . sa*
     duidui. . . . *ni sa rui duidui tiko kina vakalevu na nomu vosa ni*
     kaya ko iko e [ ] nicava ni . . . e ca na bula vaka i lavo. . . .
     That is what I am talking about. . . . that is what I am talking
     about . . . it is different. . . . that it is very different from your
     saying that . . . the money life is bad. . . .

MANU

047 *[Sega!*
     (No!

048 *Au ma ta kaya e ca na bula vaka i lavo]*
     I never said the money life was bad.)

SAKIUSA

049 . . . *ka vinaka na bula vaka i taukei.*
     . . . and the taukei life-style good.

MANU

050 *Au ma ta kaya!*
     (laughs) I never said it!

051 *O ma ta rogoca na ka au kaya?*
     (laughs) You couldn't hear what I said?

SAKIUSA

052 *E na matai ni kedatou sa qai tekivu.* . . .
     At first, when we began. . . .

MANU

053 *[Sega!]*
     (No!)

SAKIUSA

054 . . . *o a kaya ni ca na bula vaka i lavo.*
     . . . you said that the money life was bad.

MANU

055 *[Sega, sega, sega, sega.]*
     (No, no, no, no.)

SAKIUSA

056 *Ia qo ko sa qai veisautakina tale!*
     Well and here you then change about again!

MANU

057 *E sega, sega.*
     No, no.

058 *Raica, au a kaya vakaoqo e na nodatou veitalanoa: e na kena soli na meca i, kei na ka e da bulia na i taukei, na kena soli, na kedrau e duidui.*
     I said like this in our discussion: that the giving of this thing, and the thing we taukei make, its giving, their difference.

059 *Ia, me'u kaya vakadodonu vei iko, na kedrau duidui koi: a yaba, eda . . . eda valata, a gatu, e da kesata, o ya e da cakava e ligada.*
     Well, I'll say it straight for you, the difference of the two: the mat, we . . . we make, the tapa sheet, we stencil, these we make by our hands.

060 *A tapioke e da tea, a kawai e da tea. . . . ia, a tapako kei na sede e da ta' tea!*
(laughs) A cassava, we plant, a kawai we plant. . . . well, tobacco and the cent we don't plant!

SAKIUSA

061 *Ia, e vakasamatakina. . . .*
Well, think about. . . .

MANU

062 [(laughs)] ( )

SAKIUSA

063 *. . . ia, mo qai vakasamatakina mada iyei, e na veigauna sa oti e da lako yani ga da kerea, ai. . . . kele mai . . . e dua la'ki qoli na wekada, ka lako yani. . . . "mada kemudou e dua na ika oqori. . . . mada, tavale, e dua na ika oqori . . . mai Tione mada a ika oqori. . ."*
. . . well, please then think about this, in previous times, we just went out and asked for. . . . anchored here . . . one of our relatives went fishing, and go out. . . . "please you all, a fish here. . . . please, cross cousin, a fish here . . . here Tione, a fish please. . . ."

MANU

064 *[hu, hu. . . .]*
(hu, hu)

SAKIUSA

065 *. . . ko na kauta sara ga.*
. . . you will just take it.

066 *Ia ni kua ko na kauta tiko yani a sede me laki saumi na ka e yei.*
Well, today you will carry out a cent to go pay for this thing.

067 *E sega ni ko na vosa rawa kina baleta na meca keda dau veisolisoli. . . . ka e kauta tiko na ka e da veisolisoli. . . .*
You will not be able to speak about it because the thing we buy and sell. . . . it has become something we buy and sell. . . .

MANU

068 *[Me yaga ondra yadra]*
(because their wakefulness is useful)

SAKIUSA

069 *. . . Vata kei na sede me vaka ko kaya tiko oqo.*
along with the cent, as you are saying.

MANU

070   *Me yaga nodra yadra kei na sokotaki waqa.*
(laughs) Their wakefulness and their boat sailing are useful.

071   *Au kaya.* . . .
I say. . . .

SAKIUSA

072   *[Au sa qai druka e dina e na mataqali vakasama ka tu vei iko.]*
(I am truly dismayed at the kind of thinking you have)

MANU

073   *. . . e vaka evei?*
. . . and what about it?

074   *E cava e dua na ca e tubu?*
(laughs) What harm grows from it?

SAKIUSA

075   [both together] *E vakaoti walega na gauna e na nomu dredre.* . . .
baleta . . . kevaka e tauri vakamalua, o drau veisausaumi kei Mo.
Just wasting the time by your laughing. . . . because . . . if (you)
take it easy, you two exchange with Mo.

MANU

076   *E sega.*
No.

077   *Veitalia ga na ( ) veisausaumi.*
Never mind exchange.

078   *Au burogo kina!*
(laughs) I am selfish about it!

079   *Au bureitakina!*
(laughs) I refuse it!

SAKIUSA

080   *O na bureitakina.* . . . *e tautauvata ga.* . . . *e levu na gauna ni ko*
sa dau tiko i yei, au dau rogoca ni o lako yani vei Tiko Maciu. . . .
o drau veiwekani kei Tiko Maciu.
You will refuse it. . . . it is just the same. . . . for the long time
you have been here, I have often heard that you went over to
Tiko Maciu. . . . you (two) are relatives, with Tiko Maciu?

MANU

081   *Io, keirau veiwekani kei Tiko Maciu.*
Yes, we (two) are relatives, with Tiko Maciu.

SAKIUSA

082 *Ia, a luvena o Mo.*
Well, his son is Mo.

MANU

083 *Io, e vaka e vei?*
Yes, so what?

SAKIUSA

084 *Ia, e vaka sara ga ni levu sara a gauna o dau lako yani vei koya ko
laki kerea mai kina e so na ka e tea, me dau kaya no mai
vakayagatakina.*
Well, it's like very often indeed you go over to him you go and
ask for something he plants, you say you want to use it.

MANU

085 *A cava, a cava?*
What, what?

086 *Kaya mai!*
Tell me!

087 *A cava?*
What?

SAKIUSA

088 *E rawa ni dou. . . .*
Can we. . . .

MANU

089 *E rawa ni vala dai?*
(laughs) Can we be lying?

SAKIUSA

090 *Oi, e sa vinaka.*
Oi, that is good.

091 *Au nanuma ni na rogoca tale ga ko Tiko na nodaru veivosaki tiko
oqo, ia e na qai vakadinadinatakina.*
I think Tiko will be hearing our discussion here again, well, he
will then confirm it.

092 *Ia sa vinaka kevaka e dai, baleta au rogoca walega na kena i
tukutuku.*
Well, that is good if it is a lie, because I only heard tell of it.

093 *Ia kevaka e dina e sa na bau dua na ka lasa. . . .*
But if it is true it will sure be an amusing thing. . . .

MANU

094 [A cava, a cava]
     (What, what?)

SAKIUSA

095 . . . *ni a solia na ka ma i a na nomudrau veiwekani.* . . .
     your relative has given things.

096 *Ia a luvena ko sa qai mai bureitakina tiko kina na tapako.*
     And you then are refusing tobacco to his son.

MANU

097 *Wawa, wawa!*
     Wait, wait!

098 *A cava, a cava Mo solia vei au?*
     What, what has Mo given to me?

099 *Kaya mai!*
     Say it out!

SAKIUSA

100 *Sa vinaka.*
     Good.

101 *Sa balavu tiko na gauna ni veivosaki.*
     Our discussion is getting long.

MANU

102 *Sega.*
     No.

103 *Mo kaya mai.*
     You say it out.

104 *Sa macala tiko ga na nomu daidai!*
     (laughs) Your lying will be clear!

Conflict Management, Gossip, and Affective Meaning on Nukulaelae

Niko Besnier

THIS IS A study of the structure and content of talk about interpersonal conflict and its management on Nukulaelae, a Polynesian atoll of the Tuvalu group in the Central Pacific. The main goal of this paper is to outline an ethnography of Nukulaelae conflict and conflict management at the interpersonal level based on analysis of talk about conflict and conflict management. The following questions underlie this enterprise: What type of situation is recognized as an interpersonal conflict? Are interpersonal conflicts on Nukulaelae resolved or managed? How is this achieved? How do the ways in which conflicts are perceived and managed relate to ethnopsychological assumptions (Kirkpatrick and White 1985) according to which Nukulaelae Islanders interpret and evaluate each other's behavior?

The method adopted here relies heavily on the microanalysis of talk about two conflict situations and their management. Through a detailed study of the strategies used to communicate *affective meaning* in talk about conflict, I attempt to discover the nature of the *norms* and *cultural processes* that come into play in conflict and its management on Nukulaelae.

This study develops as follows. The first section is a discussion of three sets of methodological assumptions that background this paper. Following this is a brief description of the setting of the situations under study. The next section situates the two conflict cases in a general description of conflict management on Nukulaelae from a broad ethnographic perspective. This is followed by the presentation of the conversational data, their analysis, and a discussion of the relationship of the macroethnographic analysis of conflict to the microanalysis of the conversational data.

Conflict, Gossip, and Affect:
Some Preliminary Remarks

This study is grounded in a set of basic theoretical and methodological assumptions about three areas of inquiry: the relationship of conflict situations to other types of cultural situation; the communication of normative notions in everyday talk; and the role of affect in language.

Much of the current anthropological literature on conflict (from interpersonal frictions to large-scale social disputes) emphasizes that conflict be seen as integral to social order (Beals and Siegel 1966 and Comaroff and Roberts 1981, for example). Geertz (1973) summarizes this approach: "Social conflict is not something that happens when, out of weakness, indefiniteness, obsolescence, or neglect, cultural forms cease to operate, but rather something which happens when . . . such forms are pressed by unusual situations or unusual intentions to operate in unusual ways" (1973:28). Conflict is thus most fruitfully studied as an integral part of the social system of the culture in which it occurs.

In his insightful analysis of social conflict and crisis in a Samoan village, Shore (1982) goes one step further in integrating conflict with the ambient social order: "Social conflict," he points out, "may be understood as possessing its own degree of order and interpretability" (1982:181). An important corollary to this view is the fact that conflict situations are valuable heuristic situations to gain insights into emic notions of norm and of social order as construed by the individuals involved in the conflict situation.

A second assumption underlying this study is that, through talk, interactants constantly "negotiate" (define, alter, manipulate) the norms, attitudes, and perceptions they share as members of the same society.[1] In Garfinkel's (1967) words, "interacting individuals' efforts to account for their actions—that is, to represent them verbally to others—are the primary method by which the world is constructed." (cf. McKellin's discussion of Mills's 1984 argument for the social construction of motive, this volume.)

This assumption is particularly appropriate to the study of gossip, a verbal genre that focuses on breaches of convention and on questions of propriety and norm. Gossip, then, is a special case of the politics of language use in general (Myers and Brenneis 1984, Brenneis 1984). Haviland proposes that gossip is "a primary metacultural tool" (1977:170) through which cultural rules are manipulated:[2]

> Through gossip people not only interpret the behavior of others, but also discover other people's interpretations; they can thus learn cultural rules at a distance. Through dialogue, gossip allows rules to change: it redefines the conditions of application for rules, thus keeping them up to date.

Thus gossip, "at once text and native commentary on texts" (Keesing 1974:93), is an invaluable context in which to study the ways in which individuals construct their cultural world. Gossip, furthermore, falls into the category of "ethnopsychological discourse" (Kirkpatrick and White 1985). As such, it is a primary source of data on folk theories which are the basis for *explanations* of, and *inferences* from, the behavior of others.[3] It is worth mentioning here that this paper is one of the first attempts to analyze the microscopic structure of naturally occurring gossip data. Unlike most analyses of gossip in the literature, which are either based on nonlinguistic data or on elicited linguistic data, this paper is based on gossip data *as it occurs* in the culture in focus.

My third assumption concerns the role of affective meaning in language. Irvine (1982), with others before her, recognizes three distinct, but mutually interactive, functional components to meaning: a referential (propositional) component, a social component, and an affective component (Lyons 1977:50 uses the terms "descriptive," "social," and "expressive"). The affective level is that through which speakers communicate feelings, moods, dispositions, and attitudes toward the propositional content of the message, the situation, the social context of the interaction, and so on. As pointed out by Ochs (1986), affective meaning pervades discourse, even where the general tone of the discourse is one of emotional detachment, as in, say, academic writing.

The three levels of meaning are of course intimately interrelated. Affect may be lexicalized (i.e., communicated through lexical devices whose sole purpose is to encode affect); but it may also be encoded in the syntactic structure of an utterance alongside the referential functions of syntax. Affect communication, thus, is a multichannel phenomenon (Irvine 1982:38–39) intimately (often inextricably) intertwined with referential and social meaning.

Clearly, the different channels through which affect may be communicated have different characteristics. An affective interjection such as "alas!" or "hurray!" communicates affect more clearly, less opaquely, or, to borrow a term from functional grammar (Haiman 1980, 1983), more *iconically* than syntactic devices with equivalent meanings. This fact appears to hold for all languages and cultures. Thus, the choice of "strategies," "tactics" (Bailey 1983), "channels" (Irvine 1982), or "keys" (Goffman 1974) that speakers of a language are constantly faced with in communicating affective meaning is a loaded factor in and of itself (cf. Bakhtin 1980 on the importance of "the speaker's choice of a language"). For further discussion of language and affect in a Nukulaelae context, see Besnier (1989a).

I have presented in this introduction three sets of assumptions about seemingly disparate questions, namely, the nature of conflict in the context of social order, the "meaning" of gossip, and the significance of affective meaning in verbal communication. These three notions will be interwoven in this discussion, in which correlations will be established between the speaker's choice of strategy in communicating affect in gossip about conflict and Nukulaelae ethnotheories of interpersonal conflict and conflict management.

The Setting

Nukulaelae is a small, isolated atoll of the Tuvalu group (formerly the Ellice Islands). Its population of 310 is predominantly Polynesian in origin, culture, and social organization, although it has received some influence from neighboring Micronesian Kiribati (formerly the Gilbert Islands).

The population of Nukulaelae is concentrated on the islet of Fagaua, which bounds a circular lagoon to the west. The very small size of the islet (three-fourths of a mile long and 800 feet

wide) makes for crowded living conditions. The main reason for
the concentration of the population on a small islet is the fact
that Fagaua has the most propitious land for the cultivation of
swamp taro, the staple cultigen that thrives in large artificial
muddy pits.

The decision-making powers on Nukulaelae are shared between an Island Council (*fono pule*) and a council of elders (*fono
o toeaina*). In addition, the Congregational pastor (*faifeau*) holds
a great deal of prestige on the atoll. He is the heir of the highly
mystical and respected position created by a succession of
Samoan missionary teachers who dismantled the traditional
chiefly system and established a virtual theocracy, based on their
interpretation of the Scriptures, that lasted almost ninety years
after the coming of Christianity to the island in the 1860s (Brady
1975; Munro 1982; Goldsmith 1988). The pastor's political influence is mostly covert, and depends largely on the individual
pastor's charisma and personal ambition.

The economy is based on the severely limited land resource
typical of atoll environments: swamp taro, breadfruit, coconuts,
and bananas. Land, as on most of the other atolls of the Tuvalu
group, is owned either individually (nominally by the head of
each household) or through a complex system of relatively strong
and relatively weak "claims" to corporate land shared by related
households (who are said to *kai tasi* 'eat together'). A claim to a
piece of land gives a particular household access to the resources
it produces (essentially coconuts and byproducts). Briefly, the
strength of a claim is proportional to the genealogical closeness
to the direct senior male descendant branch of the kin group (the
land tenure system, highly oversimplified here for want of space,
has been thoroughly described for Tuvalu in general by Brady
1970, 1974 and for the northern island of Nanumea by Chambers
1975, 1983).

In contrast to the severe land shortages on the other atolls of
the group that give rise to what Brady (1970) calls "land hunger,"
Nukulaelae's land problems are minor. Nevertheless, access to
land resources is an important underlying element of many interpersonal conflicts, like one of the situations discussed here, and is
the topic of many everyday interactions.

Conflict and Conflict Management on Nukulaelae

Daily life on Nukulaelae is characterized by a great deal of verbal interaction about other people's behavior, which I shall refer to as gossip (see Besnier 1989b for further discussion). These interactions usually include statements on specific normative notions, such as what constitutes appropriate reactions to particular situations or appropriate conduct in particular settings. In these gossip events (the term "event" is used here as a particular case of Hymes's 1974 notion of "speech event"), Nukulaelae Islanders betray a very strong prescriptive attitude toward other individuals' behavior and an acute sense of ridicule.

The environment in which these interactions take place is carefully controlled. They may only occur between close relatives or within a circle of close "friends," individuals who perform work and spend leisurely hours together. It is inappropriate to initiate gossip activities in the presence of individuals who do not fit this description. Gossip activities are thus marked as *private events.* Whether gossip may take place or not thus defines a *private arena* (to borrow Turner's 1974 term), clearly distinguishable from a *public arena.*[4] This public-private distinction is salient in Nukulaelae daily life. In the public arena, interpersonal interactions tend to be precoded and behavior essentially formulaic; spontaneity is associated principally with the private arena.

Attitudes toward gossip activities are ambivalent. While gossip is often condemned publicly as antisocial behavior, the same individuals who condemn it in the public arena often engage in gossip activities in appropriate circumstances. Gossip is a socially accepted activity as long as it is confined to the private arena. Individuals who are in the habit of engaging in gossip activities indiscriminately are strongly stigmatized (*pona*) as having "talking mouths" (*gutu faipati*).[5]

Cultural explanations for the inappropriateness of gossip activities in the public arena typically involve the fact that gossip often leads to interpersonal confrontations. Public confrontations and, more generally, the display of private (personal) identities in the public arena are seen as threats to the established social order. Responsible adults must maintain a state of mutual acceptance

and general harmony (*feaalofani* 'to feel empathy for each other',
a term borrowed from Samoan) when interacting with each other
and must avoid directly confrontative behavior as much as possible. Responsible adults should not let their emotions and internal states interfere with their social relationships and affect
others. A responsible person is calm, unemotional, unaffected by
the environment, and noninterfering. In contrast, a child or a
mentally deviant individual (*fakavalevale*) is erratic and unpredictable, is driven by emotional reaction to the environment, and
by attempts to interfere with social order so as to meet individual
needs. Variants of the same ideology are found in other Polynesian societies, such as Samoa (Duranti 1984, this volume;
Shore 1982), Tahiti (Levy 1973), and, in slightly different terms,
the Marquesas (Kirkpatrick 1983).

A consequence of the avoidance of interpersonal disharmonies
is the fact that the Nukulaelae social system is not well equipped
to handle the interpersonal conflicts that do arise. In contrast to
A'ara (White, this volume), Kwara'ae (Watson-Gegeo and Gegeo,
this volume), and contemporary Hawaiian cultures (Boggs and
Chun, this volume), all of which exhibit well-defined and highly
specialized disentangling situations (*graurutha*, *fa'amanata'anga*,
and *ho'oponopono* respectively), Nukulaelae culture does not
recognize a "disentangling" context to deal with interpersonal
conflicts. There is no clearly recognized event exclusively associated with the *resolution* of interpersonal conflicts. These are
managed rather than solved (cf. Lindstrom, this volume).

Feelings of anger, antagonism, and displeasure directed to another individual as a result of nonmanaged interpersonal conflict
are viewed as potentially disruptive, particularly when the individuals involved belong to the same household (*kaaiga*) or
broader kin group. The "bad heart" (*loto maasei*, a term used in
line 06 of transcript B) that arises between relatives as the result
of an intrafamilial conflict is likely to affect the outcome of a fishing expedition, for example.[6] Both the display and the harboring
of antagonistic feelings are seen as negative and potentially
harmful elements on Nukulaelae, as among the A'ara, Kwara'ae,
and Hawaiians discussed elsewhere in this volume.

When the conflict is seen as serious, as in the case of theft or of
physical wrong, and the interactants do not belong to the same

kin group, they usually refer the situation to a Western-style court (*fono fakamasino*). The court is presided over by the island judge (*faamasino*), whose function is similar to that of a justice of the peace in American society. One person takes the other to the monthly court meeting (*ave ki te fono*), where both parties usually end up being lectured by the judge, quite severely at times, and ordered to pay fines and retributions. This type of conflict management will not be discussed in this paper.

Intrafamilial conflicts like the two conflict situations discussed below are kept as much as possible within the private arena. Chambers (1975) reports similar patterns from the northernmost island of Tuvalu, Nanumea. Her discussion stresses the importance of the public-private dimension in the management of conflict on Nanumea:

> Relatives are expected not to quarrel with each other, though of course they do from time to time. Quarrels which do occur within an extended family are kept as quiet as possible, as most Nanumeans are reluctant to take a relative to court, even to secure right to land they believe should be theirs. Most of the public quarrels that do occur, however, involve relatives, and both relatives and non-relatives rush to the scene, the former to stop the fighting or to take sides, the latter to enjoy the show. There is little privacy, of course, and extended family groups do all they can to 'avoid publicity' in regard to their affairs (1975:43).

An intrafamilial conflict *must* be managed if it begins to affect other individuals or events not directly related to the conflict situation. Such is the case when individuals from outside the kin group become involved in the conflict or when a cause-and-effect relationship is established between the "bad heart" (*loto maasei*) harbored by an individual and an unfortunate event. Thus, a conflict is recognized as such only when it affects someone or something in the public arena. Only then will an attempt to manage the conflict be made. Thus, as on Santa Isabel (White, this volume), a conflict situation will be disentangled only if there is a *specific* reason to do so.

Conflict managements of this type usually take place as the individuals involved *faipati fakallei* 'talk thoroughly' (see transcript A, line 22). This type of interaction is not exclusively associated with conflict management; *faipati* 'to make word(s)' is the general term for any talk or conversation focused on a specific topic. This term contrasts with *sauttala* 'to chat', which refers to interactions not focused on a specific topic. The two transcripts on which this paper is based are of *sauttala* about *faipati fakallei* interactions.

The emphasis of conflict management through *faipati fakallei* is on the reestablishment of a harmonious front between the individuals involved (*feaalofani* 'to feel empathy for each other') and on the fact that the conflict has not succeeded in affecting their reciprocal social identity in the public arena (this fact is stressed at several points in the transcribed narratives in transcripts A and B below). During the management talk, the conflict is typically declared to be *off record* as far as the relationship of the public identities of the interactants is concerned.

Conversational Transcripts

This section presents the two interpersonal conflict situations on which this discussion is based. Here I introduce the information necessary to contextualize the conversational transcripts on which the analysis is based.

The transcripts are of two spontaneous conversations about unrelated interpersonal conflict situations. These conversations take place between Kelisiano and Feue (Kelisiano's name will be abbreviated to K hereafter, and Feue's to F; all names are pseudonyms). Each of the situations had taken place a few days before. Both had involved K, a man in his forties. Unlike many men of his generation on Nukulaelae, he is not a *matai* (head of a kin group), because his father, a man of great influence on the island, still holds the position as the senior member of the kin group. K's interlocutor, F, is a matai in his early fifties and a distant cousin of K. F and K spend most of their leisurely hours (*taafao*) together and are fishing partners. Their relationship is one of close friendship, in a pattern characteristic of the rather exclusive interpersonal bonds that Tuvaluans of all ages establish with each other.

Both conversations take place in the storage hut behind F's kin group's kitchen hut. In both situations, F, K, and I had just returned from our daily fishing expedition. The setting is private and very relaxed. The conversation touched on a wide variety of topics, from the most trivial to the most scandalous. The transcripts presented in transcripts A and B are part of a much longer conversation. Topic shifts are usually marked by long pauses (up to twenty minutes of silence) or may be forced by a third party's arrival within earshot. These two interactions are prototypical examples of the casual conversations (*sauttala*) that occupy an important part of every Nukulaelae Islander's everyday life.

The interactors in the gossip sessions were not aware that their conversation was tape-recorded, but subsequently gave me permission to use the recordings for my research. The two interactions were recorded in the general framework of a sociolinguistic study of conversational discourse on Nukulaelae. The story line of the first interaction (transcript A) reads as follows: Luisa, a young woman married to an important member of the community,[7] finds out that several of her banana trees have been chopped down. She knows that K had worked in the vicinity of those trees on the same day and accuses him of having chopped them down, which he has no right to do since he does not belong to same kin group.[8] In fact, the culprits are Maataio and Tito, who belong to Luisa's *kai tasi* (group of land-owning households) and thus have the right to destroy the trees. Fearing a direct confrontation with K, Luisa goes to an influential member of the community, Saamasone, with the request that K be punished by being barred from taking communion the following Sunday. Timooteo mentions the request to K, who then seeks Luisa. In the meantime, Luisa had learned that her original accusation was false. When she finally meets K at Olataga, a small settlement on an islet across the lagoon from Fagaua, she apologizes to him for her rash conduct.

The second interaction (transcript B) concerns a conflict involving K and a close female relative of his, Saavave. The conflict takes place in the wake of K's daughter's wedding, which was to involve, like all weddings on Nukulaelae, many days of feasting and entertainment, in which the entire island community participates, and considerable labor (fishing, gardening) and money to purchase rice, kerosene, and other imported goods from the island store. To help with the expenses, relatives of K working on Nauru (a phosphate-producing island in the Central Pacific, on which small contingents of Tuvaluans are employed as temporary workers) had wired a $150 money order. The money was clearly intended for the *fakalavelave* 'family event', but was addressed to three people who are closely related to the four senders. One of them is K's father's classificatory sister Saavave, who took it upon herself to pick the money up from the telegraph office and to divide it up among the three recipients, including $50 for her own use. She is confronted by her own relatives and is made to return half of the money to K. This forces her to confront K, who subtly ridicules her; she then blames the senders for not having made clear that the money was communal.

Analysis

In this section, the gossip narratives transcribed in the appendix are analyzed with respect to five affective strategies. Patterns are sought in the ways affect is communicated in the gossip session about the two conflict situations. As will be seen, the gossiper uses specific channels to communicate his attitudes and emotions, all of which are characteristically low in iconicity.

Informational Structure of the Narratives

Two analytic components to the narratives can be distinguished, as is traditionally done in the literature on discourse structure (Labov and Fanshel 1977, for example): a main story line, what Grimes (1975) calls the "event"; and background materials, comments, and details (or "collateral information"). These two components are interwoven in the conversation, with the hinges easily identifiable. Among other things, the linguistic devices used in marking these hinges change the "footing" (Goffman 1981) of the interaction.

Prosody is the linguistic level at which these changes are most commonly marked. Several examples from the first transcript will serve to illustrate. For instance, an increase in voice intensity (italicized in the free English translation) marks a shift from main story line to background material:[9]

(TRANSCRIPT A)

15   *Aku muna   ttaa, ((laughs)) (2.0)*   I said, "come on, am I crazy
     my   words hey!   or what?"
     A   ko   au nei   e- (0.6) e(i)
     and Foc I   this Nps
     he tino   fakavalevale? (0.
     a   person crazy

16   *E   TONU laa   i*   It is true that I gardened
     Nps true   then that   in that area. [. . .]
     au ne sseu i   koo. [. . .]
     I   Pst hoe at there

Similarly, a change in both tempo and pitch accompanies a return from a set of collateral remarks to the main event line in the
following excerpt:

20   *[. . .] ko   Timooteo e::*   [. . .] while Timooteo's
             Foc Timooteo Nps   [banana trees] are up above
     nofo ki luga.   [on the edge of the garden
     stay to top   pit].

21   *((high pitch, fast)) (Ak)u muna i:o!*   I said, "all right!"
                           my   words yes

Nonprosodic devices include changes from direct to reported
speech and vice versa, as in lines 36–37 and 39–40.

36   *Au ne toe   logo fakamuli aka   fua*   "I heard [the truth] just
     I   pst just hear recently   then just recently."

37   *((louder)) Peelaa ko te   o-*   So that when she got upset,
                like   Foc the   [. . .]
     tena osotiiga [. . .]
     her   attack

39   *Logo au kaiaa mo   ko:: (0.3) ko*   But more recently, what do I
     hear I   why? that Foc   hear? that Tito and Maataio
     Tito eiloa   mo   Maataio   were the ones that [chopped
     Tito indeed and Maataio   down those trees] . . .

kolaa ne hai nee laaua a:: (3.0)
those Pst do Erg they-2 Cnt

40 *Muna mai. Koo hee:ai- hee:ai he*   (She) says to me, "there is
    words Dxs Inc Neg   Neg   a   nothing, no rancor between
    mea e: (0.7) onosai e:i-.   us any more"
    thing Nps   rancor Anp

Shifts from and to reported speech often interact with turn changes in the gossip session itself; in the following examples, K ends his turn with a reported string, and F begins a new turn with a nonreported string which initiates a clarification (side-comment) sequence:

(TRANSCRIPT A)

41 *K: (M)una: au, (0.7) fakatau*   K: I say, "let us forgive each
        say   I   exchange   other now."
    fakamaagalo nei taaua.
    forgive   now we-2
    ((laughter, 1.8))

42 *F: (Tee)laa heeai he (t)- koe e:*   F: So that there is no- . . .
        thus   Neg a   you Nps   You should have said that
    hai mo: (ko) ttoo   [you were leaving] the
    say that Foc the+garden   banana plantation for
    futi   o: ttoeaina. ((laughter))   [her] old man!
    banana of the+old-man

(TRANSCRIPT B)

11 *K: Aku muna, ka: ne   aa*   K: I said: "what are we doing
        my words but some what?   [standing here and] talking
    laa ttou pati e hai,   about this, the money has
    then our-3 words Nps say   already been split up
    ((falsetto)) mo   koo oti laa ne   between us by Saavave [of
                  because Prf   then   her own accord] . . ."
    vae vae nee: (0.3) Saavave:,
    divide divide Erg   Saavave

12   F: ((mid-high pitch, falling)) Te   F: That thing [the money]
                                  the   is not hers to take [. . .]
     mea   teelaa seeai   sena mea
     thing that Neg her thing
     a   ia [. . .]
     of her

Note that most of the main story line is in the form of directly reported speech. The story, in essence, is told in the form of a dialog. What K is performing is what Bakhtin (1978) and others have called "dialoging." I shall return presently to the significance of this strategy.

Having established the distinction between main and collateral information, I shall now turn to the distribution of affective meaning among these two components. More specifically, I shall focus on where and how K communicates *negative* affect (condemnation, ridicule, annoyance, and the like) in his account of the conflict and its management.

The first significant fact to be noted is that K *avoids* issuing any overt value judgments on, or condemnations of, his opponents in the two conflict situations he describes. This is particularly true of the collateral part of his narrative. At no stage in the course of the long search of collateral discourse quoted in lines 16–18 of transcript A does he state an opinion on the situation described:

16   *E   TONU laa   i   au ne sseu*   It is true that I gardened
     Nps true   then that I Pst hoe   in that area
     i   koo (1.5)
     at there

17   *a   ko futi   kolaa ne hai*   But those banana trees were
     but Foc banana those Pst do   [cut down] by Maataio and
     eiloa   n(ee) Maataio mo:: (0.9)   Tito.
     indeed Erg   Maataio and
     mo   Tito (2.3)
     and Tito

18   *I   au hoki eiloa   maafaufau*   I also thought [as I was
     because I also indeed think   gardening] about– that

peenaa ki:: (0.7) me   io   those banana trees were
thus   about   that belong-to   theirs, right?
laatou a: futi   nee?
hey   Cnt banana Tag

19   *He:ki ai   eiloa   heaku futi*   So I didn't [chop down] any
     Neg Anp indeed my   banana   banana tree–
     ne:: (1.0)
     Pst

20   *ne mea i- a   ko:*   The [chopped-down]
     Pst thing at and Foc   banana trees that I dragged
     futi   kolaa ne:: (0.8) ne: laga   to the side are Timooteo's;
     banana those Pst   Pst drag   theirs [Luisa's] are down
     eiloa   nee au keaate:(a) e   below [in the garden pit],
     indeed Erg I   away   Nps   while Timooteo's are up
     io   t- Timooteo, (1.1) mo   above [on the edge of the
     belong-to   Timooteo   because   garden pit].
     ko olotou futi   e   tai
     Foc their-3 banana Nps almost

     ttuu   ki lalo   ko Timooteo e::
     stand to bottom Foc Timooteo

     e::   nofo ki luga.
     Nps stay to above

In contrast, F intersperses K's narrative with short turns (essentially, verbal "engagement displays"—Goodwin 1981) whose affective meaning is negative in regard to evaluation of the
reported events. In line 23 of transcript A, for instance, F
punctuates the end of part of K's narrative with a heavily affect-
laden interjection:

23   *F: Ttaahh!* =   [Scandalized] That's
     Exc   outrageous!

In the examples below from transcript B, F is more explicit in his
evaluative judgment of K's opponent and makes a highly normative set of remarks, after which K expresses agreement:

12 *F: ((mid-high pitch, falling)) Te*   F: That thing [the money] is
                               the   not hers to take, it is some-
    mea   teelaa seeai sena mea   thing [that was sent] on
    thing that   Neg her thing   account of the family
    a ia   me   se mea //   event [the wedding], it was
    of her because a thing   primarily sent to you.
    (i te)   fakalave = // = lave ne
    for the family-event   Pst
    aumai // loa // kiaa koe.
    send   indeed to   you

13 *K: // Peelaa nee? // // mm! //*   K: That's it, right? Hmm!
    thus   Tag   Exc

42 *F: [. . .] Te tonuga lo: laa*   F: The truth of the matter is
    the truth   indeed then   that it [the money] should
    te mea   laa   teenaa see   not have been given to
    the thing then that   Neg   Saavave but it should have
    tuku fua kiaa Saavave ka:e::   been handed over to
    give just to   Saavave but   Kelisiano because it was sent
    ttau eiloa   o   peeofu Kelisiano   on account of the family
    must indeed Cmp pay   Kelisiano   event [the wedding], right?
    me::-   ne aumai ki te
    because Pst send for the
    fakalavelave nee? =
    family-event Tag

43 *F: = Mm.*   K: Hmm.
    Exc.

In several instances, K appears to be about to issue an abstract evaluative judgment on his opponent, an explicit indication of how F is to evaluate matters. In each instance, however, he stops short and replaces the evaluative remark with a conversational device that I have elsewhere called the "three-dot phenomenon" (Besnier 1982); that is, information whose sharedness among the participants in a conversation is assumed and thus need not be stated overtly (see Cicourel 1972 for a discussion of the "unspoken elements" of a social interaction). In line 36 of transcript B, the "three-dot phenomenon" is realized as a chuckle and the noncompletion of a turn, both at the phonological and syntactic levels:

36 *Aku muna koo atuli eiloa   a*   I figured she got chased out
    my words Inc chase indeed Cnt   by her ((chuckles)) [i.e., by
    ia n(ee) thenahhh ((chuckles))   her family, for having done
    she Erg her   something wrong].

The only overtly prescriptive pronouncements that K utters are statements through which he establishes his own credibility. Significantly, these are part of the narrative itself, not side comments addressed to F, and they are clearly framed as reported-speech strings; observe, for example, the following two excerpts from transcript A:

15 *Aku muna ttaa, ((laughs)) (2.0)*   I said, "come on,
    my   words hey!   am I crazy or what?"
    A   ko au nei e- (0.6) ei(i)
    and Foc I   this Nps
    he tino   fakavalevale? (0.7)
    a   person crazy

31 *Kiloko, (2.2) au he tino   eiloa-*   "You see, I am a man who
    you-see   I a person indeed   always knows, like, <u>given</u>
    E   ILOA LLEI faeloa   nee au   <u>my social position,</u> [who
    Nps know well constantly Erg I   always knows] whether
    peelaa te:: (2.0) i luga i oku   what I do is [right or]
    thus the   from my   wrong.
    tofi, (1.1)   i te mea kaa
    social-position on the thing Irr
    hai nee au peelaa hee llei. (0.8)
    do Erg I like   Neg good

32 *Kae ilo   nee au a   futi   a*   And I [also] know which
    and know Erg I Cnt banana Cnt   banana trees are yours."
    koutou.
    you-3

Furthermore, the credibility-establishing sequence of line 15 is worded as a rhetorical question ("Am I crazy?"), and that of lines

31–32 includes a phrase (*i luga i oku tofi* 'from the perspective of my social duties/position') which, inserted at the beginning of the quoted turn, stresses the *socially recognized* and nonnegotiable nature of K's credibility.

The rhetorical strategy of K's discourse is clear: had credibility-establishing statements been included in the collateral part of the narrative and hence directly addressed to F, his audience might have inferred that K *needed* to establish credibility in this context. As part of the quoted narrative line, and with the support of the two rhetorical devices noted in the previous paragraph, the only possible inference is that K needs to establish his credibility only for the sake of faithfully reporting his verbal interaction with his two opponents. K's "assertive rhetoric" (Bailey 1983) is devastatingly powerful.

Prosodic Structure

When K reports his own portion of dialogs, his soft and unexcited prosodic patterns are geared to convey the impression of calm, thoughtfulness, and level-headedness, as in his response to the initial accusation in transcript A:

13　*((mid-high pitch, whisper)) Io? (0.4)*　　"Oh? And why?"
　　　　　　　　　　　　　　　yes

　　I te aa?
　　why?

21　*((high pitch, fast)) (Ak)u muna*　　I said, "all right!"
　　　　　　　　　　　　my　words

　　i:o!
　　yes

K's own reported discourse is characterized by relatively long conversational turns and complex sentence structures uninterrupted by pauses. This is particularly clear in the straightening-out sequence with Luisa.

27　*Aku muna　Luisa, lle:i, (0.3)*　　I said, "Luisa, good [I am
　　my　speech Luisa　good　　　　　glad we are running into

i au ne m- manako kee: because I Pst want Sbj *fetaui taaua i Fagaua kae:-* meet we-2 at Fagaua but *mea aka laa koe koo tele* thing then then you Inc run *mai ki Olataga. (1.2)* Dxs to Olataga	each other], because I very much wanted to meet you on Fagaua but- the thing is that you had come over here to Olataga.

28 *Ko au fua e: faipati atu kiaa* Foc I just Nps speak Dxs to *koe ki luga i te: (0.3) peelaa mo* you about the like *tau: fekau ne avatu nee* your message Pst transmit Erg *Samasone.* Samasone	I just wanted to talk to you about, like, your complaint that [I heard about] through Samasone."

K's self-reported discourse thus has many features characteristic of planned discourse (Ochs 1979). The production of
spontaneous discourse with planned characteristics is a skill associated with public speaking, which is performed exclusively by
senior male members of the community. K's use of planned features in his self-reported turns associates his role in the reported
conversation with the social attributes of the most responsible
and powerful members of the community.

In contrast, when reporting his opponent's turns, K conveys the
impression of an erratic, emotional, unpredictable individual
through the use of short stretches of repetitive, choppy discourse,
as in lines 29–30 and 40 of transcript A and line 29, transcript B:

29 [continuation from 28 above]
(2.2) ((high pitch)) Muna mai io-,
              say   Dxs yes
((fast)) io- io-! ((laughter))
      yes yes
	She says, "Yes, oh, yes- yes-!"

30 *(Muna)hh a tou fafi(ne)!* say Cnt your woman	That's what she said, the woman!

40   *Muna mai. Koo hee:ai- HEE:ai he:*   [She] says to me, "There is
     say   Dxs Inc Neg   Neg   a   nothing- no harbored feel-
     mea   e: (0.7) onosai   *e:i-*   ing between us any more."
     thing Nps   harbor-feelings Anp

(TRANSCRIPT B)

29   *((high pitch)) Muna mai heeai laa*   She says, "I did nothing
              say   Dxs Neg   then wrong, they were the ones
     hoku ssee   i   ei, (0.5)   that did something wrong."
     my   wrong in Anp

     ((mid-high pitch)) e   ssee   eiloa
               Nps wrong indeed

     ko: ko   laatou.
     Foc Foc they-3

K's communicative intent may be analyzed in the light of the Davitz's (1964) model of affective meaning. Focusing on the subjective perception of affect in discourse, Davitz notes a strong correlation between what is perceived as passive feelings and low pitch, soft voice, and a slow rate of speech; in contrast, subjectively active feelings are associated with high pitch, flaring timbre, and a fast rate of speech.

K exploits these correlations in conjunction with one of the most salient characteristics of dialoging: the fact that, through reported speech, "I can appropriate meaning *to my purpose* [. . .] by ventriloquing others" (Holquist 1983:4; emphasis added). K presents himself as emotionally self-controlled, a characteristic equated with maturity on Nukulaelae, as pointed out above. In contrast, K presents Luisa and Saavave, his two opponents, as erratic speakers, lacking self-control, and, hence, immature.

Word Choice and Syntactic Structure

Two of the most covert and most effective channels for encoding affect are word choice and syntactic structure. The affective component of these two channels is covert because the primary function of words and syntax is the communication of referential meaning. Affect is always present in description, whether of a high or low degree of iconicity. The overlaying of affective meaning in the lexical and syntactic structure of discourse is a tactic that involves what Bateson terms "camouflage" (1972:414).

Next, I shall investigate the affective use of three classes of lexical and syntactic strategies: the marking of syntactic and pragmatic role within the clause; nominal reference; and emphatic and moderating adverbs. (This list by no means exhausts the affective exploitations of lexical and syntactic choice in the two transcripts.)

As described in Besnier (1986), much pragmatic information is encoded in the syntactic structure of a Tuvaluan sentence. The many possible word-order variations, for example, are distinguished from each other by the relative pragmatic salience of the nominal constituents of the sentence and by the semantics of the different case-marking patterns associated with each word-order combination.

One of the main features of this system is the fact that fine distinctions can be made in the degree of agentivity of the subject of the clause (i.e., the degree of responsibility of the agent in the action or state described by the verb). In lines 30–31 of transcript A, quoted above, for example, the ergative case-marker *nee* denotes high agentivity (Besnier 1986). Its use stresses the high degree of involvement of the agent in the action described. Note that this case-marker is used three times in the same short stretch of reported speech; in each case, the subject is a first-person singular pronoun. The case-marking strategy used in this stretch of discourse stresses the high degree of responsibility of the narrator in the situation described.

Similarly, in Nukulaelae Tuvaluan, the recipient nature of an indirect object may be emphasized through the use of the deictic adverb *atu* 'toward the recipient'. This contrasts with the marking of indirect objecthood through overt expression of the noun phrase without the adverb and through presence of the adverb without an indirect object. K uses the "emphatic" syntactic strategy in line 28 of transcript A, where both the adverb *atu* and the indirect object *kiaa koe* are present:

28	*Ko au fua e: faipati atu*	"Let me just talk to you
	Foc I just Nps speak Dxs	about the:, like, the com-
	kiaa koe ki luga i te: (0.3)	plaint that Samasone told
	to you about the	me about."

peelaa mo tau: fekau ne avatu
like your message Pst transmit
nee Samasone.
Erg Samasone

Not surprisingly, the subject of this clause refers to K, and the indirect object to Luisa, K's opponent. This strategy emphasizes the recipient (and, thus, powerless) position in which Luisa finds herself in the reported interaction.

Nominal reference in Tuvaluan may be expressed in a variety of ways, including zero-anaphora, the least "informational" (i.e., the least definite, the most opaque, and potentially the most ambiguous) referential strategy available (Besnier 1985). K makes frequent use of this referential strategy when talking about his opponents, as in the examples below from transcripts A and B:

(TRANSCRIPT A)

25	*((high pitch)) au naa e vau*	I was [walking along and]
	I then Nps come	came to [the level of]
	i te:: (0.3) fale o: Elekana	Elekana and Manatu's
	at the house of Elekana	house, and there she [Luisa]
	mo Manatu- ((high pitch)) e nofo	was!
	and Manatu Nps stay	
	atu i ei!	
	Dxs at Anp	

(TRANSCRIPT B)

33	*Tuku mai te:: ((high pitch)) mea,*	(She) then gives me the
	hand Dxs the thing	thing [the money], turns her
	mea, ffuli mai (eiloa) ttua:	heels, and leaves.
	thing turn Dxs indeed the+back	
	koo hano	
	Inc go	

In several instances, the same individuals are referred to by full noun phrases, but K chooses a descriptive noun phrase, *tou fafine* 'your woman', instead of a proper name. This is illustrated in lines 29–30 of transcript A and in lines 16–18 of transcript B below. This expression, which is often used in Nukulaelae gossip along with its equivalent *tou tagata* 'your man', has clearly sarcastic undertones.

16	*Fakalogo au nei ((chuckling)) ki* hear I here to *te mea a Ioopu e fai mai* the thing of Ioopua Nps say Dxs *kiaa Saavave, (2.0) galo aka* to Saavave disappear then	I overheard what Ioopu told Saavave,
17	*(2.0) galo aka tou fafine,* disappear then your woman	then the woman [Saavave] disappeared.
18	*maaua laa mo Lusi e llaga* we-2 the with Lusi Nps weave *pola i tena paa, koo vau* baskets at his coop Inc come *tou- tou fafine.* your your woman	[Later, while] Lusi and I were weaving coconut- frond baskets near his chicken coop, the woman [Saavave] came by.

Note also the reference made by F to Luisa's husband as *te toeaina* 'the old man' in line 42 of the first transcript. This term, which usually has a neutral connotation, is used sarcastically here, in that Luisa's husband is neither of an age nor of a social position to be called a *toeaina* 'elder, old man'.

The connotation of K's consistent use of referential expressions low in informationality when talking about his opponents is that, for him, these can be described, like nonhuman entities, with nonproper noun phrases. The general affective perlocution is thus unmistakenly negative.

K's use of adverbials is also striking. When reporting his own turns, he uses in several instances emphatic adverbs: *eiloa, loa* 'indeed [etc.]', *faeloa* 'always, constantly', and *llei* 'well, very much'. An example of this occurs in transcript A at the beginning of his report of his straightening-out conversation with Luisa:

27	*Aku muna Luisa, (2.0) lle:i, [...]* my words Luisa good	I said, "Luisa, good, [...]."

Other examples occur a little later in the same conversation:

31   *Au he tino   eiloa- E   ILOA*   "I am a man who always
     I   a   person indeed Nps know   knows, like, given my social
     LLEI   faeloa nee au peelaa te::   position, [who always
     well always Erg I   like   the   knows] whether what I do is
     (2.0) i luga i oku tofi, (1.1)   is [right or] wrong."
           from   my social-position

     i   te   mea   kaa hai nee au
     on the thing Irr   do Erg I

     peelaa hee   llei. (0.8)
     like   Neg good

33   *Tee(l)aa laa ((mid-high pitch))*   "So, I did not [chop down]
     thus   a single banana tree of
     HEEai eiloa   he futi   o: koutou   yours."
     Neg   indeed a banana of you-3

     ne:: n-
     Pst   Pst

Besides their referential function as markers of emphasis, these adverbs convey the impression of a determined and self-assured speaker, precisely the presentation of self (Goffman 1959) K strives for through his narrative.

In the same manner, K reports Samasone's original overture by including the moderating adverb *hua* 'just, only', which serves as a dampener on the initial secondhand accusation. This accusation, incidentally, is worded more as a piece of transmitted information than an accusation, thus already putting into question Luisa's credibility as the initiator of the accusation:

12   *((whisper)) au e   ssili atu hua*   "I just want to ask you
          I   Nps ask Dxs just   about Luisa's request [...]"
     kia koe i   te:: (1.8) fekau
     to   you about the   message

     nei a: Luisa ne hai mai [...]
     this of Luisa Pst say Dxs

K presents himself as being on the same footing as Samasone,

who is, as stated earlier, an influential member of the community.
The picture is clear: through subtle lexical and syntactic
choices that *appear* to be dictated by referential considerations, K
manages to present himself as having characteristics of a mature
and responsible personality. In contrast, the lexical and syntactic
descriptions of his opponents' actions and speech are charged
with negative affect.[10]

Conversational Structure of the Reported Interactions

Conversation analysts have shown that interactors organize
their conversations to reflect the relative social power between
them (much of the research on this topic is based on data from in-
tergender conversation: West and Zimmerman 1983, Leet-Pellegrini 1980, for example). Conversation opening, topic changes,
and pair-part initiation, for instance, are predominantly controlled by the interactant with greater power or greater access to interpersonal control. This fact appears to be universal.

Significantly, the reported dialogs that form part of K's narrative have many of the features of an interaction between unequals. K attributes to his own reported turns a number of
features of the speech of dominant conversationalists and
presents his interactors' turns as those of subordinate interactors.[11] In the first transcript, he is the one who opens the reported
interactions with his opponents, as in lines 26–27, which is the
beginning of the straightening-out dialog with Luisa:

26 *Maatou mo   Uili mo Paka. (0.3)*   I was with Uili and Paka.
    we-3   with Uili and Paka

27 *Aku muna Luisa, lle:i, [. . .]*   I said, "Luisa, good, [. . .]."
    my words Luisa good

Similarly, his last interaction with Saavave in the second
transcript begins with a question-answer "adjacency pair"
(Schegloff and Sacks 1973), whose first part, again, K utters:

19 *Ia! (1.6) Aku muna, he aah? (1.0)*   "Yes," I said "what is it?"
    Exc   my words a what?

20   *Konaa te:: tau:: te   luafulu*   [she says] "Here are the::,
      there   the your the twenty   you::r, the twenty-five
      lima taalaa.   dollars."
      five dollar

Lastly, in transcript A, it is K who initiates the "forgiveness" sequence. He uses a reciprocal clause, indicating that forgiveness is to be "exchanged" rather than addressed to him alone. This is an illustration of what Bailey calls a "rhetoric of compromise" tactic (1983:144–77):

41   *(M)una: au, (0.7) fakatau*   I said: "let us forgive
      say   I   exchange   each other now."
      fakamaagalo nei   taaua.
      forgive   now we-2
      ((laughter, 1.8))

This short analysis of the structure of the verbal interactions between K and his two opponents as K reports them shows again that, through the covert communication of affect, K presents himself in the narratives as a powerful, self-controlled, and, generally speaking, empathy-worthy individual.

Laughter

Finally, K punctuates his narratives with laughter and chuckles in what appears to be a highly systematic fashion, the purpose of which is the communication of an affective meaning congruent with that conveyed by the other factors reviewed in this section.

Many authors have stressed the extreme polysemy of laughter (Apte 1985; Chapman and Foot 1976, for example), a fact that cultural actors are well aware of (as witnessed by the rich conceptions of laughter types found in many cultures). While it is often difficult (if not impossible) to attribute a specific meaning to laughter where it occurs, the very *presence* of laughter may be interpreted as a significant factor (Besnier 1983a). In particular, affect communication is recognized as the most salient function of laughter.

K both laughs and *invites* laughter (Jefferson 1979) in two types of contexts. In one, laughter punctuates a self-reported turn in which he is forced by the conflict situation to issue a face-threatening statement. In line 41 above, for example, K is placed in the face-threatening position (both for him and, in particular, for his opponent) of having to initiate a forgiveness sequence. In the example below (first transcript), he is forced to save his own face in the reported dialog by asking a rhetorical question bearing on his sanity and social behavior:

15   *Aku muna ttaa, ((laughter)) (2.0)*   I said, "come on, am I crazy
      my words hey!   or what?"
     A   ko au nei e- (0.6) e(i)
     and Foc I   this Nps
     he tino <u>fakavalevale</u>? (0.7)
     a person

In both examples, laughter appears to invite an appreciation of the ridiculous nature of the whole situation Luisa created between them.

    The second context type is more transparent. K laughs and invites laughter when reporting an opponent's turns or when describing an opponent's actions as illustrated in examples from both transcripts:

(TRANSCRIPT A)

29   *((high pitch)) Muna mai io-,*   She says, "yes, oh, yes- yes-!"
                say   Dxs yes

30   *((laughter)) (Muna)hh a   tou*   That's what she said,
               say   Cnt your   the woman!
     fafi(ne)!
     woman

(TRANSCRIPT B)

36   *Aku muna koo atuli eiloa   a*   I figured she got chased out
     my words Inc chase indeed Cnt by her [family, for having
     ia   n(ee) thenahhh ((chuckles)) done something wrong].
     she Erg   her

In both contextual types, laughter is used as a channel to communicate negative affect. The target is either the conflict situation in general, which, in both cases, was initiated by the other party, or K's opponent.

Discussion

In this analysis I have examined types of affective meaning filtered through five different channels in conversations about two conflict situations. In the following discussion, I bring together the patterns observed in the conversational data with the more general ethnographic description given previously.

How does the channeling of affective meaning reflect the cultural ideologies that come into play in interpersonal conflicts and their management? In this enterprise is rooted the notion that a gossiper is "a complex filtering mechanism" (Haviland 1977:61). In other words, how the gossiper exploits rhetoric (in the broadest sense of the term) for "the conscious manipulation in a covert way of the feelings and sentiments of others" (Bailey 1983:24) is intrinsically interdependent with what a conflict situation *represents* in the culture in question.

It is important to note, first of all, that the gossiper's rhetorical manipulations are not limited to his audience in the two situations under study. In addition to K's obvious intent to have F believe him and side with him in the two gossip sessions, K also manipulates the presentation of self of his two opponents. Thus, as is the case in dialoging in general (Bakhtin 1978, 1980), K juggles between two contexts of reference: that of the ongoing conversation and that of the reported conversation. Through talk about his two opponents' actions, K modifies at will the nature of their positional identities (or social selves). He is also more or less in control of his audience's affective relationship toward the reported events and its protagonist. The two gossip situations under study are thus prime illustrations of the ways in which reality may be actively negotiated through talk.

The main conclusion that transpires through the analysis of the conversational data is the fact that K carefully avoids issuing any overt judgment on his opponent in the two conflict situations or on the conflicts themselves. Instead, from the beginning of the gossip sessions, he appears to take for granted the fact that his opponents have presented themselves in a clearly negative light. He then further reinforces this fact through covert affective devices or subtly manipulates his audience (which is only too willing to cooperate) to voice the judgments and articulate the norms at play. Bailey's (1983:223–24) remark that the effects of rhetoric are neutralized once detected as rhetoric is pertinent here. K's rhetorical strategy is to communicate his own feelings and attitudes through covert communicative channels that are low in iconicity. These covert communicative channels are also minimally marked for evidentiality, in that the author of the discourse may not readily be held accountable for the affect communicated in his discourse (Besnier 1983b).

Through the use of these covert affective channels, the presentation of self for the different protagonists of the two incidents is, on the one hand, one of poise, calm, and controlled demeanor for K himself and, on the other hand, one characterized by irrationality, unpredictability, and lack of self-control for his two opponents. As pointed out in the ethnographic characterization of conflict and conflict resolution developed earlier, a responsible adult (i.e., an individual in control of his emotions) does not, by definition, allow interpersonal strifes to reach a level at which they must be managed. Such an individual keeps his private self in the private arena and places above all other concerns the maintenance of harmony (*feaalofani*) in interpersonal relationships in the public arena. In contrast, an irrational, irresponsible, and unpredictable (*fakavalevale*) individual will let emotions surface and affect events and other individuals. Such an individual fails to recognize the boundary between the private and the public as a fundamental cultural fact.

This is precisely one of the recurrent themes in the two gossip sessions. By initiating the two conflict situations, K's opponents fail to exhibit the interpersonal decorum necessary for the maintenance of *feaalofani* in the public arena. What the disentangling conversations must achieve is the reestablishment of this decorum, which is achieved by declaring the conflict situations as being *off record* in the public arena.

Conclusion

This study has investigated the common grounds among three areas of inquiry: cultural notions of interpersonal conflicts and their management on Nukulaelae; the role of gossip as data and as a tool for the manipulation of norms; and the communication of affect in verbal interactions. The starting point for this analysis was a characterization of conflict and of the ways in which conflict is managed on Nukulaelae. Relevant to this endeavor is the question of what can be learned about conflict and conflict management from the ways in which they are represented verbally by one Nukulaelae Islander to another. More specifically, I have addressed the role of affect in such a representation.

It was found that attitudes toward interpersonal conflict situations and the cultural processes that come into play in conflict management can be identified through a detailed analysis of conversational interactions *about* conflict and conflict management. The choice of affective strategies used in such interactions "betrays" the norms and processes associated with conflict and conflict management in Nukulaelae. These findings stress the potential importance as ethnographic data of cultural actors' narrative efforts to represent events. Indeed, as shown in this study, the cultural perception and evaluation of a situation, of an individual's behavior, and of the characterization of a cultural event such as conflict are intimately dependent on the ways in which these are verbally represented.

Finally, this study is a contribution to our understanding of the potential disjunction (cf. Ervin-Tripp 1972) of affective and referential meanings. Affective meaning is often opaque and low in iconicity in discourse (compared to referential meaning). This study identifies why and how Nukulaelae Tuvaluans *exploit* this characteristic of affect to "hide" the gossiper's covert rhetorical manipulation of an audience.

Notes

Acknowledgements. The research on which this study is based was conducted on Nukulaelae between 1980 and 1982 and in 1985, with funding from the National Science Foundation (grant No. 8503061). Thanks are due to the government of Tuvalu and the people of Nukulaelae for permission to reside and conduct research on the atoll. This study benefited greatly from comments, suggestions, and criticisms from several participants to the Pitzer College Conference, particularly Sandro Duranti, Karen Ito, Elinor Ochs, Andy Pawley, Bambi Schieffelin, Karen Watson-Gegeo, and Geoff White. Ed Finegan's input was very valuable, and Jacob Love provided useful editorial comments. Any misinterpretation is mine.

1. In the context of this view, the notion of norm sharedness is problematic. Wallace's (1961) theory that norms are "owned" by the individual and not defined by the group is more in harmony with the hypotheses expressed above.

2. The functional account of gossip as a device that defines and maintains group membership, originally proposed by Gluckman (1963), is not at variance with the views expressed here.

3. This view underlies Firth's (1967) functional study of what he terms "rumour" on Tikopia.

4. Irvine (1979) cautions against taking the public-private dimension as a unified and dichotomous descriptive tool in the characterization of communicative events. The terms *public* and *private* are used here as labels for two types of communicative event that appear to be socially real for Nukulaelae Islanders. They are primarily defined in terms of setting (home vs. *maneapa* 'meeting house') and participation (within and without the kin group). The distinction is not claimed to be a valid comparative tool.

5. The same expression is used to refer to individuals who are in the habit of committing blunders, such as cracking risque jokes in the presence of individuals who are in an avoidance relationship to each other *(fakammalu).*

6. Local theories on the exact nature of the cause-and-effect relationship between the conflict and such unfortunate events are, however, never clearly articulated.

7. Some of the background details will be kept as vague as possible, as more detailed descriptions would betray the identity of the concerned individuals. A rather large number of individuals are named in the two transcripts; only the individuals with major roles in the two

conflict situations are introduced here.

8. Chopping down banana trees has interesting connotations. It is a serious crime on Nukulaelae, not only because bananas, which grow slowly and painfully on coral atolls, are a prized food, but also because chopping them down is an activity that individuals perform in amok-like fits of rage, which are classified under the rubric of *fakavalevale* 'demented, inappropriate' behavior on Nukulaelae (see Noricks 1981 for a discussion of *fakavalevale* on Niutao, an island of Northern Tuvalu). While the situation reported by K does not involve an accusation of such behavior, this important connotation is worth noting.

9. Transcriptions quoted as examples combine the Tuvaluan orthography devised in Besnier (1981) and the ethnomethodological transcription conventions summarized in the appendix, which also lists the abbreviations used in interlinear glosses. The translation attempts to recreate the general flavor of the conversation and at times deviates from the literal meaning of the Tuvaluan original. To ease the comprehension of certain passages, additional information in the translation is provided in single brackets (such as, for example, at turn transitions in reported dialogs, which are signaled in the Tuvaluan dialog solely by intonation). The two transcripts in the appendix are less detailed than the passages quoted in the paper. Pauses, intonation contours, and voice quality are not marked in these two transcripts. The marking of overlaps and latching, however, has been kept.

10. Other lexical strategies confirm this evaluation, such as, for example, the sarcastic use of the two verbs of motion *tele* 'to run' in line A:27 and *ffuli ttuaa* 'to turn one's heels [lit.: one's back]' in line B:33 to refer to Luisa's and Saavave's movements respectively.

11. It is of course the case that both reported interactions are cross-gender interactions. Other reported conversations in my corpus of gossip data, however, confirm that Nukulaelae gossipers often use the same dominant–subordinate features in the reporting of conversations between same-gender interactors.

References

Apte, Mahadev L.
1985   Humor and Laughter: An Anthropological Approach. Ithaca, NY: Cornell University Press.

Bailey, F.G.
1983   The Tactical Uses of Passion: An Essay on Power, Reason, and Reality. Ithaca, NY: Cornell University Press.

Bakhtin, Mikhail M. [Valentin N. Vološinov, pseudonym]

1978 Discourse Typology in Prose. *In* Readings in Russian Poetics: Formalist and Structuralist Views. Ladislav Matejka and Krystyna Pomorska, eds. Pp. 176–96. Ann Arbor, MI: Michigan Slavic Publications (originally published 1929).

1980 The Dialogic Imagination: Four Essays. Michael Holquist, ed.; Caryl Emerson and Michael Holquist, translators. Austin: University of Texas Press (originally published 1935).

Bateson, Gregory

1972 Steps to an Ecology of the Mind. New York: Ballantine Books.

Beals, Alan R., and Bernard J. Siegel

1966 Divisiveness and Social Conflict: an Anthropological Approach. Stanford: Stanford University Press.

Besnier, Niko

1981 Tuvaluan Lexicon. Funafuti: U.S. Peace Corps.

1982 Repairs and Error in Tuvaluan Conversation. Unpublished typescript. Department of Linguistics, University of Southern California.

1983a Au e Kata Me e Valea: Knowing When to Laugh on Nukulaelae. Paper presented at the Annual Meeting of the Association for Social Anthropology in Oceania, New Harmony, IN.

1983b On the Accountability of Reported Information: Effective and Affective Intent in Nukulaelae Gossip. Paper presented at the Annual Meeting of the American Anthropological Association, Chicago.

1985 The Local Organization of Zero-Anaphora in Tuvaluan Conversation. Te Reo, Journal of the Linguistic Society of New Zealand 28:119–47.

1986 Word Order in Tuvaluan. *In* FOCAL I: Papers from the Fourth International Conference on Austronesian Linguistics. Paul Geraghty, Lois Carrington, and S. A. Wurm, eds. Pp. 245–68. Canberra: Pacific Linguistics C-93.

1989a Literacy and Feelings: The Encoding of Affect in Nukulaelae Letters. Text 9:69–92.

1989b Information Withholding as a Manipulative and Collusive Strategy in Nukulaelae Gossip. Language in Society 18:315–41.

Brady, Ivan A.

1970 Land Tenure, Kinship, and Community Structure: Strategies for Survival in the Ellice Islands of Western Polynesia. Ph.D. dissertation, Department of Anthropology, University of Oregon.

1974   Land Tenure in the Ellice Islands: A Changing Profile. *In* Land Tenure in Oceania. Henry P. Lundsgaarde, ed. Pp. 130–78. Honolulu: University Press of Hawaii.

1975   Christians, Pagans and Government Men: Culture Change in the Ellice Islands. *In* A Reader in Culture Change, vol. 2 (Case Studies). Ivan A. Brady and Barry L. Isaacs, eds. Pp. 111–45. New York: Schenkman.

Brenneis, Donald

1984   Grog and Gossip in Bhatgaon: Style and Substance in Fiji Indian Conversation. American Ethnologist 11:487–506.

Chambers, Anne F.

1975   Nanumea Report: A Socio-Economic Study of Nanumea Atoll, Tuvalu. Victoria University of Wellington Rural Socio-Economic Survey of the Gilbert and Ellice Islands. Wellington: Victoria University of Wellington.

1983   Exchange and Social Organization in Nanumea, a Polynesian Atoll Society. Ph.D. dissertation, Department of Anthropology, University of California, Berkeley.

Chapman, Anthony J., and Hugh C. Foot, eds.

1976   Humour and Laughter: Theory, Research, and Applications. London: John Wiley.

Cicourel, Aaron V.

1972   Basic and Normative Rules in the Negotiation of Status and Role. *In* Studies in Social Interaction. David Sudnow, ed. Pp. 228–58. New York: The Free Press.

Comaroff, John J., and Simon Roberts

1981   Rules and Processes: the Cultural Logic of Dispute in an African Context. Chicago: University of Chicago Press.

Davitz, J. R.

1964   The Communication of Emotional Meaning. New York: McGraw-Hill.

Duranti, Alessandro

1984   Intentions, Self, and Local Theories of Meaning: Words and Social Action in a Samoan Context. Technical Report 122. La Jolla: Center for Human Information Processing, University of California at San Diego.

Ervin-Tripp, Susan
1972 On Sociolinguistic Rules: Alternation and Co-occurrence. *In* Directions in Sociolinguistics: The Ethnography of Communication. John J. Gumperz and Dell Hymes, eds. Pp. 213–50. New York: Holt, Rinehart and Winston.

Firth, Raymond
1967 Rumour in a Primitive Society. *In* Tikopia Ritual and Belief. Pp. 141–61. Boston: Beacon Press.

Garfinkel, Harold
1967 Studies in Ethnomethodology. Englewood Cliffs, NJ: Prentice Hall.

Geertz, Clifford
1973 Thick Description: Toward an Interpretive Theory of Culture. *In* The Interpretation of Cultures: Selected Essays by Clifford Geertz. Pp. 3–30. New York: Basic Books.

Gluckman, Max
1963 Gossip and Scandal. Current Anthropology 4:307–16.

Goffman, Irving
1959 The Presentation of Self in Everyday Life. New York: Anchor Books.
1974 Frame Analysis: An Essay on the Organization of Experience. New York: Harper and Row.
1981 Forms of Talk. University of Pennsylvania Publications in Conduct and Communication. Philadelphia: University of Pennsylvania Press.

Goldsmith, Michael
1988 Church and State in Tuvalu. Ph.D. dissertation, Department of Anthropology, University of Illinois at Urbana-Champaign.

Goodwin, Charles
1981 Conversational Organization: Interaction Between Speakers and Hearers. Language, Thought, and Culture Series. New York: Academic Press.

Grimes, Joseph
1975 The Thread of Discourse. The Hague: Mouton.

Haiman, John
1980 The Iconicity of Grammar: Isomorphism and Motivation. Language 56:515–40.

1983 Iconic and Economic Motivation. Language 59:781–819.

Haviland, John B.
1977 Gossip, Reputation, and Knowledge in Zinacantan. Chicago: University of Chicago Press.

Holquist, Michael
1983 The Politics of Representation. The Quarterly Newsletter of the Laboratory of Comparative Human Cognition 5:2–9.

Hymes, Dell
1974 Foundations in Sociolinguistics: An Ethnographic Approach. Philadelphia: University of Pennsylvania Press.

Irvine, Judith T.
1979 Formality and Informality in Communicative Events. American Anthropologist 81:773–90.
1982 Language and Affect: Some Cross-Cultural Issues. *In* Contemporary Perceptions of Language: Interdisciplinary Dimensions. Heidi Byrnes, ed. Pp. 31–47. Washington, DC: Georgetown University Press.

Jefferson, Gail
1979 A Technique for Inviting Laughter and Its Subsequent Acceptance Declination. *In* Everyday Language: Studies in Ethnomethodology. George Psathas, ed. Pp. 79–96. New York: Irvington.

Keesing, Roger M.
1974 Theories of Culture. Annual Review of Anthropology 3:73–97.

Kirkpatrick, John
1983 The Marquesan Notion of the Person. Studies in Cultural Anthropology Series 3. Ann Arbor, MI: UMI Research Press.

Kirkpatrick, John, and Geoffrey M. White
1985 Exploring Ethnopsychologies. *In* Person, Self, and Experience: Exploring Pacific Ethnopsychologies. Geoffrey M. White and John Kirkpatrick, eds. Pp. 3–32. Berkeley: University of California Press.

Labov, William, and David Fanshel
1977 Therapeutic Discourse: Psychotherapy as Conversation. New York: Academic Press.

Leet-Pellegrini, Helena N.
1980 Conversational Dominance as a Function of Gender and Exper-

tise. *In* Language: Social Psychological Perspectives. Howard
Giles, W. Peter Robinson, and Philip M. Smith, eds. Pp. 97–
104. Oxford: Pergamon.

Levy, Robert I.
1973 Tahitians: Mind and Experience in the Society Islands.
Chicago: University of Chicago Press.

Lyons, John
1977 Semantics. Volume 1. Cambridge: Cambridge University Press.

Mills, C. Wright
1984 Situated Action and Vocabularies of Motive. *In* Language and
Politics. Michael J. Shapiro, ed. Pp. 13–24. Oxford: Basil Blackwell (originally published 1940).

Munro, Doug
1982 The Lagoon Islands: A History of Tuvalu 1820–1908. Ph.D. dissertation, Department of History, Macquarrie University.

Myers, Fred, and Donald L. Brenneis
1984 Introduction: Language and Politics in the Pacific. *In* Dangerous Words: Language and Politics in the Pacific. Donald
Brenneis and Fred Myers, eds. Pp. 1–29. New York: New York
University Press.

Noricks, Jay
1981 The Meaning of Niutao Fakavalevale (Crazy) Behavior: A Polynesian Theory of Mental Disorder. Pacific Studies 5(1):19–33.

Ochs, Elinor
1979 Planned and Unplanned Discourse. *In* Discourse and Syntax.
Talmy Givón, ed. Pp. 51–80. New York: Academic Press.
1986 From Feeling to Grammar: A Samoan Case Study. *In* Language
Socialization Across Cultures. Bambi Schieffelin and Elinor
Ochs, eds. Pp. 251–72. Cambridge: Cambridge University
Press.

Schegloff, Emmanuel A., and Harvey Sacks
1973 Opening Up Closings. Semiotics 7:289–327.

Shore, Bradd
1982 Sala'ilua, a Samoan Mystery. New York: Columbia University
Press.

Turner, Victor
1974 Dramas, Fields, and Metaphors: Symbolic Action in Human

Society. Ithaca, NY: Cornell University Press.

Wallace, Anthony F. C.
1961   Culture and Personality. New York: Random House.

West, Candace, and Don H. Zimmerman
1983   Small Insults: A Study of Interruptions in Cross-Sex Conversations Between Unacquainted Persons. *In* Language, Gender and Society. Barrie Thorne, Cheris Kramarae, and Nancy Henley, eds. Pp. 102–17. Rowley, MA: Newbury.

Appendix

Abbreviations

1. Transcription Conventions

(1.2)	length of significant pause in seconds
word-	abrupt cut-off
word	forte volume
WORD	fortissimo volume
hhh	exhalation
.hhh	inhalation
wo::rd	non-phonemic segment gemination
?	rising pitch (not necessarily in a question)
,	slightly rising pitch
.	falling pitch (not always at the end of a sentence)
!	animated tempo
=	turn latching
//	beginning and end of turn overlap
((text))	information for which a symbol is not available
((high))	dominant pitch level of utterance string
((creaky))	voice quality
( )	incoherent string
(word)	conjectured string

2. Interlinear Morphological Glosses

Art	article	Nps	non-past
Ben	benefactive conjunction	Prc	precautionary
Cmp	complementizer	Prf	perfective
Cnt	contrastive marker	Pst	past
Dxs	deictic adverb	Sbj	subjunctive conjunction
Erg	ergative case	Spc	specific

Exc	exclamation	Tag	tag question marker
Foc	focus marker	Trn	transitivizing suffix
Inc	inchoative	2	dual
Neg	negative verb	3	plural
+	morpheme boundary		

Transcript A

KELISIANO

01 *Annafi eiloa nei faatoaa fetaui eiloa maaua mo Luisa.*
Luisa and I finally met just yesterday.

FEUE

02 *I hee?* =
Where?

KELISIANO

03 *I:-. Teelaa // loa i Olataga. // =*
A:t- over there, on Olataga.

FEUE

04 *// I:: Olataga? //*
O::n Olataga?

KELISIANO

05 *A ko te mea laa ne: fet- e: hai mai a Samasone, kia aku, koo oti ne hano- koo oti ne fano ki Olataga.*
The thing is that we met- . . . Samasone had told me that she had gone to Olataga.

FEUE

06 *I te aa: laa?*
What for?

KELISIANO

07 *I au naa e tipa atu i suaa taeao- te as(o)saa, au e hano o koukou i tua, nei fua!*
(not answering directly) I was walking along the other morning-on Sunday, I was going to take a bath in the ocean, just recently!

08 *Te assaa teelaa ne hai ei te mataaupu kiaa Timooteo mo: Teake?*
(remember) that Sunday on we talked about which Timooteo and Teake?

09 *A ko te suaa assaa.*
Well, the following Sunday.

10 *Io oo! teenei te assaa eiloa teenaa!*
    Yes, that was it! that very Sunday!

11 *Hanatu naa au-, i au e sae atu i te fale o: Timooteo i te feituu ki*
    tua, a koo fakafetaui ifo Samasone au.
    I was going along-, and then came behind Timooteo's house, and
    (that's where) Samasone came down to meet me.

12 *sss! Au e ssili atu hua kia koe i te:: fekau nei a: Luisa ne hai mai*
    kee taaofi kow i te:: te faamanatuga.
    Hey! (he said:) I just want to ask you about Luisa's request that
    you should be prevented from (taking) communion.

13 *Io? I te aa?*
    (I said:) Oh? And why?

14 *Me i te tala teelaa ne hai i: i: i futi kolaa o: laatou ne taa nee au.*
    (He said that) it was about a story to the effect tha:t tha:t tha:t I
    chopped down some banana trees of theirs.

15 *Aku muna ttaa, a ko au nei e-e(i) he tino fakavalevale?*
    I said: come on, am I crazy or what?

16 *E TONU LAA i au ne sseu i koo.*
    It is true that I gardened in that area.

17 *A ko futi kolaa ne hai eiloa n(ee) Maataio mo:: mo Tito.*
    But those banana trees were (cut down) by Maataio a::nd Tito.

18 *I au hoki eiloa maafaufau peenaa ki:: me io laatou a: futi nee?*
    I also thought (as I was gardening) about- that those banana
    trees were theirs, right?

19 *He:ki ai eiloa heaku futi ne:: Ne mea i-*
    So I didn't (chop down) any banana tree-

20 *A KO: FUTI KOLAA NE:: NE: LAGA EILOA NEE AU KEAATE:(A) e*
    io e io Timooteo, mo ko olotou futi e tai ttuu ki lalo, ko Timooteo
    e:: nofo ki luga.
    THE (CHOPPED DOWN) BANANA TREES THAT I DRAGGED TO
    THE SIDE are Timooteo's' their (Luisa's) banana trees are down
    below (in the garden pit), while Timooteo's are up above (on the
    edge of the garden pit).

21 *(Ak)u muna i:o!*
    I said: all right!

22 *(Tee)naa laa au ne: hai kee hano au kee faipati fakallei aka i ei,*
    ae logo aka a:u ne ttagi- i te tagi a: Luisa teenaa maa- fooliki-,
    koo:: oti eiloa ne oko ki::
    Then I thought that I should go and have a good talk with her
    (Luisa), but then I heard that Luisa senior- (I mean) junior had

already sent a complaint (and that the complaint) had reached
the ears of. . . .

FEUE

23   *Ttaahh!* =
      (Scandalized) That's outrageous!

KELISIANO

24   = *kiaa Tito. Ki:- kee hano ki te faka:-*
      (reached) Tito's ears, that he should go to the:- . . .

25   *Teenaa laa i te- annafi, kkai aka maatou, au naa e vau i te:: fale*
      o: Elekana mo Manatu- e nofo atu i ei!
      So, on- (I mean) yesterday, after eating, I was (walking along
      and) came to (the level of) Elekana and Manatu's house, there
      she (Luisa) was!

26   *Maatou mo Uili mo Paka.*
      I was with Uili and Paka.

27   *Aku muna Luisa, lle:i, i au ne m- manako loa kee: fetaui taaua i*
      Fagaua kae:- mea aka laa koe koo tele mai ki Olataga.
      I said: Luisa, good, I wanted to meet you on Fagaua, bu:t then
      you ran over here to Olataga.

28   *Ko au fua e: faipati atu kiaa koe ki luga i te: peelaa mo tau: fekau*
      ne avatu nee Samasone.
      I just (want to) talk to you about the: like, the complaint that
      Samasone told me about.

29   *Muna mai io-, io- io!*
      She says, yes- oh, yes- yes-!

30   *(Muna) hh a tou fafi(ne)!*
      That's what she said, the woman!

31   *Kiloko, au he tino eiloa- E ILOA LLEI faeloa nee au peelaa te:: i*
      luga i oku tofi, i te mea kaa ha nee au peelaa hee llei.
      You see, (I said,) I am a man who always knows, like, given my
      social position, (who always knows) whether what I do is (right
      or) wrong.

32   *Kae iloa nee au a futi o koutou.*
      And I (also) know which banana trees are yours.

33   *Tee(1)aa laa HEEai eiloa he futi o: koutou ne:: ne: n-*
      So, I did not (chop down) a single banana tree of yours,

34   *Futi konaa ne hai eiloa nee Maataio mo:: mo Tito.*
      Those banana trees were (chopped down) by Maataio a:nd, and
      Tito.

35   *Muna mai, kiloko, koe e: fakamolemole eiloa.*
      She says, look, please do forgive me.

36   *Au ne toe logo fakamui aka fua.*
     I heard (the truth) just recently.

37   *Peela ko te o- tena osotiiga i te ttaimi muamua, me e taku mai mo*
     ko au.
     So that when she got upset the first time, she said that I was the
     one who chopped (the banana trees down).

38   *Teelaa eiloa ne ave loa tena:: fekau kiaa Samasone kee taaofi aka*
     laa au e- Ae fakamuli aka:,
     And then she just sent over a request to Samasone that I be pre-
     vented (from taking communion) because I- . . . But more recently,

39   *Logo au kaiaa mo ko:: ko Tito eiloa mo Maataio kolaa ne hai nee*
     laaua a::
     what do I hear? that Tito and Maataio were the ones that . . .

40   *Muna mai. Koo hee:ai- HEE:ai he: mea e: onosai e:i-?*
     She says to me: There is nothing- no harbored feelings between
     us any more.

41   *(M)una au, fakatau fakamaagalo nei taaua.*
     I say: let us forgive each other now.

FEUE

42   *(tee)laa heeai he (t)- koe e: hai mo: (ko) ttoo futi o: ttoeaina.*
     So that there is no- . . . You should've said that (you were leav-
     ing) the banana plantation for (her) old man!

Transcript B

KELISIANO

01   *A temotou kaaiga i ttaeao hh, a te mea a Isala, ne tuku i ei kee*
     hano o sukesuke nee ia te:- ttupe a maaua mo Saavave teelaa ne
     (In) our family this morning, Isala (was angry) because she had
     gone to look into that money of mine and of Saavave (the
     money) that . . .

FEUE

02   *// (? teelaa ne) hanatu kiaa Paulo! =*
     That's why she went to Paulo?

KELISIANO

03   *= Teelaa! Teelaa: e ha- =*
     That's it, that's it, she s-

FEUE

04   *= Saavave Timooteo mo Tema mo:: // Ioopu. //*

(It said that the money was for) Saavave, Timooteo, Tema and Ioopu.

KELISIANO

05 // *Ioopu.* //
(And) Ioopu.

06 *Kai laa, muna mai a ia ko ia e maasei tena loto ia Elekana kaati laa hee: hee loto malie ki te mea: (a) Kelisiano teelaa loa hee:-*
We ate, and then she (Isala) she says she feels angry at Elekana because she probably wouldn't agree to do what Kelisiano said to- . . .

07 *Teenaa laa e hano a ia o sili me e isi eiloa te mea a: Ioopu i:- hai atu laa kiaa Paulo, muna a: Paulo, m(o) ko Timooteo eiloa m( ). Ko Timooteo, ko Tema, ko-*
So she went over to ask whether Ioopu's (money) had (arrived), and Paulo said to her, Paulo said that it was for Timooteo and . . . Timooteo, Tema, and- . . .

08 *Hanaifo laa ki gaatai- ka ne vau mua Sina.*
She went down toward the lagoon, and then Sina came over.

09 *Vau, fai mai kia aku, a ko au laa ne toe logo hoki ia Elekana i ttaeao,*
She came, and said to me, but I heard again about it this morning from Elekana . . .

10 *Hai mai me iaa ia ne logo iaa Isala.*
He had heard about it through Isala.

11 *Aku muna, ka: ne a laa ttou pati e hai, mo koo oti laa ne vae nee: Saavave:,*
I said, what are we doing (standing here and) talking about this, the money has already been split up between us by Saavave (of her own accord). . . .

FEUE

12 *Te mea teelaa seeai sena mea a ia me se mea* // *(i te) fakalave = // = lave ne aumai* // *loa* // *kiaa koe.*
That thing (the money) is not hers, to take, it is something (that was sent) on account of the family event (the wedding), it was primarily sent to you.

KELISIANO

13 // *Peelaa nee?* //
That's it, right?

14 // *mm!*
// hmm!

15 *Teelaa laa ko Ioopu k(oo) kalaga mai telotou me(a).*

Then Ioopu started scolding (Saavave).

16 *Fakalogo au nei ki te mea a Ioopu e fai mai kiaa Saavave,*
    I overheard what Ioopu told Saavave,

17 *galo aka tou fafine,*
    then the woman (Saavave) disappeared.

18 *Maaua laa mo Lusi e llaga pola i tena paa, koo vau tou- tou fafine.*
    (Later, while) Lusi and I were weaving coconut-frond baskets
    near his chicken coop, the woman (Saavave) came by.

19 *Ia! Aku muna, he aah?*
    Yes, I said, what is it?

20 *Konaa te:: tau:: te luafulu lima taalaa.*
    (She says,) Here are the: your twenty-five dollars.

21 *Aku muna ttee:-*
    I said, come on!

22 *A tino naa kaa llogo mai eiloa i tauhh mhheahh (nahh)*
    You wait, when people start hearing about what you've been up
    to . . .

23 *au e (fai) fakaloiloi,*
    I was just kidding her.

24 *Muna mai te ssee laa*
    She says, they were the ones that did something wrong- . . .

25 *hee: uaeelesi mai laa peelaa::-*
    they didn't cable to (tell us who the money was for) . . .

FEUE

26 *(Ei!) te mea laa // e hai ki te // aavaga, ka ne aa ana-*
    Come on! The money was for the wedding, what else does she
    want . . .

KELISIANO

27 *// Aku muna*
    // I said,

28 *A ko: ia Paulo e hai mai mo ko laa- koo: toko tolu eiloa.*
    And Paulo told me that there were three people (on the
    telegram).

29 *Muna mai heeai laa hoku ssee i ei, e ssee eiloa ko: ko laatou.*
    She says, I did nothing wrong, they were the ones who did some-
    thing wrong.

30 *Uaeelesi ma-.*
    They should've cabled.

31 *a ko aku muna- a ko tau pati e (taulagi) mai*

And then I said- What you are telling me sounds pretty fishy to me,

32   *ia Paulo teelaa e hai mai me toko tolu eiloa o t- kolaa e saina mai i luga i te:- Timooteo mo: (Io-) Tema mo Ioopu.*
Paulo told me that there were three people whose name appeared on the (telegram)- Timooteo, Io-, (I mean) Tema, and Ioopu.

33   *Tuku mai te:: mea, ffuli mai (eiloa) ttua: koo hano.*
She then gave me the money, turned her heels, and left.

34   *Hanatu nei Lusi ssili atu teehee Saavave,*
Lusi came (a bit later) and (I) asked (him) where Saavave was,

35   *Muna mai e: galo i te umu.*
He said that she was not in the cooking hut.

36   *Aku muna koo atuli eiloa a ia n(ee) thenahhhh // (   )*
I figured she got chased out by her (family)

FEUE

37   *// Ko te fia pule:: aa::-*
She just wants to play the boss . . .

38   *Teelaa hoki au ne ita kiaa Paulo,*
I was displeased with Paulo

39   *aku muna kae fano laa koe o tuku mai kiaa:- Saavave?*
I said (to him), why did you give (the money) to Saavave?

40   *Ko te mea e hanatu kae fanatu kaa hano mo ko:ulua, nee?*
Because if she went over (to collect it) she should've gone with you, right?

41   *Koo hai oulua igoa i ei, te uaeelesi teelaa.*
(Because) both of your names were written on that telegram.

42   *Teenaa laa aku m- te tonuga lo: laa te mea laa teenaa see tuku fua kiaa Saavave ka:e:: ttau eiloa o peeofu Kelisiano me::- ne aumai ki te fakalavelave nee? =*
So that I said- . . . the truth of the matter is that it should not have been given to Saavave but it should have been handed over to Kelisiano because it was sent on account of the family event (the wedding), right?

KELISIANO

43   *= Mm.*
Hmm.

Allegory and Inference: Intentional Ambiguity in Managalase Negotiations

William H. McKellin

> A Man's life of any worth is a continual
> allegory—and very few eyes can see the
> Mystery of his life—a life like the scrip-
> tures, figurative.
>
> JOHN KEATS

THOUGHTS AND INTENTIONS are quintessentially private. They are hidden from the scrutiny of others. Those around us construct our probable intentions from our past and current behavior. Others also use their assumptions about social relations to create motives for our actions. C. Wright Mills (1984:16) stated that, "Genetically, motives are imputed by others before they are avowed by the self" (cf. Besnier, this volume). Mills also recognized the strategic social importance of assigning motives to behavior and the role of society in controlling the range of motives available to its members:

> When they appeal to others involved in one's act, motives are strategies of action. In many social actions, others must agree tacitly or explicitly. Thus acts often will be abandoned if no reason can be found that others will accept. Diplomacy in choice of motive often controls the diplomat. Diplomatic choice of motive is part of the attempt to motivate acts for other members in a situation (Mills 1984:17).

Attributing intentions to others to create publicly recognized meanings or motives is a necessary, though potentially dangerous task. The basic stuff of disputes, social conflict, and reconciliation is the authority or control of motives, the social meanings assigned to actions. Disputes often erupt when legitimate interpretations of social ideals come into conflict in changed contexts (Scheffler 1965). Then, private intentions, social roles, and their corresponding motives and actions are no longer predictable, but ambiguous and difficult to interpret. In these situations, people may clarify, negotiate and redefine, or even sever their social bonds.

Among the Managalase of Papua New Guinea, the issues that precipitate arguments, illness, and fights are only the symptoms of more fundamental social turmoil. In the following analyses I examine the management of conflicts involving ambiguous intentions and uncertain motives. The cases are open to examination because resolution failed. If they had been successful, the negotiations might easily have passed unnoticed by most members of the community, and the underlying issues would have been successfully concealed.

Managalase avoid open displays or discussions of individuals' supposed intentions; they recognize that individuals' thoughts are often illusive, ambiguous, and imperfectly understood by others. They avoid situations in which their own intentions are the focus of public contention. Although people privately gossip about others' activities, they hesitate to assign motives and control others' actions directly. Consistent with the ideals of this egalitarian society, they prefer to address contentious issues by presenting their own proposals or interpretations of affairs indirectly. They elicit responses from others through metaphors, diagnoses of illness, and dreams.

Metaphors and allegories are an important medium for this discourse of action and motivation. Allegories are the trial balloons or political Rorschach tests of social relations. The ambiguous nature of metaphors and allegories gives both the speaker and the audience equal footings to negotiate specific issues as well as the general framework of social relations. This mediation requires neither authoritative leadership nor the intervention of third parties.

This study examines conceptions of social life and of rhetoric that shape the Managalase approach to dispute containment and resolution. It focuses particularly on the role of the metaphorical genre of allegory in "disentangling" conflicts. Through metaphors speakers and their audiences create a montage of different motives to coordinate, rather than homogenize, their views of society.

Ethnographic Background

Approximately five thousand Managalase inhabit the lush ridgetops of the Hydrographer Plateau between the low coastal mountains and the spurs of the Owen Stanley Range in Oro Province, Papua New Guinea. Villages range in size from about 50 to 250 people. Each village is a sociopolitical unit linked by kinship, marriage, and exchange ties to communities throughout the region. The size and composition of each multiclan village reflects the historical flow of people through marriage, and the shifting political alliances of those who own the surrounding land. During the course of an individual's lifetime, the village to which he or she belongs may move and undergo fission and fusion. Despite these changes, one's claims and use of gardening and hunting lands remain more or less intact.

Managalase, like their Orokaiva neighbors, maintain simultaneous membership in several named clans (McKellin 1980; Schwimmer 1972). Cognatic affiliations tie people to the clans of their maternal and paternal grandparents. Members of the same clan assume their ancestors or predecessors were genealogically related, gardened and hunted together, or cooperated in exchanges.

Kin groups, *agan*, serve as the basic social, economic, and political unit below the clan level. *Agan* are brother- or sister-hoods centered on the activities of coresident siblings. Locally resident members of the *agan* are trustees for other nonresident kin, particularly their sisters who are dispersed by marriage. *Agan* members combine affiliation with both parents' clans through a malleable combination of three types of bonds: (1) consanguinity; (2) joint ownership and use of gardening, hunting, and fishing territory (and associated commensal ritual obligations); and (3) mutual assistance in affinal exchanges.

Thus siblings, parallel cousins, cross-cousins, and others linked by territorial and exchange ties may act as kin, comembers of the same clan in some contexts. Or, in other settings, some of the same people may be exchange partners (McKellin 1980). *Agan* are identified by plant emblems derived from the names of male or female apical ancestors one, two, or three generations removed.[1]

Each person's identity in time and place grows out of kin ties and community relations. Ties to kinsmen and affines, ancestors and predecessors bind kinsmen and women together into a coeval community. Spirits are active participants in the community, assisting gardeners and hunters. They also protect their successors from foreign spirits and sorcerers. Reciprocally, the successors give ancestral spirits offerings of food from gardening, hunting, and affinal exchange feasts.

Social continuity is also visibly represented by one's children and other portions of one's *tin* 'estate' or 'inheritance'. A person's estate also includes territory. This consists of gardening and hunting land, the trees that mark them, and pools and rivers. It also encompasses rights to perform myths, legends, clan histories, some forms of magic, and songs.

Communities are destroyed or disrupted by prolonged disputes and by marriages within groups. Changes in kin-group alignments are reflected in self-imposed prohibitions on visits with adversaries, in new preferences in gardening and exchange partners, and in modified land claims. Ultimately, if kinsmen are not reconciled, there is a realignment of ties with ancestors as the community of spirits is also divided.

This study examines the role of metaphors as mediators in Managalase negotiations or, to use the term employed elsewhere in this volume, disentangling. In the two disputes that I describe, the ostensible subjects of controversy are pigs and tradestore goods, women and children. In the background, however, are fundamental issues about the construction and maintenance of individual identities and of relations between groups and communities.

The *Kaven* and Managalase Personhood

Managalase liken the historical and social ties among individuals to the growth of vines. They take root in one spot, but as they grow, they send out runners which put down new roots. Social groups send out offshoots with each marriage and new roots with each new generation of children. Within this social framework, the self is conceptualized as both the physical and spiritual aspects of an individual, his or her *kaven* 'soul-substance'. This substance is the fusion of blood and semen traced through both maternal and paternal ancestors. From conception however, each individual is distinct. Varying degrees of shared procreative substance form the initial ties among siblings and parallel and cross-cousins.

The *kaven* pervades the body and extends beyond it in the form of body heat, odor, and secretions. The *kaven* exudes an aura around an individual, defining his or her "personal space."[2] Even the warmth of a seat retains the *kaven* of an individual. The *kaven* is separated from the body during dreams, during some illnesses, and at death. Attacks by foreign or bush spirits or even ancestral spirits may be responsible for causing illness and death. The locus of a person's *kaven* is the *oj* 'heart' or site under the sternum. Emotions such as happiness, boredom, and grief are the fluttering, fatigue, and pain of one's *oj*. Managalase state that it is impossible to see into the *kaven*, into the thoughts and feelings of others. Public attributions of other's *uihe* 'thoughts, memories, and intentions' and of other's emotions are considered intrusions into another's personal space. The soul or spirit is only visible to *asi'in* 'mediums, curers'.

The state of a person's *kaven* is revealed indirectly through a person's speech, health, capacity to provide yams, pigs, and game for exchanges, and his or her cleverness and self-control. Invasions and impingement of a person's *kaven* by ancestral and bush spirits, magicians and sorcerers cause illness and perhaps death and retribution. Adults age and grow feeble as their substance and strength are depleted by conceiving and rearing children (McKellin 1985).

Good health is dependent on sharing food with the ancestral spirits, who validate one's identity and provide protection. Spirits, however, are not simply passive or benign. They can demonstrate their dissatisfaction with their successors by using shared substance to penetrate a person's space and abducting or stifling their *kaven*. Dissension among a man's living kinsmen who are dissatisfied with their exchanges is an invitation to ancestral spirits to cause accidents and illness among the living. A wife is also a target of her ancestors' displeasure if her husband's feasts are inadequate. Their spirits may make her or her children sick or prevent her from bearing children. Similarly if a sorcerer, a spirit from an alien group, or a bush spirit penetrates a *kaven*, the victim loses control of his or her *kaven* and may become sick or deranged or die. A person may even commit suicide without awareness of his or her own actions (McKellin 1985).

Magic and the diagnosis of illness also reveal the state of a *kaven*. Virtually all men and many women know magic to assist them with activities such as gardening, fishing, and hunting. Despite the widespread possession of magical power, Managalase are equivocal about its use. Possession of particular forms of magic is revealed when mediums diagnose sources of illnesses. In the diagnosis, the curer may attribute a victim's illness to discord with either a magician or a spirit. If a magician is identified, the patient asks the magician to reclaim control of his or her *kaven*.

Uncontrolled displays of emotion, of the *oj*, are dangerous. People fear public outbursts of anger, particularly by magicians. An individual who is unable to keep his or her *kaven* in check is dangerous, even if he or she is not violent. An angry magician's "hot" *kaven* can cause illness, accidents, and death. Men who are known for their power and magic control their *kaven* and their anger to avoid accusations following others' misfortunes. In several instances men who appeared to have lost their tempers in heated arguments shielded themselves against future accusations by exclaiming, *Na bazeve!* 'I'm not angry!' in the course of their tirades. These statements highlighted the tension between individuals' visible emotional states and socially acceptable interpretations of their motives.

Concepts of self and personal space have important implications for interpersonal and public politics and also provide a strong rationale for the use of figurative speech. Unlike the Trobrianders discussed by Weiner (1983) who legitimately control others by actually invading personal space, Managalase see coercion as a breakdown of social obligations and restraint. The implicit threat to cause illness and death is one of the few means of direct illicit control that a person can wield over another. Therefore, Managalase approach power, particularly magical power, with ambivalence and caution.

In a community composed of autonomous fellow villagers, enduring, stable social relations require respect for personal space and parity in personal power. This individual sovereignty is preserved by subtle persuasion rather than explicit coercion. The misuse of power and attempts to control others by infringing on their personhood causes illness and injury, destroys kin groups and affinal alliances, and eventually kills the community.

The Politics of Exchange

Exchanges between villages provide men and women with opportunities to demonstrate their strength and increase their prestige. Risks increase as men and women extend their exchange relations. Big-men depend upon and seek the assistance of kinsmen. Yet, they cannot demand cooperation from them. The big-man/magician's capacity to cause illness among both his supporters and his partner's associates haunts each transaction. Exchanges express the strength of the big-men who sponsor feasts and coordinate their timing, and they demonstrate the vitality of the community.

Monogamous marriages and the accompanying exchange of bridewealth provide the foundation for individual, interclan, and regional alliances. Men exchange with their wives' kin and with members of the groups into which their sisters and other cognatically related kinswomen marry. Simultaneously, women exchange with their brothers, their wives, and the married female members of their kin group.

Exchange partners should have comparable social stature. They are expected to have the skill and magical strength to provide the food, goods, and dancers for feasts. Men in an exchange partnership increase their prestige by meeting their reciprocal obligations rather than attempting to embarrass or bankrupt each other. Here, as elsewhere, the short-term difference in stature between the givers and recipients of feasts alternates within a wider framework of upwardly spiraling prestige for both parties (Salisbury 1963). In the long term, the fortunes of partners are linked. Failure of one partner to meet an obligation also threatens the position of the other.

Exchange partnerships are not dyadic. Simultaneous membership in several clans creates a dense web of ties for social identity and political exchange. From one point of view, multiple affiliations provide individuals with the opportunity to develop a wide range of exchange relations. These ties extend not only through their sibling group, but also through their genealogically or geographically more distant parallel and cross-cousins.

From another vantage point, however, expanding exchange relations bring increased pressures to meet competing obligations. A man must choose among his partners each time he gives a feast, fulfilling his obligations to a few while postponing exchanges with others. Here the relative power of a man's partners becomes problematic. Furthermore, he has to select men to co-sponsor feasts. New exchanges threaten the maintenance of old alliances. The strategies of coordinating exchanges and the intricacies of timing feasts take on greater importance.

The speed with which a man responds with a reciprocal feast indicates the degree of respect he has for his ally. Instant reciprocity, however, is not polite. It belittles the partner's earlier feast by the ease with which it is matched. Alternatively, extended delays suggest that the obligations to other partners with higher prestige or more threatening magic take precedence. Therefore, the timing of exchanges is an important subject of negotiation. This is one of the key issues in the eventual breakdown of relations in the first case study.

The second case study demonstrates the problems of determining which cross-cutting clan affiliations are the most strategic for participation in particular social activities. Failure to maintain ties may redefine an individual's social identity and may even result in violence.

Social relations have become increasingly complex since the introduction of coffee as a cash crop in the late 1950s. To avoid disputes over coffee gardens, the government, intending to strengthen the traditional system, unintentionally imposed an African-modeled patrilineal land-tenure system. The contradictions between this new system and the traditional bases of social organization have increased the ambiguity of land titles, kin affiliations, and marital alliances. The resulting confusion has undermined traditional criteria for kin group membership, raised intergroup tensions, and aggravated disputes. Exchanges demonstrate the power of individuals and communities. Partners should be equally powerful men and women. They should respect the established power and obligations of others and cooperate with their partners in planning feasts. Partners are hesitant to challenge each other's generosity or sense of timing openly because this might jeopardize their own alliances and personal social investments. Managalase exchange partners, like Western banks, hesitate to force their large, socially significant debtors to default on their obligations.

Failures of partners to resolve problems about the nature or timing of an exchange result in broken alliances and mutual accusations of personal weakness and incompetence. Failed exchanges often end in attacks from one's ancestral spirits or those of one's affines. They may also lead to violence within and between villages.

Taking the Hidden Path

Direct threats to the person and his or her social and political ties are mediated by curers and indirect forms of communication— dream interpretation, symbolic tokens, pantomime, and allegorical oratory.

Diagnoses of illnesses by mediums and their spirit familiars frequently identify unsettled relations as precipitating causes. Metaphorical modes of communication, *suara kuaraman*, are the most commonly used means for conducting negotiations and mediating contentious issues. Managalase compare *suara kuaraman* to a circuitous, hidden path through the bush, in contrast to a more direct, public walking track to a destination. *Suara kuaraman* is the verbal counterpart of *suara mahan* 'indirect exchange' in exchange relations. In the latter, the principal recipient of a feast redistributes food and goods among his supporters. Just as the supporters of principal guests at a feast receive food and goods indirectly through an intermediary, indirect discourse enlists metaphors as mediators between the speaker and his audience.

In addition to their roles in negotiations, metaphorical forms are used by the Managalase to gently inform relatives of deaths, to surreptitiously warn kinsmen or allies of possible attacks, and to politely criticize affines and kinsmen. Metaphors are also used in emotionally charged situations to distance the messenger from the message. The men and women who have achieved renown in exchanges also demonstrate their cleverness by trading allegories with their exchange partners. Thus, allegorical rhetoric combines aspects of secrecy, politeness, and competitiveness.

Dreams in which dead relatives communicate with their living relatives are classed by some as indirect communication and by others as direct. The ambiguity stems from the fact that though dreams are not considered metaphorical, they require interpretation, like *suara kuaraman*. They are however, non-metaphorical communication. For proper interpretation, informants state that a dream should occur several times. The repeated portions of the dream are the most significant for an interpretation.[3] Exegeses of dreams, like many allegories, tokens, and pantomimes, are constructed in discussions with kinsmen.

Genres of metaphorical communication and dreams employ related metaphorical figures and themes. *Ha'a* 'allegories' are the most common form of metaphorical communication, similar to the "veiled speech" used by Highlanders (Strathern 1975; Goldman 1983). Indirect discourse in Managalase is fashioned from conventional metaphorical figures and characteristic plots. For example, an allegory about betel nut usually refers to a marriage arrangement or the exchange of a pig. Likewise, a betel nut with designs cut into the peel may be a token that can convey the same messages. In addition to allegories, tokens, pantomimes (which act out the plot of an allegory), and some songs are also considered metaphorical.[4]

Other metaphors are not as widely used and known as the betel nut example. Many groups, clans, or related sets of clans have their own metaphorical forms that have distinctive applications. The Bun 'ora clan, for example, talk about sugarcane in allegories about marriage. The Mejakan of Uganomo village use stories about particular vines to indicate acceptance or rejection of an invitation to a feast.

The Managalase preference for indirect forms of communication over open negotiation and confrontation reflects their ambivalence toward public displays of power and coercion. They assume that one individual should not impose his will or opinion

on another. A person should not embarrass his kinsmen and affines or cause them to lose face by pointing out their weaknesses.
Metaphorical forms help to maintain the autonomy of the person
and sustain interchanges among equals.

Nevertheless, Managalase see indirect discourse as potentially
threatening. They describe allegorical communication as *bisivi*
'trickery' or *aboimahinan* 'questioning'. The person who initiates
an allegorical dialogue is only indirectly responsible for its outcome. Allegories are particularly threatening if the speaker addresses the allegory to a specific individual and requests an
interpretation.

Metaphorical discourse is inherently enthymematic. It requires
the audience to make inferences to complete its message. If a
Managalase story or token is interpreted as metaphorical, it also
requires a response. The response places the intended audience in
the delicate position of partially revealing his or her assessment
of the situation. The reply is made without certain knowledge of
the intentions of the speaker who initiated the interchange, but
nonetheless advances a jointly constructed statement of those intentions.

Metaphors separate the initial, hidden intentions of performers
from the final, socially negotiated and constructed relations and
motives of all of the participants. Allegories are ambiguous. They
point toward social goals, the end of old relations or the beginning of new ones, without making them explicit.

When a person tells a story or gives an item, how does the
audience or the recipient know if it was intended to have hidden
meaning? Managalase men and women are often uncertain about
what is intended as metaphorical and what is literal, commonplace, or slightly irrelevant. Whenever possible they avoid comment by stating, *Na barubaren* 'I don't know enough'. Silence is
safe and noncommittal.

Managalase especially scrutinize stories and items given by
men and women who have extensive exchange relations. These
people have had the opportunity to hone their use of indirect discourse.

The structure of stories also provides clues to their intent, as do
marks on some tokens (McKellin 1984). But, almost every man
and some women I spoke to had a tale of being "tricked" into

marriage or an exchange because he or she did not recognize an allegory or token.

Another key to identifying metaphorical communication is the state of the relation, or the potential relations, between the speaker or giver and the audience. If the intended audience believes that some aspect of the relationship with the performer is open to reassessment, indirect discourse can proceed. The meaning of the story or token unfolds as the participants disentangle or alter their social relationships.

The events that occurred in Siribu Village before, during, and soon after my research in 1976–77 provide two related cases that demonstrate the social and historical aspects of Managalase mediation through metaphorical communications. The issue in the first case concerns the communicative significance and the social implications of genres of indirect discourse. The second case examines the process of weaving social interpretations from ambiguous intentions.

The Historical Setting

Siribu Village has undergone considerable fission and resettlement in its recent history. Siribu was actually composed of two villages, Jinebuina and Kavan, when I first worked there in 1976–77. Jinebuina was the older, established settlement, and Kavan was its offshoot.

Jinebuina was founded in the mid-1960s by the area's new village constable (later village councilor) and aspiring big-man, Makai. Until its dissolution in the late 1970s, the settlement stood on a ridge along the rim of the plateau. The hamlet was keyhole shaped with several houses forming a circle in a small clearing on the top of a hill. Twice as many houses, in two lines, ran down the hillside and formed a distinct segment of Jinebuina. By Managalase standards, Jinebuina was large, with approximately 250 inhabitants.

Initially, Jinebuina was divided socially as well as geographically into two factions that roughly corresponded to individuals' most salient clan affiliations.[5] Those who lived in the clearing at the top of the hill identified themselves predominantly as members of Bun 'ora, Misaj, and Kuba 'ora clans and their attached affines and dependents. Below them, in the houses on the hillside, were people of Doho 'ora, Samoij, Guroij, and Eko 'ora. This division of the village also reflected the residential patterns prior to the move to Jinebuina.[6]

When I arrived in 1976, the village was approximately twelve years old. Its composition had altered dramatically from the time of its founding. Three years earlier the settlement at Kavan had been formed after a dispute broke out within the Bun 'ora clan over the timing of a mortuary feast. The uncontained dispute erupted into a riot and divided the whole community. The Councilor's younger brother, Magua (who plays an offstage part in the second case) was one of the casualties of the melee. He was flown to the provincial hospital unconscious after Baho (who tells the allegory in the second case) hit Magua over the head with a large wooden broadsword and fractured his skull. Magua recovered, later to become councilor on the death of his brother. His creased and scarred forehead, however, was a constant reminder of the battle and the unresolved hostilities among fellow villagers.

As a consequence of the fight, several of the families who had lived at the top of the hill moved to live with other kinsmen and affines in the lower portion of the village. A number of families, including Baho's, left Jinebuina altogether to found a new village at Kavan.

Kavan was about a fifteen-minute walk away from Jinebuina on a path that passes through the old abandoned village sites of Huaja, Siribu, and Biria. Before the fight, Kavan was just the site of a few families' garden houses, surrounded by stands of sugarcane and bananas. It had grown from its initial population of about thirty people into a sizable village of about one hundred people by 1984 when I returned. The composition of Kavan also changed recently following the final abandonment of the village site at Jinebuina.

Jinebuina and Kavan were two villages inextricably woven together by their networks of clan affiliations. For generations, members of these two factions have been bound together by kin ties through cognatic descent, shared interest in territory, and joint obligations to common sets of affines. The fight that divided Jinebuina did not sever the links between clans nor did it totally end amicable relations. It did, however, force a reassessment of the priorities given to each relationship.

In the following two examples of negotiations that preceded the dissolution of Jinebuina, men attempted to defuse growing dissatisfaction between people of the two factions and to reconcile the combatants. These performances are particularly illuminating in that they failed in their apparent social or political goals. The following brief account of an exchange that started at the beginning of my fieldwork introduces the significance, and the ambiguity, of Managalase rhetoric.

The Sprouting Coconuts

The first example demonstrates that acknowledgement of the genre of communication is itself significant. The "case of the sprouting coconuts" occurred at the beginning of my fieldwork. It was my first exposure to Managalase metaphorical rhetoric. In this example, the parties attempted to test the current health of their social relations. This was done behind the facade of deciding whether some sprouting coconuts, given in a feast, had metaphorical significance.

Russell and his Bun 'ora kinsmen, who lived at the top of Jinebuina, prepared a feast for Jubo and other affines who lived in the houses below them on the hillside. The day before the feast I inspected the cooked food and the large litters for food made from saplings. The litters were heaped with yams, taro, sugarcane, betel nut, and coconuts. I went from litter to litter, trying to match the names of the givers to those of the recipients. When we came to the litters with sprouting coconuts placed on top, the young men who accompanied me explained that the coconuts had special significance. The man who was giving one of these litters, Russell, refused to discuss the coconut sprouts. He suggested that I ask one of the recipients, Savas, Jubo's senior kinsman, for their meaning.

The next morning, after the dancing, eating, and presentation of food, I followed their advice. I asked Savas to explain the significance of the sprouting coconuts. I did not realize the implications of my request. He summed up his understanding of the token by expanding on the point that being given coconuts ready for planting (rather than eating) was an expression of dissatisfaction with the exchange relation—implying that the plantings would eventually produce exchangeable (and consumable) fruit.[7]

> SAVAS: This is what they (our in-laws) said (with the coconuts). "Your coconuts only have water in them so take these and plant them, then later, give us back sprouting coconuts to eat." This is what they would tell us after giving us the coconuts. . . . The boys asked me the meaning and I said, "We chew watery betel nuts and eat watery coconuts that are not dry inside—they haven't ripened, fallen down, and sprouted." That was what the allegory said and I told them.

What did the sponsors mean by giving sprouting coconuts? Savas and other recipients saw the coconuts and attempted to establish motives for their affines from their knowledge of rhetorical convention. When I asked Jubo, Savas's collaborator in the exchange, what the coconuts meant, he suggested a more specific interpretation. He speculated that since sprouting coconuts ready for planting were used, rather than some other token, they were expressions of a growing dissatisfaction with the imbalance in marriages between the two factions in recent years. In particular, the recent elopement of (recipient) Jubo's youngest brother with the daughter of (giver) Paulus, Makai's brother, was on everyone's mind.

Alternatively, another man suggested that the coconuts might refer to pigs. The coconuts may have been a complaint that Jubo and Savas had not cared for pigs properly and had not raised pigs for exchanges.

Sometime later I discovered that a request for a coconut by a dying person conventionally means that, rather than leaving his pigs to his successors for their exchanges, his or her spirit will kill and eat the pigs. If the message referred to pigs, the distinction between watery coconuts and solid, sprouting ones, may have been a comment on the age of Jubo's and Savas's pigs. The choice of interpretation was not resolved, because that evening Makai, the leader of the sponsor's faction, responded.

Makai denied there was a message behind the gift of the sprouting coconuts. He assured Savas that they were not dissatisfied with him as their exchange partner. The sprouting coconuts, he claimed, were obtained at a feast the preceding week. These were the only coconuts available for this exchange. His explanation seemed plausible, and it was apparently accepted by Jubo and Savas. Nothing more was said publicly about the matter at that time.

A year passed, Makai had died, and preparations were under way for another exchange between the same sets of villagers. Savas and his *agan* and Matag, a man of the Bun 'ora faction that had given the coconuts, planned a pig exchange that would also include gifts of food and tradestore goods. Matag and his associates were worried. They privately expressed doubts that Savas was really prepared for the exchange. The pig that Savas planned to give escaped to the bush while Matag's slept and grew fat under his house. Savas's pig was as scrawny as Matag's was fat.

The first public recognition of difficulties between the two groups came when Savas's wife was attacked by a severe headache and backache just days before the feast. Maive, a village medium, was asked for a diagnosis.[8] His spirit familiar found that her illness was caused by the spirit of her dead Bun 'ora father, who had abducted her *kaven*. Her father was displeased because she had failed to care for the pig he and his kinsmen were to receive.

The two pigs were exchanged, killed, and eaten. Matag made his gift first, followed a week later by Savas's feast. Not only was the pig that Savas gave less fatty than Matag's, but Savas was not able to provide the same quantity of tradestore goods for Matag. Clothes, kitchenware, and linens were promised by his exchange associates, but there was no sign of them.

Matag's supporters waited anxiously for the delayed tradestore goods. They planned to use them in an exchange with another village. Matters came to a head when Paulus, one of Matag's prominent associates (and Makai's older brother), publicly berated Savas for his continued delay. Paulus recalled the sprouting coconuts. He claimed that they were given as a warning. The coconuts, originally considered metaphorical by Savas, but denied by Makai, were recalled and reinterpreted by his brother a year after their presentation. Both the diagnosis of Savas's wife's illness and the incident over the coconuts indicated mismatched motives and intentions. Initially, Savas placed Russell, Matag, and the other givers in a difficult position by defining the nature of the interchange as metaphorical and giving an interpretation. His interpretation made it appear that they had criticized him publicly. At the time, Makai, aligned with the givers, attempted to defuse the tension by disavowing the motives assumed by Savas's metaphorical interpretation of the coconuts. This was considered proper to maintain the public perception of equivalence between the partners.

Later, after Makai had died and Paulus had assumed his role in exchanges, the whole alliance faltered because of the incomplete exchange. Paulus reinterpreted the coconuts to make their message relevant to the changed social conditions. He presented a complete list of grievances. His speech seemed to compress all of the perceived social inequalities in wives, pigs, and goods into the figure of the coconuts.

Relations continued to decline further until finally Savas, Jubo, and their Doho 'ora, Samoij, and Eko 'ora kinsmen began their move to Kavan and Biria in 1978. Small affinal exchanges continued to occur between the two for, as they put it, the sake of the children and their relations with ancestral spirits. Their political interdependence declined, and the community at Jinebuina declined.

Coconuts, Genres, and Metacommunication

The case of the sprouting coconuts reveals the nature and significance of genre in indirect discourse and the process of interpretation. The negotiation over the genre of the coconuts—indirect and metaphorical or direct and literal—was significant because it defined the nature of communication. Recognition and acceptance of the genre of the coconuts constituted metacommunication (Ruesch and Bateson 1951). Whether the coconuts were accepted as simply coconuts or as indicators of something else set the frame for the interpretation given by Savas. The ambiguity itself portrayed the unsettled state of relations between the two major factions of the community.

Russell and Matag, who were responsible for placing the coconuts on the litters in the first place, refused to comment on their significance. That, they said, was Savas's responsibility as the recipient. Russell and Matag did not give clues about the nature of the gift or the possible situations that were relevant for interpreting their tokens. Russell did not run the risk of a public rebuff by a literal interpretation. All he had done was give Savas coconuts. If he wanted to press a point, he could try again with another token or an allegory under different circumstances.

Savas, on the other hand, was forced to decide if some aspect of his relation with the Bun 'ora faction composed of Matag, Russell, Makai, and Paulus was at issue. If he had said that the coconuts were just coconuts, with no metaphorical significance, he would have denied there was a need to clarify the bond of mutual respect and obligation between him and his affines. With the attention that I drew to the event, with my innocent question, he might have decided that this was not the time to examine their mutual obligations. However, by accepting the coconuts as metaphorical tokens, Savas indicated that he assumed that the state of the relationship needed renegotiating.

Makai's public denial of indirectness on the other hand, sidestepped the challenge to the status quo. Nonetheless, given the state of affairs between the two groups, some members of the audience did not take the denial at face value.

Makai's death left the direction of Bun 'ora affairs in the hands of his brothers, Paulus and Magua. Once the initial parity between Savas and his exchange partners ended, polite, indirect criticisms turned into open hostility and mutual accusations. The poor performance by one group in the exchange raised questions about the strengths of their *kaven*. In the end, Paulus publicly denounced Savas as a man who was losing his strength and unable to maintain his place in the exchange network.

Paulus and his Bun 'ora kinsmen also suffered. Savas upset their timing for another feast in which Paulus and Matag were hosts. They could not produce the necessary goods for their other exchange partners, having received little from Savas, thus bringing their own strength into question.

This case demonstrates that genres play a pivotal role in negotiating meaning. The conventions of genre bring together the structure of the text and the social relations of the participants (see Jameson 1981). In the case of the coconuts, the oscillation between indirect (covert) and direct (overt) discourse indicates that the contract between the performer and his audience was not settled. The participants had to negotiate on two levels simultaneously. On the one hand, they needed to reach an understanding of their own relations and the motives they ascribe to one another. On the other hand, they must also negotiate a genre of communication and its conditions of use.

Culturally defined genres and motives form the pragmatic context of communication. Paine (1976) has noted that before a social transaction can occur, the participants must come to a common assessment of the nature and process of the exchange. The case of the coconuts demonstrates that this is true both in social transactions and communicative exchanges. The metacommunicative role of indirect discourse in this case is to work within cultural concepts of person and power to define the nature of specific relations and exchanges. It does this by constraining the social context and the pragmatic conditions of the interchange.

In this case, communication in a metaphorical genre was appropriate as long as the parties were equals and had similar assessments of each others' motives. The public failure of Savas and his associates frayed the bonds of mutual obligation and personal respect, expressed in terms of perceptions of *kaven*. The metacommunicative message of indirect genres was no longer appropriate for the participants' unequal social status.

The Lost Dog? or Looking For Cane?

A second case provides a good example of the process of negotiations within the allegorical mode. The interchange that follows, between Baho and his kinsmen,[9] occurred toward the end of my stay in Jinebuina in 1977, but just before the final interpretation of the sprouting coconuts.

Baho, who was living at Kavan as a consequence of the riot that split the village, came up the path and entered Jinebuina in the morning just as people were preparing to leave for their gardens.

Baho was the guardian of his dead brother's adolescent daughter. Her suitor lived in Jinebuina. The young man had come to Kavan and was staying with some of his relatives for several days. The morning of the speech, Baho awoke to find that his brother's daughter and the young man had eloped—disappeared into the bush during the night.

When Baho arrived in Jinebuina that morning, he walked straight to the house of Nevil, the boy's guardian. Nevil was sitting in his doorway facing the mall with a number of his neighbors (and Baho's kinsmen) nearby. Directly opposite Nevil on the other side of the mall, a man named Kivide sat on his front steps holding one of his children. Baho's older brother, Maive, who was Nevil's next-door neighbor was sitting on the ground with two brothers: Dajahare and Tanai. All of these men were Baho's kinsmen and represented his various kin-group affiliations: Nevil (Kuba 'ora), Kivide (Bun 'ora), and Maive, Dajahare, and Tanai (affiliated with both Kuba 'ora and Bun 'ora). The missing boy was one of Nevil's Kuba 'ora charges.

After taking some betel nut to chew, Baho addressed all of them from in front of Nevil's house. In the following allegorical narration, Baho employed two related metaphors: dogs and the scenario of following a path (blocked by a tree) to collect cane. The former invoked an image of loss or theft (possibly referring to the elopement), while the latter signified a possible (but obstructed) reconciliation with kinsmen.

> BAHO: Before, I raised many dogs when I lived in Jinebuina. I raised many dogs, went up into the mountains, caught game, brought it back, and ate it. Then, a little while ago we fought; (I) went down there (to Kavan) and my dogs died. Because I was living down there, I didn't see that a big wind came and blew a tree over. So, I thought I might go and get some black cane (for a weaving belt), prepare it, and maybe catch some game or pull out some yellow cane (to weave a design in the belt.) I thought I would go up (to my usual place) look up and see the cane standing there. I would climb up and get the cane and prepare it. I would go up, see the game, get some black and some yellow cane, prepare them and return home, so I went up the path. But the path was blocked (by a fallen tree) so I stopped, thought I would prepare the black cane, get some game to eat and leave (without the yellow cane). I went back (home), found (another kind of yellow cane), prepared it, used it in my weaving and came up here. I am finished.

Without hesitation, Kivide replied.

KIVIDE: Baho told a story. Did you understand it? Baho left something of his here. You (pl.) stole it, so he has come up here to look for it, and he has asked that whoever has seen it not wrap it up and put it away, but let him see it. If something of yours dropped, we would bring it here, put it down, and ask who it belongs to and give it to you. We should help him by bringing out (the thing that he has lost) and putting it here. Now they should give it to him quickly. If I was walking around and saw a small knife, spoon, or something else that dropped and was lying there, I wouldn't take it and keep it. I would take it quickly to the owner and give it to him. Others might try to trick him. If I (had something) that fell on the ground and the owners were looking for it, I would tell them and give it to them. If they didn't know where it was, I would get it quickly. Listen to me; you heard that he was looking for something and has asked you to look for it. He brought something here, put it down, and someone took it; that is why he has come up here to ask us. Whoever took it, don't wrap it up and put it away, but find it and give it to him quickly to finish this. He is looking for something, he said. I am finished.

Nevil, still seated, responded.

NEVIL: I haven't seen one of my dogs and am looking for it. I was looking for it when Roti (Baho's wife) came here chasing it. I was looking when Roti came up here to speak to me. "Your dog is staying down there (near Kavan). Isn't that why you are looking around?" she asked. That is what I heard and (why I have spoken). Now, perhaps (the story) is finished.

When Nevil was finished, Dajahare gave an interpretation for the audience, which included me.

DAJAHARE: Nevil told a story. I will explain it. I will explain. A dog that he fed did something, so he has told an allegory about it. He thought about the story and then spoke. A boy from here went down and got a wife, and we didn't see what happened, so (Baho) came up here and told us the story we have just heard. Baho came up here looking for the dog that he had fed game. He wants his brothers and cousins to chase it with him. So, Nevil spoke, we heard him and I have explained what he was thinking when he spoke. It was a dog of Nevil's; one that he had fed. Nevil had raised the dog, and they went around together. He went around with it, but the dog stayed down there with relatives when he came back. That person went there; stayed with them and ate. They gave him food and game. Those people who are looking for them gave food and game to eat. The dog stayed and ate and thought, "They will go." They went looking (for him), but the dog stayed there. "Your dog went down there and stayed with us," they said. They thought, "Who gave the dog scraps of food to eat? What did it smell?" They went looking, and I stayed here looking and have now found it. This (interchange) is finished now.

At the end of the interpretation, Dajahare turned to Baho, who replied:

BAHO: I got what I was looking for.

Baho seemed satisfied. After this exchange Baho went to his brother Maive's house and sat chewing betel nut and joking with his Jinebuina kinsmen. Their talk around the hearths in Jinebuina that night was about an event that would further tie them together: the impending marriage between Baho's brother's daughter and Nevil's guardian son. There was also speculation about the timing of the marriage feast and bridewealth exchange.

This interchange between Baho and his audience shows first that they accepted the metaphorical nature of his story and its initial metacommunicative implications. Also, they crafted an understanding of his story that appeared to be mutually acceptable to all parties.

Baho stated that he got what he had sought. Baho accepted Kivide's understanding of the story, and he acknowledged Dajahare's interpretation. Nevil's response that the dog was his also seemed to fulfill Baho's expectations.

Baho used the conventional figure of a dog in his allegory. His interlocutors built upon this metaphor. They developed responses around the dogs that Baho had raised when he was in Jinebuina and Baho's apparent search for his brother's daughter, her suitor, and those responsible for providing the bridewealth for the marriage. In the process, they placed themselves in relation to the figures in the story.

The replies and interpretations focused on dogs, which are common Managalase metaphors in everyday speech, songs, and allegories. Though dogs can be helpful to a hunter, they are typified as promiscuous thieves who steal game even from their masters. The loss of a thieving dog is the theme of a song about land which Baho shares with his Bun 'ora kinsmen, including Kivide, Russell, and Paulus. This characterization of dogs also appears in nonmetaphorical legends and well-known myths. In allegorical convention, a dog indicates a loss or theft, as suggested by Kivide.

What was lost or stolen? The audience's understanding of this aspect of the story hinged on Baho's role as the guardian for his deceased brother's adolescent daughter. Men in this position are always wary of elopements because they upset their strategy and timing of marriage alliances. The basic questions, however, concern his intentions in telling the story and the motives imputed by his audience.

Marriages are legitimized by a feast and the gift of bride-wealth. These exchanges mark the acceptance of the young people's informal relationship by their parents and kin. Though Managalase are almost puritanical about premarital sex, and sexual relations are virtually equated with marriage, parents may refuse to let liaisons lead automatically to marriage because of the political ramifications. Baho not only came looking for the couple, he also sought the bridewealth and feast that would legitimize the marriage.

Despite the seemingly amicable conclusion to this interchange, the timing of the marriage was disastrous for Baho's kin-group ties and exchange partnerships. Though still a member of Bun 'ora, Baho remained estranged from his Bun 'ora kinsmen as a consequence of the fight that split Jinebuina. Since then, he had worked to strengthen his Kuba 'ora ties by gardening and hunting with them and by assisting them in exchanges. This destroyed his carefully built bonds with his Kuba 'ora kinsmen. The marriage demanded that Baho and Nevil's kinsmen from the Kuba 'ora clan choose which clansmen to support. The marriage threatened to isolate Baho from his most important kin affiliations and jeopardize his ability to fulfill his exchange obligations.

As a member of the audience, I thought I recognized another message in the story. If the dogs were taken metaphorically, what was the significance of the path, the fallen tree, and the cane? My suspicions were aroused because Baho had told me the previous week that a reconciliation feast was imminent between himself and Makai's faction of the Bun 'ora clan. My research assistant, Baho's nephew, also thought that there might be more to the story, but he said we would have to wait and see.

An analysis of the story's structure suggests that two meta-phorical themes were woven together—the dogs, on the one hand, and the tree, path, and cane on the other. Each potential metaphor, the tree, the path, and the cane was repeated several times to highlight its significance in the story (McKellin 1984). Baho's audience could use either one of the two themes or both together in forming an interpretation.

Cane was used in the second set of metaphors. Cane is a com-mon figure in allegories about accepting or rejecting invitations to feasts. There is also a Bun 'ora song that has a plot similar to that of the allegory. In the allegory, the cane metaphor and the plot might both be used for their allusion to Bun 'ora and to the hunting land that Baho had not visited since the fight. The tree also played a critical role in this allegory. Trees provide individ-uals and groups with their identifying plant emblems. Named trees, *marura*, share their names with people. An ancestor's old garden sites are remembered by the fruit and nut trees planted there while the gardens were under cultivation. In myths, people turn into trees and leaves and back again. Trees are also frequent-ly used as figures in metaphorical communication. In most inter-pretations of allegories I heard, fallen trees referred to weakened or dead people. The tree in this allegory, blown over by the wind and blocking Baho's path, probably represented a person who had died.

Paths connect gardens, villages, groups, and individuals. They are social ties. In allegorical convention, paths frequently refer to genealogical ties, the routes to sources of knowledge and to paths of action. In Baho's allegory, the path led back to Bun 'ora and the social context in which he told the story.

After Baho and his allies had migrated from Jinebuina to Kavan, Baho imposed a prohibition on himself. He had promised not to return to the upper portion of Jinebuina where he and his former associates, now opponents, had lived together. He also cut himself off from his gardening and hunting territory on Bun 'ora land. He was separated from his trees, cane, game, and his ancestors who inhabited the land. His path to them was blocked. He also excluded himself from participation in exchanges with many of his clan-mates.

Self-imposed restrictions like Baho's are quite common after a serious dispute or fight. They are lifted when the disputants stage reconciliation feasts and renew their commensal relations. One of Baho's opponents, Makai, who was also the village councilor, had been trying to arrange a reconciliatory feast between Baho and his own Bun 'ora faction. Makai did not want to preside over the dissolution of the village he had created. Baho had told me several months before his speech that the reconciliation feast was imminent. Although Makai died before he could complete the arrangements, Baho told me the week before his speech that he expected amity to be restored soon.

In the allegory, the metaphor of the tree may represent any one of three men who where "felled": Matag's dead brother, at whose mortuary feast the fight started; Magua (Makai's brother), who was knocked unconscious and almost killed by Baho; or the recently deceased Makai. The tree in the story most likely referred to Makai because of his importance to Baho at the time.

Reconciliation appears to be the intent of this portion of the allegory about the tree, the path, and the cane. Was it composed to reawaken the negotiations for a reconciliation feast so that Baho could rejoin his Bun 'ora kinsmen? For the reconciliation, Baho needed help from his Kuba 'ora and Bun 'ora kinsmen from whom he had been estranged.

The two sets of metaphors—the dogs and the cane, tree, and path—are ambiguous. Baho's allegory referred not only to the elopement but also to negotiations for reconciliation. In their responses, however, Baho's audience totally ignored the possible significance of the fallen tree and the blocked path and concentrated on the dog metaphor or the marriage of the young couple.

The evolution of the allegory's meaning did not end with Baho's interchanges with his Bun 'ora and Kuba 'ora kinsmen, Kivide, Nevil, and Dajahare. The importance that Baho placed on the path, tree, and cane in the second portion of the allegory became clearer in a speech he made four days after he issued his first allegory. Standing on the steps of another Kuba 'ora kinsman's house, Baho attacked his previous audience—his former exchange associates. He berated them for not helping him and accused them of not treating him as a kinsman. They had not assisted him in arranging the reconciliation. Baho left Jinebuina after his speech, stating that he would never return.

Baho's failure in these negotiations reflected differences in the participants' social and political goals. For Baho, reconciliation had high priority because of the impact that the marriage of his brother's daughter would have on his exchange relationships. My research assistant, the brother of the girl who had eloped, explained that if the marriage and bridewealth exchange took place before Baho was reconciled with his Bun 'ora kin, then he could not include them among his party at the exchange. He would lose an important chance to reestablish his bonds with his Bun 'ora kinsmen. Meanwhile his Kuba 'ora kinsmen would become his affines.

Baho's kinsmen from Jinebuina, on the other hand, were busily arranging a feast with a neighboring village. At the time, their own exchanges took priority over helping Baho with his reconciliatory feast. They did not share Baho's sense of urgency in responding to his allegory. Furthermore, though most of his Bun 'ora kinsmen, like Kivide, were no longer hostile toward Baho, Magua still spoke harshly about the fight. Magua was not fully prepared for the reconciliation and without him the feast was destined for failure.

The reconciliation feast Baho sought never did occur. Within two years of Baho's speech, the village of Jinebuina was disbanded. Savas and his kinsmen prepared to leave after the breakdown of their alliance with Paulus's Bun 'ora agan, and the deaths of other participants in the fight changed social realities and made a formal and complete reconciliation impossible. Paulus, however, one of Baho's few surviving Bun 'ora opponents, now needed Baho's support. When I returned to the area in 1984 I found Paulus's and Baho's houses standing side by side. Paulus said that he had asked Baho (through an allegory) to rejoin his surviving Bun 'ora kinsmen, though it was done without a formal reconciliation feast. Baho said that Paulus had picked up the path of his earlier dog allegory.

Ambiguous Intentions and Coordinated Motives

How do metaphors and allegories communicate meaning? In the first case, we saw that the genre itself is metacommunicative and indicates that a particular social relation obtains between participants. Within this context, how do men and women compose and understand indirect, metaphorical discourse?

Managalase contrast allegories' fictive nature with that of everyday accounts of events, myths, legends, and other stories that are assumed to be true. Myths and legends are true by definition. Everyday stories are generally assumed to represent general knowledge and the transparent intentions of the speaker. The audience assesses the veracity of a story based on their perception of the speaker's knowledge and motives.

Common narratives and conversations in Managalase are consistent with the principles that Grice (1975, 1978) has posited for English conversation. The meaning of an utterance is dependent upon audience identification of the speaker's intentions. Allegories, however, are figurative. Managalase describe indirect communication as *bisivi* 'trickery' and *irakata venan* 'deception'. The Managalase concept of metaphor is partially consistent with Grice's identification of figurative uses of language as violations of conversational maxims, particularly the maxim that governs the quality of information. (Baho's allegory, however, does not fit Grice's criteria.[10])

If meaning is based on the audience's identification of the speaker's intention, then, to comprehend a metaphor, according to Grice, it is necessary for the listener to first recognize the violation of a maxim. Then the listener must establish the speaker's intention by searching for specific implications of the metaphor.

Searle (1979) contends that fictional discourse has two levels of intentions. The intentions on the first level are expressed through the conventional rules of genre, the metacommunicative nature of discourse. The second level includes the specific intentions of the text of the speech act. Searle's position goes part way in recognizing the importance of the conventional framework of nonliteral discourse. But, like Bloch's (1975) treatment of the context of oratory, Searle does not adequately deal with the problems of identifying metacommunicative frameworks of communication.

Wilson and Sperber (1981) and Sperber and Wilson (1982) expand Grice's treatment of relevance to provide a more comprehensive framework for interpreting figurative language. They replace the maxims concerning the quantity and quality of information with the pragmatic obligation of the speaker to be relevant. They contend that relevance, rather than cooperation, is the guiding principle of communication. The relevance of an utterance is determined by its perceived context—the hearer's beliefs, assumptions, and memory of events (Wilson and Sperber 1981). Working from the assumption that an utterance is relevant, the audience uses its background knowledge to fill in inferences that make it understandable and coherent.

What is relevant for the speaker and his or her audience in Managalase rhetoric? Allegories and other tokens are designed to evoke past, present, and future assumptions about individuals, their kinship relations, and alliances. They enable the speaker to test others' perceptions of social relevance without making any commitment to the audience.

In most narrative genres, the text surrounding metaphors provides a context for their interpretation. In Managalase allegories the context is less obvious. The social contexts in which relevances are sought are perceptions of self, background knowledge about others, especially about the roles and associated motives available to them, and the conventions of genre.

In the two examples presented, the sprouting coconuts and Baho's allegory, the audience determines independently the relevance of the social and political context that they believe the speaker is trying to evoke. In the case of the coconuts, the initial relationship between the two parties was indexed in their choice of indirect discourse.

Going beyond the general framework of metacommunication and social relations, how are particular metaphors amalgamated to mediate specific issues? When I was learning to tell allegories, I tried out my compositions on my informants. I asked them if the story was an adequate metaphorical statement of a particular message. The answer I usually received was, "These are your own thoughts, and the story could have that meaning. If people can't understand your story, that is their problem. You could always tell them another story if they don't understand this one." The speaker's obligation to the audience is limited.

The audience has almost equal freedom in understanding and interpreting stories. This latitude extends to choosing which of the speaker's possible intentions will be recognized and translated into publicly interpreted motives. The meanings of metaphors require the active participation of the audience (Paine 1981; Lindstrom, this volume). Metaphors describe—they do not in themselves make assertions. Therefore, in genres of indirect discourse the speaker's intentions are not authoritative. Allegory is unlike many genres where the listener is subordinate to the speaker.[11] Ultimately, meaning does not simply rest in the recognition of the speaker's intentions; it requires the coordinated motives of the participants. Indirect discourse puts the intentions of the speaker and the audience on an almost equal footing. Metaphors are the medium through which communicative equality is established between speaker and hearer.

This parity is particularly important in negotiating the basis of social interaction in an egalitarian society. Allegories allow the speaker and his or her audience to test sets of assumptions about personal and political relations without assuming responsibility, imposing obligations, or demanding compliance. Allegories are a form of rhetoric with almost total deniability.

While allegories preserve the equality and independence of audience and speaker, they are also dangerous. Managalase state that allegories are subtle acts of *aboimahinan* 'questioning', in which the processes of understanding and interpretation are reflexively examined. The audience must not only consider the probable intentions of the speaker, but, more importantly, they must examine their own intentions.

When the audience responds or presents an explanation, men and women must consider which of their private intentions they are willing to make public by assigning a meaning and motive to the speaker's allegory. In the process of interpretation, members of the audience present themselves in particular relations to the speaker and take on appropriate motives. Young people with limited experience are justifiably cautious and hesitant about interpreting allegories, particularly if they are the target. Some men who did respond said that they found they had unwittingly agreed to marry.

The case of the sprouting coconuts shows that the mode of communication and interpretation of figurative language do not need to be determined at the beginning of the interchange. The metacommunicative contract between performer and audience may still be under negotiation. The meaning of the token or allegory may be left pending until the end of the negotiation (Werth 1981). If the framework for the interchange is acceptable and the negotiation is successful, then the narrative will be taken as metaphorical. Otherwise, it will be treated as an interesting, odd, slightly irrelevant, or nonsensical story (McKellin 1987).

The goal in the interchange is to take inaccessible, often ambiguous intentions and transform them into coordinated, but not necessarily common motives. Shared assumptions and intentions are not necessary for social action. If agreement were necessary for dispute management, attempts to resolve controversies would disappear under accusations of blame and provocation. Metaphorical tokens draw out possible compatible motives for the participants rather than imposing a solution upon either party. In the process of reconciliation, the metacommunicative framework of equality and respect for person and the position of others is achieved; no other conditions are necessary.

Conclusions

The Managalase preference for indirect modes of dispute management and communication through metaphors and allegories reflects their concepts of self and community. Village members, fellow kin, and affines provide the sociopolitical universe in which individuals find themselves. Spirits of ancestors and predecessors further extend their social universe.

Each person's unique fusion of historical and social ties both differentiates and binds individuals in kin groups and communities. The health of individuals and the survival of communities are dependent upon preserving these social and historical relations. However, among the Managalase as in many other societies, tensions, disputes, and conflict grow out of unfulfilled expectations, competing priorities, and different interpretations of social obligations.

In this setting, where each person has a high degree of autonomy, resolving disagreements requires tact and discretion. Attempts to control or otherwise intrude on the self of another may cause illness or death. Disentangling can only proceed if there is parity between the negotiators, just as partners in affinal and political exchanges should also be equals. Healthy exchange relationships between partners increase the prestige and strength of both men. The same is also true of speakers. If they can resolve matters through metaphor, they enhance their renown by displaying their knowledge, self-control, and cleverness.

In indirect discourse, metaphors and allegories intervene between the participants. Allegorical stories and tokens are mediators, like spirit familiars and curers. The initial choice of indirect discourse is itself a metacommunicative expression of the perceived equality of the participants. As we have seen in the two examples in this study, once the balance between peers is disrupted, metaphor and allegory break into direct, presumptuous demands or dissolve into open criticism.

Indirect discourse is important in dispute resolution and negotiation because it enables the parties to separate metacommunication about social relations from particular issues under negotiation. Allegories also enable individuals to experiment with abstract representations of cultural ideals and real social relations without requiring public commitment. A request can be refused without undermining the social bonds between people. Like the Samoan *fono*, the social meanings of figurative language unfold through time (Duranti, this volume).

The Managalase preference for metaphor, allegory, and other modes of indirect communication in disentangling is consistent with their ambivalence toward public expressions of personal power. Genres of indirect discourse do not give authority to the speaker's intentions over those of his audience. Meanings are jointly constructed, protecting the participants from direct public confrontation. This symmetrical relationship between speaker and audience in metaphorical communications is similar to that of the participants in the A'ara *gruarut'ha* (White, this volume), but contrasts with the asymmetrical relations between psychotherapist and patient (Labov and Fanshel 1977) or between the participants in Kwara'ae *fa'amanata'anga* (Watson-Gegeo and Gegeo, this volume) or Hawaiian *ho'oponopono* (Ito 1985; Boggs and Chun, this volume).

The preference for allegorical rhetoric also reflects aspects of the Managalase self. Metaphors mediate between ambiguous private intentions and publicly espoused motives. Both the speaker and the audience must reflect upon the social relations they are willing to acknowledge before they engage in public interpretations. Metaphors provide a buffer between the self, sheltered within an individual's personal space, and one's position in clan history or involvement with others. The ambiguous and enigmatic nature of metaphorical discourse enables political life to proceed without publicly resolving questions of blame and responsibility. Those are issues of personal intention that ultimately cannot be resolved. The ambiguity of metaphor shields and obscures knowledge of immediate intentions while still allowing the coordination of day-to-day activities that require limited agreement for cooperation.

Social and linguistic interactions, like disentangling, do not require common intentions and shared interpretations. They do demand mutually relevant, socially constructed motives. Allegorical representations preserve individuals' heterogeneous intentions while constructing a mosaic of meanings that regenerates the premises and conditions of Managalase social life.

Notes

The research on which this paper is based was funded by grants from the Social Sciences and Humanities Research Council of Canada (1975–78) and the Spencer Foundation (1984–85). I would like to thank the members of the Pitzer Conference on Talk and Social Inference for their helpful comments on an earlier version of this paper. Particular thanks are due to the editors of this volume, Geoffrey White and Karen Watson-Gegeo, D. Olson, Richard Salisbury, Dan Sperber, Karen McKellin, and an anonymous reviewer for their comments. The deficiencies that remain are mine.

1. The plant-emblem system is similar to that of the neighboring Orokaiva (Williams 1925, 1930; Schwimmer 1972).

2. This term is taken from Weiner's (1983) discussion of Trobriand speech and magic.

3. This is similar to the pattern of repeated information in allegories (McKellin 1984).

4. Songs and their interpretations are kin group property. Group members do not necessarily agree on the literal or metaphorical aspects of all songs.

5. The clan affiliations of the individuals mentioned and the participants in the two cases are given below. The clan names are listed in order of their priority as most frequently stated by these individuals and most relevant to the discussion of the two cases. Where two clan names are separated by /, this indicates that the individual claims and exercises equal affiliation in these two clans.

Savas	Eko 'ora,	Doho 'ora,	Samoij	
Jobo	Samoij,	Eko 'ora,	Arene 'ora	
Russell	Bun 'ora,	Garidija,	Manoiva 'ora,	Misaj
Matag	Bun 'ora/	Sarosija,	Misunija	
Makai	Misaj,	Bun 'ora,	Misunija	
Magua	Misaj,	Bun 'ora,	Misunija	
Paulus	Misaj,	Bun 'ora,	Misunija	
Baho	Bun 'ora/	Kuba 'ora,	Ugese	
Maive	Bun 'ora/	Kuba 'ora,	Ugese	
Kivide	Bun 'ora,	Garidaja,	Kuba 'ora,	Misaj
Nevil	Kuba 'ora	Alene 'ora,	Bun 'ora	
Dajahare	Eko 'ora,	Kuba 'ora,	Bun 'ora	

6. A residential history of the Siribu people reveals a long pattern of village fission and fusion comparable to that described by Watson (1970) for the Tairora. At contact in 1904, the two sets of clans lived separately, the Bun 'ora faction at Huaja and the Doho 'ora faction near Biria. Prior to the Second World War, they came together at the insistence of the government to form a joint village at Siribu. This village survived until the late 1940s, when it split into two villages: one located near the old village at Huaja and the other at Biria. It was from these villages that Makai drew together people to form the settlement at Jinebuina.

7. Statements in this section and for the following case are given only in English translation. A full vernacular transcription is available from the author upon request.

8. Though Maive was a member of Bun 'ora clan, he was not involved in this feast because of his involvement in the fight that split the village.

9. See note 5 for the kin-group affiliations of the participants.

10. The dogs in the story were treated metaphorically by his

audience despite the fact that Baho actually did raise dogs when he lived in Jinebuina. This was a point of concern when the story was originally told and caused some people to focus on the second set of metaphors for their private interpretations.

11. Grice's contention that a speaker's intentions are authoritative has been challenged by examinations of other nonconversational genres (Du Bois 1987; Duranti 1988).

References

Bloch, M.

1975 Introduction. *In* Political Language and Oratory in Traditional Society. M. Block, ed. London: Academic Press.

Brown, P., and S. Levinson

1978 Universals in Language Usage: Politeness Phenomena. *In* Questions and Politeness. E. Goody, ed. Cambridge: Cambridge University Press.

Du Bois, John W.

1987 Meaning Without Intention: Lessons from Divination. Papers in Pragmatics 1(2): 80–122.

Duranti, Alessandro

1988 Intentions, Language, and Social Action in a Samoan Context. Journal of Pragmatics 12: 13–33.

Goldman, L.

1983 Talk Never Dies: The Language of Huli Disputes. London: Tavistock.

Grice, P.

1975 Logic and Conversation. *In* Syntax and Semantics, vol. 3. P. Cole and J. Morgan, eds. New York: Academic Press.

Grice, P.

1978 Further Notes on Logic and Conversation. *In* Syntax and Semantics, vol. 9. P. Cole, ed. New York: Academic Press.

Ito, K.

1985 *Ho'oponopono* and the Ties that Bind: An Examination of Hawaiian Metaphoric Frames, Conflict Resolution and Indigenous Therapy. Culture, Medicine and Psychiatry 9: 201–17.

Jameson, F.

1981 The Political Unconscious: Narrative as a Socially Symbolic

Act. Ithaca: Cornell University Press.

Labov, W., and D. Fanshel
1977 Therapeutic Discourse: Psychotherapy as Conversation. New York: Academic Press.

McKellin, W.
1980 Kinship Ideology and Language Pragmatics Among the Managalase of Papua New Guinea. Unpublished doctoral dissertation, University of Toronto.
1984 Putting Down Roots: Information in the Language of Managalase Exchange. In Dangerous Words: Language and Politics in the Pacific. D. Brenneis and F. Myers, eds. New York: New York University Press.
1985 Death and Loss of Life: Aging and Passing Away Among the Managalase. In Aging and Its Transformations: Moving Toward Death in Pacific Societies. D. Counts and D. Counts, eds. Lanham, MD: University Press of America.
1987 Pragmatic Metaphors in Papua New Guinea: Reading Between the Lines in an Oral Culture. In Le Conte. P. Leon and P. Perron, eds. Ottawa: Marcel Didier.

Mills, C. W.
1984 Situated Action and Vocabularies of Motives. In Language and Politics. M. Shapiro, ed. Oxford: Basil Blackwell (originally published in 1940).

Paine, R.
1976 Two Modes of Exchange and Mediation. In Transactions and Meaning: Directions in the Anthropology of Exchange and Symbolic Behaviour. B. Kapferer, ed. Philadelphia: ISHI Press.
1981 The Political Uses of Metaphor and Metonym. In Politically Speaking: Cross-Cultural Studies of Rhetoric. R. Paine, ed. Philadelphia: ISHI Press.

Ruesch, J., and G. Bateson
1951 Communication: The Social Matrix of Psychiatry. New York: Norton.

Salisbury, R.
1963 Ceremonial Economics and Political Equilibrium. VIe Congres international des sciences anthropologiques et ethnologiques, tome 2. Paris: CISAE.

Scheffler, H.W.

1965 Choiseul Island Social Structure. Berkeley: University of California Press.

Schwimmer, E.

1972 Regional Communications Systems in Papua New Guinea and the Problem of Social Boundaries. Toronto: Mimeo.

Searle, J.

1979 The Logical Status of Fictional Discourse. *In* Expressions and Meaning. J. Searle, ed. Cambridge: Cambridge University Press.

1983 Intentionality: An Essay in the Philosophy of Mind. Cambridge: Cambridge University Press.

Sperber, D., and D. Wilson

1982 Mutual Knowledge and Relevance in Theories of Comprehension. *In* Mutual Knowledge. N. V. Smith, ed. New York: Academic Press.

Strathern, A.

1975 Veiled Speech in Mt. Hagen. *In* Political Language and Oratory in Traditional Society. M. Bloch, ed. London: Academic Press.

Watson, J.

1970 Society as Organized Flow: The Tairora Case. Southwestern Journal of Anthropology 26: 107–24.

Weiner, A.

1983 From Words to Objects to Magic: Hard Words and Boundaries of Social Interaction. Man 18: 690–709.

Werth, P.

1981 Relevance. *In* Conversation and Discourse. P. Werth, ed. London: Croom Helm.

Williams, F. E.

1925 Plant Emblems Among the Orokaiva. Journal of the Royal Anthropological Institute No. 35.

Williams, F. E.

1930 Orokaiva Society. Oxford: Oxford University Press.

Wilson, D., and D. Sperber

1981 On Grice's Theory of Conversation. *In* Conversation and Discourse. P. Werth, ed. London: Croom Helm.

PART IV

TANGLED DISPUTES AND STRAIGHT TALK

Straight Talk on Tanna

Lamont Lindstrom

ON TANNA, an island of southern Vanuatu, people unsnarl conflict in talk. They convene debates, which take place at circular kava-drinking clearings, in order to produce true or "straight" talk. This polemic product is a consensual decision, public account, or settlement between disputing parties. Metaphorically, conflicts are tangles of contradictory claims, statements, and versions which speakers attempt to unravel (see White, this volume). Conflict (or *trabol* 'trouble' in the local litigious terminology debaters bring to their meetings from Vanuatu Pidgin English[1]) must be unknotted. The truth must be straightened. At meetings, debaters attempt to *-fi* (open, untie, loose, free) or *-oser(i)* (unwind, unroll, disentangle, resolve) 'trouble'. When disputants agree, they *-oseri ia nagkiariien* 'untangle talk.' When they do not, they sometimes accuse one another of *-ouini atihi nagkiariien* 'knotting the talk' (see Appendix, Transcript A, 074).

Debates in egalitarian Melanesian societies aim to generate reconciliation and consensus (see, for example, cases reported in Epstein 1974). The importance of consensus stems, in part, from Melanesian dispute-settlement structures in which, typically, no participant has the authority to adjudicate the issue. Third parties at a debate must rely on moral suasion, on shaming, and on rhetorical skill to resolve a dispute. The importance of consensus also relates, in part, to Melanesian notions of interpersonal equality which make problematic most acts of "representation" (cf. Myers 1986). People are disinclined to speak for others who are their social coevals. Similarly, they avoid *public* speculation about the details of another person's intentions or the tenor of his feelings. Rather, adult men generally possess the right to speak for themselves.

At Tannese dispute-settlement meetings, people must work to

disentangle conflict collectively in order to produce a cooperative agreement. These products are public accountings (meanings, definitions, interpretations, versions) and also, sometimes, decisions (dispute settlements, plans for future group action, etc.). A consensus supposes that people share the interpretive versions they have produced in debate. Moreover, if the meeting has taken a decision or resolved a dispute, participants are also supposed to agree about the course of future action whether this is the location of a garden or the fining of some consensually-defined-to-be-guilty party.

Consensus definitionally presumes a climax. Some agreement is reached. It presumes people achieve, reach, find, arrive at, create, or negotiate accounts and decisions. These various English metaphors which describe the production of consensuses allude to several different processes of decision making and imply a number of kinds of consensual decisions. Some consensuses are "found." As with a Quaker "sense of the meeting," participants expect consensus, here, to flow from collective group will—a will that people discover through assembled cogitation and talk. Other consensuses are "negotiated." This sort of collective account or decision, unlike the former, in that no participant is supposed to have violated personal conscious or will, is a negotiated compromise—a lowest common denominator of individual desire. This consensus and the processes of "negotiation" which establish it presume the operation of individual or factional, rather than group, will. Bailey (1965) describes consensuses of this sort within Indian decision-making bodies. Here, the problem is not to "find" the collective meanings, truths, and interests presumed to exist, but to cut a deal that all participants can support.[2]

Consensus may imply, then, either an indivisible collective sentiment or the sum (rather, negotiated lowest common denominator) of individual interests and versions. These conceptualizations of consensus are also ideological. They represent and legitimize processes of decision making for those involved. Whether or not they model accurately how people actually resolve conflict, produce group decisions, and generate and maintain shared meanings is another question. In Tannese debate, speakers work to produce shared, public, and consensual meanings about the particulars of conflict and its appropriate resolution. This they call "straight" talk, or truth. One may seek to triangulate the meanings of a statement, or of dispute itself, within a space defined by individual intention, shared convention, and contextual interaction. On Tanna, public meaning (i.e., "truth") depends, ideologically at least, on the latter two of these points. People cooperatively determine the consensual truth as they untangle conflict.

Conflict, as an analytic category, is itself rather conflicted. The term labels a miscellany of emotional states, interpersonal behaviors, and intellectual misunderstandings. "Trouble," on the island, reveals itself in behavior that ranges from complete interpersonal avoidance to the propinquity of a physical punch-up. For purposes here, within the confines of a debate, I assume conflict to be the existence of a number of competing and contradictory stories or truth versions. Speakers may decry the existence of these preconsensual, conflicting accounts during a debate as in Transcript A:

021   I am not adding anything to the debate, but I want to know how many statements (words) are there here?

022   Five or six?

Consensus, conversely, is the production of a single public accounting, be this an interpretive truth or a decision to act. By untangling their stories, people expect also to unsnarl associated conflicted emotions and interpersonal relations. Tangled words are both the symbolic cause and tropic representation of conflict. The occurrence of "speech" (*nagkiariien*) is a metaphor for the existence and playing out of dispute (Lindstrom 1981b:385). People fight with words. Speech is, however, also the mechanism of disentangling dispute. Although newly reconciled disputants mark conflict termination with an exchange of material goods, the work of resolution itself demands that people first exchange words in debate. Their goal is the production of a consensual account. Once they stop putting forth conflicting versions, protagonists achieve silence, or the untangling of *nagkiariien reraha* 'bad talk' which concludes debate.

Islanders conceive of local debate processes and products more in terms of the finding—rather than negotiating—of consensus.

Metaphors of discovery parallel those of disentanglement in local fashions of talking about debate. Figuratively, people speak of debates as voyages through space rather than as competitions or warfare in which individual interests contend. They speak of the meaningful or decisive products of debate as "arrived at" rather than compromised (Lindstrom 1983; cf. Lakoff and Johnson 1980). These tropes of motion govern people's working descriptions, if not also their understanding, of the processes of talk and decision "making." Speakers "proceed" (Appendix A:122, B:64), "voyage" (A:028), or "fly" (A:063, 105) along an argument; they "descend" (A:055) in detailed statements; they "surmount" (A:072, 098) a debate when the group's "canoe" (A:036) arrives at its destination.

Debates are collective voyages of disentanglement; all travelers reach the same truth terminus. Metaphorically, at least, consensus flows from the joint interaction of speakers. It is not a balancing of individual interests or a compromising of wills. People arrive at consensus and resolve conflict when they have straightened talk. The truth exists; it just needs untangling. Produced consensual meanings—as in proper Quaker style—are the sense of the meeting, of the group as a whole.

To some extent, these consensual truths and decisions are indeed the emergent and joint productions of those present at a debate. Disputants cannot resolve many sorts of social conflict unless all sides take part in appropriate debate. The fact of their production (disentanglement or discovery) in public discourse accords these accountings and decisions a value greater than that of individual versions or resolutions. In debate, people declare publicly the truth of the matter and also their resumption of good relations with antagonists.

Even so, although local metaphors of truth untangling and discovery in some ways accurately characterize the interactionist production of consensual public accounts and decisions, these figures also hide and thus help reproduce relations of social, communicative, and interpretive inequality. Insofar as the public reality of a person's intentions and statement meanings are group-determined, rather than self-determined, he renounces some control over the interpretation of what he intends and what he has said. Everyone is not equal in this renunciation. Certain speakers maintain greater control over public meaning. They manage and direct consensus more easily inasmuch as people metaphorically perceive disentangled accounts and decisions to be "found," not negotiated, and insofar as people situate statement meaning in communicative interaction among speakers, not in individual speaker intentionality.

Situating the locus of statement interpretation and truth in the group, rather than the individual, effects and reproduces relations of power and inequality. A real (or even metaphorical) interactionist basis of truth generation, as opposed to an individual intentionist basis, transfers control of truth from individual to "group"—an already constituted system of relations of domination. This essay discusses Tannese debate, the ultimate decisiveness of its consensual productions, the witnessing of debate statements, and the enunciation of truths. Debate is more than a political procedure that sometimes resolves intergroup conflict. It also permits the management of truth. Disentangling is here one of the "mechanisms that make power possible" (Myers and Brenneis 1984:4).

Tanna

Tanna has a population of twenty thousand people who speak five related Austronesian languages and live in scattered hamlets and villages. Houses circle central kava-drinking grounds everywhere shaded by magnificent banyan trees. These drinking grounds are symbolic centers within cultural geography. Here, men gather daily to prepare and drink kava, people stage exchange ceremonies and dances, and speakers and listeners convene to make important group decisions and tackle social disputes. People call these debates *nagkiariien* 'speech'; they also refer to debate by the Bislama (Vanuatu Pidgin English) term *miting*.

Village co-residents—the men who drink kava together at one clearing—are for the most part members of a small number of local "name-sets" which regulate individual rights to surrounding lands. Members of these lineage-like structures control finite sets of male and female personal names with which, recycling appellatives over the generations, they nominate their successors. Although people entertain notions of patrilineal descent and parenthood and symbolize kinship with the metaphor of shared blood, they recruit additional local group members by naming rather than by the facts of birth. Although there are certain inherited titles on Tanna, real power rests in the hands of big-men, who achieve their position through a reputation for knowledge and also through material largesse. People support a big-man in order to gain access to the material help he can provide and access to the knowledge he has.

Wider structures of "tribe" and moiety do not today often serve to organize everyday discursive interaction. The common action groups on the island are families, village bodies, kava-drinking companies, and those congregations of believers who consume one or another body of local doctrinal knowledge. Several Christian denominations claim Tannese adherents, with Presbyterians greatest in number. In addition, the John Frum movement has attracted followers in varying numbers over the past fifty years. At present, about half the island's population continues to subscribe to John Frum discourse.[3] Throughout much of the island, residential and kava-drinking groups tend to be doctrinally homogenous. People who live together and drink kava together also, consuming the same truth, vote and pray together in the same political parties and churches.

Debate

The subjects of island debate are varied. The agenda of some meetings concern the making of a decision (whether or not to pen up local pigs, to vote in a national election, etc.), and others the settlement of a dispute (over land, familial discord, exchange inequalities, etc.). Islanders take most group decisions informally, particularly as men meet daily for kava drinking. If a dispute occurs between two members of the same local group, it typically is addressed by informal mechanisms of gossip and moral suasion, although co-residents may also convene a village debate to address the problem (see Appendix, debate B). If a decision or dispute involves people from an area wider than the local kava-drinking group, however, leading men involved set a date for a meeting and send messages of invitation to third parties to come *witnis* 'witness' the debate between protagonists. Debate is the only available mechanism to resolve conflicts or make decisions that concern more than one local group. Even if disputants pursue additional strategies, such as social avoidance, the warfare of the past, or reports to police and governmental authority, they nevertheless must at some point still address the problem in face-to-face debate.

Meetings convene around 10:00 o'clock in the morning, depending on the distance participants must travel. In most cases, "witnesses" are summoned from neighboring kava-drinking groups. If leading men deem the problem to be serious, however, or if it concerns a number of local kava-drinking groups, or if they wish to add to the dignity and repute of an occasion, they may summon powerful men from some distance away. These witnesses are older and respected leaders of local groups and are also leaders of the several politico-religious organizations on the island, including the Christian churches, the John Frum movement, the custom John Frum people, and the Kapiel movement. Some leading men are active witnesses. They attend debates throughout their region. Others restrict themselves to meetings that discuss problems closer to home. In that public speaking is a main criterion of personal prestige and the *miting* the principal arena for political action, virtually all island leaders are active debaters.

Men attending a debate sit along the periphery of the circular kava clearing. Arcs of the periphery are owned by certain of the local groups involved. These arcs are situated near the point of egress of the trails, or "roads," which link kava ground to kava ground. Protagonists, consistent with island dualism, sit at antipodal points facing each other across the clearing. Those who witness their debate mediate this dualism, positioning themselves between the sides.

Debate usually begins with a discussion of side issues. After talk has begun to flow, someone will bring up the main problem at hand. If this problem is minor, the focal antagonists may themselves make the initial statements. If things are more serious, however, and emotions engaged, supporters who are more likely to keep a cool head will carry the early debate, setting forth their version of the dispute or problem. The principals may join in later in the day. To speak, men stand and walk toward the center of the clearing (Lindstrom 1981b). They hold the center until they are done expositing and then return to the periphery to sit. Speaking continues until about 4:00 P.M., when men need to begin the day's kava preparation or their return journeys to reach home villages before nightfall in time to consume kava there. People presume that a decision will be found, or a dispute settled, in one day's meeting—before dusk, in fact, so that kava preparation may properly begin.

Meetings always include more listeners than speakers. Women have no right to public speech and sit behind men on the periphery of bush and clearing (between nature and culture) as befits their political and cosmological status. Although all men may speak, and will certainly do so at some meeting or another that touches their interests, generally at any one meeting only about one-third of those present actually speak. Of this number, a few men dominate most of the communicative interchange (Lindstrom 1981b). This is especially true of important debates attended by up to several hundred people.

Access to speech demonstrates knowledge and therefore symbolizes and maintains a person's political power (Lindstrom 1984). This has a number of consequences. Younger men involved in the delicate game of power acquisition boldly or tentatively add their two cents worth. They risk public disdain. Already influential men may for the same reason produce gratuitous speech to recall their position and power to public attention.

Data and Methods

Illustrative data for this paper are taken from three meetings that occurred in 1982 and 1983. One of these (debate B), involving a dispute between in-laws residing within a single local group, took place in a village rather than at the local kava-drinking ground. Bounds of topic relevance in debate are very wide. Numerous charges, countercharges, innuendos, and accusations fly. The principal and originating dispute in this case, however, occurred between a man's wife and his parents. Tonga cursed her parents-in-law after they intimated she was a deplorable wife and mother. Uiuai and Iati, principals in a second debate (A), disputed the ownership of a plot of ground. This became a public and conflictive issue when Iati slashed down a number of banana suckers Uiuai had planted on the land. The third meeting (C) was more strategic discussion than debate. One local group met with its supporters before the kava hour to review its position regarding a second group's improper use of local roads to transport exchange goods.

I recorded debate with a shotgun microphone and, in consultation with men who had participated in these meetings, produced subsequent transcriptions. We together penetrated some of the rhetorical and illocutionary intent of debate statements as well as their grammatical and metaphoric complexities. Tannese debate rarely takes the form of question/answer or other sorts of adjacency pairs, as in the Fijian Indian *pancayat* described by Brenneis (this volume; and see Goldman 1983:19). Instead, speakers deliver statements in which they often address a number of points and fellow speakers. Debaters do refer to statements made by previous speakers and do pose questions. As the floor is self-acquired, however, topical and speaker interactions often are not adjacent. One to several other statements by other speakers may have occupied the floor in the meanwhile. The statements in the appendix are thus excerpted from the course of debate.

Dispute Irresolution

Tannese debates generate decisions and plans to which participants seemingly consent (cf. Myers 1986). The consensual products of these debates, however, do not necessarily indicate much about the future course of behavior of those who consent. As with Huli disputing, speech is "never-ending" (Goldman 1983:282). The decisive product of many meetings, consensual though this may be, frequently has little effect on the behavior of the consenters in following days. Decisions, sometimes taken quickly in the face of a rapidly approaching kava hour, are also quickly ignored. No meeting participant has executive powers to enforce the decisions and truths discovered in debate. This lack of power correlates with consensual as opposed to other sorts of decision making (see Bailey 1965:9).

For example, the decision of debate A, based on the presentation by both sides of historical and genealogical knowledge relevant to the land plot in question, went in Uiuai's favor. His opponent Iati—although he joined this discovered consensus in the end—managed rhetorically to register his opposition to the fairness of the witnesses present and thus to the enunciated decisive product of the meeting. Others who attended observed that this "consensus," which all present, including Iati, had found, would not last long. They expected Iati to bring up the dispute sometime in the future. In fact, this particular plot of land had been a bone of contention for many years, "since before I began to shave" as Uiuai observed in debate, and had several times been at issue in a meeting. This presents an apparent problem. What is the use of finding and enunciating interpretive or decisive consensuses which people frequently disregard?

Island debaters sometimes ask themselves this same question. Those who attend debates again and again to make the same consensual decision over and over can become rather annoyed. Kieri, witnessing the discussion about misuse of exchange roads (Transcript C), complained:

001   If it is like that, this is the last time we come out and hear you
       talk all the time in our faces here at the kava-drinking ground.
002   I say you three have never acted (on your decisions).
003   This is the last time.
004   If you three reopen the debate if he wrongly exchanges feasts
       along your road, this is the last time that we will sit out here at
       the kava-drinking ground for you three to discuss it.
005   You three are like women, I say.
006   You three are like women, afraid to do anything.
007   Let some of us do it.
008   Stop talking endlessly.

This was rhetoric, however. People continue to call meetings to readdress the same issues and witnesses continue to attend meetings to re-enunciate the same consensuses.

In that the Tannese consider representation of political equals to be illegitimate, only those who take part in communicative exchange and arrive at a resulting consensus have responsibility for that decision. Any obligation to support a meeting's decision rests only on those people present during its making. This implies that people meet to discuss only those issues that are, in fact, potentially solvable. To forestall resolution of a dispute, all one party has to do is to refuse to attend a debate (see Goldman 1983:189). Debaters discover consensus, in effect, only when disputants are willing to consent. The presence of both sides signals a willingness to entertain resolution. The opposition between physical presence/absence is a crucial one in Tannese culture. One's presence signals participation in both short- and long-term political relations as well as a commitment to public, consensual truths.

Disputants, therefore, must first convince their opponents to attend a debate in order to resolve conflict. People sometimes hide their true agenda in order to bring the other side to a debate. During debate, they also attempt to manage the agenda in order to prevent opponents from bringing up additional problematic areas where they are vulnerable. Uiuai, during debate over the disputed land (Transcript A), so objected to Nikahi's attempt to relate this issue to a marital exchange dispute:

091 You are digging up (another topic here).

092 I ask myself how do I harm the children?

093 We two will talk sometime about it, let this problem lie.

In this debate, Uiuai himself had gulled Nikahi and Iati into attending the event by implying that they would only discuss the destroyed banana trees. Upon arrival, they discovered that Uiuai actually planned to debate the larger question of land plot ownership and had arranged for a number of third parties to attend. Had Iati and Nikahi known this, they could have sent their regrets. Iati decried Uiuai's strategy:

014 I say that we did not know the meeting is about this (land dispute).

015 Of we all, only we two came.

016 If we two had brought supporters to sit one-by-one like these men here, and we had questions, we could have asked them (drawn upon their knowledge).

017 You all are sitting and listening (witnessing), right?

018 But I didn't summon you, you who are sitting and listening to judge.
019 I say all his men, he brought them all here.
020 Me, my men are not here so that, if I had a question, one of my supporters could answer it.

Having arrived at the debate, Iati could only walk away if he committed himself to a more serious disruption in his relations with Uiuai and his supporters. Walking out of a meeting once it has begun denotes an alarming collapse in local relations. Rather than actually leaving in a huff, an acceptable recourse is *symbolic* absence signaled by silence. A disputant who perceives that things are not going his way may stop talking and refuse to present his whole case; he keeps secret some of the relevant knowledge he could muster. The meaning of silence, however, is ambiguous and problematic. It also signals the end of disagreement and the achievement of a consensus. Moreover, the consumption and experience of kava by men of a kava-drinking group also occurs in silence. Avoidance of speech during kava intoxication marks male group solidarity and the absence of dispute (Brunton 1979; Lindstrom 1981b). Because of this, when maneuvering to establish a favorable outcome, speakers will often instruct opponents to *stop talking*: further speech spoils the "consensus." Uiuai, for example, berated his opponents thusly:

072 I've finished the talk, Nikahi.
073 Stop attacking the consensus.
084 I already explained everything in my statements.
085 Stop striking the talk (attacking my asserted consensus).

The ambiguous meaning of silence permits subsequent manipulation of a person's participation in a consensus. When a participant stops talking, at the time people of course understand whether his silence signals the end of debate and arrival at a consensus, or whether it denotes his withdrawal from debate into a symbolic absence. Witnesses may also take a disputant's silence to indicate that he has exhausted his supply of relevant knowledge and debating points. Thus, Nariu, witnessing the debate between Uiuai and Iati (Transcript A), noted:

052 Old man Uiuai.
053 Perhaps you think I am against you.
054 Let me clear this up, please listen.
055 This morning, you produced a story (knowledge of land plot history), you went into details.
056 You produced this history in detail.
057 But listening over there we heard nothing, listening to the other side we heard silence.

In future, however, a disputant may claim that his consensual or ignorant silence was actually the silence of symbolic withdrawal, implying a withholding of further knowledge pertinent to the problem at issue. Since he was at least symbolically absent, he may thereby evade responsibility for whatever repellent consensus the meeting achieved. Uiuai, for example, explaining why he had failed to make claim to the land in question at a previous discussion declared:

059 When we debated at Iatkuriari I didn't bring this up because Rasiang was against me like you are now.
060 I will explain now.

In terms of the contractual model discussed above, a consensus is a form of promise. Those involved in the negotiation of a consensual truth or decision have some responsibility to act within its terms. In a Western contractual reading, consensuses constrain future behavior. On Tanna, however, a contextual interactionist production of statement truth, rather than truth's location in individual intention, makes both promises and decisive consensuses rather iffy. An audience does not base its interpretation of a statement upon a reading of speaker intentionality. Words mean, speakers may not. Similar descriptions of the weightlessness of promising have been reported from other Pacific cultures. Korn and Korn (1983:445) note that, on Tonga, "there is no institution of promising." Supportive utterances "are not regarded by Tongans as committing the speaker to the performance of the action" (1983:447). Instead, they are expressions of solidarity meant to preserve a relationship (1983:450; see Duranti 1984:13-16).

On Tanna, although people have a concept of individual intentionality and various mechanisms to assess this, like Tongans and Samoans, they have no word for promise. Nor do they have a specific term for consensus (viz., *-ni sumun* 'say together', *-ni kwatia* 'say singly', *-ni niteta* 'say the canoe/group'). A person's statements about his intentions do not always accurately predict his future acts. To the extent that meaning is "seen as the product of an interaction (words included) and not necessarily as something that is contained in someone's mind" (Duranti 1984:14), words may provide information about a person's *present* state. While he is interacting in one social context, his interpretations, intentions and behaviors are constrained by the meanings being publicly produced. These words, however, are less certain readings of future actions. A person will then be constrained by different interactional contexts, involved in generating a perhaps different set of truths.

In some societies, debates discover no consensus; they are nonclimactic and there is no journey's end (Gewertz 1977:345, Brenneis, this volume and 1984:82). Given the non-contractual notion of consensus on Tanna, one could say that no real climax occurs here either. Without the controlling effects of true promises upon behavior, disputes often are not permanently disentangled through talk. Speakers, in an absolute sense, neither mean what they say nor say what they mean. Still, most Tannese meetings at least end in silence—one or both of the sides stops talking and, ideally, acquiesces in the witnesses' final statements. The dispute is at least temporarily resolved, and a public decisive and interpretive consensus achieved.

This public resolution, even if immediately violated, has a further, less temporary effect. Debates function to end social avoidance between disputants (see White, this volume; Besnier, this volume). Like Tongan promises, consensuses do not always oblige and direct participants' future intentions and thus often fail to disentangle completely a substantive issue. But consensuses do symbolize and restore ongoing relations between antagonists. Avoidance is an immediate response to a serious conflict between two individuals. If the parties are members of the same kava-drinking group, resolution of dispute is immediate. If not, one or both of the disputants moves out of the area. If dispute occurs between individuals living at some distance, the dispute and resul-

tant social avoidance may never be resolved. If dispute occurs between individuals of neighboring kava-drinking groups, the parties involved will assiduously avoid meeting each other. When
they desire to end avoidance or otherwise find avoidance no
longer possible, local leaders schedule a meeting and summon
witnesses. Renewed interaction between disputants first occurs
the morning of the meeting. An achieved consensus regularizes
relations between the two and each may now talk with the other,
drink kava at the other's ground, and the like.

In that the bounds of topic relevance at meetings are extremely
broad, each side is usually able to charge the other with some
outrage or another. In that one function of meetings is to end
avoidance between disputing parties, witnesses are not in the
business of adjudicating verdicts of guilty or innocent (see
Goldman 1983:108). Labels such as these make more sense in
societies where people worry more about intentionality. Instead,
witnesses find enough diffuse blame to smear both disputing
sides and usually 'fine' (Bislama: *faen*) each a pig and a kava (see
Goldman 1983:195). At the end of the day, these bilateral fines
are prepared and consumed by the collective debate participants.[4]

Enunciation

If debate often fails to settle finally particular matters of contention, it more successfully settles the truth. In this, meetings are a
procedure that reproduces relations of inequality and power.
Inasmuch as meetings are the mechanism for termination of
avoidance, people depend on those who witness a debate to
repair their relations with economically and politically necessary
others. A person's social relational viability depends on the
mediation of powerful third parties. Moreover, Tannese consensuses, weak and shoddy as these may appear, are public disserta-
tions in which the powerful generate and manage interpretation
and public truth. As Brenneis notes, meetings produce a public
accounting of a specific conflict and also the truth of its disentangling (1984:79; see also Lederman 1984:97; Weiner
1983:163; Firth 1975:42). In the process of untangling or discovering a consensual account, speakers also enunciate statements that rehearse more general truths about persons and

conflict. Here, debate "creates an axiomatic universe of meanings that may have implications for future situations" (Brenneis and Myers 1984:19; see Bentley 1984:643).

There are a number of different kinds of participants present at debates with different subjective rights to speak. Women and young men usually remain in the audience. They lack personal qualifications to make statements; these belong to socially powerful men. In addition, a number of distinctions exist within the group of active debaters. This group includes protagonists and their supporters as well as a number of witnesses. These latter remain in the audience during most of the debate. If they take to their feet in the early going, it is usually to admonish or instruct other speakers in custom and decorum. This speaking demonstrates both their knowledge and their power so to admonish. Typically, witnesses offer their contributions near the climax of discussion. Here, they attempt to enunciate the sense of the meeting and to give a reading of the event, and thus straighten conflicting interpretation and opinion into a public truth (see Brenneis 1984:75; Goldman 1983:172).

Third parties (like Tannese witnesses) are common in dispute-settlement systems (see Boggs and Chun, this volume; Hutchins, this volume; Watson-Gegeo and Gegeo, this volume). They serve to mediate dyadic opposition. Gewertz, describing Chambri disputes, for example, notes "experts (all old men of the first or second ascending generations) were called as eyewitnesses to arguments, migrations of individuals between clans, name endowments and deaths from sorcery" (1977:345; see Comaroff and Roberts 1981:111; Brenneis 1984:74; Hutchins 1980:58). Unlike judges, however, witnesses have no official authority to weigh evidence, adjudicate responsibility, and arrange recompense or punishment. Their power to interpret the sense of a meeting and enunciate a consensus depends upon their particular positions within other social relations of inequality.

People realize that a witness's enunciation of an emergent consensus is shaped by his wider social roles, relations, and interests and thus may differ from another's. Disputants attempt, therefore, to stack the witness box. Each side sends invitations to third parties they know or suspect will favor its position. Witnesses may also self-select. The bane of some disputants is the uninvited know-it-all. Kieri, although the brother of a strong supporter of Uiuai, so self-selected himself to be a "neutral" witness, stating (Transcript A):

002 All right, one should appoint some judges to sit and weigh the debate.
003 Weigh the debate of you two to determine whose position is strong and whose is weak.
004 This is what we will determine here.
005 It is wrong for everyone to talk (at first) for who will judge (enunciate a final consensus)?
006 Debates are like this.
007 One should appoint some men to sit back (and witness).

After Iati expressed some reservations about Kieri's impartiality, he added:

008 Sorry, I am interrupting the talk, but we perceive your feeling that we are all on Uiuai's side as we judge.
009 No, it isn't thus.
010 A custom meeting's fashion is thus:
011 We sit and weigh your two positions.
012 It isn't that we only support Uiuai there.
013 We are here for both sides.

Tumhien, a second of Uiuai's witnesses, also asserted his impartiality:

035 My two younger brothers may think that I come to help Uiuai or I come to help you two, but I come to listen to the talk of both of you, of the three of you.

Powerful witnesses more easily enunciate truth to the extent that "meaning is NOT conceived of as owned by the individual" (Duranti 1984:14) but is rather discovered and untangled in debate. As in Duranti's analysis of the interactive production of meaning during Samoan *fono*, "meaning is a mosaic that no one can compose by himself" (1984:14). In debate statements, for example, tag questions are common, marked by *ua* ('or', a shortened form of *ua rekɨm* 'or not'). Tag questions of this sort reflect an interactional rather than intentional locus of statement truth. Speakers syntactically demand audience participation in the production of shared interpretations.

The interactive debate context on Tanna, however, subsumes definite relationships of inequality and domination. Certain spokesmen fill in more of the mosaic than others. Since people find truth interactionally, individuals have less control of how their words are publicly interpreted. One may imagine a sort of communicative interaction that generates multiple and divergent truths, none of which possesses more social legitimacy and exchange value than another. In Tannese debates, however, participants work to produce a *single* story. People evaluate and interpret the statements and versions others offer. They do this in order to make common knowledge, a singular public version, a consensus.

The production of shared truth, as opposed to individual interpretive readings of debate statements, requires enunciation. Someone must enunciate exactly what the emergent truth is in order to make this public. It is here that individual interest and intent may creep back in and, by shaping emerging truth, effect the reproduction of social relations of power. Here, the powerful do represent powerless women, children, and politically insignificant men who rarely speak at meetings.

When remarking on the statements of coevals, speakers take note of their right of self-representation. Kauke, for example, prefaces a statement he makes about Tonga's dispute with her in-laws (Transcript B):

001   They two will speak, but as for my (thoughts) I will tell all.

Male speakers are much less circumspect in avoiding representation of another if this is a woman or male follower. Witnesses not only enunciate the sense of a debate, they sometimes go further to also enunciate the public sense of specific *statements* made by speakers with less right than they to mean what they say. After an unusual speech by a classificatory grandmother in defense of Tonga, her son Kwaniamuk hastened to enunciate a reinterpretation of her words (Transcript B):

060 Let me say this, explain a little about what she said.

He then proceeded to suggest a true account of what his mother's statement was.

Even when someone requests information of a woman's internal state, a male spokesman may step in to enunciate this to the audience. A rather powerless man, Isaac, for example, requested that Tonga herself explain her problem with her in-laws:

064 Tonga should explain her thoughts (head), but you big-men have gone and turned off the discussion.
065 We don't know if that is her opinion or not.
066 Let her say all that is in her heart.
067 The one sitting and thinking about it (Tonga) was agitated and came running to brother-in-law.
068 Let her tell all her feelings, let us hear all.

Kwaniamuk, not Tonga, responded to Isaac and interpreted Tonga's head and heart:

069 This thing, this anger, we all know this anger.
070 I say we all know anger like this, that if two people are sitting and the husband catches (a pig), this causes anger.

Later in the discussion, Rapi also enunciated his own interpretation of Tonga's true intentions and feelings:

090 Tonga loves her husband, as I have already said.
091 She really loves her husband.
092 She doesn't want to see blame in his eyes.
093 It is according to the wisdom of the ancestors:
094 Where his heart is there both their hearts are.
095 We big-men are through with this thing.

He then called for silence and closure of debate (i.e., acceptance of his interpretation):

096 Three men, it is enough (debate).

Speakers' use of various devices of indirection—common throughout Oceania—also facilitates the capture and enunciation of truth by the powerful (Brenneis 1984:78; Strathern 1975:199; Weiner 1983:700). Such devices, including indefinite pronominals, metaphors, vagueness, ambiguity, and the like, weaken an individual speaker's control of the public meaning of his words. These words are thus more amenable to appropriation, interpretation, and enunciation by others (Rosaldo 1984:135; Atkinson 1984:50). In situations where there is no publicly enunciated interpretation, multiple and ambiguous truths may result from indirect speaking. On Tanna, however, where the powerful enunciate an interpretation, indirection is redirected.

Iati, for example, attempted to elicit support from Kwaniamuk and Kauke, two of his kava-drinking mates who, however, were also members of Rapi's landowning corporation. Rapi, here, was Uiuai's principal witness. Kwaniamuk's reply to Iati's request that he make a statement as to his knowledge of the details of land-plot ownership was indirectly ambiguous (Transcript A):

108 A, we two haven't spoken, big-men, let me say a little about why we can't talk about this.
109 Let me explain why we can't talk about this.
110 You heard he hasn't said anything, let me explain.
111 He won't speak because of respect/shame.
112 However, you two insist on talking.
113 You two insisted on talking about it.
114 This is socially dangerous talk.
115 If you don't say anything, then we two also won't talk about it.
116 Make your statements however you please.

Kwaniamuk intimated that no one ought to be discussing the problem "out of respect," but that Uiuai and his supporters might say what they pleased. He hoped, through ambiguity, to avoid offending both sides by supporting neither. Rapi and Uiuai, however, redirected his indirect statement. They reinterpreted his claim to the middle ground as full support of their own position:

117 You two hear that talk; big-men, who supports you?

118 First-rate statement there, first-rate talk.
119 My man.
120 If you talk, talk about it like Kwaniamuk has. First rate.

Toward the end of a debate, witnesses begin to enunciate a possible consensus and attempt to legitimate this (make it the public version) by calling for silence and the end of talk. The number of witnesses present at any debate depends on the size and concern of the meeting. Witnesses themselves decide when to attempt to enunciate the public truth. Many of their attempts miscarry; other speakers continue to produce conflicting statements. Nikahi, for example, rather early attempted to close the land debate (Transcript A):

100 Okay, the debate is over.
101 The big-men will finish the meeting.

Rapi similarly stated that he would summarize the dispute between Tonga and her in-laws (Transcript B):

014 Good, the debate is sufficient, the debate is enough, I will sum up.
015 Uiuai, you be a witness.

Disputants, if they desire to end avoidance with each other, signal their present, contextual support of the consensual truth that witnesses are enunciating. Iati, for example, conceded (Transcript A):

146 In my opinion those who are judging should stand up (witness) and stop bringing up new debating points.
147 This is my thinking about it.
148 I say the judges should sum up; I agree to whatever they say about it.
149 I say that whatever statement the judge makes is okay.
150 Whether a person is only a land user or an owner.
151 And what about the land.
152 The judge will say once/finally.

153   If they say to me "I will push him off it," all right.
154   This isn't bad.
155   I accept, I have only use-rights.
156   I'll get out, okay.
157   We do not oppose it (the consensus).
158   The consensus (talk) is good.

Witnesses (or "judges") close meetings by enunciating the public sense of what emerged in communicative interaction. Control of enunciation of emergent truth permits the powerful to appropriate the words of others. In so doing, they manage the generation of common knowledge. This truth consists, as in the dispute between Iati and Uiuai, of particularistic details of history, of genealogy, and of rights to economic resources. Thus Iati, who came to the meeting to talk about the sabotage of banana trees, left having participated in an emergent consensus that reassigned ownership of the land plot itself.

Truth also consists of more general cultural interpretations and expectations. Witness Kieri, here, in addition to enunciating the fact that Iati lost the land, also rehearsed expectations of balanced reciprocity (Transcript A):

121   They two manage everything (control the disputed land).
122   They now say that you two must give up the land plot.
123   All right, give that up.
124   Now in my opinion, because they say you must leave that place, give up the plot, they two have injured you.
125   For their behavior.
126   They once told you that land was yours.
127   They should remedy their misleading you.
128   Now that they say you must get out, they must give you something.

Tumhien, similarly, rehearsed general evaluations of island traditions while enunciating the untangled truth of the matter:

141   Let us also follow custom.
142   Custom tells us what to do; you two think about this.

143 Now we debate according to the fashion of chiefs and custom.
144 Custom tells us what to do.
145 It speaks to us three.

Finally, the truth also consists of those public expectations that maintain particular systems of domination. Among these, on Tanna, is the definition of a "good" daughter-in-law. Tonga had gone over the head of her in-laws to ask Rapi, the big-man of a neighboring village, to convene and witness a meeting. Her agenda (complaints against in-laws for not helping her with child care; against her husband for not building her a decent house and for adultery) was only fleetingly raised by discussants. Rapi, and other witnesses who closed the debate, enunciated and redirected the problem to be an uppity daughter-in-law. Thus, debate ended as witnesses admonished Tonga (and daughters-in-law in general) to obey her in-laws and not to curse them.

Conclusion

On Tanna, the powerful enunciate the truth of statements and the sense of debates. Islanders do not seek the truth and import of a statement in speaker intent. An interactive, rather than intentional, locus of truth as well as speakers' use of various forms of indirection allow enunciaters to appropriate, represent, and redirect the truth and manage, thereby, common knowledge. Decisive consensuses—like promises—may not, in fact, indicate much about the future behavior of those consenting. Many consensuses last only as long as does the particular context of their generation. Individual self-interest and self-meaning are liable to revision and redirection in a different interactive context. Nonetheless, even if enunciation does not permit the powerful to determine specific future acts of particular individuals, it does permit those who disentangle conflict to manage public truth.

Moreover, the consensuses found and enunciated by witnesses (and stored in their memories) become facts that must be taken into account in future meetings that address the same, or similar, issues (see Goldman 1983:153). Although the truth value of a particular past consensus may shift contextually, the fact that it exists publicly is a legitimate debating point that disputants may raise in future discussions. Those who witnessed the stale disputes of the past achieve an additional basis of influence, controlling as they do knowledge of once-enunciated consensuses, when these disputes are recontended.

An interactive disentangling of truth necessarily implies some degree of individual alienation from self-meaning and self-interest. This is, however, an unequal alienation. Interactional interpretation proceeds, on Tanna, in a context of existing social structures of domination. The shaping of emergent public truth in debate—the enunciation of consensus—maintains and reproduces, in fact, these existing structures (Myers and Brenneis 1984:19; Myers 1986; Duranti 1984:17; Bentley 1984). By witnessing and publicly enunciating the truth, the powerful manage something of the social construction of others' reality.

Notes

Acknowledgements. I would like to thank Lawrence Rosen and the members of a 1984 National Endowment for the Humanities Summer Seminar on the Anthropology of Law, the Area Studies Fellowship program of the East-West Center, Geoff White, and Donald Brenneis for advice and support during the writing of this paper.

1. Debaters use a number of Bislama (Pidgin English) terms in their statements. The meaning of these words, although derived originally from English, is not necessarily the same as their English cognates. In some cases, Bislama terms translate available indigenous terms; in most, however, they reflect innovations during the past century in traditional dispute-settlement structures, such as "fine," "judge," "witness," or "constitution." People infuse many parts of their indigenous language vocabulary with Bislama etyma. In some cases, as with debate, this is a metamessage that signals the importance of the communicative event.

2. Presumptions of negotiated consensus no doubt correlate with the importance of "consent" in Western political thinking. A consensus is the totalized form of a number of individual consents—a voluntaristic social contract each participant makes during communicative interaction (Partridge 1971:78; Steinberg 1978:72).

3. A number of religious and political organizations are currently active on the island (Lindstrom 1981a). For many years the most successful of these has been the John Frum movement (Brunton 1981; Gregory and Gregory 1984).

4. If disputants, however, are closely related (as were Tonga and her parents-in-law and Iati and Uiuai) and the meeting thus attended primarily by other kin, people may be satisfied merely with distributing blame and ending avoidance, foregoing a fine. They thus save themselves the expense of killing pig and digging kava to repair long-standing, multiplex relationships. They rely on less expensive markers of avoidance resolution.

References

Atkinson, Jane
1984 "Wrapped Words:" Poetry and Politics Among the Wana of Central Sulawesi, Indonesia. In Dangerous Words. D. Brenneis and F. Myers, eds. New York: New York University Press.

Bailey, F. G.
1965 Decisions by Consensus in Councils and Committees. In Political Systems and the Distribution of Power. New York: Praeger.

Bentley, G. Carter
1984 Hermeneutics and World Construction in Maranao Disputing. American Ethnologist 11:642–55.

Brenneis, Donald
1984 Straight Talk and Sweet Talk: Political Discourse in an Occasionally Egalitarian Community. In Dangerous Words. D. Brenneis and F. Myers, eds. New York: New York University Press.

Brenneis, Donald, and Fred Myers
1984 Dangerous Words: Language and Politics in the Pacific. New York: New York University Press.

Brunton, Ron
1979 Kava and the Daily Dissolution of Society on Tanna, New Hebrides. Mankind 12:93–103.
1981 The Origins of the John Frum Movement: A Sociological Explanation. In Vanuatu: Politics, Economics and Ritual in Island Melanesia. M. Allen, ed. New York: Academic Press.

Comaroff, John, and Simon Roberts
1981 Rules and Processes: The Cultural Logic of Dispute in an African Context. Chicago: University of Chicago Press.

Duranti, Alessandro
1984 Intentions, Self and Local Theories of Meaning: Words and So-

cial Action in a Samoan Context. La Jolla: Center for Human Information Processing.

Epstein, A. L.

1974 Contention and Dispute: Aspects of Law and Social Control in Melanesia. Canberra: Australian National University Press.

Firth, Raymond

1975 Speech-Making and Authority in Tikopia. *In* Political Language and Oratory in Traditional Society. M. Bloch, ed. New York: Academic Press.

Gewertz, Deborah

1977 On Whom Depends the Action of the Elements: Debating Among the Chambri People of Papua New Guinea. Journal of the Polynesian Society 86:339–53.

Goldman, Laurence

1983 Talk Never Dies: The Language of Huli Disputes. London: Tavistock.

Gregory, Robert, and Janet Gregory

1984 John Frum: An Indigenous Strategy of Reaction to Mission Rule and Colonial Order. Pacific Studies 7:68–90.

Hutchins, Edwin

1980 Culture and Inference: A Trobriand Case Study. Cambridge: Harvard University Press.

Korn, F., and S. Korn

1983 Where People Don't Promise. Ethics 93:445–50.

Lakoff, George, and Mark Johnson

1980 Metaphors We Live By. Chicago: University of Chicago Press.

Lederman, Rena

1984 Who Speaks Here? Formality and the Politics of Gender in Mendi, Highland Papua New Guinea. *In* Dangerous Words. D. Brenneis and F. Myers, eds. New York: New York University Press.

Lindstrom, Lamont

1981a Cult and Culture: American Dreams in Vanuatu. Pacific Studies 4:101–23.

1981b Speech and Kava on Tanna. *In* Vanuatu: Politics, Economics and Ritual in Island Melanesia. M. Allen, ed. New York: Academic Press.

1983   Metaphors of Debate on Tanna. Naika: Journal of the Natural Science Society of Vanuatu 12:6–9.

1984   Doctor, Lawyer, Wise Man, Priest: Big-Men and Knowledge in Melanesia. Man (n.s.) 19:291–309.

Myers, Fred

1986   Reflections on a Meeting: Structure, Language and the Polity in a Small Scale Society. American Ethnologist 13:430–47.

Myers, Fred, and Donald Brenneis

1984   Introduction: Language and Politics in the Pacific. *In* Dangerous Words. D. Brenneis and F. Myers, eds. New York: New York University Press.

Partridge, P.

1971   Consent and Consensus. New York: Praeger.

Rosaldo, Michelle Z.

1984   Words that are Moving: The Social Meanings of Ilongot Verbal Art. *In* Dangerous Words. D. Brenneis and F. Myers, eds. New York: New York University Press.

Steinberg, J.

1978   Locke, Rousseau and the Idea of Consent: An Inquiry into the Liberal-Democratic Theory of Political Obligation. Westport: Greenwood Press.

Strathern, Andrew

1975   Veiled Speech in Mount Hagen. *In* Political Language and Oratory in Traditional Society. M. Bloch, ed. New York: Academic Press.

Weiner, Annette B.

1983   From Words to Objects to Magic: Hard Words and the Boundaries of Social Interaction. Man 18:690–709.

Appendix

The following are statements in translation excerpted from the course of three lengthy debates. I present the statements in sequential order although few were discursively adjacent as ellipses indicate. Where useful, I provide literal translations and commentary in parentheses. A transcription of vernacular statements is available upon request.

Transcript A. Land dispute, Uiuai and Rapi vs. Iati and Nikahi, 2 June 1983

KIERI

001 Excuse me, sorry (for interrupting), the cause of the debate that we two spoke of this morning is why we all have come to this meeting.

002 All right, one should appoint some judges to sit and weigh the debate.

003 Weigh the debate of you two to determine whose position is strong (large) and whose is weak (small).

004 This is what we will determine here.

005 It is wrong for everyone to talk (at first) for who will judge (enunciate a final consensus)?

006 Debates are like this.

007 One should appoint some men to sit back (and witness).

     [. . .]

008 Sorry I am interrupting the talk, but we perceive your feeling that we are all on Uiuai's side as we judge.

009 No, it isn't thus.

010 A custom meeting's fashion is thus:

011 We sit and weigh your two positions.

012 It isn't that we only support Uiuai there.

013 We are here for both sides.

IATI

014 I say that we did not know the meeting is about this (land dispute).

015 Of we all, only we two came.

016 If we two had brought supporters to sit one-by-one like these

men here, and we had questions, we could have asked them (drawn upon their knowledge).

017 You all are sitting and listening (witnessing), right?

018 But I didn't summon you, you who are sitting and listening to judge.

019 I say all his men, he brought them all here.

020 Me, my men are not here so that, if I had a question, one of my supporters could answer it.

[. . .]

NARIU

021 I am not adding anything to the debate, but I want to know how many statements (words) are there here?

022 Five or six?

023 These two men stood and gave their statement about it.

024 But you two haven't responded.

025 Let them end (win) the debate.

026 Nikahi stood up (stated) four times, right?

027 You claim to control everything but you haven't explained (your arms go about).

028 Why don't you two give statements which indicate (voyage along) what you know.

029 Moreover, Iati stood twice to support Nikahi.

030 So you two should respond.

031 You two explain yourselves.

032 You two don't want Iati to keep (the land).

033 Let this result from your behavior.

[. . .]

TUMHIEN

034 A, a, you two men, sorry, I've sat a long time and haven't spoken.

035 My two younger brothers may think that I come to help Uiuai or I come to help you two, but I come to listen to the talk of both of you, of the three of you (both sides).

036 In debate these two men, who are our big-men, both say that they lead the group (stand in the canoe).

037 They two would guide the group (canoe).

038 But they are splitting the group; my talk is finished (I make my point).

039 I witness in my ignorance, but the two men who guide the group (canoe) have split the group.

040 The stories they put forward (before) were false.

041 They two have now enumerated everything of you three such that you must act as one family.

042 They two speak correctly that you two occupy (that other land).

043 Let they two occupy this land.

044 I have a question about what they are saying, my brother.

045 Our fathers indicated that you go stand there (control that land).

046 I have heard your name here (associated with the disputed land).

047 This is the story they two once put forward.

048 But I say to you, my brother, I say this is his kava-drinking ground which has associated lands.

049 You two should not steal, let us three proceed correctly (straightly).

050 To procure our food, one established that you my brother go live there, you live correctly there but you don't come (and claim rights) here.

051 My question concerns this kava-drinking ground, where is its land?
     [. . .]

NARIU

052 Old man Uiuai.

053 Perhaps you think I am against you.

054 Let me clear this up, please listen.

055 This morning, you produced (descended into) a story (knowledge of land-plot history), you went into details.

056 You produced the history in detail.

057 But listening over there we heard nothing, listening to the other side we heard silence.
     [. . .]

UIUAI

058 Listen.

059 When we debated at Iatkuriari I didn't bring this up because Rasiang was against me like you are now.

060 I will explain now.

061 Do you understand or are you ignorant?

062 Rasiang was against me and wanted to kick me out of there when he came to establish the land boundary.

063 Now, I refuse that decision, the one you are bringing up (flying) now.

064 Look there.

065 The land of Iatkuriari goes this way, climbs upwards, and curves around thusly.

066 You have no land rights there, only Nouar is there.

067 You use that land in the name of Nouar.

068 You obtained that land when one fought you (your namesake ancestors) and you ran off and came here and one gave (use-rights) to you.

069 Thus I say I return to stand behind your rights.

070 But for this (disputed land), you came and we held onto you, gave (use-rights) to you, gave you women, you gave us yours and we gave you ours (along with use-rights to the land plot).

071 Now, get yourself out of here.

072 I've finished (surmounted) the talk, Nikahi.

073 Stop attacking the consensus.

NIKAHI

074 Uiuai, I am not tangling (knotting) the talk.

075 I am only saying what you told me.

076 You told me everything about what the ancestors did concerning land and women.

077 I don't know about the land, the women are all dead and they may or may not have had that coconut plantation (previously mentioned) in the valley.

078 This is what you stated, I was ignorant of it, I didn't know.

079 I don't know if that coconut plantation belongs to you people, or if you have none in the valley.

080 The women are all dead.

081 I was ignorant of what I stated (before you told me).

082 You explained everything, you did everything.

083 If there is a coconut plantation there, it is because you say so, I don't know anything about it.

UIUAI

084 I already explained everything in my statements.

085 Stop striking the talk (attacking my asserted consensus).

086 You are making things bad for the two of us.

087 Giving your knowledge (head).

088 I will straighten out your knowledge.

089 I have already explained it correctly and clearly.

090 I insist on my (rights) but you say we are harming the children (future marital relations between the two families).

091 You are digging up (another topic here).

092 I ask myself how do I harm the children?

093 We two will talk sometime about it, let this problem lie.

094 I heard you say to me "friend, let me sweep you off" (the land).

095 You were against me then.

096 Now, I remain on my side.

097 You stay on yours.

098 I've concluded (surmounted) the debate, what do you say?

099 Stop attacking the decision.

NɨKAHI

100 Okay, the debate is over.

101 The big-men will finish the meeting.

102 However, I say, you have returned to your tribe.

103 Now the men have agreed for you to return to Iakarui name-set.

104 You and the rest have agreed for you to return to Iakarui.

105 However, as we argue (fly), I recall that you are living on my land in the valley.

106 And you fight me for the land at Iakuvnoua.

107 I don't know but if you've joined them (and no longer need my valley land), good.

     [. . .]

KWANIAMUK

108 A, we two haven't spoken, big-men, let me say a little about why we won't speak.

109 Let me explain why we can't talk about this.

110 You heard he hasn't said anything, let me explain.

111 He won't speak because of respect/shame.

112 However, you two insist on talking.

113 You two insisted on talking about it.

114 This is socially dangerous talk.

115 If you don't say anything, then we two also won't talk about it.

116 Make your statements however you please.

RAPI

117 You two hear that talk; big-men, who supports you?

UIUAI

118 First-rate statement there, first-rate talk.

119 My man.

RAPI

120 If you talk, talk about it like Kwaniamuk has. First-rate.

[. . .]

KIERI

121 They two manage everything (control the disputed land).

122 They now say (proceed) that you two must give up the land plot.

123 All right, give that up.

124 Now in my opinion, because they say you must leave that place, give up the plot, they two have injured you (given you something heavy).

125 For their behavior.

126 They once told you that land was yours.

127 They should remedy their misleading you.

128 Now that they say you must get out, they must give you something.

129 If you think what I say is not proper, it's okay.

130 But this is my opinion about it.

131 It is because of their telling that story that you now are in trouble.

132 Thus I say let them pay you a fine.

[. . .]

TUMHIEN

133 A, brother, you have made a statement which follows something in the Bible.

134 I consider you if you are homeless; but if you talk like that (threatening to cut off relations), then I may ignore you too.

135 If people do you wrong you should forgive them.

136 If someone calls out as he comes past your kava-drinking

ground, you should call to him to come and stay with you.

137 Don't say that you will keep up the argument, I say to you brother, to both my brothers.

138 Let us three proceed in the way of our church.

139 Let us talk according to the church.

140 This is our affiliation.

141 Let us also follow custom.

142 Custom tells us what to do; you two think about this.

143 Now we debate according to the fashion of chiefs and custom.

144 Custom tells us what to do.

145 It speaks to us three.

[. . .]

IATI

146 In my opinion those who are judging should stand up (witness) and stop bringing up new debating points.

147 This is my thinking about it.

148 I say the judge(s) should sum up; I agree to whatever they say about it.

149 I say that whatever statement the judge makes is okay.

150 Whether a person is only a land user or an owner.

151 And what about the land.

152 The judge will say once/finally.

153 If they say to me "I will push him off it," all right.

154 This isn't bad.

155 I accept, I have only use-rights.

156 I'll get out, okay.

157 We do not oppose it (the consensus).

158 The consensus (talk) is good.

Transcript B. Discussion of marital discord, 25 May 1983

KAUKE

001 They two will speak but as for my (thoughts) I will tell all.

002 First of all, I don't dislike them.

003 She went and acted in that fashion.

004 My son helped her catch a small sow and kill it on the ridge.

005 I told Tonga to do down (and help with the pig).

006 Listen to me, listen to me, don't act in that way, go down (and help).

007 But I spoke for nothing, telling her uselessly.

008 She behaved (badly) as we are saying.

009 I don't dislike her.

010 I married her to my son.

011 I am content.

012 However, if she behaves this way, she wrongs me.

013 Although I spoke to Tonga she didn't listen to me, she didn't listen to me.

[. . .]

RAPI

014 Good, the debate is sufficient, the debate is enough, I will sum up.

015 Uiuai, you be a witness.

016 Our children often ignore our advice.

017 According to that stated in our constitution, a chief possesses the right if he acts correctly, but not if he acts wrongly.

018 In the law, if a person strikes another, I think carefully about it and say whether this was justified or not.

019 However is okay that he beat her.

020 Father's namesake (Kauke Ouihi) agreed that Uopu should hit her.

021 It is wrong according to law, but he thought that it was his right to determine that he should beat her.

022 I am going to agree that one of you (properly) hit her.

023 I have considered this thoroughly.

024 However I give this warning that you remember that it is forbidden to do this without my agreement.

025 Perhaps all of us sitting here see that that person did wrong.

026 Chiefs, all you witnesses (members) agree that he beat her (correctly), but if you don't report it and you do it without the chiefs' agreement—you alone decide to beat the wife of your brother— now this is what I am forbidding today.

027 That is the last of that.

028 In future if, for example, this spouse (makes trouble) and all of us chiefs, witnesses and members perceive the wrong, you chief, you agree that her spouse strikes her legitimately.

029 As for this case of ours, it is good to let this be the last.

030 Kauke saw her wrong.

031 Point number two.

032 The behavior of her two mothers, Kouia and Ritia.

033 I controlled the marital exchange of whatshername.

034 It isn't Kamti and Vani and Iau who arranged the exchange, Iau sitting there, but I gave Kouia to those three, my exchange partners on the next ridge.

035 She was exchanged for Noka, thus Riki belongs to us three.

036 She copies Kouia's manner, herself running away twice.

037 It would be well for her to return back, return back.

038 I asked Nimoia to come (to the debate), but he isn't here.

039 Perhaps Uiuai hears and will tell him to hold onto her.

040 Blood is working and affecting things.

041 She is not the exchange token of any person here.

042 She comes here, her place is here, but he should hold onto her and think about his custom.

043 That's it.

044 You warn Nimoia about what I say.

045 Tomorrow, Riki on the next ridge must not get loose and come over here to trouble our young people, my charges, my family.

046 I say that Nimoia must keep her on the next ridge.

047 That's it.

048 As to a small possible fine, I yield this to you, it's up to you two (to decide).

049 Tonga and father's namesake.

050 You two consider it.

051 If you decide to do something small, just do it.

052 You two decide everything.

053 It is up to us in custom and will be so for our grandchildren, it is up to us.

054 That's it, I say that you two will consider a bit what you will do about that talk (Tonga's cursing).

055 If you say okay, then do it or if it is bad or whatever, do a little something.

056 Whatever you two see in custom.

057 We are poor nowadays, but if you figure there is a spare fowl, you two might bring it or bring a small pig, it depends on you;

that's it.

058 Let's leave one-by-one.

059 Uiuai, why don't you make a statement.

[...]

KWANIAMUK

060 Let me say this, explain a little about what she said.

061 When they were bathing our grandson, all of them acted incorrectly.

062 They all here and that one sitting there all acted wrongly then.

063 Perhaps that's the talk (cursing) you will speak about.

[...]

ISAAC

064 Tonga should explain her thoughts (head), but you big-men have gone (proceeded) and turned off the discussion.

065 We don't know if that is her opinion or not.

066 Let her say all that is in her heart.

067 The one sitting and thinking about it (Tonga) was agitated and came running to brother-in-law.

068 Let her tell all her feelings, let us hear all.

[...]

KWANIAMUK

069 This thing, this anger, we all know this anger.

070 I say we all know anger like this that if two people are sitting and the husband catches (a pig), this causes anger.

071 They catch one of their pigs at the feeding trough and kill it.

072 If a woman catches a pig to give away, both have worked to feed it.

073 A woman to give away a pig doesn't go get one of her father's, not one of her father's but gives away one which belongs to her and her husband, and also one of their kava roots.

074 They two kill one of their pigs.

075 It is like that, it is like that.

076 However, she went and stirred up the talk which Margaret said.

077 We and Kauke did drink the kava of her and Uakui (and owe Uakui a pig and kava in return).

078 We all drank the kava, but we are waiting for Kauke to say when to reciprocate that.

079 But you said she said we are sitting about, as I have said, feeding animals, feeding fowl, feeding pigs (slow to reciprocate).

080 Thus, she is angry and wants to reciprocate by killing her pig, or for her husband to kill his pig.

081 You go and decide by yourself to kill one of your pigs or a woman or man goes to kill one of their pigs because the troublemaker is pestering them.

082 Tonga, what is the cause of your anger?

083 I see a sow in the valley.

084 Explain.

085 I don't see you carry that thing (child) and go down ever to the valley.

086 You are only angry because of Uakui's pushing.

087 You hear Margaret's talk and you are angry.

088 Explain the cause of your anger.

RAPI

089 Kwaniamuk is talking, sorry (for interrupting).

090 Tonga loves her husband, as I have already said.

091 She really loves her husband.

092 She doesn't want to see blame (accusations) in his eyes.

093 It is according to the wisdom of the ancestors.

094 Where his heart is there both their hearts are.

095 We big-men are through with this thing.

096 Three men, it is enough (debate).

Transcript C. Discussion of misuse of exchange roads, 3 August 1982

KIERI

001 If it is like that, this is the last time we come out and hear you talk all the time in our faces here at the kava-drinking ground.

002 I say you three have never acted (on your decisions).

003 This is the last time.

004 If you three reopen the debate if he wrongly exchanges feasts along your road, this is the last time that we will sit out here at the kava-drinking ground for you three to discuss it.

005 You three are like women (female animals), I say.

006 You three are like women, afraid to do anything.

007 Let some of us do it.

008 Stop talking endlessly.

009 It's like this.

010 What if you three are afraid when he comes by again?

011 Sometime he'll come again.

012 Will you behave like that always?

013 Will you three take no action because of it?

014 Let it be up to you three.

015 I say this is the last time.

016 If there is another time, you three must not complain again about it in our faces here at the kava-drinking ground.

017 Let's drink kava and leave one-by-one.

018 This is my statement, go ahead and fear them.

Getting It Straight in Trobriand Island Land Litigation

Edwin Hutchins

WHEN RIGHTS in a Trobriand Island garden pass from one person to another, the garden is conceived as moving across social space. Over time, as generations come and go, gardens trace out paths in their movements among persons and groups (*keda*: "path of social movement," literally, "road"). Extending this metaphor further, Trobrianders say that the path of a garden must be "straight" (*duosisia*). A straight path is one that can be clearly accounted for in terms of the culturally recognized patterns of transfers of rights in land. Straight paths are good, because they are strong and do not encourage challenges from others. "Tangled" (*nigwa nigwa*) paths are dangerous because they open the door to conflicting claims to the land and because they may cause the land to "disappear" unjustly from the sight of those who have legitimate claims to it.

Land litigation cases arise when there are conflicting claims to the right to use a garden plot. The central goal of the litigation activity for the community as a whole is to arrive at a straight path for the garden; that is, to produce an account of the history of the garden and perhaps prescribe a future for it that fits the principles of transfers in rights over land. The goals of the individual litigants are to produce credible accounts of the history of the garden that culminate in the litigant's legitimately holding rights in the land.

Litigation occurs in a village court, which consists of public testimony, commentary by "bailiffs" and a pronouncement by the village chief. Court proceedings culminate in the chief's statement about which path is most "straight," most in line with cultural principle. Such a judgment may establish rights in land and become a basis for action, such as gardening or subsequent transfers. The possibility of a definitive outcome, articulated in the chief's public summary of a "straight path," gives Trobriand land litigation a character different from other cases discussed in this volume, such as the land debates in Tanna described by Lindstrom. However, the contrast is one of degree rather than kind, as will be seen below.

Conflicting claims concerning rights to land in the Trobriands arise for many reasons. It is important to note at the outset that there is no more valuable resource in Trobriand life than land. Every mature person is embedded in a complex web of relationships in which control of rights in land or access to land figures prominently in meeting obligations to others. Land is the root of power and success. It is worth fighting for.

Yet, in a nonliterate society, there is no hall of records in which rights to land can be recorded, so rights to this most valuable resource are secured only by the agreement in the community that they exist. They are thus a completely social construction, and when a person's right to a piece of land is challenged, the only way to maintain that right is to defend it in public. A defense of rights in land is accomplished by presenting an account of the history of the land: a digest of its movement through social space. This movement is marked by events: exchanges of valuables, lifelong gardening relationship, deathbed proclamations, and the like, so a litigant must not only describe the path of the land, he must also recount the events that caused the land to move through the hands it did. Events, alas, are often inherently ambiguous. Just as words depend upon context for their meanings, so do the meanings of symbolic actions. The meaning of any particular exchange event is not contained in the event itself, but must be established with respect to prior exchanges and relationships. If one is not privy to the required background knowledge, it is easy to misinterpret the meaning of an event, or less benignly, by manipulating the understood context of an event, one can change its meaning. Knowledge about events and relationships, therefore, is essential to understanding events in the social world and in constructing the kinds of compelling histories of pieces of land that secure rights in them. Knowledge is clearly power, but knowledge is not uniformly distributed. Older Trobrianders often lament that their potential heirs do not know the histories of their lands and that they may consequently lose them to those who can invent a more compelling (even if untrue) story. For this reason, it is felt to be important to promote knowledge of a descent group's land within the group and to inhibit its transmission to others wherever possible. Finally, the application of the "law" itself is not always clear-cut. Even if we agree on the events that have occurred and on the meanings of those events, there may still be differences of opinion about what is the relevant principle for understanding the relations among the events.

It is on this rather slippery social surface, then, that Trobrianders struggle to gain or maintain access to that which is of paramount importance. The actual conduct of a court case is, to a large extent, concerned with managing the process by which ambiguities are resolved through the construction of public accounts. A straight path must be found for the garden. But this process is complicated by both the importance and the uncertainty of the outcomes.

Because there is so much ambiguity in the interpretation of events and their meanings and such an uneven distribution of knowledge, litigants cannot always anticipate what line of argumentation their opponent will take. It is therefore considered vastly preferable to make one's own presentation to the court after having heard the opponent's presentation. That way, one is in a position to construct a strategy that is tailored to that of the opponent.

This also permits one to decide what to reveal and what not to reveal in court. Since knowledge is power, one would like to win the case while making public as little of one's specialized knowledge as possible. Finally, because land is so important, publicly discussing the plans and motives of individuals with respect to land inevitably risks open displays of anger. The threat of loss of land itself is obviously very disturbing. One may be facing the prospect of not being able to meet established or promised obligations to one's most important relations. But losing in court means not only losing the land, but losing esteem as well. To bring a case and lose it is, under the most charitable interpretation of one's peers, evidence of social ineptness, and less friendly observers may conclude that one has lied.

So, a subsidiary goal of the conduct of litigation is to control volatile emotions and aggression while dealing in public with understandably sensitive issues. The management of strong emotions and disruptive displays during the course of an actual court session is accomplished in a variety of ways, both explicit and implicit. On the one hand, participants themselves recognize the need to control hostility by commenting about the importance of maintaining decorum and avoiding certain extraneous topics. On the other hand, the entire organization of the court as a social event works toward that end by orchestrating which speakers have rights to talk on which topics at what times in the proceedings.

Getting the path straight requires that the history of the garden and the litigants be brought into the public eye, but doing this can also bring up tangential issues that are not the focus of the case. Further, in the conduct of land litigation, knowledge can be political power (cf. Lindstrom, this volume). A litigant will need to provide whatever evidence is required to support his claim to the contested garden, but may not wish to discuss the status of other related gardens where his knowledge and someone else's ignorance may in the future be the basis of a claim to those lands. There is therefore a tradeoff in the conduct of the court between going into enough detail to resolve the case at hand unambiguously and to the satisfaction of all involved, while still avoiding the opening of old wounds, the introduction of extraneous issues, or forcing the revelation of knowledge that derives its political potency from its limited distribution. Finally, when a straight path has been found for the garden, the decision of the court must somehow be made to stick; it must become the new social reality of the community.

In this study I will show how people seek to accomplish these multiple goals of land litigation by examining recorded discourse from an actual case. In previous work, I have analyzed the cultural premises of Trobriand Island land tenure and illustrated their operation in another land litigation case. For the discussion here I give only a brief outline of land tenure principles (see Hutchins 1980 for more detail). My purpose is to describe a case of land argumentation as both a course of reasoning and an interactively produced social reality. I begin with an overview of land principles that must be understood to comprehend the arguments, opinions and decision put forward in the case and then describe the case in point as it developed during a village court. Having shown how litigants construct accounts to achieve the primary goal of acquiring land rights (finding a straight path), I then go on to discuss the means employed to accomplish the subsidiary goals of managing hostility and establishing a social reality most likely to give the decision lasting effect.

Setting and Fieldwork

For an anthropological audience or, for that matter, any social science audience, the Trobriand Islands need little introduction. These islands, located about 120 miles north of the eastern tip of the Papua New Guinea mainland, have become widely known through the writings of Bronislaw Malinowski (e.g., 1922, 1935). The thirteen thousand inhabitants rely primarily on subsistence agriculture for their livelihood. Land is of utmost importance in the Trobriands because all wealth and power are ultimately rooted in land.

The status of Trobriands chiefs (*guyau*), who resemble other Melanesian big-men in many respects, derives from hereditary claims within local descent groups, *dala* (see Powell 1960, Weiner 1976:45). While certainly less formal or hierarchical than Polynesian chieftainship, Trobriand leadership exhibits ranked positions distinguished by gradations of power over people and resources. Of significance for this study, chiefs act as managers of *dala* land, with village and district chiefs exerting regional influence.

Malinowski gave a thorough account of the uses of land and how it was tied up in myth and tradition, but when it came to describing how people actually acquired and defended rights in land he was silent. I have elsewhere (1980) developed an ethnographic description of the major concepts addressed in actual cases of land litigation (see also Powell 1956 and Weiner 1976 for descriptions of Trobriand land tenure). Analyses of the wider range of social goals pursued in land litigation, and of underlying understandings about conflict, are almost entirely lacking.

During my fieldwork in the Trobriands between July 1975 and September 1976 I recorded six village court cases. These included three cases of land litigation and three dealing with claims to other resources. As in a previously published analysis of one of the three land cases, the data for this study consist primarily of my transcription of court proceedings in the Trobriand language. This transcript, in English translation, is shown in the appendix. (A transcript of vernacular statements is available upon request.)

The Village Court

Land litigation cases are heard in the central clearing of the village. These village courts are a syncretic convention combining the traditional village airing of disputes with a hearing protocol and authority structure introduced first by the British and later by the Australian colonial governments. The present method of hearing civil cases such as land disputes in a court presided over by the chief (*guyau*) of the local district grew out of the obvious inability of government officers to make culturally meaningful decisions. The *guyau* not only has the authority to back up court decisions with effective sanctions, but he also possesses knowledge of the *liliu* 'sacred myths' needed to evaluate group claims to particular parcels of land.

Although village courts are nominally presided over by the highest-ranking chief (*guyau*) of the district, who lends his authority to the decision, the actual conduct of the case is controlled by a number of men who are referred to as members of the court ("bailiffs"). They are important leaders of the village, some of whom have served as village councilors during the period of district councils under the Papua New Guinea government. As will be seen, the role of the bailiff is critical to the conduct of the case and the formulation of a public account of a "straight path." Not only do the bailiffs control turn-taking as they call upon witnesses, but in recapitulating testimony and in rendering an opinion they are the primary shapers of the court consensus. In the village I studied, the *guyau* had suffered a stroke and was considered to be a bit dull-witted. A more capable *guyau* would certainly exercise more influence relative to the bailiffs than the one I observed. In this case, the *guyau* retained the authority of his office, and his pronouncements bore the weight of chiefly decree, yet it was the bailiffs who instructed the *guyau* in the proper judgment to be rendered at the conclusion of the case.

Court cases are usually initiated by a complaint to the village bailiffs. A compelling complaint is one put forward by a group of litigants, most commonly related as kin. If the disagreement cannot be settled among the prospective litigants, the bailiffs ask the litigants who their witnesses will be. The bailiffs then set a date for the court, ensuring that relevant witnesses and the district chief will be present.

The overarching structure of a case typically unfolds as testimony, followed by opinion and then decision. A case begins with position statements by the principal litigants, establishing the main point(s) of disagreement. This is followed by the testimony of witnesses who are called upon to give evidence because of their knowledge about particulars in the case and their relationships to the principals. Just which individuals hold relevant testimony is usually known by litigants, bailiffs, and audience alike, with bailiffs calling upon those persons to ensure that sufficient detail is made public to construct an adequate history (path) for the garden.

After witnesses have spoken for both sides, one or more of the bailiffs will give an opinion. Once the bailiffs have given their opinions they generally restrict further presentation of evidence and instruct the chief, who then puts forward the court's decision. As noted above, the chief's "decision" is more of a pronouncement of an account formulated by others than a judgment rendered from chiefly wisdom. The pronouncement, coming at the end of the court proceedings, helps establish a publicly acknowledged social reality by lending rhetorical and political force to the bailiffs' opinions.

Principles of Trobriand Land Tenure

In the Trobriand view of things, all of mankind is divided into four major exogamous matrilineal clans. Within each major clan there are a large number of subclans (local descent groups) called *dala*. With regard to rights in land, the *dala* is the relevant corporate entity. There are two types of rights in land: use rights and rights of allocation. In principle, the rights of allocation of a garden reside in perpetuity with a single *dala*. I will refer to such a *dala* as the "owning" *dala*, but the reader must remember that

Trobriand ownership is not the same as ownership in our society. The right of allocation is the right to determine who shall next hold rights in the garden. Use rights in a garden are the rights to cultivate the garden or have someone cultivate it and the right to control the disposition of the produce of the garden. In general, rights in land are always transferred in response to a presentation called *pokala*. *Pokala* comes in many forms and may be a part of many types of Trobriand exchange relations. The garden rights received in response to *pokala* are called *kaipokala*.

Given these two types of rights in land and the restriction that the right of allocation of a garden does not leave the owning *dala*, there are six legitimate forms of transfers of rights in land:

1. The prototypical form is where *pokala* is presented within a *dala*, say from a sister's son to a mother's brother, and both the right of allocation and use rights are given in return.

2. A second type of transfer occurs when the use rights in the garden are allowed to leave the owning *dala* in response to *pokala* from another *dala*. This most frequently happens when a father gives use rights in a garden to his son in return for the son having gardened for the father throughout his life. This lifelong gardening relationship is called *kaivatamla*. It derives from the name of the poles up which the yam vines climb as they grow.

3. When use rights in a garden go outside the owning *dala*, the right of allocation over the garden remains in the owning *dala* and can be transferred within the *dala* in response to *pokala*.

4. Once the use rights in the garden have gone outside the owning *dala*, they can be allowed to stay there after the death of the person who held them if one or more of his heirs presents the owning *dala* with a payment called *katumamata*. *Katumamata* literally means "to cause to wake up." This is a metaphorical reference to waking up the agreement between the two *dala* that "fell asleep" when the holder of the use rights died.

5. Another possibility when the use rights have gone outside the owning *dala* is that they can be recovered by the owning *dala*. To accomplish this, the owning *dala* presents the *dala* of the use rights holder with a *pokala* payment called *katuyumali*, which literally means "to cause to return."

6. Finally, if there is only one descendant remaining in a *dala*, all of the rights in gardens held by his predecessor go to him

without the requirement of any *pokala*. This is the only circumstance under which it is possible for rights in land to change hands without the payment of any *pokala*. However, under exceptional circumstances, all rights in a piece of land may pass from one *dala* to another. If a *dala* dies out completely, a circumstance called *wokosi*, the land must pass to another *dala*. How that happens is the essence of this case. Land may also pass permanently from *dala* to *dala* as reparation for homicide—an event also touched upon by the case to be presented.

Trobriand agriculture is a rotating slash-and-burn system. Every village controls a number of large fields, each containing up to a hundred individual plots. Every year, a large field that has lain fallow for at least six years is chosen for cultivation. A large communal work party builds a fence around the entire field, and then individual gardeners go to work on the individual garden plots in the field.

The garden cycle consists of declaring one's intent to garden by slashing small spaces at the corners of the garden, *sikwali*; cutting down the brush in the garden plot, *takaiwa*; burning the cut brush, *gabu*; weeding, *pwakova*; planting the plot, *sopu* or *vali* depending on the crop; cultivating the garden plot, *bagula*; harvesting the plot, *tayoyowa*; and eating the produce, *kamkwam*. The activities of cutting, harvesting, and eating are the basis for a persistent shorthand reference to using the garden and having someone use it on one's behalf. Thus, the transcripts of litigation are rife with statements about people cutting and eating gardens where mention of those activities is actually a synecdoche for the entire gardening cycle.

Background to the Case of Pakaraii vs. Kanioivisi

There is really only one garden at issue in this case, although at the end of the case, the dispositions of three others will be clarified as well. A brief reconstructed history of the garden prior to the hearing of the case follows.

Everyone involved agrees that the garden was originally held by Kamlosiu, a man of a *dala* in the Lukwasisiga clan. Kamlosiu was of the generation of the parents of the villagers who are now elderly. The details of the original transfer of land are sketchy, I believe because they involved reparations for a homicide. In any case, the first transfer discussed in the case is not disputed by these litigants. The first transfer of this land was from Kamlosiu to Modoumli. Modoumli is also a Lukwasisiga man, but of a different *dala* than Kamlosiu. At a late stage in the case, there is some talk about the details of this transaction, but people are discouraged from talking about it. That occurred is taken as given, and several risks involved in pursuing it in the context of this case will be discussed below under the heading of controlling hostility. This appears to have been a transfer of both the rights of allocation and the use rights in the garden across *dala* lines. So the first step in the path of the garden moves it to Modoumli as the sole holder of both the right of allocation and the use rights. This state of affairs is acknowledged by both litigants and is shown in Figure 1.

There are two interesting relations to Modoumli with regard to this garden. First, Modoumli's son, Tokuyawabu, made gardens for him all his life, that is, had a *kaivatam* relationship with Modoumli, and by virtue of having done so was granted rights to Modoumli's holdings. Among these were the use rights to the garden in question. The other interesting relation concerns Gumkwadewa. Gumkwadewa is the sister's son of Modoumli and therefore stands to inherit from Modoumli whatever holdings he has in land. Since the use rights in these gardens are held outside the *dala*, Gumkwadewa should be the successor to the rights of allocation of those gardens. Because Gumkwadewa is the last living representative of his *dala*, the rights pass to him without his having to provide *pokala* to Modoumli. Upon the death of Modoumli, the title to the garden was split, with Gumkwadewa holding the right of allocation and Tokuyawabu holding the use rights.

Because Modoumli had allowed the rights in the garden to go to Tokuyawabu, Gumkwadewa was powerless to recover the garden in Tokuyawabu's lifetime, but would stand to recover it upon the death of Tokuyawabu. Gumkwadewa and Tokuyawabu disputed the rights to use this garden while they were both alive, and each time Tokuyawabu prevailed. The question of the wisdom of those earlier decisions is raised in this hearing. In any case, it is clear that villagers attribute Tokuyawabu's victories at

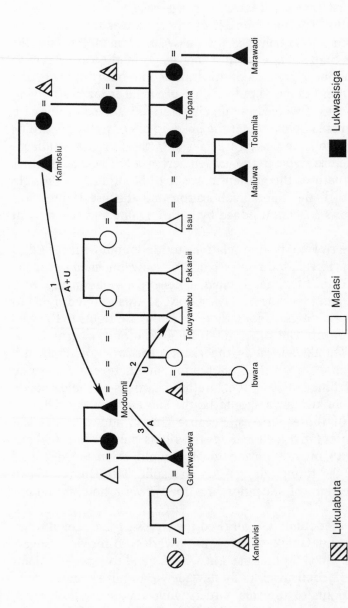

FIGURE 1. The undisputed portion of the history of the garden. Use rights and the right of allocation are given to Modoumli by Kamlosiu (1). Modoumli's son, Tokuyawabu, gardens for his father for decades and is given use rights in the garden in return (2). The right of allocation must stay in the *dala*, and so it passes to Gumkwadewa, the only surviving member of the *dala*, on the death of Modoumli (3).

Lukulabuta

Lukwasisiga

Malasi

least in part to the fact that he was a powerful and intimidating man, while Gumkwadewa was meek and somewhat inarticulate.

While Tokuyawabu was using the garden, Kanioivisi had been adopted by and was gardening *kaivatamla* for Gumkwadewa. On the strength of that relationship, Gumkwadewa, who realized that he might never actually be able to use the gardens in which he had rights, told Kanioivisi that upon Gumkwadewa's death, Kanioivisi would have use rights to the gardens.

Gumkwadewa died before Tokuyawabu, so Gumkwadewa—as the last representative of his *dala*—was unable to recover the rights in the garden. With the death of Gumkwadewa, a problem arises. What becomes of his right of allocation in this garden? There is no one remaining in his *dala* for it to pass on to, and none of the original owners of the garden (Kamoliu's *dala*) either approached him in life or appeared at his mortuary ceremony to recover the rights. He had declared his intention to recover the gardens and pass their use to Kanioivisi but was unable to see this come to pass because he died too soon. At the time of the death of Gumkwadewa, then, use rights in the garden are held by Tokuyawabu, and the status of the right of allocation in the garden is unclear.

During Tokuyawabu's lifetime, his younger brother, Isau, had gardened for him and stood to inherit his holdings. Isau had actually cultivated the garden contested in this case on several previous occasions.

When Gumkwadewa died, Mailuwa and Marawadi *sagali*'ed on behalf of their classificatory father, Tokuyawabu, to "wake up" the use-rights relationship. This should allow Tokuyawabu to keep the garden until he dies.

Tokuyawabu died in March of 1976. At the mortuary ceremonies for Tokuyawabu, Kanioivisi made payments to Tokuyawabu's kin (the Malasi people in Figure 1) on behalf of Gumkwadewa's *dala* to recover the use rights in the garden. Thus, Kanioivisi acted as if Gumkwadewa were still alive, or at least that the right of allocation resided posthumously with Gumkwadewa, whom Kanioivisi represented.

In July of 1976, when it came time to cut the season's garden plots, the garden here disputed was among those in the garden field to be prepared by the village. Tokuyawabu's classificatory younger brother, Isau, declared his intention to use the garden by marking it (*sikola*). Kanioivisi disregarded the markings and sent Gumkwadewa's son, Libai, to cut the garden in preparation for burning. When Isau discovered this had happened, he got together with his brothers and made a complaint to the village court bailiffs. This is how the case came to be heard on August 6, 1976.

How Are Straight Paths Discriminated from Crooked Ones?

Every litigant who takes a case before the court believes that there exists a credible path that conforms to the principles of land tenure and that culminates in him or the party he represents having rights in land. Litigants often do not know the details of their adversaries' claims before the litigation begins and must convince themselves that their claims can withstand the assaults of others. Once the litigants have presented their positions, it is the job of the court to decide which, if either, is a legitimate claim. Straight paths are discriminated from crooked ones by applying knowledge of the principles of land transfers to the events described in the paths presented by the litigants.

The case begins with the position statements of the two litigants. This is followed by the testimony of specific witnesses who are called to testify because of their relationships to the principal figures in the case. After a number of witnesses have spoken, Kwaiwai (a "member" of the court and heir apparent to the *guyau*) offers his opinion/analysis of the case. In a more typical case, once a member of the court has given an opinion, no more testimony would be heard. Because of the difficulty of settling this case, however, additional testimony is solicited. It is during this period that the tradeoff between getting enough evidence to settle the case and letting the case get out of hand must be monitored. Here there is a mixture of evidence and opinions. Finally there is the decision of the chief (*guyau*).

Pakaraii's Path

The path proposed by Pakaraii emerges in his presentation, although only vaguely since only two of his statements refer to transactions in the history of the garden. He mentions the original *pokala* transaction between Kamlosiu and Modoumli, (see transcript, 15–16) and he refers to Tokuyawabu's use of the garden in statement 21. The rest of the account of how the garden got to Tokuyawabu's hand is left to be inferred by the listener. The remainder of his brief presentation deals with why he moved out of Modoumli's group. Tiliewa, the bailiff who is most active in the conduct of this case, indicates in his recapitulation of Pakaraii's presentation the unstated intent of Pakaraii's idea: that the garden should remain for the present in the hands of Pakaraii's Malasi *dala*. The combined contribution of Pakaraii and Tiliewa to the construction of a path for the garden is shown in Figure 2. This path is elaborated in the testimony of Ibwara, Isau, and Mailuwa. By the time these three have testified, a complete path will have been described. Although their testimony follows Kanioivisi's presentation, let us deal with it now and reveal the shape of the path they propose. Ibwara fills in the details of the *katumamata* payment given at the *sagali* for Gumkwadewa. That is intended to secure the rights in that land for the Malasi people until the death of Tokuyawabu. Isau dwells on the aspect that is of greatest importance to him, Tokuyawabu's declaration that Isau shall hold the land when Tokuyawabu dies. Of all the testimony given with regard to this path, Mailuwa's is by far the most complete. His path would lead the garden back to its original Lukwasisiga owners by way of the Malasi brothers of Tokuyawabu. In statements 166–86, he covers all of the links except that by which Tokuyawabu acquired the land. That link can of course be assumed and inferred from the fact that he is talking about Tokuyawabu's deathbed disposition of the gardens.

Together the statements of these people constitute the description of this proposed path of the garden.

Kanioivisi's Path

Kanioivisi's path is shown in Figure 3. In his first presentation to the court, statements 35–95, he reveals this path by traversing it several times at varying levels of detail. In his first passage, statements 38–50, he goes once around the structure emphasizing the justification for the garden moving to him from Tokuyawabu. In statements 51–56, he goes around the path again, this time with emphasis on the future path of the garden back to its original Lukwasisiga owners. Statements 57–60 claim that what Pakaraii proposes will cause the garden to go off the path and disappear. Statements 64–78 provide more detail on how the garden moved from Modoumli to Tokuyawabu and why it should move on from Tokuyawabu to Kanioivisi. Statement 79 ends the path and again describes a return of the garden to its original Lukwasisiga owners. Statements 82–89 cite the general principle by which that should be the ultimate resting place of this garden and why it cannot remain in any one *dala* until it has returned to the Lukwasisiga. Kanioivisi finishes with a statement (93) intended to show that Pakaraii has no business talking about this garden.

Following the testimony of Ibwara, Isau, Mailuwa, and a somewhat irrelevant presentation of Mulapokala's ideas by one of the members of the court, Kanioivisi speaks again. His second presentation is given in statements 220–312. He begins with a hypothetical counterfactual situation in which it would make sense to Malasi people to state a claim to the lands. But that is known not to be the case and Kanioivisi leaves it to the listeners to make the plausible inference that since that is not the case, the Malasi people have no claim to the land. In statements 237–39 he gives another quick tour of his path:

237 Buyers, the old Lukwasisiga men were the buyers.
238 The buyers of these gardens are of a different *dala*. They bought them, ate of them, and they go around and come to me.
239 These gardens will emerge later.

In statements 247–49 Kanioivisi attacks the link between Isau and Tokuyawabu in Pakaraii's path. This link represents the first place, chronologically speaking, where the two paths differ. He argues that confusion would result from proceeding that way. In statements 253 and 254 he gets to the heart of his objection to Pakaraii's path.

253 He (Pakaraii) is a Malasi, I am Lukalabuta, they are Lukwasisiga.
254 We are caretakers. It is not our thing, no.

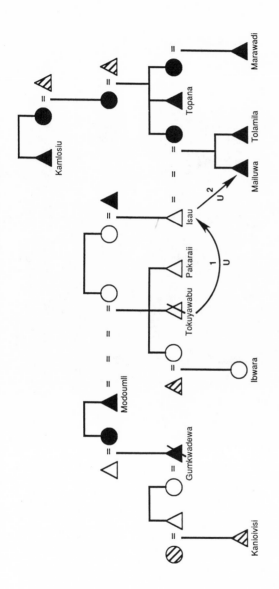

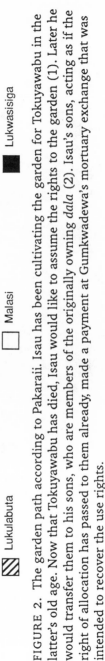

FIGURE 2. The garden path according to Pakaraii. Isau has been cultivating the garden for Tokuyawabu in the latter's old age. Now that Tokuyawabu has died, Isau would like to assume the rights to the garden (1). Later he would transfer them to his sons, who are members of the originally owning *dala* (2). Isau's sons, acting as if the right of allocation has passed to them already, made a payment at Gumkwadewa's mortuary exchange that was intended to recover the use rights.

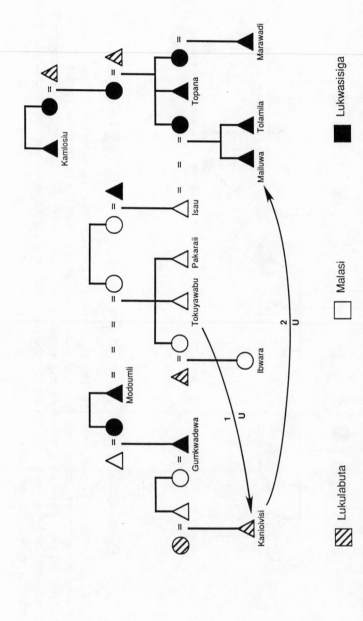

FIGURE 3. The garden path according to Kanioivisi. Kanioivisi claims that Gumkwadewa tried to recover the use rights to the garden from Tokuyawabu. If he had succeeded, he would have given use rights in the garden to Kanioivisi in return for a lifetime of gardening (1). Kanioivisi will return the use rights in the garden to the original Lukwasisiga owners in return for additional *katuyumali* payments (2).

Kanioivisi and Tokuyawabu were both caretakers of the garden. The implication of this is that neither of them has the authority to decide to whom the rights in the garden shall pass. This is stated explicitly in statements 299–300.

299 They are not our Malasi things, they are not our Lukalabuta things.
300 I will not give them to my kinsmen, he shall not give it to his kinsmen.

In statements 260–93, Kanioivisi gives the details of Gumkwadewa's *pokala* relations to other men. This does not contribute directly to the issue of the path of this garden, but it is a display of the completeness of Kanioivisi's knowledge of Gumkwadewa's holdings and *pokala* relations. This lends credibility to his claims regarding this garden. In statements 294–99, he touches again on the path from Modoumli, through Tokuyawabu and himself, eventually returning to the Lukwasisiga *dala*. In statements 309–11, he swings once more all the way around his path using the device of simply naming the people who stand as social locations along the path of the garden. In his last statement (312) he poses a question for the court: which path shall it be? Perhaps he who would have it disappear has sucked you in?

We now have two complete paths for the garden. Both of them start in the same place in the past and end in the same place in the future, the Lukwasisiga *dala*, but they differ in the social territory they cover in between, including the immediate present.

Kwaiwai's Opinion

Kwaiwai is the first to address the issue of which of these paths is appropriate. He asks the bailiffs to say what they think the crux of the case is. Tiliewa responds (statements 444–53) with a clear summary of the two paths shown in the figures above, adding that in a conversation with Mulapokala, one of the senior men of the Lukwasisiga *dala*, Mulapokala had proposed the same path that Pakaraii proposed in court.

Kwaiwai is a smart man, successor to the chief of Tukwaukwa village. He can speak some English, and in this analysis, he uses the English word *culture*. He says there are two paths here and he wants to see Kiriwina culture preserved whichever one they go down. He summarizes the two paths in a sentence each.

475   He thinks that Modoumli has died and Modoumli's *kaipokala* will just run to Gumkwadewa, (from) Gumkwadewa (to) him (Kanioivisi).
476   Pakaraii's thought is that their father's *kaipokala* will run to Tokuyawabu, when Tokuyawabu dies, (on to) Isau.
477   Because of *kaivatam*.

And neither of these paths is completely satisfactory in his view. He goes on to say why:

478   And therefore, I think we members have erred, because we were not forceful while Tokuyawabu and Gumkwadewa were alive.
479   Members we have erred.
480   If we had been strong when the living Gumkwadewa resided with Tokuyawabu, we would have cut this case off then.

But given that that was not done, it is still possible to line up one of the proposed paths with Kiriwina culture, and Kwaiwai proceeds to do so while drawing with a stick in the clay of the central clearing of the village.

484   But we will line up this road, culture, this Kiriwina road (Kanioivisi's path).
485   Not this road (Pakaraii's path).

These sentences and the others in Kwaiwai's speech (see transcript) highlight what seems to be a developing problem in native litigation: the introduction of other principles from Western culture. I have seen it invoked in other cases in support of arguments, but here, Kwaiwai works hard to identify Pakaraii's strategy with European—specifically patrilineal—notions and the idea of hiding the garden in his *dala*. Looking at the development of the case, I really don't think that Pakaraii or his comrades borrowed any ideas from European culture in making their case, but Kwaiwai uses that idea to discredit their argument, which is flawed in terms of the Trobriand reckoning of things.

That he does this in his capacity as a "member" of the court seems a bit ironic since the very notion of "members" of court, and the word *culture* as well as the structure of the proceedings are all borrowed from the European tradition. Traditionally, that is, before contact, disputes were reportedly settled (or not) by verbal and physical battles in public. This was not acceptable to British colonial administrators, and I suspect that it was not much liked by most Trobrianders either, since only the very powerful could succeed in such an environment. The colonial administrators sometimes tried to intercede and hear cases, but they lacked the knowledge of the details of community life and the principles of descent and land tenure required to make judgments that satisfied anyone (Malinowski 1935:103). The current syncretic style of proceeding in which a chief oversees a more or less orderly presentation is a response to the inadequacies of the previous methods.

Tovalugwa's Opinion

Immediately following Kwaiwai's opinion, Tovalugwa steps forward. He points out that they stood strong who stood with Tokuyawabu. He was a very persuasive man, but now he is dead and not so strong anymore (although he still has influence over the life of the village in the continuing mortuary exchanges and his ghost terrorized the village for months after his death [Hutchins 1987].) Tovalugwa suggests that if Tokuyawabu had died before Gumkwadewa, then Gumkwadewa would have taken this and other gardens without protest and would have passed them on to Kanioivisi. He says that the path has become twisted because of the strength of Tokuyawabu in life and that has made the proceedings slow, but the garden must return to the Lukwasisiga *dala*. He implores the people to get it straight this time and points out the consequences of failing to do so.

521 Get it straight in our time.

522 And if you are inept, it appears that (this dispute) will not lie down.

Dudawelu's Opinion

Dudawelu introduces another perspective on the case. He suggests that consideration be given to which groups have eaten this garden. He says,

563 That garden is clearly Lukwasisiga and its straightness comes running and stops (in Lukwasisiga hands).
564 He and his brother do not hide it so to speak.
565 But I want, I am thinking about eating.
566 The Lukwasisiga finished eating so to speak.
567 Modoumli finished eating.
568 Tokuyawabu finished eating.
569 Gumkwadewa has not eaten, and Kanioivisi has not eaten.
570 Today you permit it to be described.
571 It stands there, and then returns to the Lukwasisiga as their thing clear and straight.

Dudawelu advocates giving the garden to Kanioivisi for the present because, of all those concerned, he alone has not yet eaten of the garden. This is, I think, an innovative approach, and in these circumstances it coincides with the application of the underlying principles of land tenure. However, it is easy to imagine cases in which it would contradict the principles of land tenure.

Murebodema's Decision

Two more opinions are offered, one by a Malasi man, Sigaroii, and another by one of the Lukwasisiga men who stands to recover the garden eventually. Both of these opinions support the path proposed by Kanioivisi. Following these opinions, Murebodema is coached by Tiliewa, Tokuyawa, and Tovalugwa, the bailiffs in the case, in how to state the decision of the court.

MUREBODEMA

671 The *pokala* here was considerable.
672 So you younger people think it over and your recovery payments shall go.

673 Hey, if we took these issues to Vanoi (paramount chief of the Trobriands) it would be the same with him.

674 He would say, "All these things, *yolova*, *sagali*, warming up payments.

675 These are not *pokala*.

676 He cuts, he dies, he gives to his kinsmen, he cuts and dies, this is *pokala*."

677 And of course because the *dala* has died out, well quickly um, you should recover (the garden) so it comes back.

678 If there is but one man remaining, he should finish the payments.

679 Hey, this is a good path for this garden.

680 Fine, it should go to Kanioivisi for a while.

681 Because Gumkwadewa and Tokuyawabu fought all the time.

682 As if Gumkwadewa had died, and it was just between Kanioivisi and Tokuyawabu, fine let it go back for Kanioivisi to eat for a while.

683 He eats, and whatever you Lukwasisiga people are thinking, give a lot to Kanioivisi.

684 Because he gave *pokala*.

685 So give a lot, not like a *yolova* payment.

686 At Sagali we give just a little.

687 This is *pokala*, and you younger people tend to muddy these distinctions, so let Kanioivisi eat.

688 He shall touch it for a while.

689 Hey, just this.

Following Murebodema's decision, the bailiffs attempt to ensure that the decision is thought by all to be a "straight" one.

TILIEWA

690 Well people, is this how you think it should be?

691 Thus the old man (Murebodema) has chopped it off.

692 When the Lukwasisiga people make their recovery payments to Kanioivisi, he should return a bit to the Malasi people to eat.

693 Or perhaps he will keep it all to himself or return something or other.

694 He shall give them a sufficient little gift, give them something.

(Pause. There is general discussion as people begin to disperse.
Then a man appears carrying a clay pot.)

TILIEWA

695 People, as you have heard today Kanioivisi will eat, and here
     Topana already carries the small cut (the first part of the pay-
     ment).

696 We make no more litigation here.

TOVALUGWA

697 Is it straight?

     (General assent)

In the world of land litigation, where there is no hall of
records, and no source of objective "truth," the best that can be
done is to try to discover in the testimony of witnesses a path that
makes sense. I am sometimes amazed that this procedure works at
all since the uniqueness of appropriate paths is not a formal
property of the rules of land tenure. This was a difficult case to
settle because the path of the garden became tangled in the void
left by the premature death of the last survivor of the *dala*. I do
not know how frequently a *wokosi* situation develops, but my
guess is that it is an infrequent event.

Creating a Social Reality

The main way that a decision is made to stick, of course, is to
develop a public account of a straight path. Ideally, the court
looks for a path that is so obviously correct that no one would
challenge it. The path needs to be both public and culturally correct. Making it public helps prevent the garden's becoming lost
because the whole community now knows something of its history.

If there is not enough discussion of the case, people will not
find the decision compelling and will continue to think about it.
At the conclusion of one witness's speech, Tovalugwa encourages
people to speak up:

This is not the time for us to be quiet. (If we do) later we will go
out of the village and you will say, "O they twisted the talk, they

twisted it." Don't you do this. Instead, let each give straight answers to your questions, and confine your words to that.

What if we don't get it straight? We will see it in court again, just as this case was seen during the lifetime of Tokuyawabu and Gumkwadewa. The court failed to make a straight decision then, they gave in to the forcefulness of Tokuyawabu, and, for that reason, the case appears again. The inability of the court to make the decision in the previous generation is referred to by Kwaiwai in statements 478–86 and by Tovalugwa in his opinion (cited above).

So the decision is made to stick by talking and getting a straight account that is publicly acknowledged and agreed upon as correct. The tension between sufficient discussion and risking escalating hostilities is apparent in the following exchange.

TAUDABALA

547 You unravel the path (directed to the bailiffs)

548 Don't call people saying, "Someone come."

549 Nobody, you do it, its straightness has gone into your ears now cut it.

550 Stop now— here we are headed to a fight.

TOVALUGWA

551 If we cut it now, you will go to the field, but you will not burn the garden.

TILIEWA

552 It is not as if Tokuyawabu was here to tell of his *kaipokala*, or Modoumli, we would cut it if he came.

553 In this case, one of them has disappeared, the other has disappeared.

554 We must cut it off at the root.

TOVALUGWA

555 His older brother (Tokuyawabu) was very contentious.

556 Say how you hear the two of them (the litigants).

TILIEWA

557 If only Modoumli and Gumkwadewa were here, we would cut it off by virtue of his *kaipokala*.

558 But if we cut it off here, you will all think it was our [ex.pl.]
     doing.
559 We would cut it here and it would go on, split off and irritate
     the eye (as does a cinder).
560 The members shall decide and we will listen.
561 Because it is so serious, many men come forth.

A similar position was taken by Tovalugwa at the end of his
speech reported above where he cautioned that they had to get it
right this time or the case would not lie down, that is, it would
continue to cause trouble.

Soliciting all this talk does result in people getting angry.
During the hearing of the case, tempers flared on several occasions, and the bailiffs lost control of the proceedings twice. One
source of trouble was the talk of the original *pokala* from
Modoumli to Kamlosiu. Raising this issue is dangerous because it
may get the Lukwasisiga people bickering among themselves
about who should be the one to recover the garden. When mention of this *pokala* by witnesses gets people shouting, Tiliewa
responds,

375 Eaters and givers of *pokala* have already come, we will not dis-
     pute this.
376 Because the Lukwasisiga people will end up disputing this gar-
     den.

Such a decision within the Lukwasisiga *dala* should not be
made in public. Rather, it should be made in private by the senior
men in the *dala*. It is embarrassing for such intra-*dala* bickering
to appear in public.

The court attempts to control such outbursts in several ways.
The very first words spoken in the case are a set of admonitions
to the litigants and witnesses.

TILIEWA
001 (The roles of) givers of pokala and garden cutters are finished;
     today you[pl.] shall speak.
002 I beg of you, no arguments, no fist fights.
003 Yes, you should speak clearly, so that people can hear and can

chop the end off (of this case) and be done with it.
004   No deceptions, no arguments.

These seem to be rather conventional pronouncements and occur in other cases in virtually the same form. How much impact they actually have is unknown. All six of the cases of litigation I recorded included shouting matches, but I never saw a punch thrown in litigation. Outside the context of litigation, however, fist fights did occur occasionally.

A second technique used to control conflicts is to steer the discussion away from sensitive topics before they even arise. Thus, when Mailuwa rises to speak, Tiliewa cautions him to stick to the point.

TILIEWA

158   Mailuwa, you speak.
159   At this time we are already carrying long-winded talk of this garden.

MAILUWA

160   I won't say anything except about what the old man said about the garden as we sat together (in the house of the death vigil).

When all else fails, the bailiff can resort to shouting people down. Both times that the court went out of order—once when the original *pokala* was being discussed (395–98) and a second time when Ibwara broached the status of a set of gardens related to the one in question (418–34)—order was restored by the bailiffs shouting at people to leave their stupid ideas and shut up.

In addition to finding a publicly acknowledged straight path for the garden, there are two other mechanisms to make the decision of the court stick. The first is that the chief pronounces the decision of the court even though he did not formulate it himself. This chief, Murebodema, is getting a little senile and has suffered at least one minor stroke, which has left him with some paralysis and a slight impairment of speech. He is not too sharp anymore, but after being instructed by the bailiffs on what to say, he announces the decision. In spite of his weakened condition, he is a chief nevertheless, and he commands the respect of the village. There is in his announcement an implicit threat of action against those who would go against his word. He attempts to add a little weight to this pronouncement by saying that the paramount chief, Vanoi, hearing the same case would have said the same thing. Finally, the decision is made to stick by acting on it immediately. At the end of the case, Topana brings out a clay pot that is the first part of a larger payment by which he and his Lukwasisiga kin will eventually recover their garden from Kanioivisi. The idiom used to describe his action is that the small payment "nicks what it will later cut," that is, Kanioivisi's tie to the garden. This not only secures their later claim, it commits them to that course of action and undermines their claim for more immediate acquisition via Isau. This public action, then, redefines the relationships of the participants in the case to the land in question. Notice that since Isau is Mailuwa's father, if Pakaraii's path had prevailed, Mailuwa would probably have used the garden immediately himself to meet his obligations to his father. This coziness accounts for the collusion between the people of the Malasi and Lukwasisiga clans. In this case the presentation had to be made to cut the Malasi clan people out of the loop.

Conclusion

In this study I have analyzed a case of Trobriand land litigation to show the conceptual and social means by which participants in a court session pursue the multiple goals of constructing an account of garden history, avoiding overt hostility, and establishing social reality for the account judged to be a "straight path." As noted in a previous analysis of another Trobriand land case (Hutchins 1980), public argumentation of land rights affords the ethnographer an unusual opportunity to record discourse rich in participants' statements about their own reasoning and that of others. The analysis given here illustrates the coordination of processes of reasoning with the interactive management of litigation as a social and emotional event.

From the perspective of the community, the task of Trobriand Island land litigation is to settle disputes over claims to rights in land by discovering and making public a path for the garden that is culturally correct. Failure of the court to establish an accepted and culturally correct history for the garden risks the continuance of the dispute. The outcome of a land court is not so much a decision in favor of one side as it is the formulation of a public account of garden history that is articulated by the bailiffs and rhetorically underscored by the chief. In other words, the court decision is not to be found in a single turn of speaking by the chief, but in the interactive process by which a social reality is created during testimony and opinion. Seen in this way, Trobriand land cases appear more like the situational consensus described by Lindstrom (this volume) for Tannese debates.

However, several mechanisms are used to ensure that the litigants and others abide by the decision of the court. Getting a straight and unchallengeable path into the corporate awareness is the most important of these, but others include the implicit threat of action against those who contravene the chief's word and the immediate conduct of exchange events that redefine the relationships of people to the land.

Finding a straight path requires that the histories of gardens and litigants be brought into the public eye. The process of making individual or *dala* knowledge public, of making conflicting claims explicit, and of clarifying ambiguities can evoke hostility and aggression. Since Trobrianders understand that attempts to solicit talk on land matters may evoke anger, court discourse is frequently aimed as much at the problem of anger as at the acquisition of land rights. In the latter section of this discussion I have indicated some of the ways in which the goals of controlling hostility and maintaining decorum are achieved in the court context. On the one hand, the entire structure of the village court as a social event works toward these ends. The sequence of events in a court session is "scripted" to produce an emergent account backed by the authority of bailiffs and district chief. On the other hand, the structure of turn-taking and selection of topics for discussion is closely orchestrated by the bailiffs. Not only do the bailiffs make efforts to steer conversation away from sensitive topics, but they will make direct appeals that help define a desired social reality, both in the court situation and over the long term.

References

Hutchins, Edwin

1980 Culture and Inference: A Trobriand Case Study. Cambridge, MA: Harvard University Press.

1987 Myth and Experience in the Trobriand Islands. *In* D. Holland and N. Quinn (Eds.) Cultural Models in Language and Thought. Cambridge: Cambridge University Press.

Malinowski, Bronislaw

1922 Argonauts of the Western Pacific. New York: E. P. Dutton.

1935 Coral Gardens and Their Magic: A Study of the Methods of Tilling the Soil and of Agricultural Rites in the Trobriand Islands. Vol 1. New York: American Book Co.

Powell, H. A.

1956 An Analysis of Present Day Social Structure in the Trobriand Islands. Ph.D. dissertation, University of London.

1960 Competitive Leadership in Trobriand Political Organization. Journal of the Royal Anthropological Institute 90:118–48.

Weiner, Annette B.

1976 Women of Value, Men of Renown: New Perspectives in Trobriand Exchange. Austin: University of Texas Press.

Appendix

The English translation given here was prepared from a transcription of an audio recording of the court. A full vernacular transcript is available from the author upon request.

TILIEWA

001 (The roles of) givers of *pokala* and garden cutters are finished; today you [pl.] shall speak.

002 I beg of you, no arguments, no fist fights.

003 Yes, you should speak clearly, so that people can hear and can chop the end off (of this case) and be done with it.

004 No deception, no arguments.

005 Therefore the old man shall speak first (so that) we will come to know about this garden that their father held.

PAKARAII

006 I will not speak. Let the young man speak now because he went and marked (the garden) for cutting.

007 Whence (comes) this garden that he marked for cutting. That's it.

TILIEWA

008 Pakaraii wants—I told him to speak, but no, he wants Kanioivisi to say first who told him to mark that garden.

009 And then he will speak.

KANIOIVISI

010 The procedure is like this: whoever summons (the case) . . . he knows this is the way.

011 It is not as if I will sit here and speak (while) he who summoned (the case) goes later.

012 He knows what his father's things were and he should say.

TILIEWA

013 He wants . . . (to Pakaraii) he wants you to speak first.

KANIOIVISI

014 It is certainly true that I went and marked (the garden) and he should say what is on his mind.

PAKARAII

015 That garden was our[inc.pl.] father's *kaipokala* (unintelligible).

016 And they cut it of course.

017 Hey, it is not as if Tolukuyabi adopted me. He gave birth to me.

018 We lived with my father because we fought, we fought with Soriya.

019 My mother said, "You move and take your child with you."

020 I slid over there.

021 My elder brothers held and cut (the garden). Hey, they had already cut it several times.

022 I myself had already gone and was gardening (the gardens) in Tolukuyabi's hand.

TOVALUGWA

023 Is that all?

PAKARAII

024 Yes, that is all.

TILIEWA

025 Kanioivisi now you have heard his words.

026 Their father *pokala*'ed to Kamlosiu for the garden.

027 And he himself had already gone to Tolukuyabi and gardened with him.

028 Their father already gave the thing to him (Tokuyawabu) to cut until he died.

029 And he thinks it should stand for a while in the hands of the Malasi people.

030 Because their father already gave the garden to his younger brother. (Isau?)

031 So it would stand in the hands of the Malasi.

032 Good, Kanioivisi come and speak. We will listen.

033 Whoever among you witnesses knows of the garden will be listening to you speak.

034 But now Kanioivisi will say what his tabu may have told him. [90]

KANIOIVISI

035 I have nothing to say at all.

036 You all already know me, I have not one word to say.

037 I won't say anything (time for) speaking is finished.

038 Hey, he spoke the truth that this garden is his father's *kaipokala* from Kamlosiu.

039 They have finished cutting it.

040 It comes, Modoumli died.

041 Tokuyawabu held it, Tokuyawabu cut it . . . Tokuyawabu died.

042 Gumkwadewa died.

043 All of these gardens shall be in my hand.

044 Because my elder brother said, "*Wokosi*." But after Gumkwadewa, *wokosi* remains.

045 And he goes as if it is *wokosi*.

046 Yes, but *wokosi* is later. I myself am *wokosi*.

047 We say *wokosi*, I say that I am *wokosi*.

048 Because Gumkwadewa had died and gone. Yes, I will hold these things.

049 I just waited, Tokuyawabu died, all the gardens were in Tokuyawabu's hand, I will hold all of them in my hand.

050 When I have finished holding them, whoever among the owners want them—they know.

051 But these gardens were already truly purchased.

052 The old men already *pokala*'ed for them, we cannot lightly return these gardens.

053 No, they have already been purchased.

054 And it went on to the end, Tokuyawabu ate them, that's done, and today I will touch and eat of all of these gardens.

055 And whoever there is of Lukwasisiga who sees me and wants a garden, whatever you ask of me, those things will return.

056 Whatever remains, I will hold.

057 So he goes there.

058 What shall I do with his way, if we think his thought, what will become of these gardens?

059 It will turn off the path and go and lodge in (his) *dala*, it will have disappeared.

060 We will not know what has happened.

061 My tabu (Gumkwadewa) did not touch one of these gardens.

062 My tabu told me, he said,

063 Live here (with me) Tokuya . . . I think he goes later.

064 Live here, when Tokuyawabu is dead and gone, you shall touch these gardens with your hand, and eat for a while.

065 You feed me *velina* (filial duty).

066 So, Tokuyawabu fed Modoumli, he fed him and he died.

067 And when Tokuyawabu has finished eating (these gardens).

068 When his blood goes bad, you touch them.

069 Eat of them for a while. You are my mouth.

070 This is what my tabu (Gumkwadewa) told me.

071 And the Malasi shall cut them?

072 What could he be thinking that the Malasi might cut them?

073 Hey, a while back my tabu (Gumkwadewa) died, I didn't see a single Malasi (person).

074 Me, a while back Tokuyawabu died, and the Malasi people saw me.

075 I *sagali*'ed to, um, Mailuwa, I *sagli*'ed to Ibodem, I *sagali*'ed to Tolamilaguyau, eh, Ilaibisila.

076 I went there and said,

077 "Well, it's over, I think I shall touch these things with my hand."

078 I will care for these things.

079 And later whoever among the Lukwasisiga knows what is his

thing will come to me and I will give him his thing.

080 Whatever remains is mine.

081 But the buying is already finished.

082 Our elders finished the buying long in the past.

083 These gardens run.

084 They do not stand, no. They run.

085 Because of *wokosi*, they do not easily lie down, no.

086 They jump from *dala* to *dala*.

087 Where those people of *wokosi* are caring for the gardens and die, others will go, get them and bring them back.

088 We don't hold these things for nothing, no.

089 Because you already know they are Moudoumli's *kaipokala*.

090 His (Pakaraii's) father was Modoumli, but he went to Tolukuyabi.

091 He left Modoumli.

092 It was Tokuyawabu who gardened for and fed Modoumli.

093 At the time of (Tokuyawabu's) death, he (Pakaraii) did not touch one thing.

TILIEWA

094 Is that all? Kanioivisi, are your words finished?

KANIOIVISI

095 Yes.

TILIEWA

096 You have heard the old man speak and then you heard Kanioivisi speak.

097 One was instructed by his tabu, the other was instructed by his father.

098 So what have you people heard of this garden?

099 We will ask further because people (the principals) have already died.

100 But at this time, what have you heard?

101 Now, a while back Tokuyawabu left, and you speak (of it).

102 You Malasi, he forgot and moved out, what have you heard a bit [unknown] about this garden?

103 What have your elder brothers told you about this garden?

IBWARA

104 Please, I will say something because he (Kanioivisi) never . . . our elder brothers cut it.

105 They, e, he (Tokuyawabu) already. . . .

106 I asked, I said, "These your father's gardens, who shall hold them?"

107 He said, "Those that Kanioivisi, um, Gumkwadewa held, those shall not be cut, they are already Kanioivisi's.

108 Those of mine, um, hey, that I held from Modoumli, those are yours.

109 Because Toyowota heaped up yams for Modoumli, he gave him land.

110 A while back Tokuyawabu *sagali*'ed.

111 I said, "What are you doing?"

112 "We are *sagali*'ing for land."

113 I said, "O, really?"

114 They took their *sagali* payments and went and *sagali*'ed.

115 They said, "Not our younger brothers. He will *sagali* his tabu for land.

116 I will *sagali* for land.

117 "Because their father's *dala* had died out."

118 And I asked, I said, "When you die, who shall hold these gardens?"

119 He said, "These are my things, perhaps I will die and they shall go to the old man who lives (Isau) because they were our father's thing.

120 Because, um, our mother's brother (Toyowota) already made food for him (our father).

121 Hey, I know he heaped up his *pokala*."

122 And therefore I think these gardens belong to he that lives, his children already . . . ?

123 And his (Kaniovisi's) younger brother (Libai) went and marked the garden, we don't know what his younger brother had in mind.

124 He *sagali*'ed and I asked.

125 He said, "*Sagali* for land because their line has died out."

126 The old man (Tokuyawabu) said this.

TILIEWA

127 This is what your mother's brother told you Ibwara?

128 This is what the deceased Tokuyawabu told you?

IBWARA

129 This the deceased said in the presence of his son-in-law.

130 And Lagimyuwa, he said it to him also.

TILIEWA

131 However, now you have heard Ibwara speak (of what he said) while living.

132 But I want it at the end in the house (of the death vigil) whoever heard his words then shall speak.

TOKUYAWA

133 He is missing the mark, Mailuwa (should speak).

       (Tiliewa and Tokuyawa whisper)

TILIEWA

134 Mailuwa was truly a caretaker of the old man.

TOKUYAWA

135 Mailuwa and Bolibuwa shall say whatever he might have said there in the house.

TILIEWA

136 (listing names) Not his younger brothers.

137 Mailuwa and Bolibuwa and Kaulela wherever he went.

138 Didn't he hear the old man's words?

139 They have finished speaking now Kaulela (Isau) what do you have to say?

TOVALUGWA

140 (addresses Isau) Hey! Come here.

141 Tokuyawabu was staying in your house, what did he say about this garden?

142 Not all the land, just this one.

143 Speak that the people might hear you.

ISAU

144 He died, you see, and people wanted to cut that garden.

145 He said, "No, only my younger brother shall cut this garden."

146 He shall cut it and make my meal.

147 When I have finished eating, it shall return into his hand.

148 He shall hold that garden.

149 When he has finished eating it, when his blood goes bad, that

garden will return and to to the Lukwasisiga—it is their thing.

150 In the meantime, my younger brother shall eat that garden.

151 Hey, that's what he told me.

TILIEWA

152 That's it? Is that all he told you?

(Isau is deaf and does not hear Tiliewa. Tovalugwa goes out and yells in his face. [29])

TOVALUGWA

153 Is that all of the words of the deceased?

ISAU

154 Yes

TOVALUGWA

155 You have spoken, there is no more?

ISAU

156 No

TOVALUGWA

157 Stand aside.

TILIEWA

158 Mailuwa, you speak.

159 At this time we are already carrying long-winded talk of this garden.

MAILUWA

160 I won't say anything except about what the old man said about the garden as we sat together (in the house of the death vigil).

161 Me, Bolibuwa and him, the three of us.

162 A, Sigaroi went and said, "I don't want those gardens, just the one at Osesuya."

163 The old man just sat there and didn't answer one word.

164 So Sigaroi spun around and went out.

165 The three of us were sitting there and the old man said,

166 "Of those gardens, the small one I have already given to you.

167 Those others, if my blood is strong, well, Isau will feed . . . whatever he makes of a garden I will eat.

168 If not, that garden shall return to Isau's hand.

169 Not to any other."

170 This is what he said.

171 "He shall hold it in his hand.

172 When Isau comes to the end and dies, you Lukwasisiga people shall rise up and cut the garden.

173 You shall take that garden.

174 Because you [pl.] have finished the business of that garden."

175 When Gumkwadewa died we *sagali*'ed like this.

176 In the afternoon, I took a pig as my payment.

177 Marawadi took one dollar as his payment.

178 This was Tokuyawabu's *sagali* for those gardens.

179 These ones that are the old man's *kaipokala* so to speak.

180 And that's all he said.

181 He said, "Only in the old man's (Isau's) hand.

182 When he dies and it ends, and we are short, it will go to you [pl.]."

183 He said, "This whole group of things that the old man (Modoumli) took, he got by *pokala*'ing to your [pl.] elders.

184 And this was your [pl.] mistake (?) Malasi, you see it is serious and for this reason you do not touch these gardens with your hands.

185 The end of this will be Isau.

186 When Isau dies, perhaps your things will return because you have done it all right handed."

187 That's all he said.

TILIEWA

188 Tovalugwa will speak next.

189 You have heard Mailuwa.

TOVALUGWA

190 You have already heard Mailuwa's words, they have emerged.

191 Modoumli died, you see that old man (Mulapokala) told me to come and speak his words.

192 I already told Marawadi to listen to these words.

193 Tokuyawabu died, in the morning we began the *sagali* and finished.

194 Mulapokala took a clay pot. He said for Modoumli.

195 He took it and gave it as his *sagali* payment.

SIBWEKEWA

196 The older man died first, Modoumli more recently.

TOVALUGWA

197 Tokuyawabu. Yes, I suppose so.

OTHER

198 Yes, that's right.

TOVALUGWA

199 This clay pot didn't even have a sign of use on it.

200 He took it and this is what he thought:

201 He took it, not even one pot, uh,

202 They didn't release even one little plot of the old man's *kaipokala.*

203 No, a while back Modoumli died.

OTHER

204 /Gumkwadewa/Gumkwadewa.

TOVALUGWA

205 Marawadi took one dollar, Mailuwa took the pig you have already heard about.

206 So, they took those things and not one garden was released to come back.

207 [359] They held several that would be extra for his son-in-law to hold.

208 This is what he (Mulapokala) said.

209 I join this to what was said by Mailuwa about going to *sagali,* and the words of Mulapokala I have brought out.

210 Listen and consider.

211 And as the two argue, say what you think.

TILIEWA

212 You have now heard a bit of the old men's talk.

213 Mailuwa has truly told us what the deceased said.

214 Isau spoke for the deceased (Tokuyawabu), and Kanioivisi speaks for his tabu.

215 Pakaraii carries his father('s words).

216 They have finished bringing this out.

217 Who among you knows something of this garden and will speak?

MOLUGUTOLA

218 I will speak my mind.

219 Kanioivisi is not hiding this.

220 He didn't say anything about Gumkwadewa's *pokala* to Kamlosiu.

221 Pakaraii said Kamlosiu's *kaipokala* was Modoumli *pokala*'ing to Kamlosiu.

222 He said Modoumli's *kaipokala* to Kamlosiu.

223 So they have reported it, forget about it.

224 Look and go to how it is with the thoughts of the two of them.

225 This (about *pokala*) they have reported.

226 Kamlosiu, Kanioivisi named Kamlosiu.

227 If Kanioivisi was to hide it, you would fight over it . . . more and where would it go?

228 But their thoughts (are what you should consider).

KANIOIVISI

229 I think I shall speak some more, yes?

230 What shall we do with his thoughts?

231 If they were Toyowota's *kaipokala*, it would not be easy for me to touch them.

232 These gardens would be in Malasi hands.

233 It would not be easy for me to touch them.

234 I would not touch them at all, not at all.

235 Tokuyawabu was a caretaker of these gardens, I am a caretaker.

236 You have heard this.

237 Buyers, the old Lukwasisiga men were the buyers.

238 The buyers of these gardens are of a different *dala*. They bought them, ate of them, and they go around and come to me.

239 These gardens will emerge later.

240 So, shall it be clear of obstruction, or shall it disappear, how shall we unravel it?

241 No. (It was determined by) Sagali, our friends (ancestors) have served up the hairs on the end of the palm leaves (have completed every part of the *sagali* exchange.)

242 The *sagali* is finished, later I will respond, what will he do?

243 The purchase of these things is finished.

244 We don't lightly give them back.

245 They were bought.

246 Europeans are like this, we are like this.

247 We garden our gardens to feed our fathers.

248 He only eats, when he dies it does not go to his kin.

249 If his things went to his kin, they would not be easy to hold.

250 I am the conclusion of *wokosi*.

251 Tokuyawabu has finished caring for the garden.

252 He is dead and gone and I will care for this thing.

253 He (Pakaraii) is a Malasi, I am Lukulabuta, they are Lukwasisiga.

254 We are caretakers. It is not our thing, no.

255 He took care of it until he died, it has come, and I will take care of this thing.

256 When I have finished taking care of it, I will throw it back.

257 I do not hide it, I do not understand hiding.

258 For what reason would I hide men's things?

259 Some (of Gumkwadewa's gardens) were his *kaipokala* from Modoumli.

260 He *pokala*'ed to Kamlosiu.

261 For some he *pokala*'ed to Dabwai.

262 This was Modoumli's *kaipokala*.

263 Some were Marawadi's *kaipokala*.

264 This is what my tabu told me about these gardens, some were the *kaipokala* of Monasim and Tetobai.

265 All of these Modoumli reeled in and held.

266 Some he held were the gardens of Kaligaiisa and Tuyega's grandparents.

267 This is what my tabu told me.

268 I say truly he did not *pokala* to Modoumli.

269 This Gumkwadewa told me.

270 He said, "I did not *pokala* to Modoumli, I gave him no food, nothing."

271 Mosilibu and Bovaiyoma resided here and burned coconuts.

272 He went to them and said, "I stand here open mouthed.

273 Kaikwanibula and I garden for (?)

274 Who shall garden for Kaikwanibula?"

275 This my tabu told me, he said.

276 "Who shall garden? They have no women."

277 He got up and came to the old man Kaikwanibula, he told him, he said,

278 "Stay well, your grandchildren shall garden for you.

279 I will go to the old man (Modoumli)."

280 He moved to Modoumli, he got married, he loaded his yam house.

281 He stacked up one hundred, two hundred.

282 Gumkwadewa said, "This is all of my *kaipokala*, because the *dala* is dying out."

283 My tabu told me this, he said, "When they have died, you will hold these things."

284 This is why Gumkwadewa's things follow him.

285 Because I understand *wokosi*, I have fought hard.

286 If there were new generations, it would suit me to go little by little by little.

287 But I understand *wokosi* and I struggle hard.

288 My tabu said, "This is all of my *kaipopakala*.

289 But the yam house grew to heaven.

290 Who shall eat of my holdings, my *kaipokala*?

291 There is Modoumli and I hold them all by myself when Mosilibu dies.

292 The chiefs shall not touch these things.

293 I will hold things in my hands."

294 My tabu *pokala*'ed Modoumli in food. I already pokala'ed in food to Gumkwadewa.

295 Tokuyawabu has already eaten.

296 They have already finished *pokala*'ing in food to Modoumli.

297 And I have finished *pokala*'ing to Gumkwadewa.

298 The things that we [ex.pl.] hold will soon be held by the Lukwasisiga.

299 They are not our Malasi things, they are not our Lukalabuta things.

300 I will not give them to my kinsmen, they shall not give them to their kinsmen.

301 You have heard, these Lukwasisiga things will go to them.

302 By what reason?

303 He knows what are his things, he, he..these are my things here.

304 These, my things shall return.

305 We don't give them indiscriminately.

306 If we dispute the (events of) our ancestors, their *kaipokala* comes.

307 O here we would dispute well.

308 But not this, *wokosi* moves like a yam creeper.
309 Modoumli, Gumkwadewa, e Tokuyawabu, myself, Gumkwadewa—that's all.
310 Then the Lukwasisiga thing returns to them.
311 What is left over they will release.
312 Which path shall it be? Perhaps he who would have it disappear has sucked you in?

PAKARAII
313 So be it.
314 It seems to me that if Gumkwadewa had been your true father it would be appropriate for your to say this, but Gumkwadewa adopted you.

KANIOIVISI
315 Really!?
(They begin shouting over each other)

KANIOIVISI
316 It is true that my tabu Gumkwadewa adopted me.

TOVALUGWA
317 Stop, stop, let him speak.

KANIOIVISI
318 Wait, he said that Gumkwadewa adopted me.
319 It is true that Gumkwadewa adopted me, but there was *kaivatam*.
320 You have heard that.
321 If I was not nursed by my mother, then you could say, "You were adopted."
322 If I was not nursed by my mother, you could say this.
323 But everybody adopts.
324 And in my case there was *kaivatamla*.
325 You can't lightly say "Gumkwadewa adopted you."
326 As you know, however, there was *kaivatamla*.
327 If Kaligaiisa and Tokwaiyera had died then I would say,
328 "O come and pay."
329 And I would repay that man.
330 Because my mother and father died, he pulled me in, and I would repay.
331 But there was *kaivatamla*.

332 Gumkwadewa stood in the center of the village and Kaligaiisa
     took yams from their garden to eat.

333 Today (?)

TILIEWA

335 People, some harsh words have been said about this garden,
     how do you hear them?

336 People, will someone speak?

     (on coaching from Tovalugwa)

337 Lukwasisiga people shall not speak, but we affinal kin who know
     of these things shall come and speak.

338 They have finished buying them, they cut them and died, they
     came along, lived, cut the gardens and died.

339 And today the gardens emerges, what shall become of it?

340 People what is your thought?

341 One of them pulls his father the other pulls his tabu.

342 (The garden) stretches.
     :

[Statements 343–434 transcribed but not translated]
     :

KWAIWAI

435 Mister Chairman, I think they should grasp a little of my thought.

436 I won't ask questions, but I will speak my mind.

437 Molugutola spoke and I think in some respects he got to the
     heart of it, but I don't want to ask a (general) question.

438 I will ask the members (of the court).

439 I ask you, you hear the case of the two of them, and, in this case
     we say "garden."

440 Yes, you hear Kanioivisi speak, you hear Pakaraii speak, and the
     witnesses speak.

441 And I want (to know) what point you are listening for (that the
     case) snags upon, the two of you will tell me and I will speak of
     it.

442 If not, I will speak of what I have been listening for.

443 This is what I ask the two of you.

TILIEWA

444 (For) me, the old man's words were like this:

445 Modoumli pokala'ed for this garden, Tokuyawabu gardened his
     (food), it remained there by virtue of kaivatam only, it continued

on and will go will go and will stand with Isau.

446 When it is finished standing at Isau, it will jump over to the Lukwasisiga (people).

PAKARAII

447 Because Mailuwa is already there.

TILIEWA

448 This is the old man's idea like this, by virtue of *kaivatam* only.

449 And his (Kanioivisi) idea is, his tabu told him that all the things that Tokuyawabu held would return to him for him to take care of when Tokuyawabu died.

450 And he would have whoever of the Lukwasisiga that would have *pokala*'ed to Modoumli, um, to Gumkwadewa, who think of the garden going (to them), Kanioivisi shall eat the *pokala* and release the garden.

451 And the dead man's thoughts about this garden were, when his time was up it would go and slide along as he (Pakaraii) has said.

452 This garden stays by virtue of *kaivatam* only, will go and stand until Isau's time is up, and then will jump over to Lukwasisiga.

453 This is my hearing of the old man's words.

454 I went to Mulapokala to beg for a quinine tablet.

455 I asked Mulapokala (about it), Mulapokala said the same.

456 He said, "No one shall cut that garden.

457 Mailuwa shall not hold it, Marawadi shall not hold it.

458 Modoumli *pokala*'ed for it.

459 It stayed with Tokuyawabu by virtue of kaivatam only, and by virtue of *kaivatam* only it shall go to Isau.

460 It will jump over when this *kaivatam* is finished."

461 This is the road of the dead man and the old man.

KWAIWAI

462 Hey, I asked my question, chairman, I listened like this and therefore I will speak.

463 Our Kiriwina customs—culture culture.

464 In this there are two roads.

465 Today, the two of them. One road is Pakaraii's thought the source of this garden, this one.

466 He would hold the garden which is his father's *kaipokala*.

467 He wants his father's *kaipokala* to run and go into his dala.

468 Kanioivisi wants to hold this garden.

469 Kanioivisi wants to hold Modoumli's *kaipokala* so it will go into his *dala*.

470 Therefore, for this reason, the thoughts of these two fork apart.

471 One road, another road.

472 My hearing of this, I know a little something and I will say it.

473 I want our Kiriwana customs on which ever road we go down, one or the other.

474 Kanioivisi has said, his thoughts are like this as you know.

475 He thinks that Modoumli has died and Modoumli's *kaipokala* will just run to Gumkwadewa, (from) Gumkwadewa (to) him.

476 Pakaraii's thought is that their father's *kaipokala* will run to Tokuyawabu, when Tokuyawabu dies, (on to) Isau.

477 Because of *kaivatam*.

478 And therefore, I think we members have erred, because we were not forceful while Tokuyawabu and Gumkwadewa were alive.

479 Members we have erred.

480 If we had been strong when the living Gumkwadewa resided with Tokuyawabu, we would have cut this case off then.

481 Gumkwadewa was the last in the line, Kanioivisi, you (and Gumkwadewa) would be dividing (the *pokala*).

482 Members we have erred.

483 There are several missed marks in Tukwaukwa, we were not forceful with Gumkwadewa and Tokuyawabu, and therefore you see these two here today.

484 But we will line up this road, culture, this Kiriwina road.

485 (Drawing on the earth with a stick) Not this road.

486 And therefore I have unraveled it, all you members think about it.

487 That's all.

488 This road is the European's road, Edwin and them (Europeans).

489 This is the Europeans' road, we Kiriwinians, this one is our road.

490 That's all of what I heard.

:

[Statements 491–657 transcribed but not translated]

:

TOKUYAWA

658 Cut the case, you go cut it.

659 Mailuwa and Bolibuwa *sagali*'ed but it came to nothing.

660 The little pig died, it died, they didn't eat it, it just died.

TILIEWA

661 And he already gave them their share.

:

[Statements 662–670 transcribed but not translated]

:

MUREBODEMA

671 The *pokala* here was considerable.

672 So you younger people think it over our recovery payments shall go.

673 Hey, if we took these issues to Vanoi (paramount chief of the Trobriands) it would be the same with him.

674 He would say, "All these things, *yolova*, *sagali*, warming up payments.

675 These are not *pokala*.

676 He cuts, he dies, he gives to his kinsmen, he cuts and dies, this is *pokala*."

677 And of course because the *dala* has died out, well quickly um, you should recover (the garden) so it comes back.

678 If there is but one man remaining, he should finish the payments.

679 Hey, this is a good path for this garden.

680 Fine, it should go to Kanioivisi for a while.

681 Because Gumkwadewa and Tokuyawabu fought all the time.

682 As if Gumkwadewa had died, and it was just between Kanioivisi and Tokuyawabu, fine let it go back for Kanioivisi to eat for a while.

683 He eats, and whatever you Lukwasisiga people are thinking, give a lot to Kanioivisi.

684 Because he gave *pokala*.

685 So give a lot, not like a *yolova* payment.

686 At *sagali* we give just a little.

687 This is *pokala*, and you younger people tend to muddy these distinctions, so let Kanioivisi eat.

688 He shall touch it for a while.

689 Hey, just this.

TILIEWA

690 Well people, is this how you think it should be?

691 Thus the old man (Murebodema) has chopped it off.

692 When the Lukwasisiga people make their recovery payments to Kanioivisi, he should return a bit to the Malasi people to eat.

693 Or perhaps he will keep it all to himself or return something or other.

694 He shall give them a sufficient little gift, give them something. (pause)

TILIEWA

695 People, as you have heard today Kanioivisi will eat, and here Topana already carries the small cut (the first part of the payment).

696 We make no more litigation here.

TOVALUGWA

697 Is it straight?
     (General assent)

Doing Things with Words: Conflict, Understanding, and Change in a Samoan *Fono*

Alessandro Duranti

That a concrete passing of judgment in a legal question is no theoretical state-ment but an instance of 'doing things with words' is almost too obvious to bear mentioning. In a certain sense the correct interpretation of a law is pre-supposed in its application. To that ex-tent one can say that each application of a law goes beyond the mere under-standing of its legal sense and fashions a new reality (Gadamer 1981:126).

IN THEIR introduction to *Dangerous Words: Language and Politics in the Pacific*, Myers and Brenneis (1984) provide a rich and stimulating discussion of the complex relationship between politi-cal speech and social order. Without retracting to an idealist, neo-Kantian view of speech as "creating the world," Myers and Brenneis point to the importance of the pragmatic, multifunctional use of talk for a culturally adequate understanding of social pro-cesses. In this perspective, political meetings must be seen not merely as the ritualistic and inescapable reproduction of pre-defined power relationships, but as contexts that "provide for public understanding, both of specific events and of more general assumptions about the social world" (Myers and Brenneis 1984:28).

In this essay, I will discuss these processes of interpretation and social action through a study of conflict resolution in a Western Samoan social event called *fono*. I will show that Mead's (1937) analysis of Samoan society as both hierarchical and cooperative is largely correct and that the organization of talk in a social event such as the *fono* provides the participants with the necessary tools for reconciliation (see also Holmes 1987). In such a context, which shares some of the liminal qualities attributed by Turner (1974) to social dramas, the system is reassessed, the social order redefined, and change is made possible. In this context, not only do participants need to cooperate, they may also put aside rank and personal prestige in the name of a resolution that could "work."

Social Structure and Interaction:
Stratification, Competitiveness, and Cooperation

In the course of his crusade against the "myth" of Margaret Mead and everything she represented in American anthropology and history, Derek Freeman has portrayed Samoans as people who are naturally prone to conflict and constantly driven by an incurable competitiveness. Thus, for instance, he wrote:

> Situations are generated at all levels of the social structure in which, as we have seen, the omnipresent competitiveness is liable to break through the constraints of convention into open contention and conflict. . . . the rank-conscious Samoans become so deeply involved in contests that there is an ever present likelihood that participants in ritualized competition will resort to outright violence against their opponents. (Freeman 1983:142, 146)

Although Freeman is right to say that Samoans are very rank-conscious and, on some occasions, more prone to violence than one would expect from Mead's portrait, his case is overstated. Not only does Freeman not give the reader a sense of the theatrical nature of many threats and confrontations in Samoan everyday life (cf. Ochs 1988), but he seems so preoccupied with corroborating his point with details that he leaves out of the account some relevant information. For one thing, he forgets to tell us that Samoans do have institutions that deal with conflict resolution and that those institutions are, in some cases, very effective. In fact, as I will show in this study, when we look at some of the contexts for dealing with conflict in Samoan society, we find that Mead's criticized claim that Samoan society is both hierarchical and cooperative is, at least in some respects, right (cf. Gerber 1985).

Although perhaps strong in explaining history, Freeman is certainly weak in considering context (cf. Shore 1983; Weiner 1983).
Thus, for instance, he clearly misses the typically context-bound
nature of rank in Samoan society. The contextualization of rank,
as we shall see, is important for assessing the relationship between ritualized competition and social order.

Hierarchy and Cooperative Achievement

There is no question that Western Samoa is a hierarchical or
stratified society (cf. Keesing and Keesing 1956; Mead 1937;
Sahlins 1958). Rank plays an important role in Samoan social organization and in daily social interaction, as it did historically in
Hawai'i. Thus, a very basic distinction is made in Samoa between
matai 'titled people' and *taulele'a* 'untitled people'. A *matai* title is
conferred on an adult member of an extended family by a special
session of the extended kin group (*'aaiga potopoto*). A title gives
its holder control over one or more plots of land and its products
and decision power and responsibilities within both the family
and the village political structure. Thus, for instance, a *matai*
title gives a person the right and duty to sit in the village *fono*.
Among *matai*, a distinction is made between *ali'i* 'chiefs', and
tulaafale 'orators' (what Mead called "talking chiefs"). Chiefs are
typically, but not always (cf. Shore 1982), higher ranking than
orators, who are seen as their vassals. An orator performs certain
tasks for his chief and in return receives goods and protection.
Untitled people are servants of *matai* and help in carrying out
the provision of food and any kind of labor. Serving the higher-
ranking *matai* is seen by Samoans as a crucial aspect of the traditional path to knowledge and power. Finally, rank and status
differences are clearly indexed by the Samoan language, which
has a special "respect vocabulary" (*'upu fa'aaloalo*) for talking
about *matai*, their actions, feelings, and belongings (cf. Milner
1961).

The Samoan notion of rank, however, is extremely context-sen-
sitive. As pointed out by Mead,

[rank] is a not an attribute of the individual himself, but it is always observed as an aspect of the situation in which an individual

is temporarily or sometimes permanently placed. . . . the Samoans recognize status [read "rank"] in any situation. The lover who calls on a girl is treated by the father of the girl, who may far exceed him in rank as a chiefly visitor. In any group of untitled young girls, one will be treated as the *taupou* ["village virgin queen"]; in a traveling party in which no one has rank, some will be designated to act as talking chiefs, etc. (Mead 1937:286).

Mead's characterization is confirmed by a number of more recent studies. Thus, Ochs (1982) has shown that, in household interaction, caregiving is hierarchically organized so that the highest-ranking caregiver does not have to actively perform for the baby, but delegates someone else who is lower ranking to perform for her. This general pattern is applied to any given situation so that there always is a high-ranking caregiver and a low-ranking one, with the lower being the active one. If the grandmother and the mother are present, the mother might be the active caregiver; if the chief of the family and the grandmother are present, the latter will be the active one; if no adults are present, between two siblings, the younger one will be the active one.

In most cases, it is the situation that dictates the roles to be filled. Thus, in a ceremonial exchange, if no untitled people are available to carry goods or serve a guest, another *matai* will perform the task, acting as an untitled person. This sensitivity to context is sometimes carried to the extreme of having a high chief serve a lower-rank orator if no one else is there to perform a given task required by the situation or if no one else is thought capable of doing it. Rank alone does not explain how things get done. Both rank and skill must be taken into consideration, together with the situational needs. Very often in Samoa, there is a greater emphasis on "getting things done" than on who should do it.[1] As pointed out by Mead, Samoans are often more interested in the performance itself than in the individual actors.

> This separation between the individual and his role is exceedingly important in the understanding of Samoan society. The whole conception is of a ground plan which has come down from ancestral times, a ground plan which is explicit in titles and remembered phrases, and which has a firm base in the land of the villages and districts. *The individual is important only in terms of*

the position which he occupies in this universal scheme—of himself he is nothing. Their eyes are always on the play, never on the players, while each individual's task is to fit his role (Mead 1937:286 emphasis mine).

Whether we examine first the organization of a household cooking group or the organization of a village fishing expedition, we find the same principle exemplified, a number of individuals arranged in a hierarchical order, who contribute differentially according to their rank age, sex, and skill, to a total result, in which the whole group share, either directly—as in eating the food from the family oven—or indirectly—as members of a household or village whose prestige has been enhanced by the result of the labor which all have expended (ibid.:288).

The hierarchical but cooperative organization of interaction goes together with an ideology and a practice of task accomplishment as a cooperative endeavor (cf. Duranti and Ochs 1986). This point can be illustrated by the important role in Samoan interaction of the *taapua'i* 'supporter, sympathizer'. In the Samoan view, accomplishments are cooperative endeavors and the joint products of both performers and supporters. More specifically, for Samoans something is an accomplishment because of and through the recognition that others are willing to give it. The relationship between a performer and a supporter is reciprocal. The supporter recognizes the work that went into the performer's act of, for example, building a house, singing a song, fixing a broken tool, or driving a car. The performer similarly recognizes the work that went into the supporter's recognition of the performance. This reciprocal relationship is symbolically and routinely instantiated through *maaloo* 'well done!' exchanges. Should the performer receive a prize or compensation of some kind for his performance, he will have to share it with his supporters.

In this study, I will suggest that conflict management in the *fono* should also be seen as a cooperative endeavor that provides for public understanding and creates the context for change.

Ethnographic Background and Data

The data for this study were collected during one year (1978–79) in the village of Falefaa on the island of Upolu, Western Samoa.

Falefaa, which is located about eighteen miles from the capital of Apia, has a population of one thousand two hundred people divided into four sub-villages. Some one hundred Falefaa adults over the age of thirty years hold *matai* titles awarded to them by members of their extended families *('aaiga poto poto)*. Although in principle women can also be *matai*, very few women have been given the title, and only once did I observe a titled woman (an orator) participate in a *fono*.

Villagers live in traditional Samoan houses *(fale)* with no walls, or in Western-style wooden houses. Often houses are grouped together in a family compound typically consisting of a house in which people sit during the day and sleep at night, a cooking house, and an outhouse. Family compounds include one or more nuclear families related by blood or marriage.

Untitled people do most of the hard work involved in gardening (taro, bananas, breadfruit, and coconuts are the main crops), food preparation, and household maintenance. In the daytime, if not at a regular job in Apia or engaged in village or family affairs, titled men spend most of their time chatting with other *matai* in small groups, perhaps drinking kava or playing cards. A few go fishing or hunting, or work on their plantations with their young untitled relatives.

Seven important *fono* over a continuous period of four months (January–April 1979) form the basis for this study. I observed and tape-recorded these *fono*, and native Samoan speakers at Falefaa transcribed the tapes. The transcriptions were checked by me and supplemented with interviews of participants in each *fono*, especially those who had given speeches. Informal conversation and ceremonial speeches in non-*fono* contexts were also recorded for comparative purposes, and several informal interviews were conducted with chiefs and orators from the village to provide insights and evaluations of events from a Samoan perspective.

The *Fono*

There are several kinds of institutions in Samoan society that deal with breaches of social norms and could be discussed as contexts for disentangling. The word *fono* is often used to refer to a number of those institutions as well as to the actual events where people try to settle disputes or punish those who have committed a crime (cf. Duranti 1981a; Freeman 1978; Larkin 1971; Mead 1930; Shore 1982). In this study, I will limit my discussion to one particular kind of *fono*, namely, the special convocation of the entire body of titled people (*matai*)—chiefs and orators—in the village. Such an assembly usually deals with political and judicial matters involving one or more local *matai*. As typical of traditional societies (cf. Comaroff and Roberts 1981), the same structure, namely, the *fono*, acts both as a high court and as a legislative body, which can make, ratify, and abrogate laws or discuss the policy to adopt with respect to a new problem or potential conflict.

In Falefaa, *fono* take place irregularly, depending on the needs of community leaders to solve or avoid a crisis. Gathering in one rectangular house, participants seat themselves according to rank. Higher-ranking chiefs sit on either of the two shorter sides (called *tala*) of the building, and other chiefs and orators align themselves in rows on the longer sides. The seating arrangement reflects verbal interaction during the *fono* because those who sit along what is considered to be the "front" part of the house (cf. Duranti 1981a) are usually the ones who do most of the talking. The high chiefs sitting along the *tala* are expected to speak toward the end of the meeting, after the other speakers have presented their positions. A kava ceremony opens the *fono*. Several behavioral norms are followed by participants during a *fono*. For example, everyone sits cross-legged on mats, and sustained eye-contact between the speaker and audience is avoided during a speech (but see Duranti 1981b for exceptions).

Two genres of speech are used in a *fono*: *laauga* 'formal, ritual speech' (stressing shared values and information, predictable in form and content, and emphasizing common interest, agreement, and harmony) and *talanoaga* 'talk, chat, discussion' (stressing personal values and new information, less predictable in interactional style, and emphasizing personal interests, disagreements, and conflict). Elsewhere (Duranti 1981a, 1981b, 1983, 1984a) I have detailed the characteristics of both genres. Briefly, the first speech in a *fono* is always a *laauga* considered as the introduction (*tuuvaoga*), delivered by an orator who will go on to announce the agenda but cannot yet discuss the issue(s) before the *fono*.

The opening orator's speech first recognizes the work of those who provided the kava, then makes a "thanksgiving to God." Then the orator's speech goes on to refer to one or more important events in Samoan history through the metaphor of "mornings" (*taeao*) of the past, after which the orator acknowledges the dignity or sanctity of the chiefs and issues a formal greeting and praise to all the important titles of the village, one by one. The agenda is then announced, with the orator ending his speech by metaphorically referring to the wish for "clear skies," that is, for good health for the participants.

Several *laauga* speeches by other high-ranking persons may follow, using a similar format. The *fono* then moves into a phase of *talanoaga* speeches in which issues are discussed and opinions expressed. Lower-ranking titled men may participate in this phase, which sometimes approximates conversational interaction in structure (e.g., turn-taking patterns) and style.

Samoans have several expressions that succinctly characterize the way they see a *fono*. The verb *teuteu* 'make beautiful, decorate', is used in a number of metaphors such as *teuteu le tagi* 'settle the court case' (cf. Milner 1966), *teuteu le nu'u* 'make the village beautiful, settle the conflicts within the village', and *teuteu le vaa* 'take care of a relationship'. These definitions are provided both as glosses for outsiders, such as the ethnographer (cf. Duranti 1981a:29), and as reflexive statements within a *fono*, as shown below:

(1) (*Fono* April 7, 1979).[2]

CHAIRMAN

(...) *fa'auma lea makaa'upu.* ... Let's close this topic.
Keukeu lo kaakou vaa ma Lufilufi. (Let us) take care of our relationship with (the village of) Lufilufi.

Ia 'a 'e kaakou alo i luma. So that we can face ahead.

(2) (*Fono* April 16, 1979).

MANUOO

(...) *Ia fa'akasi mai le Akua* may God be with us (to help)
i le koofaa ma le ukaga ... with the chiefs' decision and the orators' decision

'o aa mea 'o fa'alekogu o le ikuumaloo, . . .	are there any problems in the district, . . .
'o le aso legei e keukeu ai mea uma. . . .	on this day everything will be settled.
'O e aa fo'i se koofaa i le kaakou (kau)aofiaga, . . .	whatever decision is going to be taken at our meeting, . . .
Ia 'o le kaakou malae aa legei e folafola ai mea uma . . .	Well, at this sacred meeting place everything will be announced . . .

As in dispute resolution in many societies, metaphor plays an important part in *fono* discourse. The word *teuteu*—pronounced *keukeu* in the phonological register used in a *fono* (cf. Duranti and Ochs 1986)—is used in expressions such as *teuteu le vao. Vao* is the high grass and weeds that grow in front of the houses (Milner 1966:313) and must be cut every so often by the young untitled men. Although *teuteu le vao* implies the action of cutting the grass, it conveys more than the simple act of cutting. It also implies a series of operations that must be accomplished in order to make the land look nice: collect the fallen leaves, cut the grass, and burn it. *Teuteu* is a reduplicated form of the word *teu*, which means, as a noun, "a bouquet of cut flowers" and, as a verb, "to put something in order" (cf. Shore 1977:161).

In Duranti (1981a:30), I gave the following interpretation of the Samoan metaphor: that a *fono* is called either when a breach of some social norm has taken place or when one is anticipated. Such a breach, either actual or potential, creates a crisis in which the harmony of village life is disrupted. "The ideal mutual love (*fealofani*) of the members of the community is suspended. The beautiful village becomes like the *vao*, the bush or forest, where tall grass and weeds grow, where men can misbehave away from the eyes of social institutions and social control. The convocation of a special session of the *fono* is the attempt to make life orderly and more predictable, to cut the weeds, the bad feelings, and to make the village beautiful again." When I wrote this, I was intrigued by the correspondence between the Samoan ideology of a *fono* and its discourse organization, but I did not pursue the analysis of the actual process of conflict resolution. In this study I will discuss the *fono* as an antagonistic framework that provides a context not only for testing the social system, as suggested by Shore (1982), but also for allowing communication to take place where otherwise no communication would be possible (Myers and Brenneis 1984). It is in fact in the process of accusing, shaming, blaming, as well as discussing possible solutions to a particular conflict, that Samoans work out other conflicts and therefore create a context for expressing and understanding more than what is being explicitly discussed. The outcome of a *fono* is a cooperative achievement, a dialogical construction of a temporary mutual consent that goes beyond the participants' individual goals and "fashions a new reality" (to use Gadamer's words in the quote above). In the process of "straightening up" a relationship, the *matai* reconsider the social order presupposed by that relationship. By defining "truth" and restoring "justice," the *matai* cooperatively define the meaning of their actions and shape their own future.

The Power of Words: Cooperative Construction of Truth and Search for Justice

Samoan ways of speaking exhibit many striking examples of an ideology and practice of interpretation in which words are not simply seen as representing some already defined world, but as shaping reality, as creating the world. There is nothing idealistic about this view, however. There is no "spirit" or conscience being objectified into the world through language.[3] There is instead a materialistic view of "words as deeds," of utterances as "acts" (cf. Austin 1962). The same verb *fai* means both "say" and "do, make"; the word *uiga* means both "meaning" and "actions" (cf. Duranti 1984b, 1988). This world view seems in fact common to many Pacific languages (cf. Lindstrom, this volume; Rosaldo 1982; Verscheuren 1983).

If words are deeds, they can be powerful and dangerous at the same time. If words shape the world, a speaker may be responsible for the consequences of what he said, regardless of his putative original intentions. Samoan orators must thus be very careful about what they say. Although a speechmaker can gain in prestige and wealth from speaking on behalf of a powerful chief or from helping out in a difficult negotiation, he may also risk retaliation for having said what might be *later* defined as the wrong thing (cf. Duranti 1984b, 1988).

These risks conflict with the stated goals of a *fono* as an arena for the reconstruction of truth and search for justice (see example 1 in the appendix). Social actors in a *fono* use different strategies to deal with this problem.

Announcing the Agenda: Recognition of the Crisis

As mentioned above, one of the first speaker's tasks in a *fono* is to announce the agenda of the meeting (cf. Duranti 1981a, 1981b). Consistent with the local theory of speech and social action briefly outlined above, the announcement of the topics to be discussed is more than the official definition of a crisis or of a crime; it is also its public constitution. Prior to the first speaker's announcement, the events to be discussed might have been a private affair, they might have had no publicly accessible interpretation. Once mentioned, they become subject to public concern. In the Samoan view, if I understand it correctly, the crime or crisis is in part constituted at the time of its announcement in front of the assembly. Given the highly stratified nature of Samoan society, if the people to be tried are higher ranking than the person who must announce the agenda of the meeting, the latter finds himself in a difficult spot. He might have to publicly accuse parties who are more powerful than he is.

One way to get out of this difficult situation is to skip the announcement of the agenda and let other, more powerful members of the assembly deal with it. Another strategy is that of being very vague and using disclaimers as to the real nature or seriousness of the conflict or crime to be discussed. (Indirect discourse is characteristic of disentangling events in several societies represented in this volume, e.g., see essays by Arno, Brenneis, McKellin, Watson-Gegeo and Gegeo, White). Finally, a third strategy is that of two or more members of the council to cooperatively work at stating the agenda so that responsibility may be diffused (see example 2 in the appendix).

Cooperative construction of an accusation, however, is not only invoked by lower-ranking *matai*, but by higher-ranking ones as well. There are times in a *fono* when even the most powerful and outspoken figures may need to borrow a voice to express disappointment. When feelings run high and it becomes increasingly difficult for an individual to "keep cool," others may come in to fill in his role or change the atmosphere with highly formal and ritual speech. The organization of interaction in a *fono*, in which one party speaks at a time and can hold the floor for an extended period of time,[4] facilitates this cooperative work at reconstructing events and assigning responsibilities. In this way, multiple resources are available for otherwise inescapable and dangerous one-to-one confrontations.

Resolution

The canonical discourse organization in a *fono* is to start with a formal and highly predictable speech that stresses the shared values and common history in the community and then to move to the more personal and unpredictable statements of the accusations and expressions of disagreement. Thus a *fono* always starts with a *laauga*, a ceremonial speech that celebrates the dignity of the participants as "gods on earth" and at the same time defines them as subject to God's ultimate will. The points of agreement among participants are also stressed, such as their will to get together and arrive at a decision that would satisfy both the chiefs and the orators. Only after the shared goals and background have been stressed do speakers get into the details of the crisis. This very same pattern is also maintained in the discussion part of the meeting, *talanoaga* 'chat, discussion', in which each speech also tends to embed the more controversial or accusatory statements within outer layers of predications about harmony, shared understanding, and wishful thinking (cf. Duranti 1981b, 1984a). The discourse organization adopted by Samoan speechmakers in disentangling contexts such as the *fono* mirrors the "old-new strategy" often discussed by psychologists and linguists interested in preferred word-order patterns across languages (cf. Clark and Haviland 1977; Chafe 1976; Givon 1979).

When Things Must Be Said:
Shaming and the Liminal Nature of a *Fono*

Regardless of the particular topic being discussed, an apology to the assembly or at least to some of its members is an important outcome of any *fono* that discusses direct or potential breaches of social norms. For this reason, one might think of the entire process of disentangling as a series of moves toward reconciliation, with the apology being one of the last steps (similar to the *ho'oponopono* process described by Boggs and Chun, this volume).

Such a process may be a long and difficult one. Events and responsibilities must be assessed to avoid making the same mistakes in the future. Thus, those making the accusation must be given a chance to state their case and display their feelings. The defenders, in turn, must show concern for the honor of the offended and the prestige of the whole community. Not only the accusation but also the apology must sound convincing. Thus, despite the explicit emphasis on reestablishing the lost harmony, as discussed above, attempts at quick resolutions of a case may be discouraged or explicitly condemned (see example 3 in appendix). Public, often prolonged, shaming may take place even when the accused is a high-ranking chief. The excerpt in (3) below, for instance, is taken from a meeting in which the high chief A. and his orator V. are being accused of having used offensive language toward the assembly during the day of the elections for the National Parliament. The senior orator who acts as the chairman of the assembly engages in a prolonged shaming invective in which the sacred honor of the village and of the chiefs is contrasted with the secular mischiefs of one of its members. In addition to rhetorical questions such as, "Is that the role of you chiefs?", we also find threats that might provoke fear in the defendants as well as in anyone else tempted to follows his steps. The phrase, "the tradition of Moamoa," for instance, refers to the old practice of expelling the offenders from the village and burning their houses and belongings.

(3) (*Fono* March 17, 1979)

SENIOR ORATOR

(. . .) 'O le gu'u legei e le se   (. . .) This is not a piece of a
fasi-gu'u   village.
Pe se gu'u e ka'alo i ai se isi.   Or a village to fool around with.

Mai le foafoaga o le lalolagi,   From the creation of the Earth,
'O Falefaa 'o le gu'u (. . .)   Falefaa is a village (. . .)

e fagagau aku ai kupu o le   (where) the kings of the country
akugu'u.   are born.
(. . .)

'Ae 'aafai fo'i 'o Lau Afioga A.   And if it was Your Highness A.
[name],   [name]

'ola! Se 'ou ke ofo.   Man, if I am surprised!
'Ou ke ofo gaa—a e pei   I am surprised—as I already
oga 'ou kaukala aku,   said

Kalu mai le foafoaga o legei gu'u,   From the beginning of this village,

ma lo'u fo'i ola mai i le lalolagi legei   and in my life on this world,

'ou ke le'i fa'alogo aa i se isi   I never heard anyone

u- aga faga faga mea leaga   who said those bad things to
le pa'ia o 'Aaiga.   the holy chiefs.
(. . .)

Ma le aofia laa legei ma le fogo   And this assembly and fono

e fikoikogu i Lau Afioga A.   is about Your Highness A.

go'o le aso le paaloka.   cause the day of the elections.

Le aso ga ma- maakagoofie.   That beau- beautiful day.

'Ua ula lea aso.   That day had been joyful.

'A 'e 'ua koa pogaa o lou afio aku   But it was spoiled by your arrival

i le mea ga iai lo kaakou gu'u akoa   to the place where our entire
                                              village was

ma 'upu 'ua lafo aku i lo kaakoou gu'u.	and (by) the words said to our village.[5]
'O le mea laa o le aofia ma le fogo.	This is the thing (= topic) of the assembly and the fono.
'O lea 'o lo'o fia maua gei le sa'o.	Here (we) will know what really happen.
po 'o Lau Afi-[CHANGE OF TAPE] (...)	whether it was Your High(ness...)
'O le mea laa lea 'o lo'o fia maua i le asoo o le kaakou gu'u.	This is what today's meeting of our village is for.
Auaa 'o 'upu ia 'ua lafo i le gu'u.	Because of those words said to the village. ....
'O aga o Moamoa e kaakau 'o iai. (...)	The tradition of Moamoa must be applied. (= a severe punishment)
A'e kaumafa i le pia, faga mea leaga aku lea.	You drink beer, say then bad things.
Faga mea leaga aku lea. Oka!	Say bad things. Man!
E fa'apegaa ea se kulaga o 'oukou 'Aaiga,	Is that the role of you chiefs?
'O 'oukou 'Aaiga e ka'i ala?	You are the chiefs who (should) show us the way?
'I mea lelei ma mea maakagofie?	Toward good and beautiful things?
OTHER SPEAKER *Maalie!*	Well said!

This is indeed harsh rhetoric, and physical violence might have erupted had these words been uttered in another context. Within the *fono*, instead, even senior, high-ranking participants seem willing to accept shaming and threats as part of the disentangling process. Their cooperation is indeed called upon not simply by mentioning honor and moral values, but, more importantly, by the threat to the system of authority they represent. Shaming is allowed if credibility must be restored. In these contexts, details are strategically brought into the discussion. Thus, speakers might engage in verbatim quotes of verbal offenses or incriminating statements if the defendants seem reluctant to recognize the seriousness of their crime. An example of this is given in (4) below:

(4) (Cont. from (3) above)

SENIOR ORATOR

(. . .) Go'u kaukala aku fo'i i legaa aso	I also spoke on that day
go 'ua 'ee afio aku i le fale.	when you had come to the house.
"A. [name], ka'akia e iai se kaeao."	"A. stop, there is some important affair (going on)."
Oi! A'o lou koe afio mai i fafo	Oh! But you came back outside
koe afo gei 'upu 'o gaa	(you) repeated those words
" 'Ai kae! Ufa! Kefe!"	"Fuck off! Ass! Prick!"
(. . .)	

Although it is my understanding that the senior orator is relying on his authority and special role in the proceedings to be able to repeat such offensive words in front of the assembly, no one is in principle immune from blame and shame. Thus even a powerful *matai* can in fact be criticized by a lower-ranking orator. The following excerpt, which presents such a case, also illustrates the more indirect, metaphorical style often found in the speech of less powerful members of the assembly.

(5) (*Fono* April 7, 1979)

TAFILI

'Ua gaepu le vai oga 'o le maka o le vai	The water is muddy because the cause of this (lit. the eye of the water)

'o Lau Koofaa le Makua.	is Your Highness the senior orator.
Le afioga ga kauave. 'O fea *'o iai?*	The opinion had been given. Where was it?
Leai. 'Ua leaga oga o ai? *Leai. 'Ua mama lava*	No. It's bad because of whom: No. It did leak
oga 'o Lau Koofaa le Makua.	because of Your Highness the senior orator.
'O le ala fo'i lea 'o le *fa'aumiumi o legei makaa'upu.*	That's the very reason of the prolonging of this matter.

Within the characteristically stratified Samoan society, this almost egalitarian, liminal nature of the *fono* points to a concern for the construction and preservation of a policy that is meaningful to more than a few powerful figures.

The political discourse within a *fono* can be viewed as operating at different levels. The very convocation of a *fono* can be seen as an astute stratagem invented by some influential party to gain allies and be granted public permission to prosecute and publicly shame those who dared challenge his authority or conspired against him. Rather than explicitly saying "so-and-so betrayed me" or "I want to punish him," a *matai* might try to build a case against his political opponent or someone related to him. His motive might indeed be retaliation or a vote of confidence from the assembly. He may indeed be driven by competitiveness or by his obsession with rank, as Freeman (1983) might argue (see above). However, once the *fono* has been convened and others are involved, the cooperative construction of truth and mutual consent might lead toward a direction unwanted by those who called the meeting. In the process of striving for power and recognition, the *matai* not only work out a solution for the issue at hand, they also provide each other an occasion for the public understanding of other viewpoints and seeing of alternative solutions. It is within such a context that change becomes possible.

A Context for Change

One of the main themes of the meetings I documented during my first stay (1978–79) had to do with the elections for the national parliament. Before the elections, several meetings of the village council centered on the issue of who should run for the election. Despite the recognized need to narrow down the selection to one candidate, three people from the village (Falefaa)—the two senior orators (Moe'ono and Iuli) and the young chief Savea Sione—ended up competing against one another and against the other candidates from another village in the same district.[6] After the defeat of Falefaa's candidates and the victory of the incumbent M.P. from the nearby village of Lufilufi, other meetings took place with several different agendas. As can be gathered from the transcripts of those meetings, however, the elections remained one of the main themes in the speeches. The defeat had weakened village unity and the relationship with the nearby village of Lufilufi. The "mutual love" was shaken. The subsequent *fono* were used for disentangling the controversial outcome of the election. One of the issues was seniority. There seemed to be some resentment from some members of the assembly against the young chief Savea, who had dared to compete against more senior *matai* and had actually received more votes than the two more senior candidates from his village. The issue, in fact, was of a more general nature and involved the relationship between "tradition" (*aganu'u*) and modern government laws (*tulaafono*). According to "tradition," senior *matai* have precedence over younger, lower-ranking ones; according to the "law," any *matai* has the right to seek election.

Things got even worse when Savea decided to take to court the district M.P. for slander. Many *matai* felt that a public confrontation in the capital's court would have reopened the wounds created by the elections and would have worsened the already shaky relationship with the M.P.'s village, Lufilufi, historically and hierarchically tied to Falefaa.

A meeting was immediately called to try to convince Savea to withdraw his accusation. Savea promised to think about it and give an answer in a few days. Given the danger, for the whole community, that his decision might entail, Savea found himself (or was this planned on his part?) in the advantageous position of being able to offer something to those very people who would have wanted to punish him for his lack of respect. The meetings in which Savea is asked to withdraw his accusation toward the M.P. represented potentially highly confrontative situations, where several powerful figures were struggling to regain control of the events while trying to strike against their political opponents.

What we see through an analysis of the transcripts is quite remarkable: Savea chooses this occasion to apologize publicly for having previously challenged the senior orators' authority (see example 4 in the appendix). Furthermore, from the very beginning, he hints that he wants to do something that would please one of his antagonists, the senior orator Moe'ono, who has asked him not to go to court with the M.P. (see example 5 in the appendix). Confronted with Savea's public recognition of his authority and seniority, Moe'ono radically changes attitude and repeatedly recognizes, in front of the assembly, Savea's wisdom:

(6) (Fono April 7, 1979)

MOE'ONO

Ia. Fa'afekai Savea.	So. Thank [you] Savea.
'O lea laa 'ua maua aku lou figagalo . . .	Now that your decision has been given . . .
fa'apegaa Savea	(let's do) like that Savea,
Ia. Ikiki lou kigo makua le koofaa!	So. You are young but think like a wise person! (lit. Your body is small but your decision is mature!)

?

Maalie!	Well said!

Whatever the original goal of the participants, the discussion is turned into an occasion for healing old wounds. One party (Savea) finally acknowledges the right of seniority, while the other party (Moe'ono) recognizes the younger chief as an equal. Harsh feelings and disagreement come under control by a common goal: the social harmony within the village and within the district. The different threads of discourse come together for a solution that would work.

After such a turning point, the participants as well as the ethnographer might have forgotten the different issues and conflicts being addressed by the assembly on that day. After all, harmony seemed both the goal and the result. The final speech by the highest-ranking chief, however, puts things into perspective again.

Summing Up: The Chiefs' Perspective

The *multifunctional* nature of the discussion is often recognized in the speech of the highest chief (*ali'i*) present, who speaks as a representative of the entire chiefly "side" or "families" (*'aaiga*). The high chief summarizes the previous discussion, commenting on the different opinions and interpreting the conflict as embedded in a wider context. What was indirectly indexed by the case officially on the agenda is often more explicitly mentioned in the high chief's speech. This is recognized by Samoans themselves who often say that whereas an orator goes "around and around" an issue, a chief talks "straight." The chief's understanding of the conflict embodies at times the recognition of alternative positions. Such a recognition is already, in some cases, the acceptance of a potential change in the political alliances or power relationships within the council.

(7) (*Fono* April 7, 1979)

SALANOA

[...] e kaua fo'i iaa ke a'u le vagaga a Moe'ogo	... Moe'ono's speech is also important for me
... e kusa ... 'o laga fa'amalamalamaga auaa. . .	... as for ... his explanation because ...
'o legei mea o le paloka, 'o le mea o le- o le mea fa'alekulaafogo	this thing of the election, it's something that has to do with the (new)

... *e:- e:-e*

e lee feaiaaka'i laa
le kulaafogo ma le agagu'u.

(you) cannot compare the (new)
laws with (our) tradition

pei laa ou ke kau maua aku i
le figagalo o Moe'ogo,

as I have gathered from Moe'ono's
opinion,

'ese le kulaafogo. 'Ese le-
le kaakou vaa ma Lufilufi.

One thing is the (new) laws.
Another thing our relationship
with Lufilufi.

[...]

'o le kuulaga laa o le- o la'u aa-

that's the position that I-

'o lo'u aa magaku ko'akasi, ...

my own opinion, ...

ma 'o lou alofa mogi fo'i lea.
Alofa iaa Savea,

and my true love, my love to
Savea.

Pe alofa i le gu'u ...

If (you) love the village ...

e iai lo'u kaofi fa'apegei=
pei oga 'ou fa'akuu aku

here is my opinion as I
mentioned before

e'ese le kulaafogo 'ese le
agagu'u.

One thing is the (new) laws,
one thing the tradition.

'Afai gei ... e- e maaloo Savea, ...

Even if ... Savea wins

i le moliaga o Igu, ... Ia.
Maaloo Savea. ...

in the court case with Inu. ...
Okay. Savea wins.

Ae 'o le 'aa aafaaiga lo
kaakou vaa ma Lufilufi.
[...]

But it will affect our
relationship with Lufilufi.

Ia. Afai fo'i e- ... 'o le
'aa faiaiga Savea, ...

Then, if by any chance, Savea
loses, ...

Ia e fa'apea oga kaakou—
kaakou afaaiga.
[...]

We are also going to be
affected/hurt.

... lafo iaa Savea e

.. leave to Savea to reconsider

feku'uga'i ai laga koofaa, ...   his decision, ...

Ia amai lekali po 'o lea le   So give us an answer and
kali la'a aumaia,   whatever the answer (we)'ll get.

Ia. Kaakoa fiafia!   Let us be happy (anyway)!

Maguia le aso!   Have a good day!

OTHERS
Maaloo!   Well done!

The public acceptance of Savea's decision, whichever will be—
"whatever your answer, let's be happy about it!"—is in fact a
recognition of his new higher position. Although such a recognition is found at first only at the level of *political discourse*, it is
eventually corroborated by the following events: at the next elections Savea was elected as the district M.P. representative.

Conclusion

Whether or not the actors' initial motivation in provoking a crisis
or getting involved in a crime is the "competitiveness" described
by Freeman (1983) as "omnipresent" in Samoan characters,
Samoans do have institutions that provide alternatives to the
"outright violence against their opponents" that Freeman
(1983:146) says is the likely outcome of almost any kind of social interaction in Samoan society. Whether or not Samoans are
really aggressive and competitive, the *fono* is at least one efficient
framework that allows them to conduct their daily life without
continually resorting to physical violence.

A question that still remains open and should be given attention is the extent to which similar frameworks work for other sec-
tors of the population such as, for example, untitled and young
people. Furthermore, we must also consider the possibility of
variation from one community to another—even within the same
island—in terms of efficiency and availability of the institutions.
A culture provides the frames, but it is real individuals who must
perform the tasks. During my fieldwork experience, I was im-
pressed by the ability of certain people to hold the village polity

together. I imagine there could be other situations where this might not happen. When we talk about social dramas, we often forget that the unpredictability of their outcomes is related to their fluid structure, which changes while we observe it, and it is often too distant before we can describe it. The careful analysis of transcripts of audio-recorded interactions may provide a useful avenue to the reconstruction of those swift moments when the ethnographers' path and that of the people they study cross, while history and personal choice merge and the future gets shaped, through words, among other things.

Notes

Acknowledgments. I would like to thank Karen Watson-Gegeo for her comments and suggestions on an earlier draft of this paper. For their friendship and patience in dealing with my intrusive presence in their daily affairs, I am particularly grateful to the chiefs and orators in Falefaa, Western Samoa, where I conducted my field work in 1978–79 and in 1981. (*Ia, fa'afetai atu i 'Aaiga ma Aloali'i fa'apea fo'i i laa'ua Matua ma le 'a'ai o Fonotii.*) Special thanks go to the Rev. Fa'atau'oloa Mauala and his wife Sau'iluma for their constant support throughout our stay in Samoa. The research on which this paper is based was funded by the National Science Foundation (NSF Grant No. 53-482-2480).

1. This cultural preference is also reflected in the syntactic structure of Samoan utterances that tend to prefer clauses with the structure Predicate–Patient (VO) over Predicate–Agent (VA) (cf. Duranti 1981a; Duranti and Ochs 1983; Ochs 1988).

2. *Transcription conventions*: I have used traditional Samoan orthography with the exception of vowel length, which is here transcribed phonemically, that is, with two identical vowels instead of a macron on a single vowel. The letter *g* (*ng* in some other Polynesian orthographies) stands for a velar nasal and the inverted apostrophe (') for a glottal stop. The transcripts were first done by local native speakers and then revised by the author in cooperation with a number of knowledgeable Samoan speechmakers. All the examples in this paper are taken from audio-recording of spontaneous (non-elicited) interaction (cf. Duranti 1981a for more information on methodology). Three dots "..." indicate an untimed pause. Three dots between parentheses "(...)" mean that a portion of the transcript has been omitted for brevity or clarity.

3. See Schaff (1973) for a review of the philosophical, psychologi-

cal, and linguistic literature on linguistic relativity and linguistic determinism.

4. In Duranti (1981a), I proposed to use the term "macro-turn" for extended turns that also comprise backchannel responses at fairly predictable moments.

5. Here "our village" means "our council," namely, the *matai*.

6. It might seem strange that each person was able to maintain his decision to run for election against the assembly's opinion. In fact, within highly stratified Samoan society, an individual's decision *must* be respected. A person's house might be burned down by the council's orders, but he cannot be forced to change his mind about something. Ultimately, no *matai* can tell another *matai* what to think or what to say, unless the latter voluntarily agrees. A Samoan saying expresses this attitude succinctly: *e le umu le isi matai i le isi matai* 'no matai prepares the oven for another matai'. Each *matai*, whether chief or orator, whether high ranking or low ranking, is ultimately sovereign over his own decision.

References

Austin, J. L.
  1962 How to Do Things with Words. New York: Oxford University Press.

Chafe, Wallace
  1976 Giveness, Contrastiveness, Definiteness, Subjects, Topics, and Point of View. *In* Subject and Topic. C. N. Li, ed. New York: Academic Press.

Clark, H., and S. E. Haviland
  1977 Comprehension and the Given-New Contract. *In* Explaining Linguistic Phenomena. R. O. Freedle, ed. Washington, D.C.: Hemisphere Publishing.

Comaroff, John L., and Simon Roberts
  1981 Rules and Processes: The Cultural Logic of Dispute in an African Context. Chicago: The University of Chicago Press.

Duranti, Alessandro
  1981a The Samoan *Fono*: A Sociolinguistic Study. Pacific Linguistics, Series B, vol. 80. Canberra: The Australian National University, Department of Linguistics, Research School of Pacific Studies.

1981b Speechmaking and the Organization of Discourse in a Samoan *Fono*. Journal of the Polynesian Society 90:357–400.

1983 Samoan Speechmaking Across Social Events: One Genre In and Out of a *Fono*. Language in Society 12:1–22.

1984a *Lauuga* and *Talanoaga*: Two Speech Genres in a Samoan Political Event. *In* D. L. Brenneis and F. Myers, eds., Dangerous Words: Language and Politics in the Pacific. New York: New York University Press.

1984b Intentions, Self, and Local Theories of Meaning: Words and Social Action in a Samoan Context. Center for Human Information Processing, Technical Report no. 122, La Jolla, California.

1988 Intentions, Language, and Social Action in a Samoan Context, Journal of Pragmatics, 12:13–33.

Duranti, Alessandro, and Elinor Ochs

1983 Word Order in Samoan Discourse: A Conspiracy Toward a Two-Constituent Pattern, Paper presented at the Summer Linguistics Institute, UCLA.

1986 Literacy Instruction in a Samoan Village. *In* Acquisition of Literacy: Ethnographic Perspectives. B. B. Schieffelin and P. Gilmore, eds. Norwood, N.J.: Ablex.

Freeman, Derek

1978 'A Happening Frightening to Both Ghosts and Men': A Case Study from Western Samoa. *In* The Changing Pacific: Essays in Honor of H. E. Maude. H. Gunson, ed. Melbourne: Oxford University Press.

1983 Margaret Mead and Samoa: The Making and Unmaking of an Anthropological Myth. Cambridge: Harvard University Press.

Gadamer, H.-G.

1981 Reason in the Age of Science. (Translated by G. Lawrence). Cambridge, MA: M.I.T. Press.

Gerber, Eleanor

1985 Rage and Obligation: Samoan Emotions in Conflict. In Person, Self and Experience: Exploring Pacific Ethnopsychologies. G. White and J. Kirkpatrick, eds. Berkeley: University of California Press.

Givon, Talmy

1979 On Understanding Grammar. New York: Academic Press.

Holmes, Lowell D.

1987 Quest for the Real Samoa: The Mead/Freeman Controversy and Beyond. South Hadley, MA: Bergin and Garvey.

Keesing, Felix, and M. Keesing

1954 Elite Communication in Samoa. Stanford: Stanford University Press.

Larkin, F.

1971 Review of the Second Edition of M. Mead's The Social Organization of Manu'a. Journal of the Polynesian Society 6:219–22.

Mead, Margaret

1930 The Social Organization of Manu'a. Honolulu: Bernice P. Bishop Museum Bulletin 76.

1937 The Samoans. In Cooperation and Competition Among Primitive People. Mead, ed. Boston: Beacon Press.

Milner, G. B.

1961 The Samoan Vocabulary of Respect. Journal of the Royal Anthropological Institute 91:304.

1966 Samoan Dictionary. Oxford: Oxford University Press.

Myers, Fred, and Donald L. Brenneis

1984 Introduction. In Dangerous Words: Language and Politics in the Pacific. D. L. Brenneis and F. Myers, eds. New York: New York University Press.

Ochs, Elinor

1982 Talking to Children in Western Samoa. Language in Society, 11: 77–104.

1988 Culture and Language Development: Language Acquisition and Language Socialization in a Samoan Village. Cambridge: Cambridge University Press.

Rosaldo, Michelle Z.

1982 The Things We Do With Words: Ilongot Speech Acts and Speech Act Theory in Philosophy. Language in Society 11:203–37.

Sahlins, Marshall

1958 Social Stratification in Polynesia. Seattle: University of Washington Press.

Schaff, A.

1973 Language and Cognition. R. S. Cohen, ed. (based on a translation by O. Wojtasiewicz, 1964). New York: McGraw-Hill.

Shore, Bradd

1977 A Samoan Theory of Action: Social Control and Social Order in
      a Polynesian Paradox. Unpublished doctoral dissertation, Uni-
      versity of Chicago.

1982 Sala'ilua: A Samoan Mystery. New York: Columbia University
      Press.

1983 Paradox Regained: Freeman's Margaret Mead and Samoa.
      American Anthropologist 85:935–44.

Turner, Victor

1974 Dramas, Fields, and Metaphors: Symbolic Action in Human
      Society. Ithaca: Cornell University Press.

Verscheuren, J.

1983 On Boguslawski on Promise. Journal of Pragmatics 7:629–32.

Weiner, Annette

1983 Ethnographic Determinism: Samoa and the Margaret Mead
      Controversy. American Anthropologist 85:909–18.

Appendix

Further examples from *fono* verbal interaction referred to in the discussion.

(1) In search of truth and justice (*Fono* March 17)

IULI

(. . .) E saa'ili aa po 'o ai ua faia   (We must) find out who said
fa'a'upuga gei.   those words.

. . . Auaa aa lee faia,   . . . because if (this) is not done,

e koe kula'i mai fo'i se isi kaimi.   it will happen again some other
                                                    time.

?

Maalie!   Well said!

(. . .)

IULI

Saa'ili le mea kogu. . . .   search for the truth. . . .

'Oga fai lea 'o le figagalo o le   So that we can fulfill the village
kaakou gu'u.   wish.
(...)

(2) Setting the topic (*Fono* April 7, 1979)

(Context: The first orator has just concluded the introductory speech
leaving out the mention of the agenda.)

FIRST ORATOR
(Ending his speech) Maguia le aofia   Good luck to the assembly
ma le fogo!   and the fono!

?
( ) kai // fekalai.   thank you // (for your honorable)
                                          speech.

CHAIRMAN
'O aa makaa'upu o le fogo?   What are the topics of the fono?
Fai mai makaa'upu // o le fogo.   Tell us the topics // of the fono.

FIRST ORATOR
'O le makaa'upu   The topic
o le aofia ma le fogo, . . . Ia e   of the assembly and the fono . . .
fa'akakau kogu lava   really centers around
i lo kaakou Falelua . . . oga pau ga   the two subvillages [fn. 3] . . .
'o makaa'upu.   That's it for the topics.

CHAIRMAN
Oi! [Conventional marker of repair   Oh!
initiation]

FIRST ORATOR
(Softly) E aa?   What?

CHAIRMAN
(Softly) 'O le isi makaa'upu o Savea. The other topic about Savea.

FIRST ORATOR
Ia. 'o le isi fo'i makaa'upu e uiga   Right. There is also another topic

i le-...   about...
le Afioga iaa Savea 'ogo 'o - 'o le   His Highness Savea 'cause- the::-
laa:-...
mea fo'i ma Fa'amakuaaigu.   thing there with Fa'amatuaainu.
Go 'ua kukulu Savea i-...   Cause Savea has complained...
i le Maaloo...   to the government...
Ia (iga) 'ua ka'ua gi fa'akosiga   Given that some (illegal) cam-
                                                paigning has been said (to have
                                                been done)

(a) Fa'amakuaa'igu i le paloka, ...   by Fa'amakuaa'ino during the elec-
                                                tions
iai fo'i gisi makaa'upu o lo'o lee   (if) there are some other topics (I)
maua ...   didn't get...
Ia. La'a maua i luma.   So, they will be brought to the
                                                floor.

?
Maaloo!   Well done!

CHAIRMAN
Ia. Fa'afekai aku [name] ...   So. Thank you [name] ...
'ua 'ee fa'amaga le fogo   for starting the fono
...

(3) The apology must be motivated (*Fono* March 17, 1979)

CHIEF
Lau susuga saa 'ee kolaulauiga   Your Highness, you have
makaa'upu.   announced the agenda.
Ia. e lee gofogofovale fo'i e   So. Not to keep sitting here for no
kakau oga-   use it is necessary to-
auaa e iloa e igei 'o igei e kupu ai le   because this one (= me) knows
fa'alavelave.   that it was this one (= me) who
                                                started the trouble.

'O lea laa 'ou ke kalosaga aku ai   So now I apologize (to you) with
ma le fa'amaulalo.   all humility.
... E leai se kagaka e sa'ogoa i   ... Nobody is perfect in this world
legei lalolagi
'afai 'o iai se sesee, ia,   if there is some error, well,
lafo mai i le koe'iga ma pau lava   Charge it to this old man and
'o le mea akoa.   that's the end of the thing.

Ia. E lee mafai e seisi oga — Well. Nobody can test this world. . . .
kofo legei lalolagi. . . .

'O le mea laa lea gao ga 'ou — That's the thing I apologize to you
kalosaga aku, — about,
i luma o lo kaakou gu'u — (truck passes by) (. . .) in front
of our village

ia e lee aogaa fo'i ga gofogofo — it is not worth it also to keep
fa'akali umi — sitting waiting forever
fa'akali umi ia. A'o lea e iai le mea. — (pulling out money) waiting
forever. So. Here is the thing
(=money).

Ia. Ga 'o ga avaku o le — So. Here is the apology to you.
fa'amaulaloga.
Po 'o lea loukou figagalo, ia. — Whatever your wish is, well,
Ga'o ga avaku (pea ia) e lee umi aa — Only give you (like) my speech is
gi a'u kala. — not that long.
E pupu'u. . . . *Kaukala sa'o.* — It's short. . . . (to) talk straight.

?
Mo'i lava. — Very true.

?
Maaloo. — Well done.

CHIEF A.
Ia 'ua uma fo'i — So it's also finished

IULI
(Interrupting by calling A's name) — Thank you for you speech, Your
A.! A.! Fa'afekai saugoa i Lau — Highness.
Afioga.
Ia. Sau se ikulaa oga e saugoa — Well. There will be a time when
mai lea, — you will say that,
Ae se'i- . . . *'o lea e le'i uma kaakou* — But let- . . . our subvillages have
foiala — not finished (speaking)
pei oga iai fo'i kuulaga ma aofia o — as there are also other positions
lo kaakou gu'u. — of our village.
Ia. 'O lau kali aku lea. I lau- — So. That's my answer. To your-
saugoago a lau afioga. — speaking of Your Highness.
(Second orator restarts his speech)

ALO
Ia. 'O lea mapu ia i le maoka le   So. It now rests in his residence
kagoa (. . .)   the holy speech (. . .)

(4) Savea recognizes his mistake (*Fono* April 7, 1979)

SAVEA
'Ae 'ou ke fa'apea aku Moe'ogo . . .   But I am telling you Moe'ono . . .
[. . .]
e aogaa lo'u . . . kapukapua'i aku   my support for the campaigning
i lalua alofaiva . . .   of you two [Senior Orators] is im-
    portant . . . [lit. 'my support for
    your fishing is useful']

(Later on, same transcript, p. 65)

[. . .] *Moe'ogo ma Iuli e aogaa*   Moe'ono and Iuli, my- my- my-
la'u- la'u- la'u
alu aku i le mea o lua . . . maliu ai   going with you two is needed . . .
ma lua- . . . fagogoka ai. . . .   (wherever) you go and fish . . .

(5) Aiming for social harmony (*Fono* April 7, 1979)

SAVEA
'ou ke kalosaga Moe'ogo   I implore you Moe'ono
'ua fusia lo kaakou gu'u i le   to strengthen our village in the
fealofagi i le asoo   mutual love on this day
ia aveavea'i le vaaega a 'o le 'upu   to continue in the way of the truth
mogi
o le aso sefulu-, koe sefulu aso   for another ten days
ia amaia le Aso Gafua iaa ke a'u   give me until Monday
'ou ke avaku le kali   I'll give the answer
'ae mo'omia kele le mea   but it is most important (to me)
'ua 'ee siligia ai lo'u kagaka.   the thing you have asked me.

PART V

EPILOGUE

The Power of Talk

Roger M. Keesing

A VOLUME of papers so carefully and thoughtfully integrated, and so well synthesized and summarized by its editors, needs no last word. The slow and gradual process whereby academic discussion gradually crystallizes into a volume attests to the value of planning and deliberation—and also to the power of talk.

If there is room for me to expand, having joined the venture at the very end, it is mainly with reference to the power of talk. First, there is the question of what we gain by such a detailed unpacking of real talk by real people in real contexts. It has become fashionable in various genres of interpretive / symbolist / postmodernist anthropology, and more generally in critical theory, to use the metaphor of text to characterize whatever it is that one interprets. It has further become fashionable to use "discourse" in the Foucaultian sense. The papers in this volume explore texts—in an earlier and narrower sense—of discourse—in an earlier and narrower sense (though one still current in linguistics). What value is there in such careful and detailed interpretation of transcripts to show how cultural meanings are created, negotiated, and iterated through talk?

A first point is that, although such analyses begin with empirical "data" in the form of transcripts of dispute resolution, interpreting how meaning is negotiated and explicating the cultural assumptions (all that need not be said) that render what is said interpretable is far from a mechanically inductive process. The authors here engage in something more like literary criticism than empiricist induction. Taking texts (in the narrow sense) as texts (in the metaphorical sense) opens up "the data" to the reader's inspection (in the sense that novels or plays are accessible, as texts); but interpreting them requires all the analyst's powers of insight and imagination, and draws on the experience of long and deep fieldwork, immersion in another people's cultural world.

Let me develop further the notion of "all that need not be said" (i.e., cultural assumptions). Conversation, and more contextually formalized genres such as those examined in these papers, create, negotiate, and manipulate meanings in terms of what the participants "know" (in a broad sense) and need not—indeed cannot—"say." I am reminded of Gregory Bateson's observation that the genome of a shark need not encode the laws of hydrodynamics: it is (in some sense) their complement. So too, talk at once establishes or creates a culture, and *assumes* it. Interpreting the transcripts of such discourse (in a way comprehensible to the nonparticipant in this culture) demands that the analyst invoke and articulate this hidden complement of cultural knowledge (and, as Hutchins shows in his paper and book [1980], its logics).

However, the reading of texts in this narrow sense places heavy demands and empirical constraints on the process of cultural interpretation. True, the reader is at the mercy of the analyst in having access only to the particular transcript the latter provides, the translation the analyst gives, and the cultural and sociological data she provides. Nonetheless, the reading must be persuasively and comprehensibly anchored in the transcript and the cast of characters.

The texts span a range in the depth and detail with which they are transcribed and explored. At one end, we find a transcript consisting of glosses of vernacular utterances. At the other (especially in Besnier's paper), we find a much more fine-grained transcript of the linguistic and conversational patterns used in local talk of "untangling." Subjecting local talk to conversational analysis, as pioneered by Sacks, Schegloff, and Jefferson and as recently applied anthropologically with great power and insight by Michael Moerman (1988), reveals both subtle cultural patterning and an apparently universal substrate. At the level of grammar, we find fascinating use of the alternative constructional patterns languages provide, to evoke scenarios that foreground agency or disguise it, specify causation or leave it implicit. Such manipulation of language to evoke images of the relationships between actors and events is critically important in contexts, such as those explored in the papers, where questions of morality, intention, and responsibility are engaged. At the level of pragmatics, we find use of alternative registers (and, as in Lindstrom's and Arno's papers, choices between the use of loan words versus vernacular forms or local dialect forms versus those of the standard language) to express relationships both between the protagonists and between the speaker, the community, and the world outside it.

Finally, we recurrently find in these texts vivid metaphoric images—"untangling," "straightening" (the Kwaio I study, like a number of other Austronesian-speakers represented here, are "straighteners" rather than "disentanglers")—of the restoration of social/cultural order. We find other schemes of metaphoric imagery as well. The burgeoning interest in conventional metaphor in critical theory (e.g., Ortony 1979) and cognitive studies (Lakoff and Johnson 1980; Lakoff 1987; Johnson 1987) has catalyzed anthropological awareness of how other people's worlds are constructed in and through metaphor. The metaphoric equivalences expressed in non-Western languages are turning out both to be partly unique and to reflect striking cross-cultural consistencies (such as recurrent patterning in what Lakoff [1987] called "image schema transformations"). These seem to be deeply grounded experientially, in ways both culturally specific and humanly universal. The spatial/physical imagery of straightening, and of paths, explicated in these papers will serve to illustrate (see also Claudi and Heine 1986 for a comparative examination of metaphor and linguistic change).

Let me now return to a broad theoretical issue explicated by Brenneis and Myers in their introduction to *Dangerous Words* (1984). There is a tension, running through these papers as well as those of the 1984 volume, between two perspectives we can take on the relationship between "political" talk (in a broad sense) and the social contexts in which it is embedded.

In one perspective, talk takes place within a framework of social and cultural structure. When disputes or conflicts create a breach in the social order, integration is restored through an airing of grievances, a public reiteration of norms, a collective construction of an authoritative or adjudicated account. The setting and format in which such resolution is achieved represents the power structure of the community—whether hierarchic and formal or egalitarian and informal. Political talk reiterates and reproduces these structures of power. Of course, there are many variants on this paradigm: functionalist, Marxist, Weberian, and so on. What unites them is the premise that a social system and a culture create and define the space within which conflict resolution takes place and the form it takes. Talk, thus viewed, sustains and reproduces a preexisting social and cultural order.

An alternative perspective, again with variant forms (social interactionalist, phenomenological, transactional, etc.), takes social interaction, and the talk which is its medium, as constitutive of the social system. A world is fashioned through talk, created through interaction. In such a view, the "structures" of society and culture, the hierarchies of power, are reifications. Structures are evanescent, social order is negotiated and contingent. In contexts of dispute resolution or public discussion, the relationships and decisions expressed in talk constitute political power and structure; they do not simply iterate or reproduce it. Moreover, political talk is political action; power is enacted and constituted through words, not simply expressed or confirmed by them.

The papers in this volume show how and why either an extreme structural perspective or an extreme interactionalist perspective is misleading and incomplete—but how each perspective illuminates crucial elements of social life. Talk at once expresses and publicly iterates structures of power and constitutes them, at once reproduces existing constellations of political relationships and transforms them.

Both of the paradigms, or collections of paradigms, I have sketched take a relatively static and narrow frame in time. If society and culture are evanescent and emergent, if interaction creates and continuously renegotiates a social world, then the past is an artifact of this ongoing process. If, in contrast, we view society and culture as comprising a relatively stable, integrated, and self-reproducing system (as functionalist and even most anthropological Marxist approaches have done), then structures perpetuate themselves, but in a timeless and bounded universe.

The contemporary Pacific environment in which the "disentangling" examined in the book has taken place is neither timeless nor bounded. A further necessary complement to the two perspectives I have sketched—one that partly for reasons of space and focus remains implicit in most of the papers—would take into account structures of power and the embodiment of power in discourse, but would see these structures, and the unfolding of interaction, as temporal, historical phenomena. Where the "societies" we study have for decades been incorporated into colonial states, and are now incorporated in postcolonial states (in the Pacific, Papua New Guinea, Solomons, Vanuatu, Western Samoa, Fiji, etc.), a historical view that situates "societies" both in time and in wider regional systems seems an urgent complement to both of the perspectives I have sketched.

I was struck, in these papers, by elements of the dispute-resolution processes that seemed to derive from colonial legal structures and from missionary ideologies and perhaps mission-taught practices. As White notes for the A'ara (among whom I did brief survey research in 1964), the procedures and ideology of "disentangling" are played out in the context of a society deeply influenced by Anglican teachings. We find as well elements seemingly constructed in emulation of colonial courts (as in the Trobriand resolution of land disputes). The strongly traditionalist Tannese described here by Lindstrom sprinkle their talk of conflict with Pidginisms, many of them reflecting the legal mechanisms of the strange Condominium of the colonial era. I have argued that even among the diehard and fiercely conservative Malaita pagans I have studied, conceptions of *kastom* and mechanisms of resolving conflict according to customary law have been extensively influenced by colonial legal statutes and court procedures (and by the power of the written Word, as indigenously perceived).

The authors represented here have no illusions that the "societies," and phenomena, they describe exist in a timeless realm, insulated from wider systems. Nevertheless, the style of representation to which we are heirs characteristically leads us to perform a different kind of disentangling, one that disengages a community we studied from wider contexts when we describe it. Our own "talk" demands a constant self-reflexivity and meta-interpretation.

If we view and represent the communities (and "societies") where we work as less bounded than the conventions of anthropological discourse dictate, then we can make a further move in exploring the politics of talk; we can examine encounters between members of a community where we work and powerful outsiders: the agents of government authority, "development," church, and so forth. Moerman's beautifully subtle interpretation of an encounter between Thai villagers and a government officer will serve to illustrate (1988:68–100). The negotiation of "culture" is more wondrous when neither linguistic code nor culture is fully shared; and the dynamics of power, expressed and negotiated through conversation, are perhaps more vividly grasped in such a context.

My point is not to question the "authenticity" of the contexts and procedures of dispute resolution. I have recently argued (e.g., in Keesing n.d.) that anthropological reverence for the "authenticity" (and virtual sanctity) of ancestral pre-European societies and cultures is misplaced. Among tribal peoples, as in colonial and postcolonial states, societies had open borders, cultures were constantly changing, and the symbolic stuff so revered by anthropologists (myths, rituals, cosmologies) served ideological ends and "class" interests. If exogenous elements contaminate "genuine" cultures, then pre-European Lau (north Malaita) culture was probably "contaminated" by Polynesian influences; so were many cultures of what is now Vanuatu. Fiji, in these terms, would have to be judged fundamentally inauthentic. My point is that to situate social and political processes within wider systems in time and space need raise no doubts about "authenticity."

We may hope that the papers collected and interwoven here, arrayed with those in *Dangerous Words* (Brenneis and Myers 1984), will inspire further exploration of how talk is used to negotiate, reproduce, create, and change social order in Pacific communities and their links to the world outside.

References

Brenneis, Donald L., and Fred R. Myers
1984 Dangerous Words: Language and Politics in the Pacific. New York: New York University Press.

Claudi, U., and B. Heine
1986 On the Metaphoric Base of Grammar. Studies in Language 10:297–335.

Hutchins, Edwin
1980 Reasoning in Discourse: An Analysis of Trobriand Land Litigation. Cambridge, MA: Harvard University Press.

Johnson, Mark
1987 The Body in the Mind: The Bodily Basis of Meaning. Chicago: University of Chicago Press.

Keesing, Roger M.
n.d. Kwaisulia as Culture Hero. Reconsidering Anthropology in Melanesia. J. Carrier, ed. (forthcoming).

Lakoff, George
1987 Women, Fire and Dangerous Things. Chicago: University of Chicago Press.

Lakoff, George, and Mark Johnson
1980 Metaphors We Live By. Chicago: University of Chicago Press.

Moerman, Michael
1988 Talking Culture: Ethnography and Conversational Analysis. Philadelphia: University of Pennsylvania Press.

Ortony, A., ed.
1979 Metaphor and Thought. Cambridge: Cambridge University Press.

Index

Library of Congress Cataloging-in-Publication Data

Disentangling : conflict discourse in Pacific societies / edited by
Karen Ann Watson-Gegeo, Geoffrey M. White.
    p.   cm.
Includes bibliographical references.
ISBN 0-8047-1692-7 (alk. paper) : $47.50
    1. Conflict management—Oceania. 2. Discourse analysis—Oceania.
3. Ethnopsychology—Oceania. 4. Dispute resolution (Law)—Oceania.
5. Oceania—Social life and customs. I. Watson-Gegeo, Karen Ann,
1942– . II. White, Geoffrey M. (Geoffrey Miles), 1949– .
GN663.D57 1990
303.6'0995—dc20   89–48716
                                                              CIP

This book is printed on acid-free paper.